9. Keep a log of problems you've fixed. A log will give you an idea of where to start when something similar occurs, and makes it easy to tell your boss what you've been doing with your time.

10. Document your network. Record the configurations of servers, workstations, bridges, and any piece of equipment that you can't reconfigure from memory in less than a minute.

11. Keep a log of problems you've fixed. A log will give you an idea of where to start when something similar occurs, and makes it easy to tell your boss what you've been doing with your time.

12. Prepare for problems in advance. Create a disaster-preparedness plan that details your strategy for recovering from theft, fire, flood, earthquake, or terrorist attack. Almost all businesses struck by disaster that don't have a plan are gone within two years. Most with a plan survive.

13. Read the documentation for your equipment. If you don't want to read the whole thing, look for exceptions to the normal behavior and troubleshooting tips. Also look at the README files on software distribution diskettes, because they may contain information that is not in the manuals.

14. Be prepared to use any available sources of information. Join the local NetWare User Group and the CNE Professional Association. Stay tuned to the CompuServe forums or the Internet news groups on NetWare. Be on the lookout for patches for your version of NetWare.

15. If you run into a dead end, don't bang your head against the wall—get help. Use one of the resources listed in Appendix A to get more information about your problem, or contact tech support.

Troubleshooting NetWare® Systems

Second Edition

GET THE BEST CONNECTIONS FROM
NETWORK PRESS™

You CAN judge a book by its cover.

This Network Press™ title is part of a new, expanded series replacing Sybex's acclaimed Novell Press® book series. With Network Press, you'll find the same dedication to quality from a truly independent and unbiased point of view. Our unique perspective guarantees you full coverage of Novell, Microsoft, and the other network environments.

Building on 20 years of technical and publishing excellence, Network Press provides you the broadest range of networking books published today. Our well-known commitment to quality, content, and timeliness continues to guarantee your satisfaction.

Network Press books offer you:

- winning certification test preparation strategies
- respected authors in the field of networking
- all new titles in a wide variety of topics
- up-to-date, revised editions of familiar best-sellers

Look for the distinctive black-and-white Network Press cover as your guarantee of quality. A comprehensive selection of Network Press books is available now at your local bookstore.

For more information about Network Press, please contact:

Network Press
2021 Challenger Drive
Alameda, CA 94501
Tel: (510)523-8233 Toll Free: (800)277-2346
Fax: (510)523-2373 E-mail: info@sybex.com

Troubleshooting
NetWare® Systems
Second Edition

Logan G. Harbaugh

The first edition of this book was published under the title
Novell's Problem-Solving Guide for NetWare Systems

NETWORK PRESS ®
SYBEX

San Francisco ■ Paris ■ Düsseldorf ■ Soest

Associate Publisher: Steve Sayre
Acquisitions Manager: Kristine Plachy
Developmental Editor: Guy Hart-Davis
Associate Developmental Editor: Neil Edde
Editor: Marilyn Smith
Project Editor: Shelby Zimmerman
Technical Editors: Jeff Bankston, James Huggans
Book Designer: London Road Design
Graphic Illustrator: Tony Jonick
Desktop Publisher: Susan Glinert Stevens
Desktop Publisher Liaison: Scott McDonald
Production Coordinator: Kimberley Askew-Qasem
Indexer: Nancy Guenther
Cover Designer: Archer Design
Cover Photographer: Greg Probst

Warranty

Sybex warrants the enclosed CD-ROM to be free of physical defects for a period of ninety (90) days after purchase. If you discover a defect in the CD during this warranty period, you can obtain a replacement CD at no charge by sending the defective CD, postage prepaid, with proof of purchase to:

Sybex Inc.
Customer Service Department
2021 Challenger Drive
Alameda, CA 94501
(800) 227-2346
Fax: (510) 523-2373

After the 90-day period, you can obtain a replacement CD by sending us the defective CD, proof of purchase, and a check or money order for $10, payable to Sybex.

Disclaimer

Sybex makes no warranty or representation, either express or implied, with respect to this medium or its contents, its quality, performance, merchantability, or fitness for a particular purpose. In no event will Sybex, its distributors, or dealers be liable for direct, indirect, special, incidental, or consequential damages arising out of the use of or inability to use the software even if advised of the possibility of such damage.

The exclusion of implied warranties is not permitted by some states. Therefore, the above exclusion may not apply to you. This warranty provides you with specific legal rights; there may be other rights that you may have that vary from state to state.

Copy Protection

None of the files on the CD are copy-protected. However, in all cases, reselling or making copies of these files without authorization is expressly forbidden.

This book is dedicated to the memory of my mother, Nyna Harbaugh.

Acknowledgments

I F YOU'RE READING THIS, it's probably because you think your name is in here. I hope it is, but if I missed acknowledging your contribution to this book, I apologize.

I would like to thank the people who made this book possible. The editorial staff at SYBEX, including Shelby Zimmerman, the project editor, Steve Sayre, associate publisher of Network Press, and Neil Edde and Guy Hart-Davis, the developmental editors, all played substantial roles in making this book happen. Marilyn Smith, the editor of this book, made it better than it would otherwise have been. Jeff Bankston and Jim Huggans, the technical editors, helped make sure that all the information in this book was accurate and that I was presenting it well.

I would also like to thank the people who have helped me learn the techniques I passed on in this book, especially Russ Mitchell, Michael Bryant, Laura Chappell of Novell Education, and Brent Loschen of NeXT, for their excellent training and support. Thanks to Jane Nulty and Pam Eaken, who let me go to all those classes, and to all the tech pubs department members who made it necessary for me to learn the techniques in the first place. Thanks to Peter Jerram and Rose Kearsley, who helped me write the first edition.

I would also like to thank my parents, who are responsible for my love of learning and of reading, which helped get me where I am today. (I'll read anything—even manuals.) My family and friends put up with me while I wrote this book.

Contents at a Glance

Introduction   *xxiii*

PART I: BASIC ELEMENTS OF TROUBLESHOOTING   1
Chapter 1: Principles of Troubleshooting   3
Chapter 2: Troubleshooting Servers   19
Chapter 3: Troubleshooting Workstations   65
Chapter 4: Troubleshooting the Physical Network   117
Chapter 5: Troubleshooting Network Printing   157

PART II: DISASTERS: BEFORE AND AFTER   **195**
Chapter 6: A Pound of Prevention   197
Chapter 7: Coping with Disaster   229

PART III: TROUBLESHOOTING TECHNIQUES FOR LARGE NETWORKS   **249**
Chapter 8: Troubleshooting WANs   251
Chapter 9: Connecting to Other Systems   285

PART IV: ADVANCED TOPICS   **303**
Chapter 10: Troubleshooting Network Applications   305
Chapter 11: Upgrades to NetWare, Hardware, and Software   321
Chapter 12: Tips and Techniques   345

PART V: APPENDIXES   **365**
Appendix A: Resources for Troubleshooters   367
Appendix B: Tools for Troubleshooters   383
Appendix C: Network Record Keeping Forms   425
Glossary of Terms   437

Index   *509*

Table of Contents

Introduction   *xxiii*

PART I   **BASIC ELEMENTS OF TROUBLESHOOTING**   I

Chapter I   **Principles of Troubleshooting**   **3**

An Approach to Troubleshooting   5
   Breaking Down the Elements   5
   Trying Different Solutions   6
Troubleshooting New Systems and Additions to Existing Systems   7
   Stripping Down to the Minimum   7
   Keeping Track of Configuration Details   7
Troubleshooting Existing Systems   8
Attitude: The Single Most Important Thing You Can Get
   from This Book!   9
Record Keeping   10
Resources for Troubleshooters   13
Aids for Troubleshooting   14
   Snapshots for Quick Reference   14
   Fault Points for Identifying Problem Areas   15
   Real-Life Stories   16

Chapter 2   **Troubleshooting Servers**   **19**

Snapshot: Troubleshooting Servers   20
Fault Points for Servers   25
NetWare Version-Specific Information   27
   NetWare 2.*x* Operation   27
   NetWare 3.*x* Operation   28
   NetWare 4.*x* Operation   29
Troubleshooting New Servers   30
   Hardware Problems in New Servers   31
   Software Problems in New Servers   39

Troubleshooting Existing Servers 44
 Hardware Problems in Existing Servers 44
 Software Problems in Existing Servers 46
 Intermittent Problems with Servers 48
Using Other Diagnostic Tools 49
Managing the Binderies or NetWare Directory 50
Upgrading NetWare 51
Troubleshooting NLM Problems 51
Using System Fault Tolerance 52
 Mirroring and Duplexing 52
 RAID for Fault Tolerance 53
 SFT Level III 54
Real-Life Stories 55
 Scenario One: Installing a New System 55
 Scenario Two: Maintaining an Existing System 60

Chapter 3 **Troubleshooting Workstations** **65**

Snapshot: Troubleshooting Workstations 66
Fault Points for Workstations 72
 Workstation-to-Network Connection Failures 74
 PC Card, Motherboard, and BIOS Failures 75
 Operating System and Software Failures 75
 User Failures 76
Troubleshooting Workstations—The Basics 76
 Checking Connections 77
 Checking for Changes 78
 Checking New Installations 78
Troubleshooting PC-Compatible Stations 79
 Troubleshooting PC Hardware 79
 Troubleshooting PC Software 85
Windows and NetWare 89
 Windows 3.0 to Windows for Workgroups 3.11 90
 Windows 95 91
 Windows NT 94
OS/2 Clients 95
PS/2 (Micro Channel) Clients 96

Macintosh Clients   96
    Macintosh Hardware   96
    Macintosh Software   101
UNIX Workstations   103
Real-Life Stories   104
    Scenario One: Installing a New Workstation   104
    Scenario Two: Maintaining an Existing Workstation   107
    Scenario Three: Another Existing Workstation   110
    Scenario Four: An Existing Macintosh   111
    Scenario Five: A Windows Workstation   114

Chapter 4   **Troubleshooting the Physical Network**   **117**

Snapshot: Troubleshooting the Physical Network   118
Fault Points for the Physical Network   120
Network Topologies   122
    Ring Topology   124
    Star Topology   125
    Linear Bus Topology   125
Data Communication Protocols   125
    IPX/SPX   126
    IP (TCP/IP)   127
    NetBEUI   127
    NetBIOS   127
    AppleTalk   128
    OSI   128
An Overview of Hardware Standards   130
    Ethernet   130
    Token Ring   132
    LocalTalk   133
    ARCnet   134
Tracking Down Cabling Plant Problems   135
    Cabling: Lengths, Termination, Grounds, Connectors,
        and Type   137
    Patch Panels, Repeaters, and Concentrators   139
    Routers, Bridges, and Gateways   140
Documenting the Cabling Plant   140

Real-Life Stories 141
   Scenario One: A New Cabling System 141
   Scenario Two: Part of an Existing Network Fails 144
   Scenario Three: An Existing Token Ring Network 146
   Scenario Four: Caring for a Growing Network 148
   Scenario Five: Fun with AppleTalk 152

Chapter 5   **Troubleshooting Network Printing**   **157**

Snapshot: Troubleshooting Network Printing 158
Fault Points for Network Printing 167
The Printing Process 169
   The Shell—Printer Redirection 170
   CAPTURE.EXE and Print Jobs—Printing Options 171
   The Print Queue 172
   PSERVER—Printing Controls 173
   The Print Server 173
   Configuration Files or Attributes 174
   Serial and Parallel Interfaces 174
   The Printer 175
Troubleshooting PostScript Printers 177
Troubleshooting NetWare for Macintosh Printing 178
Troubleshooting UNIX Printing 178
Real-Life Stories 180
   Scenario One: A New PostScript Printer 180
   Scenario Two: A Router as Print Server 184
   Scenario Three: Remote Printing with NetWare 4.*x* 187
   Scenario Four: A Single Workstation That Can't Print 190
   Scenario Five: Macintosh Printing Problems 192

PART II   **DISASTERS: BEFORE AND AFTER**   **195**

Chapter 6   **A Pound of Prevention**   **197**

Managing Backup Systems 199
   Evaluating Backup Systems 200
   Developing a Backup Plan 204
   Backing Up Workstation Data 205

Managing Power Protection 206

Evaluating Power Protection Systems 206

Evaluating System Power Requirements 207

The Quality of Your Equipment 207

Preventive Maintenance and Other Precautions 208

Getting Rid of Dust and Other Contaminants 209

Checking Connections 209

Taking Anti-Static Precautions 209

Following Manufacturer's Directions 210

Maintaining a Return Path 211

Maintaining Fault Tolerance 211

Keeping Network Plans and Logs 213

Documenting the Network 213

Logging Network Events 214

Baselining Your Network 215

Monitoring the Server 216

Using Utilities for Baseline Information 219

Training the Users 220

Protecting Your Network against Viruses 221

Elements of Network Security 222

Physical Security 223

Password and Login Security 223

Trustee and File Rights 224

Dial-in Access Security 225

Other Access Security 225

Recovering from Disaster—In Advance 226

The Recovery Plan 226

Data Recovery in Advance 227

Recovery Services in Advance 227

Chapter 7 **Coping with Disaster** **229**

Attitude: Keeping Your Head 231

Recovering from Mechanical Failure or Destruction 232

Your Emergency Kit 232

What to Try First 233

Physical Recovery 234

Data Recovery 235

Restoring from Backups 236

Recovery Services—How Much Is All Your Work Worth? 239

Recovering from Software Problems and User Errors 240

Applications and Network Access 240

Restoring Individual Files 240

Handling Other Hardware Failures 241

Reconstruction—When All Else Fails 242

Recovering from Viruses 243

Disaster Prevention Tools and Techniques: A Recap 244

Disaster Preparedness 246

Disaster Planning 246

Documenting Your Disaster Plan 247

PART III   **TROUBLESHOOTING TECHNIQUES FOR LARGE NETWORKS** 249

Chapter 8   **Troubleshooting WANs** 251

How LANs Are Connected to Form WANs 253

Connecting Multiple LANs at One Site 253

Connecting LANs between Buildings 256

Connecting LANs across Long Distances 256

Connecting LANs around the World 260

Additional Fault Points of WANs 262

Troubleshooting WAN Hardware 262

Dealing with Telecommunications Service Providers 266

Troubleshooting WAN Software 267

Network Management Tools 270

What's Available 270

Features to Look For 271

Diagnostic Tools 273

Hardware-Based Products 273

Software-Only Products 276

Managing without Diagnostic Equipment 277

Services across WANs 278

Printing on WANs 278

Managing Multiple Logins 279

NetWare Directory Services and WANs   280
   The New Structure of NetWare 4.*x*   280
   NWADMIN: The New Management Tool   283
   Troubleshooting NDS   283

Chapter 9   **Connecting to Other Systems**   **285**

Methods for Connecting to Other Systems   287
Connecting Other PC Operating Systems   289
   Windows Clients and NT Servers   290
   OS/2 and NetWare Access   292
   NeXTStep and the NetWare UNIX Client   292
   UnixWare and NetWare Support   293
Connecting Macintoshes   293
   NetWare for Macintosh on the Server   293
   AppleTalk Support on PCs   296
   IPX for Macs   296
   AppleTalk Gateways   296
TCP/IP and UNIX Connectivity   297
   NFS for NetWare Access   298
   NetWare and UNIX Permissions   300
   Troubleshooting TCP/IP Connections   301
   NetWare on UNIX Systems   302

PART IV   **ADVANCED TOPICS**   **303**

Chapter 10   **Troubleshooting Network Applications**   **305**

Applications That Access NetWare Services   306
   File Services   307
   Print Services   309
   Accessing NetWare Services from Windows
      for Workgroups 3.11 or Windows 95   312
   Accessing NetWare Services from Windows 3.1   312
Applications Running from the Server   313
   Running LAN WorkGroup   315
   Running Windows 3.*x* from the Server   316
Electronic-Mail Applications   317

	Using Networked Modems	318
	Networked Data Modems	319
	Networked Fax Modems	320
Chapter 11	**Upgrades to NetWare, Hardware, and Software**	**321**
	Upgrading NetWare	323
	Upgrading without Disrupting Work Flow	323
	Planning the Upgrade	324
	Preparing for the Upgrade	325
	Upgrading from NetWare 2.x to 3.x	328
	Upgrading from NetWare 3.x to 4.x	329
	Example: NetWare 2.15 to 3.12	331
	Example: NetWare 3.11 to 4.1	334
	Upgrading Hardware	338
	Hardware Upgrade Considerations	338
	Troubleshooting Hardware Upgrades	338
	Upgrading Software	339
	Upgrading Networking Software and Operating Systems	340
	Upgrading to Windows 95	341
Chapter 12	**Tips and Techniques**	**345**
	Tips for Troubleshooting PCs (DOS Computers)	346
	Boot Errors	346
	AUTOEXEC.BAT and CONFIG.SYS Errors	347
	IRQ Conflicts	347
	Tips for Troubleshooting Windows	349
	Windows Versions before 3.1	349
	Windows 3.1 and Later	350
	Windows 95	352
	Windows NT	353
	Tips for Troubleshooting Macintoshes	354
	Tips for Troubleshooting UNIX Workstations	357
	Tips for Troubleshooting NetWare	358
	BINDFIX	358
	PRINTCON	359

After ABENDs or Power Failures	359
Login Scripts	360
NetWare 2.*x*	360
NetWare 3.*x*	360
NetWare 4.*x*	361
Tips for Troubleshooting Printing	362
The Next Step	363

PART V **APPENDIXES** **365**

Appendix A **Resources for Troubleshooters** **367**

The NetWare Manuals and README Files	369
Other Novell Publications	369
NetWare Application Notes	369
Novell Research Reports	370
Novell Technical Bulletins	370
Magazines	370
Weekly Magazines	371
Monthly Magazines	371
Newsletters	372
Computer Select and Other CD-ROM Products	372
Books and Catalogs	373
Online Resources	373
NetWire	373
Bulletin Boards	374
BIX	376
World Wire	376
The Internet	376
Internet Newsgroups	377
FTP Sites	379
World Wide Web Sites	379
Technical Support Databases	380
The Network Support Encyclopedia (NSE)	380
Support On Site for Networks	380
The Certified NetWare Engineer Professional Association (CNEPA) and NetWare Users International (NUI)	381

	900 Numbers and Consultants	381
	Training	382
Appendix B	**Tools for Troubleshooters**	**383**
	Other Sources of Information about Tools	385
	Information Tools	386
	Virus Detection Software	387
	Workstation Utilities	390
	Diagnostic Tools	392
	NetWare Utilities	392
	Protocol Analyzers	393
	Inventory Tools	394
	Backup Tools	395
	Fault-Tolerance Systems	395
	Disaster-Recovery Tools	396
	Shareware, Freeware, and Demo Utilities	396
	Audit Programs	397
	Backup Utilities	404
	Bindery Utilities	405
	Data-Recovery Utilities	408
	Diagnostic Utilities	408
	Network Diagramming Tools	413
	Macintosh Utilities	414
	NDS Tools	414
	Remote Workstation Management Utilities	415
	Software Management Tools	415
	User Management Tools	416
	Upgrade Utilities	418
	Virus Scanners	419
Appendix C	**Network Record Keeping Forms**	**425**
Glossary of Terms		**437**
Index		*509*

Introduction

I F YOU ADMINISTER or help administer a NetWare network, troubleshooting—solving problems—is one of your primary concerns. The goal of this book is to show you how you can use a systematic approach to make troubleshooting network-related problems an easier job and avoid many of the typical trouble-shooting pitfalls.

While this approach will require some effort on your part, in collecting information about your network and then in working to understand how your network operates, it will yield both an ability to fix anything that might go wrong, as well as a very marketable skill.

Who Should Read This Book?

You don't need to be a networking expert to be a successful troubleshooter. In fact, many network administrators have been assigned the task simply because they know a bit more than anyone else in the company. Following the principles in this book will help even a relatively inexperienced administrator to isolate and correct most problems. However, to use this book effectively, you should know the fundamentals, such as:

- A basic understanding of the equipment you are working with

- The ability to open a PC and change a disk drive or install a LAN adapter

- An understanding of the basics of DOS and MS Windows (or whatever system your clients are running)

- The ability to move around the file system

- An understanding of the basics of configuring a system

You can learn more about networking topics such as these from many sources. If the manuals that came with your hardware and software are not satisfactory, there are many alternatives available in your local bookstore. Appendix A covers resources for learning more about your system.

Organization of This Book

This book is organized in four parts:

- **Part I, Basic Elements of Troubleshooting,** begins with an overview of the principles of troubleshooting, which are the underlying concepts you'll need to understand and to master the science of troubleshooting. The remaining four chapters in this part show how to troubleshoot each major component of the network: servers, workstations, the physical network, and print services.

- **Part II, Disasters: Before and After,** describes steps you can take to prevent or minimize disasters, and what to do if they strike anyway (or before you have a chance to implement the suggested measures).

- **Part III, Troubleshooting Techniques for Large Networks,** covers the issues involved with multiple LANs connected to form WANs, and heterogeneous LANs and WANs comprised of different types of operating systems and protocols.

- **Part IV, Advanced Topics,** offers some specialized information, including troubleshooting application programs running in a network environment, avoiding problems while upgrading your network, and using some tips, tricks, and techniques to solve particularly stubborn problems.

The appendixes are references that troubleshooters will find very useful. Appendix A provides information about resources, including publications, online resources, technical support databases, associations, support services, and training. Appendix B lists some of the tools available to troubleshooters, such as diagnostic tools, inventory tools, and virus-detection software. It also includes a listing of shareware, freeware, and demos. In Appendix C, you'll find forms that you can copy to use in inventorying your network and recording the configurations of your workstations, servers, and network devices. The glossary at the end of the book includes terms you are likely to encounter not only in this book but in the NetWare manuals and in other discussions of networking.

Special Features of This Book

This book has several special features to help you find and understand the information you need:

- Snapshot sections at the beginning of Chapters 2 through 5 in Part I provide a quick reference to isolating the cause of your current problem. They take you through a series of questions designed to help you find the source of the problem and direct you to the section of the chapter that has the details.

- Fault point charts and descriptions clarify all the essential links in a network chain. Each item in the fault point chain can affect the chain. The key to finding the fault points and checking them for failure is an understanding of the principles involved in that chain.

- Real-life scenarios (in Part I) describe typical problems and how a troubleshooter would go through the process of isolating the fault and fixing it. Two fictional companies and their administrators are used as examples.

- Notes, tips, and warnings throughout the book provide extra information, helpful hints, and cautions about potential problems.

A Note from the Author

Like many of you, I didn't set out to be a network administrator. I was working as a translator when someone in one of the companies I was working for had trouble with his PC. I helped him fix it, using the principles set forth in this book (which I had learned working on cars). This led to other troubleshooting and computer-related jobs. I eventually ended up at Novell and had the opportunity to learn a lot while I was there. I'm now consulting on network systems. I welcome input on this book. My Internet address is lharba@aol.com.

Basic Elements of Troubleshooting

PART

Principles of Troubleshooting

CHAPTER

OST BUSINESSES HAVE BEEN USING PCs for years, usually in the same way that typewriters were used in the past—as individual tools to enhance productivity. Now, many companies are discovering that computers can be networked in local-area networks (LANs) and wide-area networks (WANs) to increase productivity dramatically. But the resulting networks are being built piecemeal; first one department networks its computers, then another, and eventually the whole company, but not necessarily according to any overall plan.

Such networks usually consist of several different kinds of workstations—PCs running any of several operating systems, Macintoshes, UNIX workstations—all tied together through servers of one sort or another, and perhaps also tied to the old mainframe or minicomputer as well. One of the best tools for connecting various workstations and servers is NetWare. Its ability to allow many different environments to work together also makes it possible to create networks of incredible complexity.

Because the use of networks is growing so rapidly, and because training programs turn out far fewer graduates than are needed, network administrators are in short supply. Often, this means that users who know only a little more than their colleagues about computers or networks find themselves pressed into service as administrators. And administrators who began by administering a small departmental network may now find themselves responsible for a half-dozen servers and hundreds of workstations. These people may be able to set up basic configurations of their workstations or LANs, but often have little or no formal training or background in troubleshooting. This book is intended to help the knowledgeable user to understand the principles of troubleshooting, and to apply those principles to fix problems with workstations and networks.

There are many books on troubleshooting that are full of information on what to do in specific situations—if X happens, do Y. There are others that try to present the material contained in the software documentation in a more accessible way. These are useful resources, but the one thing almost never touched on is the *approach* to troubleshooting. This book is not about how to get a particular network driver to work with a particular adapter. Instead, it will show you how to isolate the cause of your problem, find the information necessary to fix the problem, and apply that knowledge.

An Approach to Troubleshooting

MANY PEOPLE INVOLVED WITH COMPUTERS and networks of computers regard setting them up and fixing them when they stop working as an arcane art. To the average user watching an expert troubleshoot and fix a system, the process might seem like magic. However, whether the expert consciously follows them or not, there are certain basic principles common to all troubleshooting.

The basic process of troubleshooting is simple to state: determine that there is a problem, isolate the problem, identify the cause of the problem, and fix the problem. The biggest difficulty in applying this relatively simple process to a LAN or WAN, or even to a single workstation or server, is caused by the enormous number of possible combinations of hardware, software, and configurations involved.

Breaking Down the Elements

The simplest approach to this complexity is to break it down: isolate the WAN into LANs; each LAN into server, workstations, and cabling; each server or workstation into hardware, DOS, and networking software; and the physical cabling into segments. Each of these subsystems can be further divided as necessary, until each element can be determined to be the cause of the problem or not.

Often, an experienced troubleshooter will have a seemingly intuitive "feel" for what might be wrong. But what appears to be intuition is usually a rapid process of elimination based on long and often painful previous experience. This experience is useful in rapidly finding and fixing a problem, but it is not essential. Most users, by following a logical and methodical approach, will be able to solve the same problem, although probably not as quickly.

Trying Different Solutions

The optimum approach to becoming a good troubleshooter is to try things out. As long as basic precautions are followed to avoid irreparable changes, experimentation is fine. In fact, this is often the way that even a highly experienced troubleshooter will approach a problem: try a few different things until the system is fixed. He or she will simply have a better feel for which things to try first—which "fault points" are the most likely to be broken.

There are a couple of basic ways to determine what things to try first, and how to continue from there. Try the simple things first. It's much easier to verify that a PC is plugged in than to disassemble it and check the hard disk to be sure it's receiving power. It's also much more likely that the PC has been accidentally unplugged than that the power connection for the hard disk has failed or worked loose. Also, don't change more than one thing at once; for instance, replacing all the cards in a PC might well fix the problem, but it won't tell you which of the cards has failed. Unless you need to get that PC back online immediately, it's better to switch cards one at a time, replacing the old one if there's no change, until the problem is isolated.

Each chapter in this book will help you to determine the most likely failure areas for your particular setup. These vary from system to system, but as you become familiar with the trouble spots for your system, you will be able to rapidly check a few items and often solve your problem within a few minutes. Not only does this save time when irate users are waiting to get back online, it makes you seem like a wizard to your boss.

Two of your best tools to determine likely areas of failure are a well-kept log and a *baseline* of the system, which is a collection of statistics that represent the normal operation of your equipment. These are discussed further in this chapter and in Chapter 6.

Almost all systems that need troubleshooting fall into one of two categories: systems that were working and have failed or new systems that don't work as expected (this includes existing systems that stopped working when something new was added). Each requires a certain basic approach, but the essential underlying principle of all troubleshooting is to eliminate possible causes of the problem until the actual cause is isolated.

Troubleshooting New Systems and Additions to Existing Systems

WഀITH A SYSTEM THAT IS NEW, or one to which something has been added, the basic approach is to achieve a minimum configuration that works, or to return to the configuration that worked before things were changed, and build from there. For instance, a networked workstation will often have a number of cards in it, which might include a network adapter, video display adapter, floppy/hard disk controller, mouse, serial/parallel adapter, expanded or extended memory board, coprocessor or accelerator card, internal modem, host adapter, and SCSI controller. Each of these can potentially interfere with the others.

Stripping Down to the Minimum

To begin with, it's best to fall back to a basic minimum, perhaps only the floppy/hard disk controller and video adapter. If the PC will boot with just these cards, then add others until you discover what isn't working, or what is conflicting with the basic system.

With new additions that cause problems, it is unlikely that the new part is defective, so the solution is usually to isolate the conflict between the new item and something in the system. Unless you have specific suspicions about where the conflict may be, the most certain procedure is to remove any extraneous parts from the system. If the new addition works with a basic system, begin adding the remaining components back in until the problem recurs.

Keeping Track of Configuration Details

It is important to keep track of each card in a PC, and what interrupts and memory segments it uses. Actually checking each card's manual and writing down what its configuration is may be the only way you will discover that it is attempting to use the same memory segment as another card. See the "Record Keeping" section later in this chapter for suggestions on how to record data about your system.

You may discover that the default configurations of all the cards in the PC will not work together. In this case, you must determine which cards have alternate configurations and how to set them, and then possibly reset the appropriate software. There are also programs that will help you determine which interrupts and memory segments each card in a system uses. See Appendix B for information about useful software.

Some network cards, like the NE2000, have more than a dozen possible configurations, but only two or three that are normally used. Unfortunately, the advisble configurations on some cards can be difficult to discover, depending on the quality of the documentation. This is also true in general of all the cards you might find in a PC. Even expensive cards may have terrible documentation; it is one of the few instances where paying more will not necessarily gain you anything.

It is also true that Plug and Play and PCI are not without their problems. Even if all the cards in the system support Plug and Play, and your operating system supports it and has drivers for the cards, things may still not work, or you may find that one card's drivers conflict with those for another card. You should check the documentation and README files on the driver disks that came with the cards to make sure that the drivers are the latest available.

If you cannot find the information you need in the manual for the card, or cannot make sense of what is there, your best bet is to find someone else who has already been through the problem and pick their brains. Possible sources of information include the manufacturer's tech support line, the dealer you bought the equipment from, your local MIS organization, the Support Alliance, various forums on CompuServe or the Internet, and the local CNE user group. See the "Resources for Troubleshooters" section later in this chapter and Appendix A for more information about various groups you can contact.

Troubleshooting Existing Systems

WITH AN EXISTING SYSTEM that was working and has failed, the basic approach is to determine what has changed. This may require a methodical approach involving swapping cards or checking connections, or it may be as simple as discovering that the user has added a new piece of software that is incompatible with other software on the system.

Talk to the user. You might ask these kinds of questions:

- Does the user know of a way to make the problem go away?

- Is there a certain time of day, a particular piece of software, or a certain server associated with the problem?

- Has the user changed the configuration of his or her PC recently?

- What was the user doing when the problem occurred?

Getting the information from a user can be difficult. Users may not remember the critical change, or may be reluctant to admit having done something that may be causing a problem.

There are a couple of things you can do to make the necessary information easier to find. The first is to keep a record of system configurations on each workstation on your network. This information can be tedious to acquire, although inventory programs can produce most of the information you will want automatically. Another useful approach is to standardize the workstations on your network as much as possible. Make sure that they are all using the same version of DOS, the same network shell and adapter, and so on.

Sometimes, the change to a system is not intentional. It may be a connection that has worked loose, a corrupted file, or a broken cable. You will still have clues to investigate, but you may need to dig for them. It is still basically a process of elimination which is determined by the break points of the system. These will be covered in the appropriate chapters in detail.

Attitude: The Single Most Important Thing You Can Get from This Book!

WHEN I MEET WITH OTHER TROUBLESHOOTERS, system engineers, or networking experts, the conversation often turns to troubleshooting, and what makes a good troubleshooter. The consensus is that the single most important ingredient to make a good troubleshooter is not knowledge, or experience, or intelligence. It is attitude. A determination to keep trying until you figure out the problem is essential. Any system that worked once can be made to work again. The critical thing is to keep trying until the problem is solved.

The biggest stumbling blocks for most troubleshooters are the mistaken impression that they have "tried everything" and the feeling that the problem is too complex—that they'll never be able to understand the problem. The first idea is usually caused by looking at the system too quickly, but it may also result from failing to consider the possible effects of elements apparently outside the problem. The second feeling can be avoided by breaking the problem down into more basic components—break a WAN into LANs, a LAN into server, workstations, and cabling plant, and so on.

You can be successful at troubleshooting as long as you are willing to keep trying. You may not be as fast at first as someone with a lot of experience or knowledge of the system, but you can get results. The more familiar with your system you are, of course, the more capable of fixing it you will be. This is one of the functions of performing the baselining and collecting the log sheets for every workstation and server on your network, as explained in the next section.

Record Keeping

T IS UTTERLY IMPOSSIBLE to overdo documentation of your network. Hours spent collecting information on your network might seem like a waste at the time, particularly to your supervisor, but it could make many, many hours of difference in the time required to get the network running again if there is trouble. It's cheap insurance.

One of the most useful aids in troubleshooting is good record keeping. It's difficult to isolate what might be causing a problem if you don't know what is in the system. Likewise, if you need to reconfigure a system back to its last working state, it's easier if you don't need to rediscover the settings that got it to work in the first place. Also, your records for a similar system and how you got it to work may give you a lead on fixing your current problem.

You should have a record of each system that includes the date it was installed and the original configuration, the dates and details of each update or addition to hardware or software, and perhaps a printout of the configuration files. Such a record can greatly simplify the problem of isolating the latest change to a system. It will be easier to keep such records if you establish a database or use a standard worksheet when you set up or modify a workstation. Figure 1.1 shows an example of a worksheet for recording server configuration data. See Appendix C for more sample worksheets.

In addition, an archive of the standard software used on your workstations can make your life much easier. It's far easier and faster to simply copy the files needed from your standard set of floppies or network directory than to copy them from the original floppies, re-create them, or regenerate them, as required.

FIGURE 1.1

An example of a server configuration worksheet

Server Configuration Worksheet
Side One

Name: _Asmodeus_   Location: _Office 1141_   Date: _3/30/96_

Internal IPX Number: _C11412385_   Department: _Marketing_

Brand/Model: _ACMA 150 Mhz Pentium PC1 Tower Award BIOS 6.11_

Support Phone Number: _408 555-1491_   Serial Number: _A11093B31_

Memory Installed: _64 Mb_ Possible: _256 Mb_ Type: _16x32 SIMM_

Board: _LAN Adapter_	**Board**: _LAN Adapter_
Brand: _3Com_	Brand: _3Com_
Support #: _408 764-6399_	Support #: _408 764-6399_
Model #: _36590TP_	Model #: _3C590TP_
I/O Port: _____	I/O Port: _____
Memory Address: _____	Memory Address: _____
Interrupt: _____	Interrupt: _____
DMA: _____	DMA: _____
Slot Number: _3_	Slot Number: _2_
Driver: _3C590.LAN_	Driver: _3C590.LAN_
BIOS Version: _1.21_	BIOS Version: _1.21_
Network Number: _1A114100_	Network Number: _2B114100_
Board: _SVGA_	**Board**: _____
Brand: _On Motherboard_	Brand: _____
Support #: _____	Support #: _____
Model #: _____	Model #: _____
I/O Port: _____	i/O Port: _____
Memory Address: _B000-B7FF_	Memory Address: _____
Interrupt: _____	Interrupt: _____
DMA: _____	DMA: _____
Slot Number: _____	Slot Number: _____
Driver: _____	Driver: _____
BIOS Version: _____	BIOS Version: _____
Network Number: _____	Network Number: _____

Disks - see other side

FIGURE 1.1 (cont.)

Server Configuration Worksheet
Side Two — Disks

Controller: Adaptec 1742B (EISA)   Int: — DMA: ____ Slot #: _4_

Support #: 510 555-3201   Driver: AHA1740.DSK

Port: — **Mem. Address:** —   BIOS Version: 6.02

Disk	Size	Heads	Cylinders	Device Code (5-digit)	Logical Device	Physical Partition	Mirrored With
Maxtor PO-125	1 Gb	15	4196	21100	1	0	1
Maxtor PO-125	1 Gb	15	4196	21200	2	1	—

Controller: Motherboard   Int: _E_ DMA: ____ Slot #: ____

Support #: 415 555-8195   Driver: ISADISK

Port: 1f0 **Mem. Address:** ____   BIOS Version: _____

Disk	Size	Heads	Cylinders	Device Code (5-digit)	Logical Device	Physical Partition	Mirrored With
Quantum IDE 105S	100	8	995	11000	1	0	—

A daily log is another useful tool for the network administrator. It can provide a history of a particular problem, making it easier to isolate things that may occur at long or irregular intervals. A good log can make it much easier to justify new purchases or upgrades; for example, if you can show that the same part has failed four times in the last 10 months. (And a log will also show your supervisor just what you've been doing with your time.)

Resources for Troubleshooters

B ECAUSE OF THE ENORMOUS NUMBER of possibilities inherent in LANs, no single book can address all the possible combinations or provide all the information necessary to understand your LAN. Among the additional resources available to you, and which I hope you will use, are:

- The NetWare manuals.

- The hardware manufacturer's manuals.

- Books on NetWare, networking, applications you may be using, and so on.

- Trade publications. Between the weekly and monthly magazines, there are thousands of pages published every month on hundreds of topics related to networking.

- Computer bulletin boards and services. CompuServe has a large section on NetWare. Any question you might have has probably been discussed on one of the forums. The Internet news groups on NetWare (such as comp.os.netware.misc) are also extensive.

- Your local NetWare user group.

- The local chapter of the Certified NetWare Engineer Professional Association (CNEPA). Even if you're not a member, you can probably get either free advice or professional help through the Association.

- Your Authorized Reseller. The dealer you bought NetWare from should have technical support personnel who can help you with your problem.

- Services from Novell's technical support, including its hotline (1-800-NETWARE), the NetWare Web page (www.novell.com), the NetWare Support Encyclopedia, and so on.

- Online or CD-ROM-based collections of information, including Micro House Technical Library, Computer Select, and the various magazines' CD-ROMs, such as Byte on CD-ROM, LAN Times CD-ROM, and others.

See Appendix A for more information about the resources available for troubleshooters.

Aids for Troubleshooting

T HIS BOOK PROVIDES A NUMBER OF TOOLS designed to help you implement the approach to problem-solving outlined in this chapter. These include a Snapshot section at the beginning of the remaining chapters in Part I, fault points that identify where things can go wrong, and real-life stories to help you put the information in context.

Snapshots for Quick Reference

The Snapshot sections in the following chapters in Part I provide a quick reference to lead you through the basic process of isolating the cause of your current problem. Each Snapshot will ask you whether the problem is with a new system or an existing one, and then take you through a series of questions designed to help you find the source of the problem. It will then direct you to the section of the chapter that discusses that part of the system, which will discuss the principles involved and get more details on how to fix the problem.

The process you should follow to isolate a problem with your LAN is in the same order as the chapters; check the server first, the workstations second, and the physical network third. Your first indication that there is a problem will often be a complaint from a user. The best course is usually to quickly eliminate the most obvious possible causes before doing an in-depth analysis. If a cursory examination shows that the user's workstation seems to be in order, then check to make sure that the server is operational.

Your first check of the server should simply be to see that it is on and responding to the keyboard. If it is, there could still be problems, but it's best to next find out how many workstations are experiencing problems, then do some simple tests to determine whether the physical connections could be causing the problem, before doing a really thorough examination of the server. It's usually faster and less likely to inconvenience lots of users to check a few other workstations than to begin working on the server.

Fault Points for Identifying Problem Areas

Rather than a typical flowchart, which cannot cover anything close to all the possibilities inherent in a network, I have developed a system that looks at the places where things can go wrong. This approach does require a certain degree of understanding of your system, but is also adaptable to any system. The idea is that there are, within any combination of different types of workstations, network interface cards, network topologies, servers, cabling, software, and so on, a limited number of points where something can go wrong.

For instance, the connection between the network card and the physical wiring is a fault point. Depending on your system, the connector may be any one of a dozen types, each with its own unique way of going bad. Rather than attempt to teach you what all of these are and how to tell if they are the problem, I'll attempt to show you how to isolate your problem to that particular fault point, and leave the rest to you.

The fault points are all the essential links in a network chain. For instance, the workstation hardware and operating system, the software and hardware that allow the workstation to talk over the cabling, the cabling system, and the server itself are all parts of the network chain that connects the user to the server. Other chains may include the chain from the user to the printer or to a modem, from the server to a remote LAN, from the LAN to another LAN, and so on. Each item in the fault point chain can affect the chain in three ways: it can fail, its links to the previous item can fail, or its links to the next item can fail. For instance, a power cord could be broken, or it could have a faulty connection to the wall socket or the power supply of the equipment it's attached to.

In every case, the key to finding the fault points and checking them for failure is an understanding of the principles involved in that chain. This does not mean that you must know and understand the seven levels of the OSI model, for example, but you should understand that the network adapter and network driver in a workstation combine to send a message through the wire to the network adapter and network driver in the server. You should also know that, depending on the type of network and whether the packet goes straight to the server or is passed along from one workstation to the next, a missing T-connector at the unused workstation in the next cube might be the problem.

For quick reference, the fault point chain for each chapter in Part I is represented as an illustration like that shown in Figure 1.2.

FIGURE 1.2
The fault point chain for
troubleshooting servers

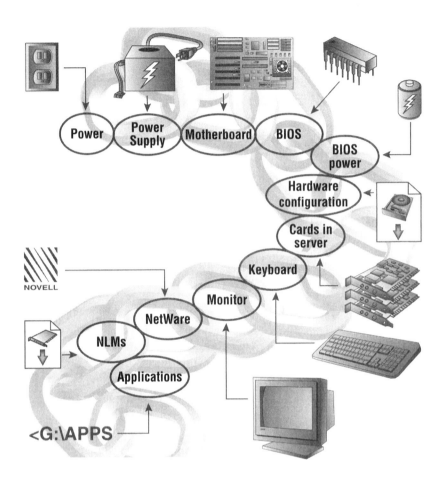

Real-Life Stories

Each of the remaining chapters in Part I will also have a narrative section
describing typical problems and how a troubleshooter would go through the
process of isolating the fault and fixing it. Two fictional companies and their
administrators will be used as examples. They combine the equipment and
experience of a number of actual businesses. Each real-life scenario includes
sections on the fault point chain and the lessons learned from the experience.

Small Company Scenarios

Itsy-Bitsy, Inc. is a small company with one building housing several departments and about 200 users. The company has one system administrator, John, who is responsible for several NetWare servers, the networking hardware, and the workstations, most of which are PCs, with a few Macintoshes. The NetWare servers include both NetWare 2.*x* and 3.*x*, and they're thinking about making the jump to 4.*x*.

John has learned "on the job," without any formal training. He has learned a good deal the hard way, and he has developed a good feel for PCs, DOS, Windows, and NetWare, as well as the basics of networking hardware. Itsy-Bitsy is a small manufacturing company, and the users are relatively unsophisticated, so John gets lots of experience in user training and in supporting applications. As a result, he has developed an interest in scripts and automation tools for installations.

Big Company Scenarios

Fran, the system administrator for Great Big, Inc., is responsible for a three-building campus, one of several sites scattered across the country. She has two assistants: Jethro, who is experienced with Macintoshes, but not particularly with NetWare, and Marilyn, whose primary area of expertise is with UNIX, although she is learning NetWare. Marilyn was formerly the administrator for the Engineering department, which runs UNIX workstations on a UNIX server. Between them, these three are responsible for 14 servers, including 2 UNIX servers, networking hardware that includes links to company sites in other cities and abroad, and about 1000 workstations, including PCs, Macintoshes, and UNIX workstations.

The internetwork is typical, having grown up from a number of departmental networks. It includes several different types of wiring and network protocols, different types of workstations in different departments, and no real program for integrating the whole mess into a coordinated whole. The evolution of this internetwork will provide examples of what to do and what not to do in planning and evolving a network.

One of Fran's big goals is to cross-train her people so that they all have a basic understanding of the different types of systems, as well as the networking hardware. With about 1000 users, she also has a deep interest in diminishing the need for user support by standardizing applications and using the most user-friendly software available. Great Big is a software development company, and most users are relatively sophisticated, the opposite of Itsy-Bitsy. But the problem that Fran faces is that many of her users are inclined to jump in and fix things, which they may or may not understand completely.

Troubleshooting Servers

Snapshot: Troubleshooting Servers

IS THIS A NEW SYSTEM?

Will the server boot DOS?

If not, first go to Chapter 3, and see the section on new workstations. The section about hardware problems in new servers, on page 31, contains information about the specialized hardware found in servers, such as multiple network adapters and hard disk adapters. For NetWare 2.x, it is not strictly necessary that the server boot DOS, but it's a good test—if it won't boot DOS, then NetWare is unlikely to load either. You may need to boot from a floppy, especially with a 2.x server.

Will NetWare load?

If NetWare won't load, the error messages that appear while it attempts to load are your best clues to the problem. For details on the loading process, see the sections on NetWare version-specific information, beginning on page 27.

If you are running NetWare 2.x and using a Novell DCB, you should also check to see if the PROM on the DCB that allows the PC to boot from a SCSI drive has been installed. If the chip has not been installed or has been installed incorrectly, the PC will not recognize the SCSI drive as a bootable disk. Look for bent pins, and make sure that the chip is facing in the correct direction. Be sure to observe static precautions when handling chips and boards! If you aren't familiar with proper static precautions, see Chapter 6 for more details.

Are some devices (such as network cards or disk drives) inaccessible after NetWare loads?

This is likely to be a hardware problem. Either a piece of hardware is not functioning correctly or the driver program for that hardware is not functioning correctly. See the section about hardware problems in new servers, on page 31.

IS THIS AN EXISTING SYSTEM?

Is the server up?

If the server is working (the screen is lit, the prompt responds to keyboard input, you can switch to different NLM monitor screens, and so on), then the problem is likely to be in either the workstation or the physical network (the cabling, repeater, MUX, and so on). You can quickly check with MONITOR or FCONSOLE to make sure that all LAN adapters are sending and receiving packets. If they are, then you should next determine how many workstations are experiencing problems. If it is only one, then go to Chapter 3 for information about troubleshooting workstations. If several or all workstations have similar problems, go to Chapter 4 for information about troubleshooting the physical network. Finally, if the physical network checks out, then you'll need to begin a deeper analysis of the server. This is covered in the section on using SERVMAN, MONITOR, and FCONSOLE, on page 44.

Can you reboot the server?

If the server does not appear to be working—if, for instance, the cursor is frozen, the screen is dark, or it doesn't respond to keyboard input—reboot the server. If the server reboots correctly, then the problem may have been a system error of some sort. Check the error message log to see if there are any unusual error messages. See the section on checking the error message log, on page 45. You should also make note of any new NLMs or new applications that may have been running on the server; if the problem recurs, they are a good place to start. See the section about troubleshooting NLM problems, on page 51.

Will the server boot DOS?

If the server reboots without error messages, but NetWare doesn't load, try just booting DOS. With a NetWare 2.x server, you will need to boot from a floppy. If the server will not boot DOS, then it is likely that the problem is a hardware failure, although it's possible that COMMAND.COM has been corrupted. See the section about hardware problems in existing servers, on page 44.

Will NetWare load?

If NetWare fails to load on a server that was working before, one of two things is likely to have happened: there is a hardware failure or the NetWare system files may have become corrupted. There are other possibilities, such as a network "storm" causing so much interference that NetWare cannot function, but the first two possibilities are the most likely.

With NetWare 3.x or 4.x, watch the messages that come up as SERVER.EXE attempts to execute. Usually, they will give you the necessary clues to determine what has failed. If you have a backup copy of SERVER.EXE, you can try replacing the one on the boot drive.

With NetWare 2.x, the problem may also be with the DCB or the EPROM on it that allows NetWare to boot from a SCSI drive. If you are using this feature, you should see a message from the BIOS on the DCB that tells you it is making the SCSI drive available as a boot drive. You should also keep a backup copy of NET$OS.EXE—it is also subject to becoming corrupted.

Can you load NetWare but not access some or all server functions?

If the server appears to be functioning but workstations cannot access it, and the physical network appears to be functional, then running MONITOR or FCONSOLE is your first step to isolating the problem. The two most likely areas of failure are the LAN adapters and the disk drive systems. See the section on software problems in existing servers, beginning on page 46.

Does the server have intermittent problems?

Intermittent server failure can be difficult to troubleshoot because there are so many probable causes, including power surges, faulty equipment, or applications running on the server or a workstation. The important thing to look for to isolate intermittent problems is what changes just before the crash. You will need to investigate by talking to users and researching records and logs. See the section about intermittent problems with servers, on page 48.

ETWARE BEGAN TO TAKE OVER the PC-networking marketplace when it was changed to run on IBM PC-compatibles rather than the original proprietary Motorola 68000-based servers. The first servers were 286-based IBM AT-compatibles, and as new chips and capabilities have become available, NetWare has grown to accommodate and make use of the new resources.

As PC-based networks have grown, the demand for more capabilities has also grown to the point that there are now superservers available. These super-servers incorporate many of the features of the mainframes they are replacing, such as the ability to replace defective cards or even hard drives without needing to turn the server off, multiple processors, and Error Correction Code (ECC) memory that can self-correct hardware memory errors. Memory and disk storage sizes have expanded by several orders of magnitude, from 640 KB of RAM, to 64 MB, to 512 MB or more, and from 10 or 20 MB hard disks to 2 GB (2000 MB) to 500 GB RAIDs.

As the speed and capabilities of servers has grown, NetWare has also grown in the services it provides. From a relatively simple file- and print-sharing service, NetWare has grown to provide access to other types of computers and computer networks, including Macintoshes, UNIX machines, and IBM mini-computers and mainframes. NetWare now supports many network protocols and dozens of network adapters, and can run on hundreds of PC-compatibles. As its capabilities have grown—because they have grown—NetWare has become much more complex and more difficult to troubleshoot. This chapter will lead you through the troubleshooting process for servers.

In general, the principles of troubleshooting workstations are equally applicable to servers. In fact, servers are usually more straightforward in basic configuration than workstations, because they aren't usually personalized with add-on software. The differences that can make servers a problem to trouble-shoot include the high-performance enhancements common to most servers, such as large amounts of RAM, large hard disks, specialized and faster interfaces, and NetWare itself. These differences are covered in this chapter; the basics of getting a workstation to work are covered in Chapter 3.

In this chapter, we'll cover:

- Tracing the fault point chain for servers

- Troubleshooting new servers

- Troubleshooting existing servers

- Using diagnostic tools

- Dealing with NetWare Loadable Module (NLM) problems

- Protecting the server with System Fault Tolerance (SFT)

Fault Points for Servers

CHAPTER 1 INTRODUCED THE CONCEPT OF a chain of fault points as a guide to troubleshooting networks and network components. Within any combination of different types of workstations, network interface cards (NICs), LAN topologies, servers, cabling, software, and so on, there are a limited number of points where problems can occur. Because a conventional flowchart cannot cover anything close to all the possibilities inherent in a network, it makes more sense to look only at those places where things can go wrong.

Figure 2.1 shows the fault chain for troubleshooting NetWare servers. Each item in the chain depends on the previous items for proper operation. For instance, the server will not operate at all without power to the wall socket. A complete fault chain would also include the connection between the wall socket and the power cord, the power cord, and the connection to the power supply. Similarly, the power supply link in the fault chain also includes the connections from the power supply to the motherboard and disk drives. The BIOS controls the motherboard and the beginning of the boot process, and it can cause failures if it isn't recent enough or if its battery power fails. The hardware configuration includes the values stored in the BIOS that tell the PC what type of floppy and hard disk drives it has, as well as the settings on the various cards installed in the server.

The cards themselves can also fail because of their connection to the motherboard, their connection to whatever device they're attached to, or because of a failure of some component on the card itself. Be aware that many cards now

FIGURE 2.1
The fault point chain for
troubleshooting servers

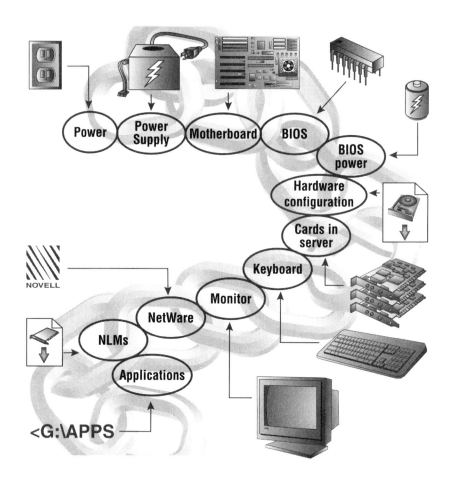

have a BIOS of their own that operates in addition to the BIOS on the mother-board, to add further functionality to the server.

A failure in the keyboard or monitor or in their cables or connections may result in a crash, a server that won't boot, or a server that seems dead when it isn't. NetWare, even though it is software, has the same three failure points:

- It can fail in its connection to previous links, such as a driver that accesses the LAN adapter or in the connection to the next item, which might be a Net-Ware Loadable Module (NLM) written for a different version of NetWare.

- It can fail internally (crash).

- It can fail because other software fails. NLMs (in NetWare 3.*x* and 4.*x*) or VAPs (Value-Added Processes, in NetWare 2.*x*) add functionality to Net-Ware, and can fail, usually causing the loss of that functionality, but sometimes causing the whole server to crash. Also, applications running on the server have been known to cause servers to crash, if they attempt to access NetWare services with an illegal function call.

NetWare Version-Specific Information

NETWARE, AS A PC-BASED NETWORK OPERATING SYSTEM (NOS), has evolved through three major versions. The first PC-based versions of NetWare needed to be generated with all operating system configurations set up in advance. These versions include NetWare 2.0, 2.0a, 2.10, 2.11, 2.12, 2.15, and 2.2, known collectively as 2.*x*. The next evolutionary step for NetWare was 3.0. NetWare 3.0 was the first version of NetWare written for the 80386 processor. It took full advantage of the additional capabilities of the 386 over the 80286, and also allowed reconfiguration of nearly every aspect of the operating system while the server was running. More recently, NetWare 3.10, 3.11, and 3.12 have been released, and all are collectively known as 3.*x*. The third evolutionary step for NetWare is NetWare 4.0. This version adds features specifically designed for large corporate networks. Later versions include 4.01, 4.1, and 4.2, known collectively as 4.*x*.

The biggest difference between the 2.*x* series of NetWare and 3.*x* and 4.*x* is that the configuration of 2.*x* cannot be changed after the operating system is installed. Versions 3.*x* and 4.*x* can be configured "on the fly," and the configuration can be changed without even bringing the server down, let alone redoing the installation. Version 4.*x* includes additional functionality for large networks, principally the NetWare Directory Services (NDS), which allows access to server functions from anywhere on a large internetwork.

NetWare 2.*x* Operation

If you're new to NetWare, you may wonder why this section is still in here, since 2.*x* is no longer being shipped by Novell. I have spoken with some poor, benighted souls who are still attempting to run the original NetWare 4.*x* (from

1987) on the original proprietary Motorola 68000-based servers. I can't be of much help to those people, but I think there are enough people still using Net-Ware 2.*x* (many quite happily!) to make this section worthwhile.

From a floppy, the loading process is this: DOS is loaded from the floppy, then NET$OS.EXE is executed, either manually or from the AUTOEXEC.BAT file. NetWare takes over completely from DOS. When the server boots from a hard disk, it boots from the NetWare cold boot loader, which is written to track 0 of the disk when the hard disk is formatted. The cold boot loader is executed when the server is turned on, and in turn executes NET$OS.EXE, which is the only operating system present—DOS is never loaded. If the server boot drive is a SCSI drive, the PROM (programmable read-only memory) on the DCB (disk coprocessor board), or the BIOS on later model SCSI adapters, is what allows the server to boot from a drive that is not supported by the PC's BIOS.

Commands in the SERVER.CFG and AUTOEXEC.SYS files allow you to automatically run VAPs, set up printers, and execute other commands that add functionality to NetWare in the same manner as an AUTOEXEC.BAT file on a workstation.

Communication buffers are used to hold data packets arriving from workstations. They don't use much memory, so set the number twice as high as you think you'll need. If you set the number too low, it will degrade network performance, because the server will ignore packets it doesn't have room for in the buffers, forcing the workstations to resend the packets. Changing the number requires regenerating the operating system with INSTALL.

NetWare 3.*x* Operation

The biggest difference between NetWare 2.*x* and NetWare 3.*x* is that 3.*x* can dynamically allocate and deallocate memory as resources or NLMs are loaded or unloaded. Figure 2.2 illustrates the differences in NetWare versions.

Some resources, such as disk drivers or protocols bound to LAN adapters, are normally loaded permanently, but some may be loaded and unloaded as needed. All remaining free memory is used for file cache buffers, which hold the files last requested, so disk access isn't required if the file is accessed again.

The loading process for NetWare 3.*x* is the same from a floppy or a hard disk. You boot the server with DOS, then run SERVER.EXE. SERVER takes its configuration parameters from the STARTUP.NCF and AUTOEXEC.NCF files. If you will be booting from a DOS partition on the hard disk, it doesn't need to be more than about 2 MB, but I recommend at least 4 MB. This will

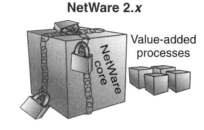

NetWare 2.*x*

Value-added processes

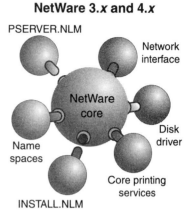

NetWare 3.*x* and 4.*x*

PSERVER.NLM

Network interface

NetWare core

Disk driver

Name spaces

Core printing services

INSTALL.NLM

give you enough room for a directory where you can place backup copies of SERVER.EXE and STARTUP.NCF, in case those files are corrupted or accidentally changed or removed. It will also give you room to grow if future versions of NetWare require more space for SERVER.EXE or the equivalent.

NetWare 4.*x* Operation

The most complex addition to NetWare 4.*x* is NDS, which uses a distributed NetWare Directory database to manage all services over a large internet. A large internet is organized logically by country, state, organization, organizational group, organizational role, and so on down the line, rather than according to what hardware is plugged in where. This means that users on a server in one building can access volumes, printers, or other services on servers in other buildings, or even other states or countries, without needing to know the other server's name or going through complex procedures to set things up first.

"Objects" are the basis of NDS; they contain information on various parts of the network, such as drives or printers. Each object contains information about who is allowed to access it, including users and groups, domains or workgroups, titles, and sites. Additional information has been added to many objects' properties to help you further identify items in your network. For example, you can record the telephone numbers and address of each user, or the locations of printers.

User accounts and groups are also set up globally, which means that users can log in to their account on any PC attached to any server and get the same services they would have on their "home" server.

The entire network structure, including servers and their volumes, can be viewed as a tree and browsed by the user. This makes it easier for users in large networks to locate resources without knowing in advance the exact name of the server or device. Files, directory structures, and volumes can be replicated and updated automatically on multiple servers, or at different sites, providing additional fault tolerance and faster access to data (local versus remote).

Other new features include:

- File migration—the ability to automatically move files that aren't being used to other media, such as optical disk, conserving hard disk space

- Automatic compression and decompression of files

- Suballocation of blocks on a hard disk, which means that on a disk with 4 KB blocks, a 512-byte file will no longer use up 4 KB

- The beginnings of protected mode operation, which in the future will prevent badly written applications from being able to crash the server

- Additional network management tools to make running the network easier and to allow the remote management of servers and their devices

- SFT Level III—the mirroring of not just disks, but entire servers

These features may make migrating to NetWare 4.*x* attractive for you, even if you have only one server and a small LAN. The file compression alone could give you another six months to a year before you need to expand your disk drive capacity again. You'll also find that the management tools in NetWare 4.*x* are much more useful than in previous versions.

The following sections cover troubleshooting new servers and existing servers, including hardware problems and software problems. These will be followed by some further details on special parts of NetWare.

Troubleshooting New Servers

THE PROBLEMS THAT AFFLICT NEW SERVERS are conceptually different from those affecting existing servers. You can generally assume that all the hardware is functional, at least until you have eliminated the other possibilities. The most common problems will be configuration errors, possibly including conflicts between hardware or software settings.

Hardware Problems in New Servers

With NetWare 3.*x* and 4.*x*, the server must be able to boot DOS before you start NetWare. With NetWare 2.*x*, it is not strictly necessary—NetWare boots from the cold boot loader on track 0 of the hard disk. However, if the server will not boot DOS, either from the DOS partition on the hard disk or from a floppy, it probably won't be able to load NetWare either. You can try to boot from a floppy if there is not a bootable hard disk in the server. If you are having problems getting the server to boot DOS, see Chapter 3, which covers troubleshooting workstations. The problems addressed here will be the specialized ones relating to server hardware and getting NetWare running.

The usual differences between a NetWare server and a PC workstation are these: a large hard disk or disks (often with more than one hard disk adapter), lots of RAM, multiple NICs, a faster processor, a faster bus, and of course, the NetWare operating system.

A NetWare server could be anything from a 386 PC with one floppy and a hard drive, one LAN adapter, and a monochrome video adapter to a high-end Pentium or Pentium Pro EISA bus or PCI bus PC, with 128 MB of RAM, an IDE disk drive adapter with 3.5- and 5.25-inch floppy drives and a hard disk to boot from, two SCSI hard disk adapters with two or more multi-gigabyte hard drives on each adapter, two LAN adapters, and a VGA monitor and adapter. As your configuration approaches the latter, it can be very difficult to set up. The following sections describe the most common hardware problem areas.

RAM (Over 16 MB)

There are two problems that may occur with large amounts of RAM. The first happens when an additional RAM board is used to add the RAM. The second is simply a function of the way some devices and NetWare itself react when there is more than 16 MB of RAM in the system. Many PCs will allow up to 128 MB of RAM on the motherboard, and some allow 512 MB or more. However, older machines that may allow only 4 MB on the motherboard will require additional boards. These boards can be difficult to configure; be sure to set the interrupts correctly and to keep the segments of RAM contiguous.

Additionally, you may need an updated driver for your SCSI adapter or NIC, or you may need to load the driver with a parameter that tells it that your server has more than 16 MB of RAM. You may also need to use the REGISTER MEMORY command to tell NetWare that the server has more than 16 MB with ISA bus PCs. With EISA bus PCs, you may need to add the following SET command to the AUTOEXEC.NCF file:

```
SET AUTO REGISTER MEMORY ABOVE 16 MB = ON
```

The default setting is ON, but some PCs may not register the memory unless you include the command in AUTOEXEC.NCF.

If you're using a 486 VL-bus server (or a 586 VL-bus server, if you can find such a thing), you may experience a driver lockup problem in machines with more than 16 MB of memory. This is an acknowledged problem with many cards, including Adaptec VL-bus SCSI controllers. If you have a situation where your server has grown to the point that you need more than 16 MB of RAM, I strongly recommend that you upgrade to either an EISA or a PCI system.

Type of Bus

A server is a problem to PC designers—a regular PC might have a floppy/hard disk adapter, an I/O board, a modem, a video board, a sound board, and a network adapter. These days, the floppy/hard disk adapter and I/O board are usually combined or integrated onto the motherboard, leaving four boards. A server, on the other hand, could have a floppy/hard disk adapter, an I/O board (also usually on one board or integrated onto the motherboard), a modem, a video board, one or two network adapters, and as many as three SCSI controllers, for a total of seven boards.

Many modern PCI motherboards have three or four PCI slots and three ISA slots. To get high performance for all the network boards and SCSI controllers, it may be necessary to go to either a dual-PCI bus system with seven or eight PCI slots or to an EISA system. The reason that some makers still produce an eight-slot EISA bus system, often with optional additional processors, is to support servers.

EISA has all but disappeared from the PC marketplace but continues to be supported as a server platform because of its board capacity. It is more of a nuisance to configure because it usually requires software, rather than being configured from BIOS as PCI is. However, an eight-slot EISA motherboard is less expensive than a dual-bus PCI motherboard, and EISA network and SCSI adapters have been available for quite a while, are well understood, and have mature drivers. If you are buying a new system, EISA may still be a good choice if you need lots of network and SCSI adapters. Just make sure that you can still get the EISA versions of the cards you want before you buy the PC.

PCI is the wave of the future. It provides a higher potential throughput and it's easier to configure. As time goes on, it will become increasingly more difficult to find EISA cards or systems. Dual-bus PCI systems will become more common and less expensive, and the problems with configuring them will be worked out. When everything works as it should, PCI can be a joy to configure, because there are no interrupts to worry about—just plug the cards in and go. Unfortunately, it often isn't that simple. Every BIOS maker seems to handle PCI configuration with different terminology and in different ways, making it difficult to even describe what works. This is a case where the manufacturer's tech support or another administrator who has set up the same configuration may be very helpful.

As manufacturers move toward the Windows 95 Plug and Play model, they seem to be assuming that they no longer need to support anything else, or even document how their cards actually work. You may find, for instance, that interrupt 12 is used by the built-in PS/2 mouse connector on your motherboard, and that it cannot be made available even by disabling the mouse. Similarly, it's now difficult to find a monochrome video board, which is all a server really needs. Many of the new video boards use a number of different areas of memory. If you're running Windows 95, this may not present a problem. However, if you're trying to use a number of other cards under NetWare, you might try using a very basic ISA VGA card (or monochrome, if you can find one) to avoid memory conflicts.

Two good sources of information about potential problems with the cards in your system and what to do about them are the README file on the disk that came with the adapter and online support resources, such as a CompuServe forum or Web page. See Appendix A for more information about resources for troubleshooters.

SCSI Adapters

SCSI stands for Small Computer System Interface. It is most commonly used as a hard disk drive interface, but is also used for many other devices, such as scanners, additional drives such as CD-ROM drives, cartridge drives, tape drives, and so on.

It is common to have two SCSI adapters in the same server to provide for mirrored drives, and possibly a third SCSI adapter for a backup tape drive. It is often the case that SCSI host adapters from different manufacturers will not work in the same PC. For that reason, it is best to use the same manufacturer's cards, and even the same model of card, when more than one adapter is required.

SCSI adapters do not interface with the PC in the same way as IDE and MFM/RLL adapters. If you wish to use a SCSI drive as a boot drive, you will need an additional BIOS, because the PC doesn't know that it should look on the SCSI adapter for a boot drive. The BIOS may be on the SCSI adapter itself, or it may be added to a network adapter to allow this. If you have multiple SCSI adapters, only one should have the BIOS enabled. In addition, you should take care that the interrupt used by a SCSI adapter is not used by other floppy or hard disk adapters, particularly if you have a motherboard with a built-in adapter. With PCI cards, look in the manual to see if the card is a bus-mastering card. If it is, it will need to be in a master slot, not a slave slot. Check your motherboard manual to see which slots are which.

SCSI Devices

The SCSI bus is a daisy chain, with up to seven devices, each connected to the next. Figure 2.3 illustrates the SCSI chain. Each device in the chain has its own unique ID of 0 through 6; the SCSI controller has an ID of 7. If you are having problems with a PC that has more than one SCSI device, make sure that all the devices have unique SCSI IDs. Duplicate IDs will usually cause the server to hang right after the SCSI driver loads. Of course, the method of removing the devices and trying them one at a time to isolate the problem applies here, too.

Termination is another major cause of problems with SCSI devices. Often, incorrect termination will cause intermittent problems. Both the first device on the SCSI chain (usually the internal hard disk) and the last device on the chain must be terminated. Problems arise when intermediate devices are terminated or when the first or last drive is not. Some devices have external switches to enable or disable termination and set the SCSI ID; with others, you must add or remove resistor packs on the internal printed circuit board. The simplest way to handle termination is to leave the termination resistors on the internal drive and remove termination from all other devices. Then use an external terminator on the last device. This allows you to add or remove devices easily.

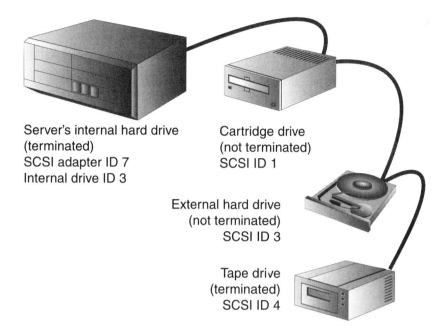

FIGURE 2.3
The SCSI chain of devices

Server's internal hard drive
(terminated)
SCSI adapter ID 7
Internal drive ID 3

Cartridge drive
(not terminated)
SCSI ID 1

External hard drive
(not terminated)
SCSI ID 3

Tape drive
(terminated)
SCSI ID 4

Under no circumstances should you ever disconnect or connect a SCSI device when it is powered up. This can damage not only that device, but any other device in the chain, including the SCSI controller or the PC motherboard. Power everything down before changing connections. This rule also applies to changing termination or manually changing the SCSI ID of a device. Some devices will allow you to change their SCSI ID with software. This, obviously, must be done while everything is on.

RAID Systems

RAID originally stood for Redundant Array of Inexpensive Disks. It is usually interpreted now as Redundant Array of Independent Disks—the disks in use are not usually inexpensive. The original intent was to put a number of small hard disks together in a way that allowed them to imitate one large, more expensive disk. Along the way, users discovered that a RAID system provides more fault tolerance and higher performance than a single drive. Now RAID systems are commonly built with high-end drives, and they may combine 28 or more drives for a 100 GB virtual drive.

There are six levels of RAID:

- Level 0 stripes data across more than one drive.

- Level 1 is essentially disk mirroring.

- Levels 2, 3, and 4 provide variations on how data is placed on several drives.

- Level 5, using at least three drives, reserves one drive as a parity drive, so that if a drive is lost, the data is maintained.

The aspects of a RAID system to be aware of when you are troubleshooting are the SCSI ID number and Logical Unit number (LUN). A single internal RAID controller with seven drives on it must have each drive at a different SCSI address, 0 through 6 (the controller is 7). An external RAID controller looks to the server's internal SCSI controller as if it were a single SCSI device. It has up to seven LUNs (actually SCSI drives) attached to it, but they are all treated as if they were one large disk. You can have up to seven external RAID controllers attached to the internal SCSI controller in the server. See the "RAID for Fault Tolerance" section, in the discussion of System Fault Tolerance later in this chapter, for more information.

If you want to save money on drives, consider RAID level 5 rather than RAID level 1 (mirroring). Mirroring costs you one additional drive for every drive you install. RAID level 5 can use one drive out of every seven to store the parity information that allows the system to be fault-tolerant.

Hard Drive Preparation

Disk drives to be used with NetWare will not normally need to be formatted before installation, just repartitioned during the NetWare installation.

Mirrored partitions should be the same size—any additional space in the second partition will be unused. There can be multiple partitions on a disk, or a single partition that spans multiple disks. Similarly, all the drives in a RAID system should be the same size. It may not be strictly necessary, depending on the manufacturer, but it's advisable.

Be careful about creating partitions above 2 GB. Some file systems cannot handle more than 2 GB in a single partition.

Multiple LAN Adapters

LAN adapters typically use both an interrupt and a memory segment. If you have more than one adapter, the adapters must not use the same interrupt and memory segment. Furthermore, different manufacturers' cards will have different sequences of interrupts and memory segments that they expect to use; thus, it is not always sufficient to set the first adapter to its first configuration and the second adapter to its second configuration. Check the manufacturer's documentation for the usable interrupts and memory segments and make sure to use different ones for each adapter.

With PCI cards, look in the manual to see if the card is a bus-mastering card. If it is, it will need to be in a master slot, not a slave slot. Check your motherboard manual to see which slots are which.

VGA Adapters

VGA adapters use both an interrupt and a memory segment. This can cause conflicts with network adapters, SCSI adapters, or any other cards in the server that use interrupts or memory segments. Be sure to check the interrupt and memory segment used to ensure that it doesn't conflict with other cards. As mentioned earlier, this information may be difficult to find for Plug and Play adapters.

Automatic Loading of BIOS into Upper RAM

Shadow BIOS, or loading the BIOS into the RAM between 640 KB and 1 MB, is intended to allow for faster execution of BIOS instructions, by execution from the inherently faster 16- or 32-bit RAM instead of from the BIOS. Problems can occur when other hardware (such as a VGA adapter or LAN adapter) or NetWare attempts to access this same area of memory.

Interrupts and EISA Configuration

Any PC with an ISA bus (or an EISA-bus PC using interrupts) has a limited number of possible interrupts. The problem is that typically there are several cards that want to use interrupts in a particular range. For instance, NICs, mouse adapters, and some display adapters, among other devices, may all want an interrupt between 2 and 5.

Things may be complicated further by cards that limit your choice to one or two of the four possible interrupts. In these cases, careful planning may be required to avoid conflicts. Of course, you should record the interrupts in use for each PC as you configure the cards in it, both to facilitate troubleshooting if it won't boot and to make it easier to add other cards later.

EISA bus PCs in bus-mastering mode no longer have a problem with interrupts. However, in exchange for the old problem, you are now faced with a much more complicated installation procedure. You will need to know the manufacturer of each card, and often the version of the card as well, and what memory, if any, it uses. Then you must run the EISA configuration utility that came with your server to tell it what cards are installed.

You often hear that PCI cards don't use interrupts. This is not really true. They actually use two types of interrupts: the A, B, C, D PCI interrupts and the mapped interrupts determined by BIOS (usually 11, 5, 7, 9). How the BIOS is set up determines whether this happens automatically and how interrupts are mapped. If you have only a couple of PCI cards, you can usually leave things on the AUTO setting and not worry about it. With several cards, especially multiple NICs and SCSI cards, things can get interesting. Be sure to read the manufacturer's documentation on what PCI interrupt you should use and what other settings might need to be changed.

Hardware Security

NetWare provides several levels of security within the operating system. However, one aspect of security that is rarely mentioned is the security of the physical hardware itself—no software can prevent someone from accidentally unplugging a server or turning it off. I recommend that your server be placed in a lockable room, and that the door be kept locked unless someone is present.

Software Problems in New Servers

Only the most basic DOS configuration is needed to set a server up. When NetWare boots, it takes over as the operating system; DOS is not used and may be removed from memory. Thus, if the server will boot with DOS, nothing further needs to be done before installing NetWare. Again, the purpose here is not to instruct you in the process of installing NetWare, but rather to help you debug that process when it fails.

NetWare Installation

The basic process of installing NetWare is a relatively simple one of copying files onto the hard disk of the server. If you have problems, they are likely to be either with the configuration of NetWare after it's installed or with the hardware. SERVER.EXE and NET$OS.EXE are essentially programs like any other. If there are errors in loading them, they will typically be due to memory errors or hardware configuration. With NetWare 2.x, you will get an error when starting NetWare if the LAN adapter or cold boot PROM is defective.

Drive Preparation for NetWare Installation

NetWare does not use a standard DOS partition for disk drives. There will be a small DOS partition on the server's boot disk with NetWare 3.x or 4.x, but the rest of that disk and any others on the system must be partitioned with NetWare partitions. You do this with INSTALL.

You can also choose to do a low-level format and test of the drive with INSTALL under 3.x and 4.x, or with ZTEST or COMPSURF under 2.x. ZTEST reformats track 0, which is used for the cold boot loader. Unless you buy the drive preformatted and certified for NetWare, I heartily recommend performing a low-level format and test with new systems. It can't hurt in any case (although it will destroy any existing data, of course), although it may take some time.

After the drive is formatted and partitioned, a Hot Fix redirection area is set up. This is used if bad blocks are encountered on the disk. The bad blocks are mapped to the redirection blocks, which are then used to replace them. If you use MONITOR, you can see the total number of blocks on the drive and the number of redirection blocks. This is normally 2 percent of the total number of blocks. You will also see the number of redirected blocks. This number starts out at zero and, ideally, will never grow.

If you notice a large number of redirected blocks, or if the number of redirected blocks is growing regularly, it is a good indication that the disk is deteriorating physically. It's a very good idea to replace such a disk at once. You may wish to try a low-level format, followed by a thorough test of the disk. However, since the cost of a disk is usually much less than the value of the information on it combined with the cost of downtime if the disk quits in the middle of a busy day (you are doing regular backups, aren't you?), it usually pays to just replace the disk.

NetWare lets you create volumes that span multiple partitions and multiple disks. This can allow you to create volumes with very large effective sizes, which can be a problem with some operating systems that may have trouble with partitions over 2 or 2.5 GB.

If you set up a volume over 2 GB, and you either cannot see the volume or it shows as a different size from a workstation, the problem is not with NetWare, but rather is an inherent limitation of the operating system of the workstation. The only solution is to decrease the size of the volume. Keep in mind that in some cases, the only problem will be that the amount of free space that the operating system shows will be incorrect. The user will still be able to access the volume and perform normal operations.

Configuration Files

Although the names of the server configuration files are not the same in different versions of NetWare, they perform the same functions. In NetWare 2.*x*, the files are SERVER.CFG and AUTOEXEC.SYS; in NetWare 3.*x* and 4.*x*, they are AUTOEXEC.NCF and STARTUP.NCF.

Keep a hard copy of these files. It is easy to change a configuration when you are trying to troubleshoot a problem, and then lose track of how it was configured in the first place. If you intend to remove a line in a configuration file for troubleshooting purposes, it may save you headaches to comment it out first, using # (the pound sign). This way, if the problem turns out to be something else, putting the line back in the file is a simple matter of erasing one character, instead of typing in a long string.

It seems ridiculous, but the most common problem with the configuration files is misspelling. Be sure that commands and parameters are spelled correctly and that the values given are within the proper ranges. Case is usually not an issue, but some parameters, especially ones relating to Macintosh or UNIX support, may be case-sensitive.

Device Drivers

Each device in a server uses a driver. For example, the driver for a Novell NE2000 card is named NE2000.LAN. Particular care must be used to make sure that the driver is the proper one for the hardware installed, and that it is the version recommended for the version of NetWare you are using. If you don't have the proper driver, you should be able to get it from NetWire.

Watch the messages as NetWare loads. If the server freezes after a driver is loaded, it may be the wrong driver or an incorrect version of the right driver. If you have two cards of the same type, you must load the device driver twice—once for each card. NetWare will usually give you the message "Driver loaded re-entrantly" or something similar, meaning that it is loading the same code from memory.

Network Address Assignments

In a WAN, especially a large one, a common problem is duplicate network addresses. The hexadecimal number used to identify the server must be unique. Fortunately, this is an easy problem to diagnose. A repeating error message will occur at the console on all servers on the LAN, with the text "Router Configuration Error: *Servernumber* is claiming my same internet address," or something similar. This is another case where having your network well documented comes in handy. All you get on the screen is the server's network number—a long hexadecimal number. If you have those numbers in a list with their corresponding servers, it'll be much easier for you to track down the other server.

Multiple Protocols

NetWare 3.11 allows you to run multiple protocols as if they were native. Protocols supported include IPX, SPX, TCP/IP, AppleTalk, NetBIOS, OSI, and

SMB. It is possible to have a number of these protocols running on the same NIC. Each protocol must be loaded and bound to the board. The LOAD and BIND commands for each board include certain parameters. If the parameters are not set correctly (if the wrong numbers are used or the spelling is incorrect), the statements may not work for that protocol.

Another possibility is that the LOAD and BIND commands work, but they conflict with other devices on your internet. This problem occurs more often in a WAN environment than with single LANs. In a single LAN, which isn't connected to anything else, the AppleTalk zone names and zone numbers, the TCP/IP numbers, subnets, and so on, that you specify are not critical. In a WAN environment, or a LAN which may someday be expanded into a WAN, these settings become crucial—they must be coordinated throughout the WAN. It is extremely important to carefully document and structure the AppleTalk zone and TCP/IP setup you use.

If the server boots, and DOS workstations can log in, but UNIX or Macintosh workstations cannot see the server, the first place to look is in the INSTALL configurations. Double-check the settings and remember that some items (for instance the Mac zone names) are case-sensitive. For more information about problems with connecting to other systems, see Chapter 9.

NetWare Permissions

There is a saying among system administrators that 90 percent or more of the day-to-day problems that users encounter on a network involve permissions. With permissions for users and permissions for groups, and ensuring that all the proper people are in the proper groups, it's no wonder these issues are complex. They are potentially further complicated by different permissions at different levels of a directory hierarchy and on the files themselves.

One of the best investments a system administrator can make early on is to study NetWare's permissions structure until thoroughly familiar with it. Particularly, make sure that you understand completely the difference between the inherited rights and trustee rights and how they combine.

Bear in mind that the way permissions flow down through the directory structure and are granted changes greatly from NetWare 2.*x* to NetWare 3.*x*. If you use both, or are upgrading from 2.*x* to 3.*x*, make especially sure that you understand the differences in how permissions are implemented.

Login Scripts

There are three login scripts that may execute when a user logs in: the default, the user, and the system. The default login script will execute if no system or user login script exists. This script should normally not be used. The system login script executes first, and should contain commands that are necessary to set up all users. The user's login script executes next, and contains the commands that configure the user's environment.

NetWare 4.*x* adds another login script for groups (called the profile login script), which takes the place of the IF MEMBER OF construction in the system login script under previous versions. This is necessary because groups are global in a network and can be accessed by members from any server. In addition, in NetWare 4.*x*, the system login script is replaced with the container login script, which is executed for members of an organization, rather than on a server-by-server basis, because users are no longer tied to a particular server.

The Dreaded ABEND Message

With a new installation, an error message beginning with ABEND means that something in your software or hardware configuration is wrong. The first thing to try is rebooting the server.

If the problem recurs, it could be caused by:

- An NLM that is incorrectly configured, corrupted, or simply badly written

- An incorrectly entered SET command

- A printer that is set up incorrectly

- A hardware problem

Try unloading all the NLMs and reloading them one at a time, checking the SET commands in the AUTOEXEC.NCF and STARTUP.NCF files for correct spelling and values within the range allowed (check the System Administration manual for details), and check the setup of all printers configured. Then make sure that the server memory is sufficient for the configuration you are running, and check the server as a workstation for hardware problems using the procedures listed in the next chapter.

Troubleshooting Existing Servers

W ITH EXISTING SERVERS, you are unlikely to run across configuration errors or interrupt conflicts, unless you have just changed something. The principal problem with existing equipment is failures, either of hardware or software. An exception to this is that some interrupt conflicts may cause intermittent, long-term problems that will only disrupt things occasionally.

You may also encounter problems as utilization of the server increases, which can be measured as:

- Traffic on and off the server

- Disk utilization

- Memory utilization, as the number of buffers utilized increases

The typical solutions here are more memory, more network speed (more or faster NICs), and more hard disk space.

Hardware Problems in Existing Servers

Other than problems resulting from changes, which you should troubleshoot using the steps outlined for hardware problems in new servers, the most likely hardware problems are not unique to servers, but are equivalent to workstation problems (see the next chapter for details on troubleshooting workstations). Many hardware problems will produce error messages, either in the system error log or when DOS or NetWare loads, which will make them easy to spot.

NetWare has the following tools that allow you to diagnose and in some cases correct hardware problems. These tools can also be used to monitor the load on the server and network and project levels that are too high, so you can upgrade the hardware before critical levels are reached.

Using SERVMAN, MONITOR, and FCONSOLE

SERVMAN (NetWare 4.*x*), MONITOR (NetWare 3.*x*), and FCONSOLE (NetWare 2.*x*) are invaluable tools for deciphering network problems. They will tell you a lot about the normal operation of the server and can help you pinpoint problems that are otherwise difficult to isolate.

For instance, if several workstations are having problems connecting with a 3.*x* server and the server is running, and you can't find any problems with the physical network, choose the LAN Information selection in MONITOR. You will be able to see whether the server is sending and receiving packets, whether there are many bad packets or collisions, and similar information. Likewise, if network performance slows down radically when there are lots of users on a 2.*x* server, and FCONSOLE shows that the Peak Used number of communication buffers is close to or equal to the number of buffers set, you should increase the total number of communication buffers. (This will require regenerating the operating system with INSTALL.)

You should also be aware of the usual state of your server, as shown in MONITOR or FCONSOLE. There are a number of particular things to look for (and record in your log for that server). See the section on baselining in Chapter 6 for details.

Using VREPAIR

VREPAIR is a very useful tool to fix software problems with hard drives. It won't diagnose a problem with the electronics of a drive, or tell you about a SCSI conflict or termination problem, but it does a good job of getting the directory entries back in sync with the files they represent.

The most important thing to know about VREPAIR is that it will handle only one set of problems at a time.

Each time VREPAIR scans a disk, it may find problems, and, if you tell it to, it will fix them. However, the process of fixing one set of problems may uncover further problems, which will require another scan. You should continue running VREPAIR until no errors are reported.

Checking the System Error Log

The system error log is accessible through SYSCON or NWADMIN from a workstation and from some of the add-on modules in INSTALL.NLM on the server. You should become familiar with typical messages that occur in the log.

Then, when problems occur, you will have a better chance of picking out the relevant error message.

Of course, the messages are in chronological order in the log, and if you know when the problem began, this will give you clues regarding which messages you should pay special attention to. Chapter 6 has more information about baselining—accumulating the statistics that your network produces normally and how to use those baseline figures to determine what is wrong.

Software Problems in Existing Servers

With existing software that has been working correctly, there are only a few factors that can cause failure. One is a faulty piece of software that causes problems when it runs, or perhaps only under certain circumstances. This could be an NLM or a user application on someone's workstation.

Another potential cause of failure is increased load on the network that causes the server to overload. This is usually due to running out of memory, which cannot be characterized as a software problem, although you can sometimes fix the problem by reconfiguring the server to allocate less memory in other areas or by unloading unnecessary features. However, software can also cause its own problems under high loads, by not waiting long enough for a response, for instance.

Corrupted SERVER.EXE or NET$OS.EXE Files

It is possible (though unlikely) for SERVER.EXE or NET$OS.EXE to become corrupted, so it is a good idea to back up this file onto a floppy. Then, if you suspect that the file has been corrupted, you can copy it from the floppy onto the server's hard disk, overwriting the existing file. If it won't fit on one floppy, another method is to create a directory on the DOS partition of the server's boot disk, and then place a copy of the NetWare executable file (NET$OS.EXE or SERVER.EXE) in it.

Other than the slight possibility of a corrupted SERVER.EXE file, the software on an existing server is only likely to cause problems if it is changed, or if some other part of your network is changed in a way that conflicts with the configuration of your server. These problems should be treated as changes—see the section about software problems in new installations, earlier in the chapter.

e an error message on the server's screen that begins with
ıat the server software has crashed. (This message appears
.reen.) In an existing system, this is usually a fluke, possibly
:ion running on the server that is misbehaving, by an NLM
ng correctly, or by a hardware memory error.
.ng the ABEND part of the message will tell you something
ı. The System Messages manual may be useful in decoding
:. If the problem recurs, try to find out which applications
workstations when the server crashed. If any of them are new
new versions, they may be causing problems with the server.
message could also be caused by a hardware problem. Make
sure that the memory in the server is sufficient for the configuration you are
running. If you have recently added new NLMs, disk drives, name spaces on
existing drives, or protocol drivers, the server may need more RAM to function correctly. Check the server as a workstation for hardware problems, as
described in Chapter 3.

Running the BINDFIX Utility

BINDFIX is a utility program in NetWare 2.*x* and an NLM in 3.*x* and 4.*x*. It
will repair many problems that occur with the binderies. For example, use
BINDFIX if a user cannot log in, you can't modify or delete a user account, a
password cannot be changed, trustee rights can't be changed, or you get error
messages on the console that mention the binderies.

Be sure to have a backup of the bindery files before running BINDFIX. If you
do keep separate copies of the bindery files, you may be better off replacing
them, rather than using BINDFIX. The names of the files you will need to back
up are listed in "Managing the Binderies or NetWare Directory" section a little
later in the chapter.

Using DSTRACE and DSREPAIR

DSTRACE (the Directory Services trace utility) tracks NDS messages between
your server and the others in your company. It will allow you to watch all NDS
messages on the screen or save them to a log file. It can be very useful for
tracing NDS errors.

DSREPAIR is the utility for repairing the NDS database when something goes wrong. Remember that it can be run on only one server's NDS database at a time. Since it also locks the server while it is repairing the database, all users will be unable to use the server. It's not something you normally want to run during working hours, unless you're having serious NDS problems.

Intermittent Problems with Servers

There are many possible causes of intermittent failure of a server, and this can be one of the most frustrating types of troubleshooting to attempt. The causes could be anything from a power surge caused by nearby heavy equipment (or even the power draws from another facility on the same power grid) to faulty equipment, to the applications running on the server or even on a workstation.

To isolate intermittent problems, look for the thing that changes just before the crash. This seems obvious but can be difficult to actually discover. Here are some starting points:

- What time does the crash occur?

- Do the crashes happen at regular intervals?

- Is there any particular software that is always in use when the crashes occur?

- Which workstations are attached every time the server crashes?

- Are there any unusual error messages in the system error log?

- Do any of the workstations get a message other than "The connection to the file server *myserver* is no longer valid"?

- Are there stages to the problem? If you can isolate events that lead up to the crash, they will give you a clue to the root cause.

Investigating some of these items will take research: talking to the users, discovering what new software has been installed on the server or workstations, finding out who was logged in, and so on. You can simplify this job considerably with the use of network inventory systems, network monitoring equipment, and other software that will help keep track of the various parts of your network and its configuration. You can manually keep track of all installed software and hardware on your server and all the networked workstations, but it's much easier to run a network inventory program regularly to get the information. There is less chance that users will forget to mention that new program they installed, too.

Of course, some problems may be impossible to isolate without some sort of network sniffer. Anyone with an installation that is larger than a couple of servers or runs more than one or two protocols should consider getting some type of monitoring software and/or hardware, as discussed in the next section.

The best resources for determining which monitoring system is right for you are the trade magazines, your local NetWare user group, and your authorized reseller.

Using Other Diagnostic Tools

MANY LEVELS OF DIAGNOSTIC TOOLS are available to the system administrator. They range from $195 software-only products that will allow you a little more capability than MONITOR, to $50,000+ WAN analyzers that will produce a map of an extended WAN, monitor traffic, inform you if anything unusual happens, and suggest solutions.

Other available software can inventory the software on each workstation on your network, upgrade all workstations on the network with the newest versions of software as they come out, and tell you what hardware is installed in the workstations. There are other programs that enhance the NetWare utilities, producing more detailed reports than MONITOR can, with tracking over time and nice formatting of the printed reports.

Although many of these products can save you time, or be invaluable in a complex WAN environment, you can often produce the same results yourself with a little advance preparation, the tools available to you in NetWare, and some deductive reasoning. For example, a protocol analyzer might be able to monitor network traffic and detect bad packets coming from a server, and notify you of the problem, which server is producing it, and where it is located. However, by assigning network numbers to servers that will allow you to identify them (office number, followed by extension, or something similar), you can get the same information by inspecting the system error logs of your servers regularly. Of course, this is more work, so if you have the money in your budget for a network analyzer, I highly recommend it.

Similarly, the network hardware or software inventory programs are very useful, especially for large networks, but you can gather the same information manually. Appendix C provides forms that you can use to enter inventory information. See Chapter 8 and Appendix B for more information about diagnostic and network management tools.

Managing the Binderies or NetWare Directory

THE BINDERIES ARE HIDDEN FILES that contain all the information you have set up on your users, their passwords, trustee rights, ownership of files, default printers, and so on. SBACKUP, NBACKUP, and other backup programs designed to work with NetWare give you the option to back up the binderies. Be careful—if you restore from an older tape, and restore the binderies, any changes you or the users have made to passwords and the like will revert to what they were as of that backup.

If you wish to back up the binderies manually, they consist of two hidden files, NET$BIND.SYS and NET$BVAL.SYS, in NetWare 2.*x*, and three files, NET$OBJ.SYS, NET$PROP.SYS, and NET$VAL.SYS, in NetWare 3.*x*. These files are located in SYS:SYSTEM.

If a user cannot log in, if you can't modify or delete a user account, if a password cannot be changed, if trustee rights can't be changed, or if you get error messages on the console that mention the binderies, try running BINDFIX.

In NetWare 4.*x*, the bindery is replaced with the NetWare Directory, under NDS. This is a much more capable way of making the services on the server available to clients, and it requires a more extensive database, with many additional properties. NetWare 4.*x* can be configured to emulate the old style of binderies to maintain compatibility with older servers and workstation shells. The NDS database is in a hidden directory, SYS:_NETWARE, in five files: VALUE.NDS, BLOCK.NDS, PARTITIO.NDS, ENTRY.NDS, and 00006f00.000. This database can and should be replicated on other servers on your network.

Upgrading NetWare

UPGRADING NETWARE USING THE UPGRADE UTILITY is usually a relatively pain-free operation. It is well documented, and this book will not go into the details of a normal upgrade. However, even in a straightforward upgrade, there are a number of things that can go wrong. *Never* upgrade without doing a complete backup of your file system first.

The most complicated part of upgrades is the changes in names and structures. In NetWare 2.*x*, SERVER.CFG and AUTOEXEC.SYS are used to run parts of NetWare; in NetWare 3.*x* and 4.*x*, the files are called AUTOEXEC.NCF and STARTUP.NCF. Permission structures—how permissions flow in the directory structure and how users inherit permissions—change considerably from NetWare 2.15 and below, to 2.2 and above, to 3.*x*, and to NetWare 4.*x*. Make sure that you understand the differences before you do an upgrade.

Another aspect of upgrades is the hardware requirements of the new system. These requirements are discussed in Chapter 11, which covers updates to network hardware and software.

Troubleshooting NLM Problems

THE INSTALLATION PROCESS for NLMs under NetWare 3.*x* and 4.*x* is fortunately very simple. Just run the INSTALL NLM, and the appropriate files will be put in the proper places on your server. Configuring the NLMs for your particular requirements is another matter. You should also be aware before you upgrade that not all 3.*x* NLMs are compatible with NetWare 4.*x*.

Each NLM comes with appropriate documentation—this book is not intended to replace the user documentation, or even to supplement it. However, the troubleshooting process may certainly be applied to NLMs that you believe are installed correctly but refuse to function for one reason or another.

There are four types of NLMs:

- Disk drivers to allow the use of different types of disk drives (*.DSK).

- LAN drivers for running different protocols on various LAN adapters (*.LAN).

- Name space modules to allow operating systems other than DOS to access and store files on the server. These include modules for Macintosh, NFS (UNIX), and OS/2 (*.NAM).

- Management utilities and server applications, such as MONITOR, INSTALL, and UPS. These allow you to configure and manage the server, or add functionality (*.NLM).

If you are having regular abends or problems with server performance, make sure that you have the latest version of all the NLMs you are using. (Updated NLMs and patches are often available on NetWire.) If necessary, reduce the number of NLMs loaded to the minimum necessary for basic server functions, and add the rest back in one at a time until you can determine which one is causing a problem or conflicting with other NLMs.

Using System Fault Tolerance

SYSTEM FAULT TOLERANCE (SFT) is Novell's method of ensuring system reliability in the event of hardware failures. SFT II protects the data on a server. SFT III allows for entire servers to be protected. The following sections describe the functions of SFT.

Mirroring and Duplexing

Both mirroring and duplexing are intended to allow the server to continue to provide file services even if a disk fails. All the data on a disk is duplicated on the mirrored disk, and if one disk fails, the other provides continued access to the data. These systems also provide the additional advantage of reducing the disk access time by half; NetWare will read or write to whichever disk is available, and then update the other in the background. Data can also be read from both disks at once, alternating blocks, which doubles throughput.

The only drawback to mirroring or duplexing is the added cost. For each volume required, two disks must be purchased; with duplexing, two controllers and two disk enclosures with power supplies are also required. However, given the relatively low cost of disk storage, this is cheap insurance against the lost time a crashed disk will cause on even a small network. Obtaining a new drive and restoring from a backup will take a minimum of hours and perhaps days, and of course, anything on the server that has been changed since the last backup will be lost as well.

The difference between mirroring and duplexing is the level of duplication of components. Mirroring uses two disks attached to the same controller and usually the same power supply. Duplexing uses separate controllers, disks, and power supplies, providing continuing functionality even if the power supply or controller fails. Figure 2.4 illustrates how mirroring and duplexing work.

FIGURE 2.4
Mirroring and duplexing

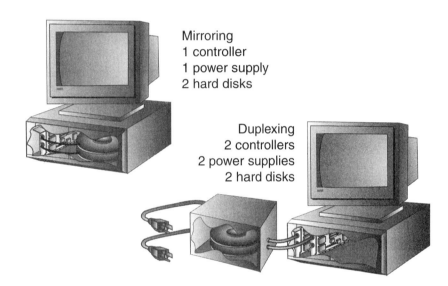

Mirroring
1 controller
1 power supply
2 hard disks

Duplexing
2 controllers
2 power supplies
2 hard disks

RAID for Fault Tolerance

RAID provides more fault tolerance and higher performance than a single drive, and more efficient use of drive space than mirrored drives. RAIDs are commonly built with high-capacity drives, and may combine 28 or more drives for a 100 GB virtual drive. Figure 2.5 illustrates how a RAID system works.

As explained earlier in the chapter, there are six levels of RAID. The most common is level 5, which uses at least three drives, reserving one drive as a parity drive, so that if a drive is lost, the data is maintained. There can be up to seven drives in a single RAID array. Since RAID level 5 uses a single drive for

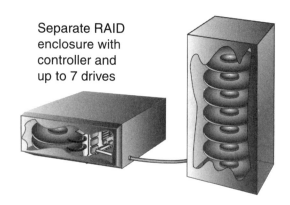

Separate RAID
enclosure with
controller and
up to 7 drives

parity regardless of how many drives are in the array, the most efficient configuration uses seven drives, which results in a total capacity of six drives, with one parity drive.

Because RAID level 5 provides the fault tolerance of mirroring with a much smaller loss of drive space (one drive in three, to one drive in seven, instead of one out of every two drives), it has become very popular. It also offers gains in speed, since data can be pulled off more than one drive at once, better utilizing the performance of the SCSI controller. Finally, as demands for capacity continue to increase, RAID provides an effective way to increase capacity. Drives can be added to a RAID relatively seamlessly, and RAID controllers can be cascaded to a capacity of one or two controllers, each controlling seven controllers attached to seven drives each, for a total capacity of 49 or 98 drives.

SFT Level III

SFT level III allows you to mirror an entire server, rather than simply the disk drives. This provides a level of fault tolerance previously available only on mainframes and minicomputers. All data written to one server is also written to the second server, which may be in a remote location. If any part of one server fails, the other server takes over. This is particularly important in mission-critical applications where any loss of connectivity might cause extensive business losses, such as in banking or airline applications. Figure 2.6 illustrates how SFT III works.

The two servers don't need to be identical, but the lowest configuration will apply to both servers. For instance, if one server has 16 MB of RAM, and the other 32 MB, they will both effectively have 16 MB.

FIGURE 2.6
SFT level III

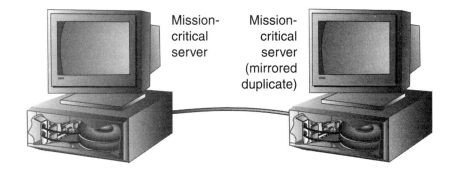

Mission-critical server   Mission-critical server (mirrored duplicate)

Real-Life Stories

THIS SECTION DESCRIBES typical problems and how a troubleshooter would go through the process of isolating the fault and fixing it. The two fictional companies introduced in Chapter 1, and their administrators, will be used as examples. They combine the equipment and experience of a number of actual businesses. These two scenarios are intended to show some representative problems often encountered when setting up or troubleshooting a server. Although you may never see these particular problems, they should give you a feel for the process an experienced troubleshooter uses to isolate a problem, determine the solution, and fix the problem.

Scenario One: Installing a New System

The administrator is installing and configuring a new system. He encounters some typical problems associated with late-model servers using large amounts of RAM and more than one hard disk adapter.

Snapshot—Scenario One

Is this a new system?

- Will the server boot DOS?

- Will NetWare load?

- Are some devices (such as network cards or disk drives) inaccessible after NetWare loads?

John, the system administrator for Itsy-Bitsy Inc., has about $25,000 of computer and components sitting in a couple dozen boxes around his office. They are the parts to put together the new high-performance server that the Tech Pubs department has been asking for this last year. Being a bright guy, and having read this book before, he is carefully observing anti-static precautions and recording the settings of all the cards, disks, and so forth as he puts the system together.

The server is a Pentium EISA-bus PC with 64 MB of RAM and an internal 1 GB IDE hard drive, one 3.5-inch floppy and one 5.25-inch floppy, two serial ports, one parallel port, and VGA support on the motherboard. It supports shadowing the BIOS in RAM. In addition, he has two external enclosures, each with two 1.2 GB hard drives, an 8 mm SCSI tape drive, two SCSI adapters, and two 16-bit Ethernet adapters. He will have two drives attached to each SCSI controller, providing full mirroring; controller, disk drives, and power supply will be entirely separate for each set. The tape drive will be added to the daisy chain on the first SCSI controller, the one that the tape drive came with. Of course, the server and enclosures will be plugged into a UPS.

As John installs the boards in the PC, he records the settings of each one on the server configuration form he copied from Appendix C of this book. The first NIC uses interrupt 3 and memory address C000. He sets the second NIC to interrupt 4 and memory address D000. Doing so ensures that there is no interrupt conflict between the cards and makes the LAN configuration easy, too; these are configurations 0 and 1 for the drivers for the NICs.

Next, John installs the two SCSI adapters. He knows that the built-in hard drive adapter uses interrupt 14, so he can choose 10, 11, 12, or 13 for the two cards. He sets them to 10 and 11, records this, and then closes up the server. He next makes sure that only the second of the two SCSI drives in the first enclosure is terminated, and that neither is terminated in the other enclosure. He has terminated the tape drive, which will be the last SCSI device in the chain for that controller.

Finally, everything is ready. He plugs everything into the UPS, attaches and secures all the cables, and crosses his fingers. He turns on the SCSI devices, then flips the main power switch on the PC. Nothing happens. Three hours later, once the UPS's battery has charged, he turns everything on again. This time, assorted fans begin whirring, the PC beeps, and messages begin appearing on the monitor.

John sees several messages, identifying the BIOS, the VGA adapter, and the SCSI adapter. Then DOS is loaded, and he is ready to begin the installation of NetWare. He brings the server up to partition the drives. However, when he starts SERVER.EXE, the SCSI adapter won't load its driver. Belatedly, John remembers seeing in the adapter's documentation that the driver must be loaded with a /v switch if the server contains more than 16 MB of RAM. A few minutes later, the driver is loaded with the /v switch and the first SCSI adapter driver loads.

However, once the second driver for the other SCSI adapter loads, John is unable to use INSTALL to partition the drives. In fact, none of the drives show up at all. He begins experimenting. He tries removing one of the cards. The other one works fine and its drives are visible to INSTALL. He reinstalls the first and removes the second. The first one works fine, too. He tries setting the cards to different interrupt settings, thinking that they might not like being on adjacent disk channels. They still won't work when both cards are installed.

Finally, he goes to a higher authority. He calls CompuServe and asks some questions in the NetWare forum. Within a short while, he gets his answer: those two SCSI adapters just won't work with each other. Maybe in the next version of the driver or ROM...

He decides to put all the drives on the single SCSI adapter that came with the tape drive, until he can get another adapter from the same manufacturer. That works fine. He is able to mount all four drives, and mirror the first two to the second two. He remembers to remove the termination from the second drive in each enclosure, so that the daisy chain of two sets of drives and the tape drive will only be terminated at the end. He also makes sure that the SCSI ID is different for all five SCSI devices.

The drives are mounted and mirrored; now it's time to load the network drivers. John loads the network driver and binds the first protocol to the card. The server hangs. John checks the settings in the LOAD and BIND statements. If the DMA channel or memory segment numbers were wrong, he should get an error message. Instead, the server just freezes. Back to CompuServe. Finally, he discovers that his brand-new NIC should be used with the updated driver supplied on the disk that came with it, rather than the file with the same name that came with NetWare. After he loads the updated driver and reboots, the NIC works fine.

After a few seconds, the server begins beeping and he sees the message "Router Configuration Error: Marketing is claiming my same internet address." Then he remembers he has already used his girlfriend's phone number for the Marketing department server's internal network number. He decides to use the system he saw suggested in this book—he uses the number of the office the server is in as the first four digits of the network number, and the extension of the phone in the room as the last four digits. Now, after he has implemented this scheme throughout his company, he'll be able to tell where error messages are coming from without needing to refer to a long list of numbers and the servers they represent, and he will know the phone number of the room the server is in, too.

After the server is operational, he loads MONITOR to check the basic statistics for the server. When he selects Resource Utilization, the first thing he notices is that NetWare is showing total memory as 16 MB. He takes the server down and checks the configuration of the server. The BIOS and DOS programs recognize the whole 64 MB, but when he starts the server again, it still only shows 16 MB. He checks several of the NetWare manuals before he finds the reference to REGISTER MEMORY in the System Administration manual. He enters the command and adds it to AUTOEXEC.NCF, and everything is fine.

Lessons Learned—Scenario One

- Remember to check the termination and ID of SCSI drives. You may not get an outright failure, but instead an intermittent problem that will drive you crazy.

- If you can't figure it out, don't spend huge amounts of time experimenting—try asking someone.

- If you're using more than 16 MB of RAM, make sure you know the implications for compatibility with other components and drivers. You may also need to change the default configurations of NetWare to recognize the memory.

- Get adapters from the same manufacturer whenever possible. Even though the standards (Ethernet, SCSI, and so on) are supposed to be the same, they aren't always implemented in quite the same way. Drivers from different manufacturers may conflict with each other, too. If you are having a conflict, you can try using the same driver for both cards. Don't expect this to work, though.

- Make sure your drivers match your devices. Check NetWire or your authorized reseller to see if you have the latest version of the drivers.

- On a multi-server LAN, be sure to have a scheme for coordinating internal network numbers and LAN numbers.

The Fault Point Chain—Scenario One

In this scenario, there are several chains, from the server to each device, and then on the server itself. The fault points below are for the hard disks. Each problem above has its own chain.

THE DISK DRIVES

- AC power from the wall.

- The power cord.

- The power supply for the disk drive.

- The power cable from the power supply to the disk drive.

- The disk drive mechanism itself.

- The terminating resistors on the disk drive.

- The data cable from the disk drive to the port on the enclosure.

- The data cable from the enclosure to the controller in the server.

- The terminating resistor on the controller. This chain could also continue instead to an internal SCSI drive in the server.

- The controller (hardware).

- The controller (configuration).

- The disk driver installed in NetWare.

THE SERVER

- AC power from the wall.

- The power cord.

- The power supply for the server.

- The motherboard.

- The BIOS configuration of the server.

- The configuration of the cards in the server (conflicts).

- Differences in implementations of SCSI on the two controllers.

- DOS.

- NetWare (SERVER.EXE).

- The disk drivers (AHA2740.DSK, OTHER.DSK).

- The formatting and partitioning already on the drives.

INSTALL sometimes has problems with drives that were previously formatted with other operating systems. The cure is to format the drives using a DOS formatter, then format them again with NetWare.

Each of these points could have made the disk drives fail to show up as available for partitioning. Some of them can be quickly verified (if the power light on the enclosure is on and you can hear the drive spin up, the first four on that chain are eliminated) before you check the others. In this case, John wasn't initially aware of the possibility that the two controllers might conflict with each other. This may happen to you, too. If you believe you have eliminated all the possibilities, then there is probably something in the chain that you've either overlooked or aren't aware of.

Scenario Two: Maintaining an Existing System

Fran, an administrator for Great Big, Inc., is faced with a server that won't respond to the prompt. She encounters a problem with a faulty NIC and then has trouble with the disk drive, probably caused by the original crash.

Snapshot—Scenario Two

Is this an existing system?

- Is the server up?

- Can you reboot the server?

- Will the server boot DOS?

- Will NetWare load?

- Can you load NetWare but not access some or all server functions?

Fran, the system administrator for Great Big, Inc., comes back to her desk after lunch. There are 15 messages from various users, saying that they can't connect to the server, or that their applications don't work, or that they can't see drive F. Fran notices that all the user complaints are from people with accounts on the Marketing server, so she decides to check that server first, before looking at all the users' workstations. She grabs the data sheet she prepared when she installed the server, which lists its hardware and software configurations, and heads for the office the server is in.

The server is on, and there is text on the monitor (nothing helpful), but the server doesn't respond to the keyboard. Even the CapsLock and NumLock keys don't respond. She checks the connection between the keyboard and CPU and tries again. Still nothing. There is a workstation in the room. She tries to connect to the server and gets the message "Server marketing is unknown at this time."

Fran reboots the server. Both DOS and NetWare load properly and the server is back online. Relieved that another crisis has been averted, she logs in as supervisor from the workstation and begins checking the volumes to make sure that everything is accessible again. After about 5 minutes, the workstation loses the connection to the server, and on checking, Fran finds that the server has hung again.

After she finishes her primal scream therapy, Fran begins eliminating possible causes. Since the server will boot and load DOS and NetWare, and it has been running fine for quite a while, it's almost certainly not a configuration problem. She is the only one with the supervisor password, and she hasn't changed anything on this server in months, so it shouldn't be a problem with an addition being configured improperly.

She notifies the department members that the server may be down for a while, and then reboots the server again, paying particular attention to the messages from the BIOS, DOS, and NetWare. There are no out-of-the-ordinary messages or errors reported. She logs in again from the workstation and quickly goes to the system error log. At the end are a number of messages relating to Ethernet configuration errors. A clue!

She quickly checks the system error log of another server on the same Ethernet segment, and it does not display the same errors. From this, she deduces that the problem may be related to Ethernet but is probably also unique to this server. She tries to log in again, and the server is down. She turns the server off and replaces the Ethernet card with a spare.

The server comes up, but now it can't mount the second volume. Fran ignores this problem for the moment—it may be the result of the freezes and powering off without shutting down properly. She logs in from the workstation and waits anxiously. Five minutes, then ten, then fifteen pass. There are no new messages in the system error log. It seems that the original problem has been fixed.

Now, it's time to get that second volume mounted again. Fran starts up VREPAIR and begins scanning the unmounted volume for errors. It finds errors and says it's repairing them. When VREPAIR finishes, Fran brings the server down correctly, then restarts it. It still can't mount the second volume. Then Fran remembers that VREPAIR should be run over and over again until it doesn't report any errors.

Unfortunately for Fran, with 20 people clamoring outside the door to know when their server will be back on line, the VREPAIR process is taking about 20 minutes per cycle with this 1.2 GB volume. However, on the fourth time through, there are no further errors reported.

When she restarts the server, the volume mounts properly, and everyone is able to log in and get to their files again. Fran reflects that it might have been faster to reformat the drive and restore the disk from last night's backup, but all the work done that day would have been lost. She resolves to talk to her manager about mirroring the drives on the mission-critical servers as insurance against this sort of problem.

Fran then logs the incident in her work log, recording the problems and solutions in case she comes across a similar situation again. She also logs the problems on the data sheet for the server.

Lessons Learned—Scenario Two

- Check to see whether a reported problem is affecting more than one user—it will help you tell whether the problem is with the user's workstation or with the server or cabling.

- Check the server's system error log regularly. Not only will this enable you to distinguish important messages more easily, you may well be able to spot a potential problem before it results in downtime.

- Remember that it may be necessary to run VREPAIR several times before all errors are corrected.

- Mirror the drives on mission-critical servers.

- Keep a log, and keep it updated. It will help you solve the problem the next time. There will be a next time.

The Fault Point Chain—Scenario Two

There are several fault point chains in this example. The first one is the original problem with the server.

- AC power from the wall. This includes spikes or brownouts.

- The power cord.

- The power supply for the server.

- The motherboard including RAM.

- The BIOS power. If the batteries wear out, configuration information is lost.

- The BIOS configuration of the server.

- The cards in the server. Each has its own chain of connections, configuration, drivers, and so on.

- The keyboard and its cable.

- The monitor, its power, its cable, and the video adapter.

- NetWare. SERVER.EXE could be corrupted, or could simply have crashed.

- The NLMs loaded when the server crashed.

- Applications running on the user's workstations when the server crashed.

In this case, many of these are easily eliminated. If there is text on the screen, obviously the server has power and the monitor is working. If the BIOS were configured incorrectly or its batteries worn out, the server wouldn't boot correctly. The keyboard responds after rebooting. Since no one has logged in yet, it couldn't be applications running on the server. This trims the list down to the motherboard, the cards in the server, NetWare itself, and the NLMs. The messages in the system error log pointed the way to the first item to check. But if there hadn't been any messages, the order of things to try (easiest to hardest) might have been this: replacing SERVER.EXE, not loading the NLMs, replacing the cards one at a time, and trying another motherboard.

Troubleshooting Workstations

Snapshot: Troubleshooting Workstations

IS THIS A NEW PC-COMPATIBLE SYSTEM?

Does the POST (power-on self test) finish without error messages?

If so, go to the next item. If not, either the system may be configured incorrectly with the SETUP program, or it may have been assembled incorrectly. Some examples of this type of error message are "RAM configuration error, block 22f," "Kybd Error 301," and "Hard disk not ready." See the section on PC configuration and the Setup program, on page 83.

Does the workstation boot without error messages?

If so, go to the next item. If not, the error messages should give you a clue as to the problem. Newer video adapters, hard disk adapters, and LAN adapters are examples of possible sources of these messages. See the section on troubleshooting PC cards and connections, on page 81.

Does DOS load without error messages?

If so, go to the next item. If not, try booting from a floppy disk. If this works, replace the COMMAND .COM file on the hard disk. If DOS still won't load correctly, see the section on troubleshooting PC software, on page 85.

Do the network drivers load without error messages?

If so, go to the next item. If not, try replacing the network drivers. If this doesn't help, the driver may be configured incorrectly. Check the network adapter version and the version of DOS in use. If everything matches, the NIC may be faulty. See the section on networking software, on page 86.

Can you log in to the server?

If there are no error messages but you cannot see the server, try to log in to another server, if there is one. Try to log in from another workstation. If the server is up and more than one workstation cannot log in, the problem is likely to be with the physical network—either the cabling itself, or one of the devices such as a concentrator or repeater. See Chapter 4 for details.

IS THIS AN EXISTING PC-COMPATIBLE SYSTEM?

Is the display readable? Does the cursor respond to the keyboard?

If so, go to the next item. If not, make sure the PC is on. Are there any status lights on? Is the fan running? If the PC is on, but won't respond to keyboard input, it is frozen. Reboot the PC. A simple test to see if the keyboard is functioning is to try the CapsLock or NumLock keys—if the indicator lights come on, the keyboard is functioning, whether the screen responds or not. If the keyboard lights respond, but the screen doesn't change, the PC may still be frozen. This type of hang is typical of software problems, usually with applications or TSR programs.

The number of possible causes for freezing are practically infinite. If the PC hangs regularly, it may be a hardware or software problem. Check for software problems first. See the section on troubleshooting PC software, on page 85.

If the screen or keyboard still won't respond after rebooting, check their connections to the PC. If they are tight, review the hardware configuration to check for interrupt conflicts. See the section on troubleshooting PC hardware, on page 79.

Does the POST (power-on self test) finish without error messages?

If so, go to the next item. If not, the chip that holds the setup data may have lost power or there may be a hardware failure. Check the configuration with SETUP. See the section on PC configuration and the Setup program, on page 83. If everything matches your configuration worksheet, see the section on troubleshooting PC hardware, on page 79.

Does the workstation boot without error messages?

If so, go to the next item. If not, the error messages should give you a clue as to the problem. Video adapters, hard disk adapters, and LAN adapters are examples of possible sources of these messages. See the section on troubleshooting PC cards and connections, on page 81.

Does DOS load without error messages?

If so, go to the next item. If not, try booting from a floppy disk. If this works, replace the COMMAND.COM file on the hard disk. If DOS still won't load correctly, the problem may be with some of the items in the AUTOEXEC.BAT or CONFIG.SYS files. See the section on trouble-shooting PC software, on page 85.

Do the network drivers load without errors?

If so, go to the next item. If not, try replacing the network drivers. If this doesn't help, the driver may be configured incorrectly. Check the network adapter version and the version of DOS in use, and install a new driver. If the new driver also doesn't work, the problem is likely to be the NIC. See the section on networking software, on page 86.

If you are using the ODI driver, make sure that the NIC driver is the latest available for your NIC. You may need to update the NIC if it is an older card. The order that the ODI shell drivers load in is LSL, DRIVER.COM (the network driver for your NIC), IPXODI, and NETx. Make sure that the NET.CFG file has the proper configuration information for the card you are using. The same is true for the VLM drivers. Make sure that you have the latest version of the DRIVER.COM driver.

Does the workstation see the server (SLIST)?

If so, go to the next item. If not, the problem may be in the connection to the physical network, in the physical network itself, or in the server. If the server is working (screen on, console prompt responds), check the connections from the network adapter to the transceiver (if any) and to the physical network. See the section on troubleshooting PC cards and connections, on page 81, and Chapter 4, which is about troubleshooting the physical network.

Can you log in to the server?

If not, make sure that the user you are attempting to log in as exists, and that the spelling of the username and the password are correct. Try logging in as another user. If this doesn't work, make sure that a station restriction has not been set up for that PC. Also see the section about BINDFIX in Chapter 2. If you are using NDS, be sure that the context is specified correctly.

Does Windows load without errors?

Once the workstation has booted, DOS has loaded, the NetWare shell has loaded, and you can connect with the network, you can be fairly sure that the workstation is functioning correctly. If Windows produces error messages, it is almost certainly because of configuration problems with Windows. See the section on Windows, on page 89.

Can Windows attach to the network?

If the workstation can connect to the network under DOS, but not under Windows, this may be caused by a setup problem with Windows. See the section on Windows, on page 89.

IS THIS A MACINTOSH SYSTEM?

Does the POST (power-on self test) finish with a tone instead of a chord?

When the POST runs, you will hear a tone when it is completed. If you hear a chord (three or more tones one after the other), the POST has failed. If the POST fails, it means you have a hardware problem. Try reseating the cards and memory in the system, and check for loose connections on the power supply, hard disk, floppy drive, and so on.

Does the workstation boot without error messages and without freezing?

As the Mac boots, you will see icons appear along the bottom of the screen. These icons represent the additional system extensions, Control Panels, or CDEVs that are loading. You can usually find the corresponding driver by looking in the System folder, the Extensions folder, or the Control Panels folder for a corresponding icon. (The view must be set to Large Icon.) If there is a problem with a driver, you may get an error message in a window on screen, or the Mac may just freeze. Either way, identify the last icon, reboot with extensions turned off (by holding the Shift key down while the Mac boots), and remove that driver, then reboot. See the section on Macintosh software, on page 101.

Do the network drivers load without errors?

The network drivers load along with the others during the boot process. You should identify the icons associated with the network drivers. The most likely cause of error messages at this point is from faulty configuration information.

Does the workstation see the server in the Chooser?

If not, check to be sure that the Macintosh name space is loaded on the server. If it is, recheck the physical connections and reboot. If it still won't work, try reinstalling the network driver. If that still doesn't work, you may have a faulty network card or LocalTalk adapter.

PC-COMPATIBLES CAN BE VERY DIFFICULT to troubleshoot, principally because of their enormous variety. There are at least seven Intel processors in use, at twenty or so different speeds; plus clone processors from other companies such as AMD, IBM, Cyrix, and Thompson; many different motherboards and BIOS versions for each processor; hundreds of different hard disks; and thousands of different cards. All this variety can make troubleshooting a maze, especially if you don't have the documentation for the PC. However, if you understand the principles of how the PC loads its BIOS, operating system, network drivers, and other software, you should be able to isolate the cause of any problem and figure out what to do about it.

Most workstations attached to Novell networks are currently IBM-compatible PCs of one type or another. However, there are other possibilities: PS/2s, Macintoshes, and UNIX workstations are the most likely. Some of the principles discussed in this chapter apply equally to all sorts of workstations, and others are platform-specific. The fault points and basics applicable to all platforms will be covered first, then specifics of IBM compatibles, Windows clients, OS/2 clients, PS/2 workstations, Macintoshes, and UNIX workstations. Once again, the "Real-Life Stories" section at the end of this chapter will lead you through some real problems, showing how they were diagnosed and resolved.

Troubleshooting servers is covered in Chapter 2. However, if problems with a server occur before NetWare loads, you should treat it as a workstation, using the troubleshooting techniques in this chapter.

Fault Points for Workstations

HAPTER 1 INTRODUCED the concept of fault points as an alternative to the more conventional flow charts. The problem with flowcharts is that they become too difficult to use with subjects as complex as a network, or even when covering the possible configurations of a workstation.

The basic fault point chain for a workstation includes the same elements for any type of workstation. If you understand the potential fault points for a workstation, you will be able to isolate any problem to a particular part of the system, then apply the concepts presented in this chapter to figure out how to fix the problem.

Figure 3.1 illustrates a typical fault chain for workstations. Each item in the chain depends on the others, and each item has three parts: the part itself, the connections between it and the preceding part, and the connections between it and the following part. For example, the power at the wall socket can be broken if the power to the socket fails, if the socket itself is faulty, or if the power cord to the PC power supply is defective or not plugged in. Similarly,

FIGURE 3.1
The fault point chain for workstations

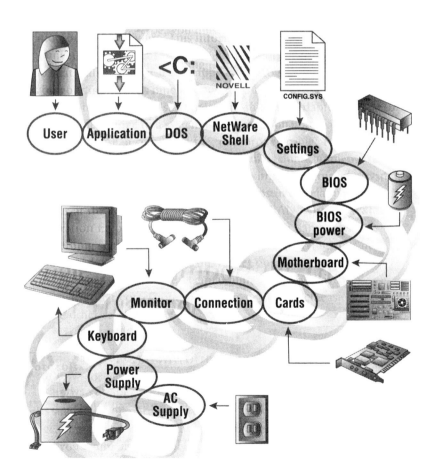

the power supply is connected to the wall by the power cord and has connections to the motherboard, the disk drives, and the fan.

To determine which of the three parts of the chain is causing the problem, you must use deductive logic. If any part of the workstation is receiving power, the power supply and the cable are probably good. If one part of the workstation is not getting power, and the rest are, it's probably the connection for that part to the power supply. If the workstation isn't getting power anywhere, check the power cord and the socket before replacing the power supply.

You might think that the keyboard has only two parts: the keyboard and its connection to the motherboard. However, the third part here is the user. If the wrong keys are pressed, the symptoms may resemble a problem with the keyboard hardware or the connection to the PC. This is also true of the monitor, but it has even more variables: it may be turned off independently of the PC, it has a power connection and a video connection, and it can also be made to seem dead by turning down the contrast and brightness.

Workstation-to-Network Connection Failures

The connection to the network is a common failure point, because of the number of possible fault points and their susceptibility to outside interference. The network connection usually consists of the connection from the NIC in the PC to a transceiver, to a concentrator or hub, or directly to the server, depending on the type of network topology.

For example, take the relatively simple case of an NIC with a thick Ethernet connection, connected to a transceiver that converts the thick Ethernet to 10BaseT, which is connected to a wall jack with a second cable. In this chain, several things can go wrong:

- The thick Ethernet cable can slip from the NIC, can become defective, or can come loose from the transceiver.

- The transceiver can become defective.

- The 10BaseT cable can come out of its socket on the transceiver, can become defective, or can come out of the wall socket.

The network connection fault points are further complicated by the fact that they are often hard to see, difficult to get at, and subject to being kicked by the user or pulled out by a janitor with a vacuum.

PC Card, Motherboard, and BIOS Failures

Each card in the PC has its own fault point chain, including:

- The connections to the bus and to whatever device it supports

- Its jumper configurations for interrupt, DMA segment, and so forth

- The matching configurations in the setup of the PC, whether in hardware or software

The motherboard has a point of failure where the power supply connects to it, and one for each service it provides, whether on a card, a parallel or serial port, the keyboard interface, the sound interface, or the memory. Each of these can typically be diagnosed by the error messages that appear during the boot sequence, or, as a last resort, by eliminating all other possible causes.

The BIOS, and the associated CMOS, holds configuration information for the PC, including the number and types of floppy and hard drives installed, the number of serial and parallel ports installed, the time, and other information. If the battery that provides power to the BIOS wears out, this information can be lost. If the BIOS is out-of-date, it may not support new floppy drives or hard drives, or it may cause problems with software, such as Windows not running in the enhanced mode with an older 386 BIOS.

Operating System and Software Failures

The PC's operating system and the NetWare software are configured with several files, including AUTOEXEC.BAT, CONFIG.SYS, and NET.CFG. Each of these files contains statements that must be spelled correctly and must also match the settings on the cards they pertain to.

The NetWare shell can fail in its connection with the PC hardware and software, by itself, or in its interface with applications. If the shell isn't configured correctly, it won't match the interrupt and memory address used by the NIC, and some shells work better than others with certain applications.

The version of DOS you use can also cause problems in one of three ways:

- By not working well with the PC hardware (unusual with versions later than 3.0)

- By not working well with applications

- By not working well with extended memory or other added features

Some applications may require a specific version of DOS. Later versions of DOS may also provide services such as memory management, networking support, and file compression.

Versions of Windows may also affect the working or performance of NetWare, depending on the version of NetWare driver you have loaded. See the section "Windows and NetWare" later in this chapter for more information.

Applications also have the same three potential problem areas: the interface with DOS, the application itself, and the interface with the user. If the application is misleading or complex, many users may mistakenly report problems that are due to misunderstanding, rather than hardware or software error. Some applications may also bypass the NetWare shell and access NetWare services directly. For more information about troubleshooting network applications, see Chapter 10.

User Failures

Finally, the user is the end point on the workstation fault point chain. Many of the problems that will be reported to you will not be hardware or software problems, but problems caused by misunderstandings—either misinterpretation of instructions or a lack of knowledge about the software.

As an administrator, the best way to deal with users is to provide some training and to encourage them to acquire training on their own. See Chapter 6, which covers ways to prevent problems, for more information about training users.

Troubleshooting Workstations—The Basics

THE BASIC PROCEDURE FOR TROUBLESHOOTING workstations follows the approach outlined in Chapter 1. Check the obvious sources of problems first, and get whatever information you can about what went wrong.

All computers work in essentially the same way. This includes PCs, Macintoshes, UNIX workstations, minicomputers, and so forth. When you turn the computer on, the system looks in its read-only memory (ROM) for instructions on what to do next. Next, it performs a power-on self test (POST) routine, then reads further instructions from a boot device (usually a hard disk, but it could also be a floppy disk, a tape drive, or even a device on the network). The boot device will load the core operating system into memory, followed by other programs that enhance the operation of the computer. These other programs include network drivers, memory optimization programs, and many, many others. If you understand this process for the computers you deal with, and the messages or indications that go with each stage, you will have a much better chance of understanding what's happening when something goes wrong.

Checking Connections

Often, the only problem with a workstation is a loose or disconnected cable. Never assume that the user has checked seemingly obvious possibilities. Check all the connections, including the keyboard, mouse, monitor, power, and network. The usual workstation has a rat's nest of cables behind it or on the floor under the desk. In some cases, especially with network connections that are relatively sensitive to loose wiring, some connections may appear to be okay—even showing a green attachment light on the transceiver—but still cause problems. The first thing to check with any installed workstation that suddenly begins having problems is that all the connections are solid.

Unless the workstation is a test or demo machine that is often reconfigured, I strongly recommend that you screw all the connections down tight. It's a pain when you need to replace something, but it lessens the chance of a user kicking something loose or of the janitor pulling out a connection while vacuuming.

Remember that all connections may not be on the workstation. If the problem is network-related and the connections seem to be okay, check the transceiver or the status light on the network card if applicable. For example, a LatticeNet transceiver has two lights: the SQE Test and the Status lights. If the SQE Test light is out, it indicates that the connection to the PC is out. If the Status light is out and the SQE Test is on, however, it indicates that the connection is broken between the transceiver and the server or concentrator.

The workstation's error message or behavior may not seem to point directly at the problem. For instance, the symptom might be a monitor that is blank or showing a fuzzy or distorted display. These symptoms might be the result of a dead motherboard, a dead display adapter, or an extreme software problem.

However, the problem might also be as simple as a video or power cable that has worked loose. Or it could be that another monitor has been placed too close to the first.

Checking for Changes

Troubleshooting workstations is the place to apply the principle of determining what has recently changed. Has the equipment been moved recently? Has anything new been added or removed? If the user says no, check connections anyway—something could have been accidentally kicked loose by the user, or a connector could have gradually worked out of its socket.

You should have a data sheet for the PC. Check it to see if the configuration on it matches the current configuration. Check to see if the fan is running; if not, either the PC is not getting power or the power supply is dead.

Ask the user if he or she knows of any way to make the problem go away. Also ask whether the problem occurs at a particular time or at certain intervals. Find out what software was running when the PC froze, and what the chain of events leading up to the crash were.

Checking New Installations

If you're troubleshooting a new installation, the same principles apply: check the obvious before trying the obscure. Make sure that the power is on and that the connections are tight before replacing the network cards.

Check the possibilities that cost you the least time or money first. It doesn't cost much to verify a power connection, but rechecking all the wiring of a network is relatively expensive.

Ideally, you should use the same type of workstation throughout the LAN, with the same kind of video adapter, network adapter, and so on. However, in real life this is usually not possible. The next best thing is to standardize on certain brands. If all your network adapters come from the same manufacturer, it will make your life simpler.

Troubleshooting PC-Compatible Stations

PC COMPATIBLES, AND WORKSTATIONS in general, have a uniform underlying structure. Figure 3.2 illustrates the basic workstation structure. No matter what components are used, the underlying structure is similar—the motherboard and operating system tie together all the assorted pieces. No matter what the CPU is, how much memory is installed, or what type of display or network adapter is installed, the basic structure remains the same. In terms of the fault point chain, this is all you need to keep in mind. Troubleshooting a problem with the display is the same whether you have a PC with a monochrome display adapter, a 486 EISA PC with a VESA accelerated XGA (eXtended VGA) adapter, or a dual-Pentium, dual-bus PCI system with lots of cards.

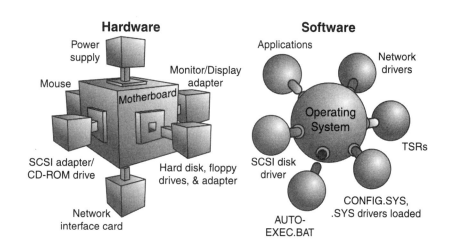

FIGURE 3.2
Basic workstation structure

Troubleshooting PC Hardware

From a troubleshooter's perspective, PC hardware does not materially change from the first 8088 PC produced in 1983 to the latest dual-processor Pentium Pro PCI system. There are, of course, vast differences in speed, size, chips, cost, and other features. However, from a functional standpoint, they are very similar: the motherboard holds a CPU chip or two, memory, slots for peripherals, a BIOS chip, a keyboard connector, and some miscellaneous odds and ends. Understand how these pieces work together on any given system, and you can apply that knowledge to any other.

Power on self test routine.

The Boot Sequence

To troubleshoot a PC effectively, you should understand the sequence of events that occur when the machine is turned on. The POST routine will run diagnostic tests on the motherboard, test the memory, and then tell you that the hard disk adapter is working and how many hard disks are connected to it. Then, before DOS begins loading, you may also see messages from some of the cards installed in the PC. Network adapters, SCSI adapters, and video cards are typical examples of cards that produce messages, although not all such cards do.

A missing boot message, or a message like "Error configuring LAN adapter," will give you helpful clues to get a PC working again, but only if you are paying close attention. These messages are often on the screen for a very short time, and there is usually no way to scroll back up the screen and review them. You may need to reboot the PC several times to get the complete text of a message. This is another time when some advance work will stand you in good stead. If all your PCs have the same configuration, or if you have become familiar with the normal series of messages that appear as each workstation boots, it will be much easier for you to spot anomalies.

Later versions of DOS and Windows 95 make it possible for you to see the messages you normally wouldn't see and choose to load or not load each command in CONFIG.SYS or AUTOEXEC.BAT:

F8

- With DOS, simply press the F8 key when you see the "Loading MS-DOS" message. It will ask you if you want to process CONFIG.SYS. You will then be able to choose to load or not load each command. Then it will ask you if you want to process AUTOEXEC.BAT. If you say yes, you will again be able to choose whether or not to process each command.

- With Windows 95, holding down the F8 key during the boot process will bring you to a menu that lets you choose to load Windows in safe mode, safe mode with network drivers loaded, or DOS mode; go through each command; boot in other modes; or load normally. See the section about Windows 95 later in this chapter for more information about this type of workstation.

Troubleshooting PC Cards and Connections

The power is on, the PC boots reliably, the status light on the transceiver is green, but the workstation won't connect to the network. What's the problem? It may still be a loose connection. Network adapters and transceivers vary considerably in the degree of tolerance they have for loose connections. It is entirely possible for the connection to be solid enough to light the status light on a transceiver, for instance, but still be loose enough to prevent the network adapter from connecting properly. Never depend on the status lights; go ahead and crawl under the desk and check the connections.

Always observe static safety precautions. Make sure that you are adequately grounded before handling the internals of any workstation. Your body generates small amounts of static electricity all the time, and walking on carpet generates enough static to destroy any computer component except the power supply. Destroying the parts you are attempting to check is self-defeating to say the least. If you don't have a grounding strap, at least make sure you touch the case of a power supply that's plugged in before handling any cards, memory modules, or the like.

If the external connections are all solid, try reseating the adapter cards. Often the cards are not secured properly and may have worked loose, especially if the connections are changed often. It may also be that the contacts on the edge of the adapter card are somewhat corroded, causing a faulty connection. If this seems to be a possibility, try rubbing the row of connectors at the bottom of the card, gently, with an ink eraser. Be sure not to get rubber shavings in the PC, and wipe the contacts off with a tissue when you're finished. Get a supply of the proper screws and make sure that all cards are screwed down.

If it's a new installation, make sure that the cards are fully seated, and that the connections are fully seated too—it's easy to mistake a good connection for a faulty one in both cases. Install all the supplied screws and cable connectors. This may be a pain initially but the effort will pay off in the long run. Never assume that two cards will work together, especially in their default settings. In fact, some cards may be impossible to use together, because neither will allow a combination of settings that won't interfere with the other.

Cards may also simply be incompatible with each other, either at a hardware level or because the device drivers necessary to access them conflict. In these cases, you should read the documentation for all equipment you plan to install and make sure that compatibility with anything else you plan to install has been established. The most common instance of this sort of problem occurs with SCSI adapters and their drivers. You should not plan to use SCSI adapters from different manufacturers in the same PC. See the section about SCSI adapters in Chapter 1 for more information.

If you need to ship a workstation, remove the cards and pack them separately. Use original packing if available. Some manufacturers will not honor the warranty if products are not returned in the original shipping containers.

Interrupt Conflicts

Interrupt conflicts are one of the potentially most confusing areas, but also often one of the most straightforward. It's usually just a matter of reading the manuals for the adapters used in the PC (assuming that the interrupts and memory segments are adequately documented). There often seems to be great resistance to reading the manual, but try it. Most manuals will, somewhere, discuss getting the card in question to operate with other cards, sometimes even specifically suggesting alternate settings for use with other specific adapters or certain software.

There are two parts to the settings on ISA cards: the memory address (a segment in RAM) and the IRQ (interrupt). The basic requirement to get cards to work together is to make sure that they use different memory segments and different IRQs.

Interrupt conflicts are primarily an issue in setting up new systems, but sometimes a conflict will produce only intermittent problems. This is especially true when the memory segments used by different cards overlap rather than using all of the same segment. For example, 16-bit video adapters usually use a larger segment than other types of cards, often including memory locations used by Windows. If some software will run but other programs will not, it may be because these programs are attempting to directly address memory in use by an adapter. This can usually be resolved in Windows by using the EMMEXCLUDE command in the SYSTEM.INI file. With other programs, it may be necessary to use a memory manager such as QEMM.

The easiest way to resolve interrupt conflicts is to reduce the number of cards in the PC to the minimum, then add the other cards back in, one at a time, until the conflict is found. Resolving it then becomes a matter of using alternate addresses where possible until the problem is solved.

EISA PCs can avoid interrupt problems entirely by using the enhanced 32-bit bus-mastering mode. However, under certain conditions, such as when the PC needs to have more than 16 MB of RAM, all the cards in the system must be

EISA-compatible, and EISA drivers must be available for all EISA cards. These cards are often more expensive, but they also provide higher performance.

PCI PCs can also avoid interrupt problems, assuming that there are no ISA cards in the PC and that the cards properly implement the PCI specification. There are issues to be aware of here, too. If the BIOS PCI configuration is set to AUTO, you shouldn't see any problems under normal circumstances. However, if it has been changed to a manual configuration, it is possible to have two cards using PCI interrupt A, B, C or D, or translating to the same ISA interrupt, which can cause problems. Another issue to look at is what version of the PCI specification is supported by the motherboard BIOS and by the cards. If they don't match, you might have problems. Finally, simply because the PCI specification hasn't been around that long, you may find an incompatibility problem, such as a high-end graphics card that won't run on a Pentium PC with a 25 MHz bus speed.

PC Configuration with the SETUP Program

Depending on the version of the PC, SETUP may be a program that you'll need to run or it may be programmed into the PC's BIOS. See your owner's manual for details if you're not sure how to run it. As an administrator, you should have copies of the SETUP.COM program for every PC that uses it. Be aware that different manufacturers and models will require different versions of the program.

Common problems with SETUP include having a device listed incorrectly or omitted from the configuration, and loss of stored parameters due to a battery failure. The information you set with SETUP is stored in a chip on the motherboard. If the battery that keeps this chip operating fails, the information will be lost. As a result, the PC may be unable to use its floppy and hard drives, may be unable to communicate with its video adapter, or may lose its connection to serial or parallel ports.

The configuration information necessary to use SETUP includes:

- The size and type of floppy drives installed (double-density or high-density, and 3.5-inch or 5.25-inch)

- The type and number of hard drives installed

- The video adapter installed

- The current time and date

The most critical item is the hard drive type. Determine the type of the hard drive(s) installed in the PC and *write it down!* In addition to your log sheet, a label in an inconspicuous place on the outside of the PC is a good idea, but at least put a label on the drive itself. Identifying the drive type incorrectly in SETUP may cause the hard drive to be irretrievably damaged and will certainly cause the information on the drive to become unavailable. If you don't know the drive type on existing PCs, use SETUP to determine it and write it down *before* there is a problem.

The latest PCs using IDE drives will normally automatically detect the type of hard drive installed. When you are configuring a new PC, you will normally enter the BIOS after you have installed the hard drive and choose the Auto Detect Hard Drive option. Depending on the size of the drive, you may have several options on how to configure it, with differing numbers of sectors, heads, and so on. This doesn't mean the drive is variable in this regard, just the translation scheme.

DOS has a limitation of 504 MB for direct hard drive support. For drives larger than that, your BIOS and your hard drive adapter must support a translation scheme to fool DOS. This is normally not a problem, but if you configure a drive in the BIOS and see that it is a 1 GB hard drive, but FDISK will give you only a 504 MB hard drive partition, it means that your hard drive controller doesn't support the EIDE (Enhanced IDE, which supports drives over 528 MB) specification. You can either replace the controller or run some software, such as DrivePro from Micro House or the Ontrack Disk Manager available with many large IDE drives.

If you are using a SCSI hard drive, you only need to make sure that the SCSI controller's BIOS is enabled. Some controllers' BIOS will work only when the controller is set to the default memory address (often 330H). This can be a handicap if you are trying to get other cards to work (such as network adapters) that also want the same memory address. The SCSI BIOS does the translation necessary to get drives larger than 504 MB to work with DOS.

Plug and Play

The idea behind Plug and Play is to make setting up a PC as simple and easy as setting up a Macintosh. Unfortunately, the execution is not that simple—at least not yet.

In some cases, you can just put the cards in any available slot, install Windows 95, and have everything work. In other cases, you may find that the slot you put the card in is not a bus-mastering slot, and that the card needs to be in a bus-mastering slot.

You may also find that the driver that Windows 95 automatically loads when it finds the card is no longer the best driver to use. In this case, you must restart Windows, then install the new driver, then reboot, then reconfigure the driver, then reboot.

Troubleshooting PC Software

PC software comprises several layers: the basic operating system, extensions and drivers, NetWare extensions, and application software. This is true of all PC operating systems. It is most straightforward with DOS. First, COMMAND.COM loads, which is the basic operating system. It loads the extensions and drivers specified in CONFIG.SYS, then the ones in AUTOEXEC.BAT. NetWare drivers may be loaded in AUTOEXEC.BAT or in another file, NETSTART.BAT, which can be started by AUTOEXEC.BAT. Finally, applications are loaded.

Windows (pre-Windows 95) adds another layer between the operating system and the application. Windows loads, and it may load a great many device drivers and extensions, controlled by a number of files including (but not limited to) SYSTEM.INI, WIN.INI, and NETWARE.INI.

Windows 95, Windows NT, OS/2, and other operating systems, such as Solaris for Intel and NeXTStep for Intel, bypass DOS completely and use their own hardware interface software. The configuration files differ from system to system, but the basic sequence is the same. A small piece of the system, known as the *kernel*, is loaded automatically because it is on track 0 of the hard disk. It then reads other files, which tell it what to load and in what order.

DOS and Its Configuration

The biggest potential problem in troubleshooting workstation software is variety. Most workstations combine one or more operating systems, various configuration files, and networking software. With PCs, for example, counting all the licensed versions, there are literally hundreds of versions of DOS; thousands of possible TSR (terminate-and-stay-resident) programs, device drivers, and other add-on enhancements; hundreds of possible configurations of IPX.COM and NETx.COM; and, of course, millions of possible configurations of AUTOEXEC.BAT, CONFIG.SYS, SHELL.CFG, and so on.

There are some basic principles to resolving software problems. If the problem is with an existing system, go back to the last working configuration. Add the new configuration in a piece at a time until you can determine the problem. It may be necessary to comment out the loading of TSRs or drivers in AUTOEXEC.BAT or CONFIG.SYS to discover which is conflicting with the new software you're attempting to install. You can also try pressing the F8 key during the boot process and choosing whether each CONFIG.SYS and AUTOEXEC.BAT command should execute.

Keeping the old versions of AUTOEXEC.BAT and CONFIG.SYS is not merely a sensible precaution, it's a necessity. Reconstructing old versions is time-consuming and may be impossible, depending on standardization, backups, and how well the system is documented. To avoid these problems, simply rename the old versions AUTOEXEC.OLD, CONFIG.BAK, or something similar. Many programs that modify these files use a similar procedure; all should.

Within an existing LAN, it's a good idea to standardize on a basic operating system. Using the same version of DOS, the same AUTOEXEC.BAT and CONFIG.SYS files, the same network drivers (and the same network cards), and the same basic login script will greatly reduce the record keeping necessary to document the network, the software necessary to install a new system or reinstall a faulty one, and the number of possible problems.

Use a virus detection program on every workstation on your network, run a virus scanner on the network itself regularly, and hold occasional sessions to educate users on viruses; and you will probably only be infected once in a while. The cost of the software and the time you spend configuring it is much less than the time and cost of restoring your server after a virus has corrupted your entire server, assuming that the backups haven't been infected, too. A workstation with a virus can sometimes be even worse than a server with a virus. The time and effort involved in determining the actual problem with an unprotected workstation that becomes infected can be enormous, and it may not be backed up, as your server is.

Networking Software

Networking software for a workstation can include the NetWare drivers (NETX.COM), ODI (Open Data-link Interface) drivers, or VLMs (Virtual Loadable Modules).

It is handy to keep a set of drivers for
'. This will make it easier to configure new
at are accidentally erased or corrupted.
to the version of DOS—thus NET2.COM,
wn as NET*x*.COM. NETX.COM (with a
Ware driver and is compatible with almost
best NET.COM driver to use with Win-
cribed a little later in the chapter.) Use
X for each network adapter in use and
don't have a copy of NETX.COM, you
ndix A).
MSNET*x*.COM use regular, expanded,
extended memory, respectively. Using expanded or extended memory will
give you more free memory in your base 640 KB, but may also interfere with Windows or other programs attempting to use these areas of memory.

SHELL.CFG or NET.CFG is the equivalent of CONFIG.SYS for the shell
(IPX.COM/NET*x*.COM). The following are a number of useful settings for
specific circumstances:

Local Printers=0   This will keep the workstation from
hanging if no ports are captured and the
user presses Shift-PrintScreen.

Preferred Server=*servername*   This will ensure that the workstation
attaches to the correct server, rather than
the one that responds the fastest.

Print Header = 255   This will allow PostScript jobs enough
header space to configure the printer
correctly.

THE ODI DRIVERS NET.CFG is the configuration file used for workstations
running RPRINTER with NetWare 2.*x* and 3.*x*. It is used instead of SHELL.CFG
with the DOS Requester under NetWare 4.*x*, and to effect changes with ODI
drivers.

The ODI drivers use a different structure than IPX/NETX. ODI is more analogous to the way network drivers are supported on a NetWare server. With the
ODI driver, LSL (the Link Support Layer driver) is loaded first. This allows you
to load different drivers for each protocol, such as IPX (IPXODI.COM) or TCP/
IP (TCPIP.COM).

The ODI drivers are loaded in the following order: LSL.COM, DRIVER.COM (a NIC-specific driver for your card), IPXODI.COM, TCPIP.COM, NETBIOS .COM, or any other protocol-specific drivers, then finally NETX.COM. There must also be an entry in NET.CFG with the following syntax:

```
LINK DRIVER IPXODI
   INT 3
   MEM C800
   PORT 2E0
```

The first line links the proper driver for your protocol to the NIC. The next three lines, which are indented, specify the interrupt, the memory address, and the port address for the card.

THE VLMS The DOS Requester for NetWare uses a group of programs called VLMs, similar to NLMs on a server. VLMs perform the same function as the earlier versions of the shell, diverting requests to access network drives or printers from being sent to the local ports, and sending them to the server. VLM.EXE is loaded first, and it then loads a number of other modules, which control the various aspects of attaching to and using the network.

The default sequence of VLMs is as follows:

1. CONN.VLM

2. IPXNCP.VLM

3. TRAN.VLM

4. SECURITY.VLM

5. NDS.VLM

6. BIND.VLM

7. NWP.VLM

8. FIO.VLM

9. GENERAL.VLM

10. REDIR.VLM

11. PRINT.VLM

12. NETX.VLM

The actual VLMs loaded and the order they are loaded in will depend on the network configuration you are using. INSTALL.EXE will automatically determine which VLMs are loaded and in what order, depending on the responses you give during installation.

The DOS Requester defaults to Ethernet 802.2, rather than 802.3, as in previous Net-Ware versions. If you have a mixed network, with some servers that won't initially be upgraded to 4.x, you should ensure that everything is using the same version, either 802.2 or 802.3.

The DOS Requester does not sit on top of DOS and intercept all disk and port traffic to determine whether it is local or intended for the network. Instead, it works with DOS. The principal difference is that the LASTDRIVE entry in CONFIG.SYS should be set to Z:, instead of D: or E:, as is typical with older shells. NetWare and DOS now use the same drive table, which means that rather than needing to know the last drive in the system so it could take the rest, as the older NetWare shells did, the VLMs recognize all the drives in the system and use the rest of the drive letters available. This has the advantage of allowing you to add drives (such as a CD-ROM) without needing to reconfigure the shell.

Windows and NetWare

I N CONSIDERING WINDOWS AND NETWARE, there are three sets of versions of Windows to look at: Windows 3.0 to Windows for Workgroups 3.11, Windows 95, and Windows NT. Each has different considerations necessary to get it to work well with NetWare.

At the time of this writing, many network managers, particularly those in larger organizations, are still buying and using Windows for Workgroups 3.11 rather than Windows 95, because they feel that the new version is not mature enough yet, especially for big networks. Users who need the 32-bit power of the new versions may be better off with Windows NT. There are a number of books on managing the upgrade from Windows 3.x to Windows 95, and upgrading won't be covered here, other than in terms of considerations from a NetWare administrator's point of view.

Windows 3.0 to Windows for Workgroups 3.11

Getting Windows to work can be difficult, particularly with older PCs. Getting it to work with NetWare can be even more difficult, for several reasons. Windows normally uses memory in locations generally reserved for DOS or hardware, including video and network adapters. As a result, Windows may interfere with the network adapter necessary to connect to the network. This can be fixed with the EMMEXCLUDE option in the [386Enh] section of the SYSTEM.INI file. Some older versions of BIOS in some systems will not run Windows 3.x at all. You can fix this by installing a later version of BIOS, either from the manufacturer or from a supplier such as Phoenix Technologies.

You may also need to update your system to the latest available network driver, a later version of DOS, and perhaps even a newer network card—and that's just to get Windows running on a workstation and able to connect to the network. Running Windows from the network is another question entirely, and best left to a Windows guru, although basic issues will be addressed in Chapter 10.

Here are some general tips for running these versions of Windows:

- Use Windows 3.1, or even better, Windows for Workgroups 3.1. These have much better network support than 3.0.

- Use IPX 3.10 or later, and NETX 3.26 or later, the ODI drivers, or the VLMs.

- Make sure NETWARE.DRV is about 125 KB. It often doesn't get uncompressed properly.

- If Windows is not running (or not running properly) in the Enhanced mode, try adding the following statement to the SYSTEM.INI file, under the [386Enh] section:

```
EMMExclude=A000-EFFF
```

If Windows runs with this setting, it means that some card or other program is using memory that Windows wants. If you can discover which part of the memory is the problem (for example C000–C800), change the EMMExclude=A000-EFFF statement to just that segment (EMM-Exclude=C000-C800).

- You might try two other statements in the [386Enh] section. These statements control the way Windows uses the hard drive and whether it accesses a potential problem area in memory:

  • `VirtualHDIRQ=FALSE`
  • `SystemROMBreakPoint=FALSE`

- Make sure that the DOS and NetWare environment settings are updated. CONFIG.SYS should have FILES= and BUFFERS= values of at least 30; and STACKS=10 is a good setting. SHELL.CFG (or NET.CFG) should have SPX CONNECTIONS=60, GET LOCAL TARGET STACKS=5 (or 10 if you'll be using IPX/SPX applications regularly), and a FILE HANDLES= setting of at least 80.

- After exiting Windows, you may get a message "Incorrect version of COMMAND.COM—reboot PC." The PC is trying to load DOS from the server, which may have a different version of DOS in the SYS:PUBLIC\DOS directory than is loaded on the PC. Put the following statement in the user's login script, or make sure that the appropriate version of DOS is loaded on the server (as mentioned earlier, standardizing on one version of DOS for all PCs on your network is a very good idea):

  `COMSPEC=C:\COMMAND.COM`

- If your network card uses IRQ 2, 9, 10 or higher with Windows 3.0 or higher, use VPICDA.386, which can be downloaded from NetWire. Replace the statement DEVICE=VPICDA with DEVICE=VPICDA.386 in your SYSTEM.INI file.

These are only a few of dozens of tips necessary to produce a smoothly running Windows environment in conjunction with NetWare. For more information, you can refer to Windows-oriented magazines, forums on CompuServe relating to Windows and NetWare, and several good books on the subject.

Windows 95

Windows 95 provides a number of exciting new features (new to the Windows platform, at least), such as filenames of up to 254 characters, multitasking, and 32-bit support for applications (more or less). It also offers the same peer-to-peer network support as Windows for Workgroups and (limited) native support for NetWare. This Windows version includes support for many more cards than earlier versions, although the generic drivers used in many cases are less than optimum; you should check the manufacturer's Web site or bulletin board for updated drivers.

There are a number of reasons that network administrators are making a less than headlong rush towards upgrading to Windows 95: it's new, somewhat untried; doesn't support NetWare 4.*x*'s NDS directly; has some problems working with NetWare 3.11 if long filenames are enabled; and doesn't offer a huge benefit until all applications are upgraded to 32-bit, which will be a long and expensive proposition in most environments.

I strongly advise you to try all your applications, network drivers, and so forth on a test set of Windows 95 PCs before you even consider moving all your users to this version. It's much easier to undo a few workstations than to convince a lot of users to give up all the neat new features they've just gotten used to when you discover that some mission-critical application won't run properly.

NetWare Clients for Windows 95

At the time this is being written, there are a number of NetWare clients available for Windows 95, including the Microsoft NetWare client that is automatically installed by Windows 95, the NetWare VLM (Shell 4.*x*), the Novell NetWare client for Windows 95, and the new Microsoft NDS-compatible Service. Each has advantages and disadvantages.

These NetWare drivers for Windows 95 will continue to evolve. See Appendix A for information about where to get the latest versions.

THE MICROSOFT NETWARE CLIENT The basic Microsoft client provides seamless integration with Windows 95, installs automatically during the Windows 95 installation, allows the user to set up a single login to both Windows 95 and NetWare, and supports 32-bit printing to any network printer. On the other hand, it doesn't support NDS. If you are still running versions of NetWare earlier than 4.*x*, this client is a good way to go.

THE NETWARE VLM CLIENT Using the VLM client requires some finagling: you must remove existing NetWare support in the device manager, then reboot in DOS mode, then install the NetWare Client for DOS/Windows, then reboot. You'll see a number of error messages about a missing driver. Ignore them. After Windows 95 is up, you'll need to use the Network Control Panel to add a NetWare workstation shell, for versions 4.0 and above. When you're asked for the locations of the files, they should be in C:\WINDOWS or C:\NWCLIENT (the default installation locations). Then you'll need to change STARTNET.BAT or add the commands to AUTOEXEC.BAT to go to the login drive, then log in, and then reboot again.

THE NOVELL NETWARE CLIENT FOR WINDOWS 95 If you're running NetWare 4.*x*, the better solution is to use the NetWare Client32 for Windows 95. You should be able to download this from NetWire, FTP it from ftp.novell.com, or use a Web browser to download it from http://netwire.novell.com. Then you'll need to uncompress the files and follow the instructions in the README file for installation.

NetWare Client32 fully supports NDS, allowing you to browse the NDS tree from the Windows Explorer. It also provides full support for NetWare login scripts and utilities, and it will probably give you higher performance than the current Microsoft driver.

MICROSOFT NDS-COMPATIBLE SERVICE Microsoft does support NDS, but to get the support, you must download the service, code-named Maple, from a bulletin board or Web server. The latest version available when this was written is 371 KB and is installed as a service. (It's an addition to the existing Microsoft Novell client, rather than a replacement, as the Novell Client32 is.) It adds NDS support, although not to the same level as the Novell client.

Support for Long Filenames

Windows 95 supports long filenames, as most other operating systems have done for a long time. However, there are some disadvantages to this support:

- You must run the OS/2 name space on a server to support long filenames. This will use more memory and a little disk space on the server.

- Any old DOS or 16-bit Windows applications will not support the long names.

If you're running NetWare 3.11, you should disable the long filename support with Windows for network drives. (In the [NWRedir] section of WIN.INI, add the line: supportLFN=0.) You could also upgrade to a later version of NetWare, which is strongly recommended.

Running Other Network Protocols under Windows 95

If you are using protocols other than IPX/SPX, there is both good news and bad news. The good news is that Windows 95 supports multiple protocols at once, and does so in a simple installation process. The bad news is that many of the drivers for Windows 95 are either old 16-bit drivers, which fail to live up to the potential of Windows 95, or first-generation 32-bit drivers, which may or may not work perfectly.

Applications and Windows 95

Any application not explicitly written for Windows 95 (or NT), and even many that were written for it, is not equipped to take full advantage of the new features of Windows 95. This may range from not being completely written in 32-bit code (even true of Microsoft's own applications) to not supporting long filenames. The best approach is to try running all of your mission-critical applications under Windows 95 before you contemplate upgrading. You should also look at the costs for upgrading your applications.

Windows NT

Many of the advantages of Windows 95 are available in Windows NT as well. The most obvious difference is that Windows NT is still using the Window 3.*x* interface. A more subtle difference is that Windows 95 is happiest with at least 16 MB of RAM, but it will run with 8 MB; NT really needs 32 MB for good performance. Also, for many applications, even first-generation 32-bit applications, Windows 95 will yield better performance in a given PC. NT provides better protection against ill-behaved programs, has a more mature set of drivers, and a modern file system.

All the caveats mentioned in the Windows 95 section apply here, too. Try before you buy, or at least before you commit to upgrading the whole network. If Windows 3.*x* is working for you, don't be in a hurry to change.

OS/2 Clients

O
S/2 IS SIMILAR TO WINDOWS in that it needs its own network drivers. The only issue addressed here will be getting OS/2 to run on your network. To do that, you need the OS/2 Requester program, which is the equivalent of NETx.COM and IPX.COM. This product is furnished with NetWare, and is available separately for older networks. Again, you should check to see that you have the latest versions of the drivers (available on NetWire or from the CompuServe NetWare forum). The Requester files include:

- LSL.SYS

- DDAEMON.EXE

- DRIVER.SYS (such as NE2000.SYS)

- IPX.SYS

- SPX.SYS

- SPDAEMON.EXE

- NWREQ.SYS

- NWDAEMON.EXE

- NWIFS.IFS

- VIPX.SYS

- VSHELL.SYS

You may also be using NMPIPE.SYS, NPSERVER.SYS, NETBIOS.SYS, and NBDAEMON.EXE if you are using named pipes or NetBIOS.

The upgrade to Warp (OS/2 3.0), or even better, Warp Connect, is well worth the cost. You get better network support and increased stability and reliability. If it weren't for IBM's famed ability to turn away developers and discourage customers, OS/2 would probably be posing a big threat to Windows 95 and NT. OS/2 is a better operating system in many ways, and it's more compatible with NetWare, if not as friendly in its interface. Unfortunately, there aren't many native applications, especially mainstream applications also available on other platforms, and hardware vendors seem to be losing interest as well—fewer support OS/2 than used to.

PS/2 (Micro Channel) Clients

MICRO CHANNEL IS AN ESSENTIALLY OBSOLETE bus developed by IBM in an effort to gain control of the PC hardware specification after the company gave the first version away. Even IBM doesn't make many anymore, and Micro Channel cards are almost impossible to find.

PS/2s using the Micro Channel bus must initially be configured and set up for each card installed, using the supplied installation utility in a manner similar to the EISA setup utility. However, after this is done, the problem of interrupts is eliminated. PS/2s use the same software as PC-compatible workstations, described earlier in the chapter.

Macintosh Clients

MACINTOSHES CAN BE ADDED SEAMLESSLY to a NetWare network, either with NetWare for Macintosh or by using MacIPX. In either case, Mac users can access NetWare file server volumes and printers as if they were attached locally.

Macintosh Hardware

Macintosh hardware is in general much easier to support than hardware for PCs. Apple makes almost all of the system units (at least for now), and the add-in cards come in a much more tightly controlled specification, which usually doesn't require any physical configuration. The newest Macs use a PCI bus similar to, but not identical with, the PC version. It, too, is easier to install than the PC version.

In addition, the system software and applications are generally easier to install and use. The Mac supports all the major protocols directly, seamlessly and more or less painlessly. Unfortunately, since PCs represent more than 80 percent of the market, many developers bring out a PC version first, and then port it to the Macintosh.

From the system administrator's point of view, there is a big drawback to the Mac. Much of the system-level operation of the Mac is concealed from the user; in fact, it is not accessible at all without special software or hardware. This makes problems more difficult to diagnose. Understanding the basic operation of the Mac, as outlined below, should make the process of trouble-shooting Macintosh clients easier for you.

Problems with the Power-On Sequence

Macintoshes will vary widely in what is displayed as they boot, but the basic boot sequence is the same for all of them: the POST runs, a memory check runs, then the basic operating system loads from the boot drive, then the extensions and Control Panels and CDEVs load. Macs are in one sense easier to troubleshoot than PCs, because they have most of the items that are added into PCs integrated into the systems. On the other hand, the operating system can be harder to troubleshoot because it is more difficult to find out what is happening at a low level.

When a Macintosh boots up, the first thing it does is run a hardware self-test. This will produce a series of tones instead of a single chord if there is a problem. Unfortunately, there are no messages on the screen during this process to give you a clue about what has happened. The length of time this process takes will vary with the speed of the processor and the amount of memory in the system—the more memory, the longer the process. This is particularly noticeable right after a memory upgrade.

After the self-test, the Macintosh looks for a disk to boot from. It will try to boot from a floppy and then from any SCSI device attached, in order of SCSI ID from 0 to 6. If it can't find a device to boot from, it displays a disk icon with a question mark blinking in the middle. If this happens, try inserting a boot floppy. If the Mac is able to boot from the floppy and the hard drive's icon shows up, try reinstalling the system—it may have become corrupted. Under System 7, this means you should move any system add-ons to another folder and delete the System folder, then reinstall from the original disks.

If the Mac won't recognize that it has a hard disk even when booted from a floppy, try using a formatting utility to locate the drive. These utilities are available as shareware and from a number of manufacturers, and will usually locate any SCSI device attached to the Mac. If the program can't find a device, either the disk is bad or a connection is faulty. Check the connections and try different cables before replacing the drive.

If the formatting utility finds the drive, you will usually have the option of writing a new driver, "refreshing" the disk (rewriting the data on each block of the disk), making a new partition, or reformatting the disk. You can usually also mount the disk manually with the utility. Try this first, then refreshing the disk, rewriting the driver, and if necessary, reformatting the disk.

After the boot disk is found, a Mac icon with a happy face appears, and then the system software is loaded. This part of the sequence is covered in more detail in the section about Macintosh software, but you should be aware that several hardware-related processes also occur here. First, after the boot disk is found, any additional SCSI devices will be mounted (see the section about SCSI devices for more details). Next, during the boot sequence, any NIC is initialized as its driver is loaded. Thus, a Mac may get partway through its boot sequence and then hang, due to a faulty NIC. This can be determined if the last startup icon that appears before the Mac hangs is the EtherTalk (or other protocol) driver. This icon will be the same icon the driver has when you select the Icon View for the folder it's in.

There are a number of startup managers that allow you to set up groups of extensions and Control Panels and control which ones load at startup. See the section about extensions in the discussion of Macintosh software for details.

Macintosh Cards

Macintoshes do not have the problem of interrupt conflicts. Simply use any and all cards that will fit in the case, and there shouldn't be any problems in terms of conflicts. However, the Macintosh doesn't use a very secure method of securing cards in the case. It is possible to unseat the card in the process of attaching the cable to it, especially with large external connectors or those where a fair amount of force is required to seat the cable in the adapter's socket. Reseat the card after attaching the cable in such cases.

SCSI Devices for Macintoshes

SCSI is the only hard disk drive interface supported on most Macs (a few of the newer ones also support IDE). It is also used for many other devices, such as scanners, EtherTalk and color video adapters for Macs with no slots, specialized video applications, and additional drives (such as CD-ROM drives, cartridge drives, and tape drives).

The SCSI bus is a daisy chain, with up to seven devices, each connected to the next. Figure 3.3 illustrates the SCSI chain for a Macintosh. Each device in the chain has its own unique ID, 0 through 6, with the Mac's motherboard (or the SCSI controller on a PC) having an ID of 7.

FIGURE 3.3
The SCSI chain for a Macintosh

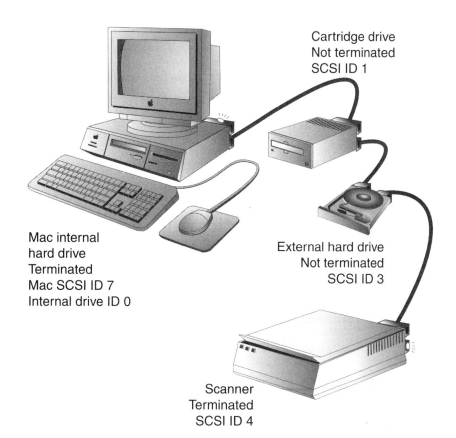

Cartridge drive
Not terminated
SCSI ID 1

Mac internal
hard drive
Terminated
Mac SCSI ID 7
Internal drive ID 0

External hard drive
Not terminated
SCSI ID 3

Scanner
Terminated
SCSI ID 4

Although you can put up to seven devices on a Mac, it is not generally a good idea. The more devices, the greater the chance of problems. The Power-Books should not be used with more than one or two external SCSI devices. This is because they use a lower-power SCSI bus than is normal, and it doesn't respond well with too many devices. If you are having problems with a Mac that has more than one SCSI device, make sure that all the devices have unique SCSI IDs. Duplicate IDs will usually cause the Mac to hang right after the self-test, or to display the disk icon with the blinking question mark. Of course, the method of removing the devices and trying them one at a time to isolate the problem applies here, too.

Termination is another major cause of problems with SCSI devices. Often, incorrect termination will cause intermittent problems. Both the first device on the SCSI chain (usually the internal hard disk) and the last device on the chain must be terminated. Problems arise when intermediate devices are terminated, or when the first or last drive is not. Some devices have external switches to enable or disable termination and set the SCSI ID; with others, you must add or remove resistor packs on the internal printed circuit board. The simplest way to handle termination is to leave the termination resistors on the internal drive and remove termination from all other devices. Then use an external terminator on the last device. This allows you to add or remove devices easily.

Under no circumstances should you ever disconnect or connect a SCSI device when it is powered up. This can damage not only that device, but any other device in the chain, including the Macintosh.

Power everything down before changing connections. This rule also applies to changing termination or manually changing the SCSI ID of a device. Some devices will allow you to change their SCSI ID with software. This, obviously, must be done while everything is on.

Macintosh Configuration

Bear in mind that some problems that seem to be related to hardware may be the result of a user having changed a setting in a Control Panel for that device. For example, on a Mac connected to the network with an EtherTalk card, the network connection will be lost if the user switches the Network Control Panel setting from EtherTalk to Built-in. Nothing in the Chooser reflects this change in the setting; the user (and you) will only see that there aren't any servers or printers available. Similarly, other devices, such as monitors and scanners, may be configured incorrectly.

Also, a device, such as a scanner, NIC, or CD-ROM drive, will often have a Startup document or Init associated with it. If this file is corrupted or removed, the device will not work. Check these items before assuming hardware failure.

Macintosh Software

In the boot process, after the boot disk is located, the system software begins to load. You will usually see a rectangular window with "Welcome to Macintosh" on it, unless the user has added a different startup screen. After a few seconds, this window will disappear, and you will see a series of icons at the bottom of the screen. These each correspond to the extension (CDEV, Init program, or Startup document) being loaded. In System 7, CDEVs (Control Devices) are stored in the Control Panels folder, and Inits and Startup documents are stored in the Extensions folder.

Macintosh Extensions

After the "Welcome to Macintosh" screen disappears, the basic system has been loaded. Everything after that is an addition to the system that was created separately. Such extensions add features to the operating system that may do anything from placing a pair of eyeballs that follow the movements of the mouse, to causing an animated character to appear out of the Trash Can and sing when a document is deleted, to allowing the use of additional fonts or enabling a network connection. A given Mac may have very few of these programs or dozens of them.

System extensions may be carefully developed pieces of software designed by a big software vendor to work within Apple's system specifications, or they may be programming exercises by college students. The important thing to know is that they are common, numerous, and can easily conflict with each other. Mac users also seem more predisposed to adding to their systems than most PC users.

Often, the only way to discover which extensions are conflicting is to pull everything out of the System folder except for the bare necessities, then put things back until you discover the conflict. In System 6, these files are all loose in the System folder, and they will be labeled Chooser document, Control Panel document or CDEV, Startup document, or simply Document. In System 7, most of these programs are stored in the Extensions or Control Panels folder.

The easiest way to minimize problems with extensions is to maintain a standard System folder, containing the system files, printer drivers, extensions, fonts, and so on, and discourage casual additions to it as much as possible. This will be difficult, but it will make it easier to recognize "foreign" extensions and resolve conflicts.

The other likely problem you will discover with Macintoshes is that the system itself is subject to becoming corrupted. This can happen more frequently than with a DOS system. If you have an intermittent problem with a Mac and are having a hard time tracking it down, consider reinstalling the operating system. Use the Installer program—don't just copy files into the System folder.

With System 7, it is usually a good idea to boot from a floppy, remove the existing System folder, and reinstall from scratch. If you do this, be sure to save anything that was added to the System folder before removing it.

Macintosh Networking

Getting a Macintosh to attach to an existing network is quite simple. If you are using AppleTalk, simply plug the connector into the printer port on the back of the Mac, turn it on, and you're connected. You may need to configure some software.

If you're using EtherTalk, install the network driver, install the network card, attach the cabling, switch to EtherTalk in the Network Control Panel, and see what appears in the Chooser. If you can't see anything in the Chooser, make sure that either AppleShare or a printer driver is selected. If so, the problem is probably the physical connection, or possibly the AppleTalk driver—either for LocalTalk or EtherTalk.

Since the network interface is built into the system at a basic level, there are normally only two things that can go wrong at the workstation: either the system itself or the network driver can become corrupted. Try reinstalling the system or network driver from the original installation disks. If neither of these work, and other Macs are able to access the devices, it's probably the network connection or the NIC.

Macintosh Printing

The basic setup of printing is as easy as networking. If the network connection works, and the printer driver works, you should be able to print from any application. Setting up Macintosh print queues and making them available to PCs as well as Macs is considerably more complex, and this setup is covered in Chapter 5.

Make sure that the same version of the printer driver is in use across your entire network, or at least in each segment using a particular printer. Even within a System version, there can be different printer driver versions, each of which can potentially conflict with the others.

UNIX Workstations

UNIX WORKSTATIONS, to an even greater extent than Macintoshes, tend to be simple to troubleshoot from the NetWare administrator's point of view. (That is, when isolating a problem with the NetWare network—UNIX itself is *not* simple.) This is because a UNIX workstation is usually an integrated package; the hardware, system software, and networking software are usually purchased together and designed to work with each other.

UNIX configuration and system administration are topics outside the scope of this book. There are many books available on every aspect of this subject.

For the NetWare administrator, there are basically only two questions with a UNIX workstation: Can it boot? Can it see the network?

UNIX workstations typically have the basic networking software and hardware built in. They usually use the TCP/IP networking protocol, which is supported in NetWare 3.*x* and above. The primary troubleshooting tools are PING, IFCONFIG, and NETSTAT, which all come with the operating system. If you can "ping" the server, you should be able to network with it. IFCONFIG will confirm that the Ethernet adapter itself is performing correctly. NETSTAT will give you information about the TCP/IP portion of your network.

If you are unable to mount network drives but can ping the server, the problem is probably with permissions—either file permissions or the authorizations in the NFS NLM setup. In fact, 90 percent of the problems with UNIX probably result from permissions being set incorrectly. These problems are covered in detail in Chapter 9.

Real-Life Stories

THESE ARE REAL-LIFE STORIES that represent the hard lessons learned by real troubleshooters in the field. Once again, the two fictional companies introduced in Chapter 1 and their administrators are used as examples. They combine the equipment and experience of a number of actual businesses. These five scenarios are intended to show some representative problems that might be encountered when setting up or troubleshooting a workstation. You may never see these particular problems, but you should get a feel for the process by which an experienced troubleshooter isolates a problem, determines the solution, and fixes the problem.

Scenario One: Installing a New Workstation

This scenario describes the process of installing and configuring a new high-powered workstation and some typical problems that might be encountered with the installation and configuration.

Snapshot—Scenario One

Is this a new system?

- Does the POST (power-on self test) finish without error messages?

- Does the workstation boot without error messages?

- Does DOS load without error messages?

- Do the network drivers load without error messages?

- Can you log in to the server?

John, the system administrator for Itsy-Bitsy, Inc., is putting together a new PC for one of his users. The system will need to run Microsoft Windows for Workgroups 3.11, as well as standard DOS applications, so it's a fairly high-end system. It includes a 75 MHz Pentium processor, 16 MB of RAM, a 1 GB IDE hard drive, a PCI Super VGA adapter and monitor, a bus mouse, Novell NE2000 Ethernet adapter, 5.25- and 3.5-inch floppy drives, and an IDE CD-ROM drive. The user also needs to have one serial port enabled for an external modem and the parallel port enabled for a printer.

John, being an experienced administrator, doesn't simply load all the cards into the PC and try to boot it. Instead, he adds the accessories incrementally. This takes a little longer, but makes it much easier to discover where the problems are. Of course, since he keeps a log of each system he sets up, he could use the log to determine which settings worked for each card if he had set up a system like this before; however, he hasn't used this combination of cards in the past.

Try loading cards into a system one at a time, even if it's a new system. This will make it easier to isolate problems when they occur.

The basic system, just the hard drive and video adapter, boots DOS just fine, so John adds the Ethernet card, being sure to record the settings for the interrupt and memory segment. The PC boots without errors again. After he installs the NetWare Shell, he tries running it to see if the PC can attach to the server. Instead, the PC freezes. After double-checking the settings on the card and the configuration of the driver, he's ready for the last resort. He reads the documentation.

The documentation doesn't appear to be helpful at first, but then John notices that there is a jumper that should be removed if the NE2000 is installed in a PC that uses the Chips and Technologies chip set. Upon checking, he discovers that the PC does in fact use this chip set. Removing the jumper fixes the problem.

He next installs the mouse. It uses one of two IRQs, 2 or 5. Since the LAN adapter uses IRQ 3 in its default setting, either would do. John chooses 5, and notes on the configuration sheet that IRQ 3 (the NIC), IRQ 4 (the COM1 serial port), and IRQ 5 are in use.

The CD-ROM drive is the last item to be added. He makes sure that the CD-ROM drive is connected to the secondary IDE interface, so he can use the Windows 32-bit disk access. After loading the driver, John is able to access the CD-ROM. It looks like the hardware configuration is done. He turns the PC off, makes sure all the screws are tight, puts the case on the machine, tightens all the screws down, reinstalls all the cables in the back, and then restarts the PC. Halfway through the POST routine, the PC hangs. After several resets, it is clear that whatever is happening is no fluke. He sighs and removes the case, then unplugs the CD-ROM, that being the last item installed.

The PC boots properly with the drive unplugged. He checks the orientation of the cable and the power connection to the drive, then restarts the PC. It boots fine. John sits and thinks for a minute. The only other thing that changed was putting the case on and screwing it down.

After some experimenting, John discovers that the PC will boot with the case on, but not when it's seated firmly and screwed down. It can be used temporarily with the case unsecured. He calls the retailer. They've never heard of such a problem but say it might be a short to the chassis somewhere. They say they'll be out to replace the PC within a couple of days.

A few days later, the PC reseller sends a technician out to fix the problem with the case. After swapping the motherboard and hard drive into a new case, the problem goes away.

Lessons Learned—Scenario One

- Keep a log of how each of your PCs is configured. Update it when you change setups. It will pay for itself the first time you are able to check a configuration without needing to take the PC apart and remove boards to verify settings.

- Read the documentation. The least you should do is look for exceptions, which are often set apart in the documentation or even in a README file on the distribution floppy.

- Make sure that neither IRQs (interrupts) nor base I/O memory segments from the different devices installed conflict with each other. Bear in mind that the size of memory used by the I/O segment may vary. Add the size of the segment to the address (remember, the numbers are in hexadecimal) to determine the next safe address to use.

- A freeze may not be caused by a card or configuration error. It can be something as simple as a sloppily manufactured case, a defective power cord, or a card or cable that isn't seated fully.

- Not all IRQs, base I/O addresses, or DMA interrupts are used by cards. For example, the serial ports, which may be on the motherboard, still use IRQs and I/O addresses, and some programs (such as Windows) may access these areas of memory, too.

The Fault Point Chain—Scenario One

Since the PC itself is running, you might think that none of it would be part of the fault point chain for this problem. However, there are a number of possibilities. For example, in this case, the motherboard was the actual cause—the NE2000 requires a different setting when used with this type of motherboard. However, other possibilities exist; for example, the problem could be caused by a marginal power supply in an older PC that wouldn't accommodate another board.

The potential faults for the first problem—the PC freezing when IPX.COM loads—were:

- The power supply to the motherboard: wall socket, power cord, power supply, and connection from the power supply to the motherboard. Faulty power can cause intermittent problems. Although it wouldn't usually become apparent at the same point in a software sequence, this could be the result of the actual activation of the Ethernet interface drawing too much power, or something similar.

- The motherboard, including the BIOS. The BIOS, especially in older PCs, is often the cause of incompatibilities with software, from network drivers to Windows.

- The NIC. This has several aspects, including the seating of the card in the bus, the settings on the card, the card's connection to the network, and the version of ROM (read-only memory) on the card.

- DOS. The version of DOS will require a specific network driver, but it can also cause problems by itself if it's corrupted or too old. As a rule of thumb, try not to let the standard version of DOS you use get more than two years old.

- The network driver. Again, don't let these drivers get too far out-of-date. Older drivers may work fine with DOS but could cause problems with newer programs, especially Windows.

Scenario Two: Maintaining an Existing Workstation

In this scenario, the administrator encounters some deceptive symptoms, then finds that an existing server is having problems at the workstation level before NetWare can load.

Snapshot—Scenario Two

Is this an existing system?

- Is the display readable? Does the cursor respond to the keyboard?

- Does the POST (power-on self test) finish without error messages?

- Does the workstation boot without error messages?

- Does DOS load without error messages?

- Do the network drivers load without errors?

- Does the workstation see the server (SLIST)?

- Can you log in to the server?

Fran, the system administrator for Great Big, Inc., gets a call from a user in Accounting. Something is wrong with his workstation; the application is running too slowly. She takes a look at the workstation. The application that's running too slowly is a word processor. She checks, and the file the user is working on is on the file server. She finds out that the user had tried to save changes to the file and the program hasn't responded to anything since. She tries to cancel the save, and eventually, after several mouse clicks, succeeds. She then saves to the local hard disk. This works quickly and normally. She then exits the program and checks the connection to the server. The server doesn't respond.

She finds the server's screen dark. The server's power light is on, and the fan is running, but the screen won't come on and the keyboard doesn't respond, even to the CapsLock or NumLock keys. She quickly checks the other workstations in the department and discovers that none of them can connect to the server. She reboots the server and gets the same result.

She begins eliminating possibilities. The monitor's power light is on, but it could be defective. She pulls a working monitor and video cable off another workstation and tries it. Nothing. She replaces the video card with the good card from the other workstation. Still nothing. In this particular chain of fault points, there is only one link left. The video system consists of the monitor, the cable, the video board, the motherboard, and the PC's power supply. The only one left is the motherboard. She swaps the server's drives and cards into another PC and starts it up. The server is back online.

Later inspection by a technician shows that the motherboard is indeed damaged, probably by a power spike. Fran uses the technician's report to justify UPSs (uninterruptible power supplies) for all servers at the site.

Lessons Learned—Scenario Two

- Workstation symptoms may actually result from network problems, either on the server or the connection to it.

- If you suspect component failure, replace the components in the chain, one at a time, with known good components.

- In an emergency, you can cannibalize one user's workstation (or your own) to replace the parts of a server. No one person's work is more critical than the whole department's. Other resources for quick temporary replacement include renting or leasing through local outlets. See your phone book.

The Fault Point Chain—Scenario Two

Since all the workstations were unable to connect to the server, the fault chain included the physical network (the cabling plant) as well as the server. However, the server is more likely to fail than the wiring, so Fran checked it first. The dark monitor and lack of response to the keyboard established that the problem was with the server. The fact that the problem repeated when the server was rebooted indicated a hardware problem, unless there had been recent changes to the NetWare configuration.

The potential faults were:

- AC power from the wall.

- The power cord.

- The power supply.

- The power cable from the power supply to the disk drive.

- The disk drives.

- The motherboard.

- The cards in the server.

- The devices connected to the cards (the monitor, the physical wiring, and so on). It's easier to check the connection on the back of a monitor than the electronics inside the monitor, and more likely that the problem is in a loose cable.

- NetWare (changes in configuration, corruption of SERVER.EXE, and so on).

- Outside interference, such as brownouts or a network storm caused by another server or network device overloading the server with bad packets.

Scenario Three: Another Existing Workstation

In this scenario, the administrator encounters a situation similar to the one described in the previous section, but with some critical differences: the administrator listens to a user's diagnosis, jumps to the conclusion that the situation is the same, and doesn't follow some basic precautions.

Snapshot—Scenario Three

Is this an existing system?

- Is the display readable? Does the cursor respond to the keyboard?

- Does the POST (power-on self test) finish without error messages?

- Does the workstation boot without error messages?

- Does the network load without errors?

- Does the workstation see the server (SLIST)?

- Can you log in to the server?

Jethro, Fran's new assistant, gets a call from a user in Accounting. Her connection to the server is down. She informs Jethro that this has happened before—she's sure it's the server. Jethro investigates and discovers that the server is apparently running, but the screen is dark. He reads the log and notes the similarities to the last incident. He decides he should swap the server's drives and cards into the other workstation in the office as quickly as possible to get the server back on line.

He flips the power switch on the server. Within seconds, cries of consternation drift through the doorway of the server room, quickly followed by the users themselves, asking why the server has gone down. Jethro, a cold feeling in his stomach, turns the server back on. The screen lights up with the normal boot messages, and the server begins to boot.

After the server is back on line, and he has pacified the users, Jethro makes two discoveries: the screen blanker in MONITOR produces a blank screen in this version of NetWare, rather than the usual bouncing square, and the cable from the first user's NIC to the transceiver has come off at the NIC.

Lessons Learned—Scenario Three

- Don't jump to conclusions and take steps you can't back out of, without trying to confirm your conclusions. If you can't think of some way to confirm your hypothesis, try to at least anticipate what could happen if you're wrong. For instance, Jethro should have checked to see if other users had connections to the server.

- Never take for granted that users know what they're talking about. Listen to them, but confirm what they tell you unless you know from experience that they are knowledgeable about PCs and networking and the setup in their department.

The Fault Point Chain—Scenario Three

A simplified chain would show the main units that could be responsible for the user's PC not being able to connect to the server:

- The workstation.

- The physical network, including the transceiver, the cabling and connectors, the repeater, the concentrator, and the connectors at the server end.

- The server itself.

Each of these fault points would, of course, have its own fault point chain. The most likely point of failure is at the workstation. Jethro's biggest mistake was not checking the workstation (either by checking the workstation itself or checking other workstations to see if they were also having problems). He should have checked the fault points in order of likelihood of failure: the workstation first, then the server, then the cabling plant.

Scenario Four: An Existing Macintosh

This scenario covers a common situation encountered with existing Macintosh setups. One of the problems the administrator encounters is in getting reliable information about what the configuration of the system should be, to compare with what it is.

Snapshot—Scenario Four

Is this a Macintosh system?

- Does the POST (power-on self test) finish with a tone instead of a chord?

- Does the workstation boot without error messages and without freezing?

- Do the network drivers load without errors?

- Does the workstation see the server in the Chooser?

When the Art department calls about a problem with one of the Macs, Fran brings Jethro along because he is familiar with Macs. One of the artists has a Mac that is hanging about halfway through the boot sequence. The user doesn't remember anything in the system that has changed recently.

They reboot the Mac again and watch the series of startup icons carefully. Just before the point at which the Mac freezes, they see an icon that neither of them recognizes. They restart the Mac from a floppy and open the System folder in Icon View. They discover the icon is from a public domain Init program that is supposed to enhance the usability of the system. The user had forgotten adding it a couple of weeks before.

Macs are easy to use, but not necessarily to administer. They often have more add-ons than comparable PCs and hide more of the operating system from the user.

Since the user isn't wedded to the offending Init, and since its behavior indicates that it may have become corrupted or be interfering with other Inits, they remove it. The system boots properly. Fran makes a note in her log to be on the lookout for this Init program in other Macs.

But there's one more thing: the user mentions that some of his fonts are no longer available. As long as Fran and Jethro are there, could they help him get them back?

This problem is aggravated by the lack of a standard for the company's Macintosh font manager—something that has been causing Fran trouble for a long time. The Macs used by the Marketing department mostly use one add-on program to control fonts, the Art department uses a different program, and other Macs scattered throughout the company may use either, or none.

When Fran checks, she discovers that this Mac is using one of the font control programs to load its fonts. The log for this Mac shows that she installed the latest version of this enhancement program a few days ago. It also shows that this Mac is using the standard set of Art department fonts in the appropriately named folder, that this folder is in the proper place, and that the program is set to open the fonts in that folder.

However, the fonts are not loading at startup. Jethro suggests using the program to load the fonts manually. When they try, they get a message saying that some of the fonts they are trying to load are already loaded. Jethro snaps his fingers—the system may have the same fonts installed in its Fonts folder. They check, and some of the fonts in one of the standard suitcases have also been loaded directly into the system.

After the fonts are removed from the System folder, the conflict goes away and the fonts all load properly. They reboot the Mac to check, and the fonts load automatically. Fran makes another note to check and make sure none of the other Macs she updated have the same fonts in two places.

Lessons Learned—Scenario Four

- When in doubt, return to a basic configuration and add Inits back in one at a time until you discover the conflict. Sometimes, you will be able to tell which Init, Startup, or CDEV is freezing the Mac by the last icon showing when the Mac freezes during startup. However, this is only one of a pair. The other file contributing to the conflict may be harder to discover, and the one you find may be necessary to the system. You can use special programs that can help you isolate and fix Init conflicts (see Appendix B for more information).

- Try to standardize on utility programs throughout the site. Use the same virus checker, the same font organizer, and so on. Doing so will cut down dramatically on problems in upgrading and supporting systems. This is important in all systems, not just Macs.

The Fault Point Chain—Scenario Four

Since the Mac was booting at least partway, the indication was that there wasn't any problem with the basic hardware. Furthermore, since the boot sequence from the hard disk was starting, the hard disk and disk driver were probably working correctly. Therefore, the next item to check was the software being loaded during the boot sequence. This is analogous to the AUTOEXEC.BAT and CONFIG.SYS portion of a PC's boot sequence.

The first item (the Init conflict) had the following fault points:

- The hardware (power supply, motherboard, any additional cards, and so on).

- The hard disk (boot device).

- The system software.

- The extensions being loaded.

- Problems with some of the cards, particularly an EtherTalk adapter. These cards aren't initialized until their extension is loaded, so the problem might appear to be with the extension, when in reality it is a hardware problem with the card.

In this case, because there was a more or less standard set of extensions in use, and because they were familiar with the normal boot sequence for their Macs, Fran and Jethro were able to identify the icon of the offending Init. However, if this had not been the case, they would have removed all extensions not supplied by Apple, and then rebooted. If the Mac had worked then, they would have added extensions back in until they identified the problem. If the Mac still hadn't booted, they would have reinstalled the system.

Scenario Five: A Windows Workstation

This scenario deals with a Windows installation on an existing PC connected to a NetWare network. The administrator deals with the Windows-related problems rather than the workstation or its configuration.

Snapshot—Scenario Five

Is this an existing system?

- Does DOS load without error messages?

- Do the network drivers load without errors?

- Can you log in to the server?

- Does Windows load without errors?

- Can Windows attach to the network?

Fran gets a call from a user who has just installed Windows and now can't attach to the network. Fran discovers that the user has installed a version of Windows 3.0 that is almost a year old.

Fran immediately removes this version from the user's PC and gets the user a new license for Windows for Workgroups 3.11. She installs Windows and copies the customized SYSTEM.INI file, the latest versions of the drivers, and shell files from the network (through DOS). She checks to make sure that the user's PC matches the standard configuration of NIC, has the memory necessary for Windows, and so on; then she launches Windows. No problems.

Lessons Learned—Scenario Five

- Windows is a complex environment that requires many specialized settings and the latest drivers. Once you get a working setup, record what you've done and try to use the same setup in any other PCs you set up for Windows. Even if this involves changing or updating the NIC, video adapter, or DOS configuration items, it will pay for itself in time saved in troubleshooting and supporting future updates to Windows.

- Try to set up a system that lets you control what the users order and install on the network. You are probably much more aware of hardware and software requirements and the latest versions of programs than most of your users.

The Fault Point Chain—Scenario Five

The basic units of the fault point chain that could have been causing Windows not to work were:

- The processor. Anything below a 386 will probably at least cause Windows to display error messages and run in real mode; and a BIOS that old may not be compatible with Windows at all. Also, PCs with less than 4 MB of memory should be upgraded before trying to run Windows. Depending on the application you wish to run, you may need as much as 16 MB of RAM.

- The BIOS. Older BIOS versions may not be compatible with Windows 3.*x*.

- Any cards in the PC. Windows uses areas of memory that some cards, especially video adapters and NICs, may be trying to use (see the discussion of EMMEXCLUDE in the discussion of Windows workstations).

- The version of DOS. A minimum of DOS 3.3 is necessary, and in general, the later the version the better.

- The network drivers. Get the latest version available. This may not be the version supplied with NetWare (even the latest version of NetWare) or with Windows. It's a good idea to check the Novell forums on CompuServe for new drivers once in a while.

- The version of Windows. Get the latest—updates are cheap, and they are usually put out for very good reasons.

- The configuration of Windows. There are many items that may need to be specially configured within Windows to get it to run on your network and with your PC, network driver, and other software. Once you get this figured out, save the WIN.INI and SYSTEM.INI files and reuse them.

Troubleshooting the Physical Network

4

Snapshot: Troubleshooting the Physical Network

IS THIS A NEW NETWORK?

How many nodes are affected? Do some of the workstations on the ring or segment work?

The first thing to do is to make sure that the server is running, and that the workstation involved is not having problems. If more than one workstation is involved, and the server is operating correctly, the problem is likely to be in the cabling plant. With a new installation, the first thing to check is that all specified work has been completed. Even with a relatively small network, there may be hundreds of wires, each of which must be properly connected, and dozens of devices which must be set properly, connected, turned on, and so on.

If some workstations are able to connect to the server but more than one cannot, the problem can be physically isolated. What do the working nodes or the non-working nodes have in common? Check to see if a ring is broken, or if all those workstations are on the same card on the concentrator. Bear in mind that it is more likely with new equipment that something has been overlooked rather than that there is an actual failure. Make sure that all equipment is connected and turned on. See the section on network topologies, on page 122, and the section on tracking down cabling problems, on page 135.

Is it only one workstation that can't connect?

If only one workstation isn't working, see if it can connect from another location. If so, then the wiring is faulty somewhere between the PC and the server.

There are several ways to isolate the fault in a wiring system without exotic or specialized equipment, although these make testing easier. Visually inspect the wiring: check that the colors of the insulation on twisted-pair wiring match at both ends of a connection, that the wiring is neat and the connectors are solidly in place, that coaxial cable connectors are solidly crimped, that the connectors are of good quality, and so on. A continuity tester will allow you to check the physical continuity of the wiring. You can make this tester yourself if you are familiar with the basics of electrical work, or buy an inexpensive model from an electronics supplier.

Also make sure that there is adequate cable to reach from where it exits from the wall to any point that the user might place the computer. Users can easily overstretch cable or pull the connector from the socket, trying to move their workstation farther from the wall socket than the cabling allows. See the section about tracking down cabling problems, on page 135.

IS THIS AN EXISTING NETWORK?

How many nodes are affected? Do some of the workstations on the ring or segment work?

When you know which workstations can connect to the server and which can't, you should be able to find the common point. Are they all on one port of the repeater or one card in the concentrator? Are they all on the same segment or ring? Are they all connecting through a bridge that may have gone down? If there are multiple NICs in the server, are all the workstations that can't see the server on one of the cards? See the section on network topologies, on page 122, and the section on tracking down cabling problems, on page 135.

Is it only one workstation that can't connect?

If only one workstation is affected, see if it can connect from another location. If so, then the cabling plant is faulty somewhere between the PC and the server. After you've isolated the problem to one station, you can begin checking the various component parts of the cabling plant between the two points. It may be the wiring, a transceiver, a board in the repeater, a faulty socket in the concentrator, or another problem in the PC-to-server wiring. See the section on tracking down cabling problems, on page 135.

Is the network experiencing intermittent faults and performance problems?

As with other parts of the network, the most difficult problems to isolate are intermittent ones. In the cabling plant, these may be caused by a variety of things, such as cables that run past fluorescent lights and loose connectors or faulty boards in workstations, servers, or other networking hardware (for example, repeaters, concentrators, or hubs). See the section on tracking down cabling problems, on page 135, or the section on punch panels, repeaters and concentrators, on page 139, or the section on routers, bridges, and gateways, on page 140.

As with other intermittent problems, you should discover what parts of the network are affected, what times of day the problems occur, what other events are associated with the problem, and any other information that can tell you what is happening when the problems occur.

HE CRITICAL ASPECT TO TROUBLESHOOTING the cabling plant is to first make sure that your problem is not actually being caused by an inoperative or malfunctioning network adapter, server, or PC. Second, you must understand the basics of your network topology. What sort of wiring do you have? What are its maximum lengths of cabling and its requirements for termination and grounds? Will one missing connection take out the whole ring? You should understand the various components that make up your cabling system: transceivers, connectors, wiring, concentrators, repeaters, bridges, and so on.

This chapter describes the aspects of the physical network you should understand, including the various network topologies, data communication protocols, and hardware standards. It also provides suggestions for tracking down cabling plant problems and documenting the cabling plant.

Fault Points for the Physical Network

HE APPROACH TO TROUBLESHOOTING introduced in Chapter 1 requires you to identify and isolate the fault points in a system. Using this approach with the physical network can be demanding, because it requires that you understand the basic processes that occur in the system. The possible variations and complexity of the cabling system can make it difficult to approach, but if you take things methodically, once piece at a time, it can be done.

The fault point chain in Figure 4.1 illustrates typical components of the cabling plant. You might not have all of these parts in your system, or you might have others not pictured here. The best way to begin to understand your network is to produce a drawing of a chain like the one in Figure 4.1, but specialized for your network. You should also make a map of the topology of your network, showing each workstation and how it is connected to the server. The various network topologies are discussed in the next section.

FIGURE 4.1
The fault point chain for
network cabling and
connections

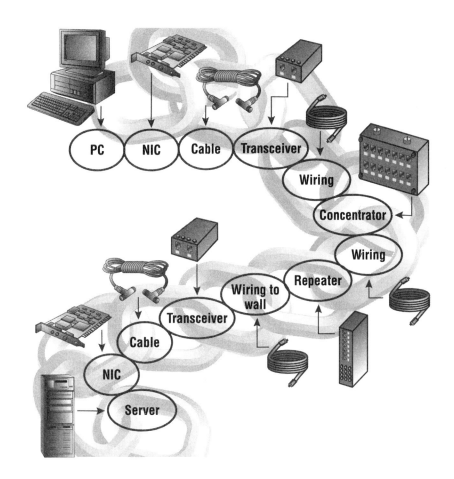

Each link in the chain can fail itself, or it can fail in its connection to a link it's attached to. For example, a cable could break or its connection at either end could fail.

In terms of the physical network, the server's fault points include the network driver for each NIC, the protocol drivers bound to each NIC, and the basic functioning of NetWare itself.

The NIC must be configured correctly, must be seated in the bus connector on the motherboard, and must have a good connection to the network wiring.

There may be one cable directly attaching the workstation to the server, or there may be several lengths of cabling between the two. In every case, the cabling must be connected properly at both ends and must be physically intact. The connectors must be properly attached to the cabling, and, in the case of twisted-pair cabling, the pairs must be connected in the same order at both ends. You must also be careful to make sure that the cabling does not run too close to possible sources of interference, such as fluorescent light ballasts.

Some systems employ transceivers to translate between two different physical types of cabling, for instance between the thick Ethernet port on a network card and the 10BaseT jack on the wall. Most transceivers have status lights to allow you to diagnose problems with the connection. If these lights are out, the transceiver is not operating. The connections on both ends of the transceiver must also be solid.

A repeater allows you to extend a network beyond the normal limitations of segment lengths. A typical setup provides one port that connects to the server and a number of ports that can be connected to different cable segments (legs). A repeater usually has status lights that show network traffic on each leg, allowing you to determine which legs are performing properly. The repeater can fail at each port connecting to the network cabling and on each internal board that provides a port, or it may fail entirely.

A concentrator, or hub, is similar to a repeater in its basic concept, which allows the total length of cabling in a network to exceed the maximum length for a single cable. A hub is typical of 10BaseT networks or twisted-pair Token Ring, and will typically have one port that connects directly to the server and one direct connection to each workstation. Depending on the type, it might fail entirely, on one port, or on one board that provides a number of ports. The status lights on the hub can help you determine which (if any) of these has happened, as can switching a problem cable to another port or board.

The workstation and its NIC are the last potential fault points in the fault chain, and they can fail in the same manner as the server and its NIC: the NIC can fail in hardware or be configured incorrectly, or its connection to the bus of the PC or the network cabling can become loose, causing an erratic connection, or its connection may come off entirely.

Network Topologies

MOST NETWORKS CAN BE CATEGORIZED into one of three types of physical topology: ring, linear bus, or star. The type of protocol doesn't necessarily indicate the topology. For example, the three most common types of Ethernet, thick (AUI), thin (10Base2), and twisted-pair

(10BaseT), use different topologies. Thick Ethernet is typically a linear bus, thin Ethernet is typically a ring, and twisted-pair Ethernet is typically a star. Figure 4.2 illustrates the types of network topologies.

The topology of thin Ethernet can also be described physically as a linear bus because the T-connector that attaches to the workstation functions in the same manner as the drop cable in a thick Ethernet setup. If the T-connector is disconnected from the workstation, only that workstation loses its connection. However, if the cable is detached from the T-connector, every workstation attached to the cable loses its connection. This is true in a thick Ethernet cabling scheme as well, but occurs much less frequently. With thick Ethernet, the drop cable is usually all that the user can reach; they usually don't have physical access to the backbone cable.

Each type of topology has a different fault point chain. A ring is the most susceptible to interruption, because if the physical links are broken anywhere in the ring, the whole ring loses connectivity. To overcome this disadvantage, some ring-type topologies combine star and ring topologies into one.

F I G U R E 4.2
Network topologies

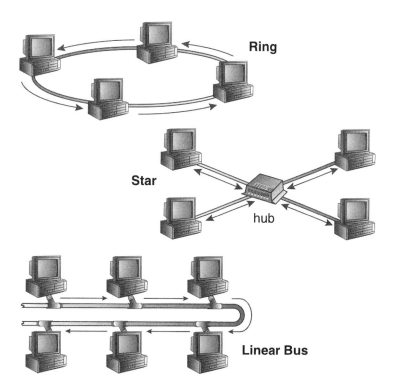

Along with the network's physical topology, you also need to consider its logical topology. *Physical topology* refers to the way the hardware and wiring are connected. *Logical topology* refers to the way that the information is sent from machine to machine. For example, Token Ring may be a star topology physically, but it is a ring topology logically. This means that you must understand the implications of both the logical and physical topologies in order to isolate the probable cause of problems. For instance, a star topology generally prevents a single break in the cabling from interrupting service to all nodes on the network. However, a token-ring network, which relies on tokens passed from workstation to workstation around a logical ring, can fail if one connection is broken, even though the physical topology is a star.

Be sure you understand the difference between physical and logical topology. A good example is Token Ring, which is physically a star but logically a ring.

Topology is the most important part of your network cabling scheme to understand. If you understand the physical and logical topology, you can isolate the fault points, regardless of the protocol running over the wire.

Ring Topology

In a ring topology, either logical or physical, every physical component of the network is typically a fault point for every connection. If one user on a thin Ethernet network (which can be considered a linear bus) disconnects his or her workstation by uncoupling the two wires from the T-connector, rather than the connector from the workstation, every workstation on the network will lose its connection. In practice, networks of this type often consist of several rings connected to a repeater, which is then connected to the server. This arrangement provides some redundancy, in that a failure in the ring usually will affect only the users attached to that port of the repeater.

With Token Ring, the topology is physically a star but logically a ring, in that a token is passed from station to station. If there is any interruption of the ring, the token will not reach the next station, and the network will go down.

The critical thing to know when troubleshooting this type of network is the location of every place where the connection can be broken by human intervention. Aside from mice chewing through the cabling, it isn't likely that the cable itself will fail. The most likely scenario is that someone has removed a connector or kicked wiring under their desk and pulled the cabling out of the jack.

Star Topology

A star topology is the most fault-tolerant topology. Each workstation is connected directly to a concentrator, which means that a break in any part of the fault point chain up to the concentrator will affect only one workstation. The two exceptions to this rule are the server and its connection to the concentrator, and the concentrator itself.

10BaseT Ethernet is the most common star topology, and it has become the most common type of network installed because of its fault tolerance and simplicity.

The biggest disadvantage of star topology is that it tends to be more expensive to install. Cabling must be pulled from every workstation to the concentrator or Media Access Unit (MAU); by contrast, a ring network needs cabling only as far as the next workstation. However, the gain in reliability is significant enough that stars have largely displaced the other topologies.

In a star topology, the fault point chain includes only the wiring between that workstation and the concentrator. If more than one workstation is involved, the workstation cabling is unlikely to be the problem. It's most likely that the problem is either with the server, its connection to the concentrator or MAU, or with the concentrator or MAU itself. Of course, this is only true unless the logical topology is a ring.

Linear Bus Topology

In a linear bus topology, there are actually two fault chains: the one from each workstation to the bus and the one from the bus to the server. If a workstation connection fails, it will affect only that workstation. An interruption of the bus will cause every connection to the server to fail. In practice, this isn't any different from a star topology if the concentrator fails; however, it is much easier to tell if this is the problem because of the status lights on the concentrator.

Data Communication Protocols

THERE ARE TWO PARTS TO THE METHOD by which computers connect with each other over cabling. The first part is the data communication protocol, which specifies how workstations within a network operating system

(NOS) communicate. Each protocol is generally associated with a specific NOS, although most NOSs now support most protocols. These protocols divide data to be sent to another computer into small pieces, called *packets*, and add a header and trailer that contain information about the sender, intended recipient, and so on. This process is carried out by the networking software.

The second part is the physical layer protocol, such as Ethernet, Token Ring, ARCnet, or FDDI. These protocols add further information in a header and trailer that determines which machine gets the packet next. This processing is mostly done by the networking hardware.

The physical layer protocol surrounds the data communication protocol, which surrounds the data. If a packet is sent from one protocol to another, the surrounding information must be translated. Since the data communication protocols are inside the physical protocols, converting them is more complex, as described later in the chapter, in the section on routers, bridges, and gateways. As an example, Figure 4.3 shows an IPX packet.

FIGURE 4.3

An IPX packet structure

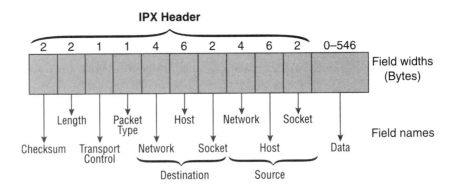

IPX/SPX

The IPX (Internetwork Packet Exchange) and SPX (Sequenced Packet Exchange) protocols are Novell's native protocols. A node address is a hexadecimal number, up to eight digits long. This number must be unique for each server and workstation.

Each LAN also has an address, called a network address. With the implementation of the worldwide IPX Internet, IPX addresses will be assigned in much the same manner as TCP/IP addresses are for the UNIX-based Internet (call 1-800-NETWARE for more information).

IP (TCP/IP)

TCP/IP (Transmission Control Protocol/Internet Protocol) is the standard protocol in the UNIX world. It was developed by the Department of Defense and is also the basis of the Internet. Internet addresses are assigned by the InterNIC. If your TCP/IP network is not connected to the Internet, and never will be, you can use any valid range of addresses. However, if there is any chance you will be connected, you should apply for an address.

A TCP/IP address has the form xxx.xxx.xxx.xxx, where each set of x's represents a number from 0 to 128. Depending on how big your company is, you might have an address of 143.xxx.xxx.xxx, 143.228.xxx.xxx, 143.228.117.xxx, or something in between, with the xxx representing available addresses for workstations on your network.

NetWare supports TCP/IP as a native protocol and also allows you to run IPX through a TCP/IP network with a process known as *tunneling*, which surrounds an IPX packet with a TCP/IP header and trailer to allow it to be routed from an IPX network, through a TCP/IP network, and back to an IPX network.

Many businesses no longer have a direct connection to the Internet. It is too great a security risk. They usually have what is known as a *firewall*—a server or router that is between their internal net and the Internet, which only (at least hopefully) allows authorized traffic in or out. With a firewall in place, the internal network numbers can be any valid range of addresses, and only the firewall router needs to have a "proper" authorized Internet number.

NetBEUI

NetBEUI (NetBIOS Extended User Interface) is the protocol used by Microsoft's Windows for Workgroups, Windows 95, and Windows NT as their native protocol. It identifies nodes by a unique name of up to 14 alphanumeric characters and divides the network into logical domains. Nodes may contain objects such as printers or disks that have been made available to the network (shared).

NetBIOS

The NetBIOS (Network Basic Input/Output System), is an application-level interface for networking primarily used by IBM LAN Server and Microsoft

LAN Manager networks. NetWare supports NetBIOS. NetBIOS nodes are named with a unique 16-character address.

AppleTalk

AppleTalk may run over Ethernet (EtherTalk), Token Ring (TokenTalk), or LocalTalk (Apple's proprietary cabling). AppleTalk devices include servers, workstations, and printers. AppleTalk Phase 1 allowed for 254 nodes on a network. Phase 2 allows multiple zones, each with 253 nodes.

LocalTalk supports only 230 Kbps, EtherTalk supports 10 Mbps, and TokenTalk supports 4 Mbps. Because of its much higher speed, EtherTalk is becoming much more prevalent.

OSI

The International Standards Organization (ISO) has developed a standard called Open Systems Interconnect (OSI). OSI is supposed to resolve the problems existing protocols have with large WANs and high-traffic loads. However, implementation has been slow; existing protocols are deeply entrenched, and most businesses are waiting until the OSI standard catches on before they implement it, which won't happen until more businesses implement the standard.

The OSI model describes standards for communication between network nodes at seven levels. The seven levels of OSI are:

- Application

- Presentation

- Session

- Transport

- Network

- Datalink

- Physical

A packet passes through each of these layers on its way from one network device to another. Each layer passes packets to the layer above and below it, but deals with only the information specific to its layer.

A packet arriving at a workstation reaches the Physical layer first. This layer processes the signal sent from another network card, interpreting the voltage changes, number of pulses, and so on to provide bits of information that are then assembled and sent to the Datalink layer.

The Datalink layer is the first layer that handles the packet as such. It may provide error correction to make sure that the packet that is arriving is the same as the one that was sent, discard defective packets, and signal the other workstation to resend the packet if necessary.

The two bottom layers together make up the hardware standards discussed in the next section. The next two layers, the Network and Transport layers, in general comprise the protocol layer, as discussed earlier.

The Network layer determines the path that a packet takes in going from the sending workstation to the intended recipient. This is the IP part of the TCP/IP protocol, and Novell's IPX also operates at this level.

The next layer, the Transport layer, provide error correction for packet routing in the same way that the Datalink layer provides error correction for the physical transmission. This is the TCP part of TCP/IP.

The four bottom layers of the OSI model are clearly defined and usually have clear analogs in any networking setup. The next three layers are not so clearly defined yet, and they may not correspond with any particular part of your system.

The Session layer deals with making and breaking connections to other systems. Protocols such as SPX and NetBIOS require that a connection to a specific other machine be made at the beginning of a session, and broken at the end of the session. Other protocols, known as *connectionless*, don't use this layer.

Connection-oriented services tend to be used when the order in which packets are received is critical, for instance, in the transmission of real-time data such as video. Connectionless services are used when the packet order is not as critical. Connectionless services provide more flexibility in delivery.

The Presentation and Application layers aren't widely used or well-defined yet. They both deal with further processing such as compression/decompression and file transfer and conversions that are necessary to allow programs to communicate.

An Overview of Hardware Standards

T O PROVIDE AN OVERVIEW of the basics of hardware standards, the following sections describe Ethernet, Token Ring, LocalTalk, and ARCnet. Each of the standards described here, and the many others not covered, has its own advantages.

The things to consider when evaluating the physical aspects of a new installation are:

- Cost of installation. Consider both the wiring required and the hardware, if necessary.

- Upgradability. Will you need to rewire your whole building to take advantage of faster technology?

- Dependability and fault tolerance. For example, a star topology will cost more for the original installation, but it will pay for itself in increased fault tolerance.

- Throughput. The rated speed of a network is not necessarily what you will experience. The load on the network, the quality of the installation, and the protocol will affect throughput. For instance, Token Ring, rated at 4 Mbps, may be a better choice than 10 Mbps Ethernet network if heavy loads are anticipated and real-time response (for automation or process control) is necessary.

- Expandability. How many more workstations can you add to the network before it chokes or you run out of ports?

- Standards. Make sure that what you buy will work with other LANs in your company and with planned future purchases. The best way to ensure this is to make sure that what you buy adheres to a published standard, such as Ethernet (802.2 or 802.3), or a well-established public domain standard, such as ARCnet.

Ethernet

Ethernet is probably the most widely implemented hardware protocol in use for PC-based LANs. It is a broadcast standard, in that each station listens for traffic and transmits if it doesn't hear anything. If two stations transmit at the same time, it produces a collision, and both stations must retransmit. Ethernet is theoretically capable of 10 Mbps, although that speed is almost never achieved under ordinary conditions. In addition to the three most common Ethernet standards, thick (AUI or 10Base5), thin (10Base2), and twisted-pair (10BaseT), there are two major new 100 Mbps versions, 100BaseTX and 100BaseVG, implemented over twisted-pair wire. There is also a standard for Ethernet over fiber-optic cable.

The three common types of Ethernet use different topologies. Table 4.1 summarizes the cabling requirements of thick, thin, and 10BaseT (twisted-pair) Ethernet.

TABLE 4.1 Ethernet Cabling Requirements	THICK ETHERNET (AUI, 10BASE5) COAXIAL	THIN ETHERNET ('0BASE2) RG-58	TWISTED-PAIR ETHERNET
REQUIREMENT	**CABLE**	**CABLE**	**(10BASET)**
Maximum overall length	2500 meters/ 8200 feet	925 meters/ 3000 feet	Number of segments depends on the concentrator
Maximum segment length	500 meters/ 1625 feet	185 meters/ 600 feet	100 meters/325 feet (from hub to station)
Maximum number of stations	100	30	Limited by the hub; can be from 4 to hundreds

Thick Ethernet

Thick Ethernet is a linear bus. This standard is uncommon, partly because, with the usual installation, the whole network must be brought down to add another station. Thick Ethernet runs over a thick (nearly ½ inch) coaxial cable with up to five trunk segments. It allows runs up to 2500 meters (8200 feet) total, up to 500 meters (1625 feet) per segment, and up to 100 stations per segment.

Thin Ethernet

Thin Ethernet is a linear bus with the vulnerabilities of a ring. Thin Ethernet is common in small installations, because the cabling is simple to install and inexpensive, with no hub required. Thin Ethernet runs over a thinner (about ¼ inch) coaxial cable designated RG-58. Thin Ethernet allows a total run of 185 meters (600 feet) per segment, up to five segments, and 30 stations per segment. Thick and thin Ethernet allow a maximum of five segments, four repeaters, and three segments with workstations on them on any one LAN. This is known as the 5-4-3 rule.

10BaseT (Twisted-Pair) Ethernet

Twisted-pair Ethernet is a star. For most business installations, it has become the wiring scheme of choice, thanks to its fault tolerance. It does require a hub or concentrator, but the cost of hubs has dropped from more than $100 per port to less than $10 in many cases.

10BaseT uses twisted-pair wiring like phone wiring, but with four pairs of wires, two pair of which are used for each connection. The maximum run from workstation to hub should not exceed 100 meters (325 feet). The total number of stations is determined by the capacity of the hubs; these may support anywhere from four to hundreds of connections. Although they are expensive, switching hubs can offer substantial performance gains over standard equipment. See the section "Patch Panels, Repeaters, and Concentrators" a little later in the chapter, for more information.

Token Ring

Token Ring is known as an IBM standard, although it was originally developed by another firm. It is usually a star topology physically, but a ring logically. A *token*, a special type of packet, is passed from workstation to workstation around a ring. Each workstation's location on the ring is a function of when it logged onto the network, relative to the others. A station can only send a packet out when it has the token. After it sends its packet, it releases the token to the next workstation.

Each workstation is usually connected by Type 1, 2, or 3 cable to a MAU, also known as the Multiple Station Access Unit (MSAU). A MAU may have 8, 12, or up to 50 ports plus the ring-in and ring-out ports.

Never connect a workstation to the MAU's ring-in or ring-out port. These are only for connecting to another MAU.

Some Token Ring networks are now being implemented over unshielded twisted-pair (UTP) cable, which is much less expensive, although more susceptible to interference. Regardless of the type of wiring, the important thing to understand is that a hardware failure will usually drop a station off the ring, losing only the one connection. However, if a problem occurs that prevents the token from being passed, then the whole ring can fail. This failure can occur if a connection between MAUs is lost, if a LAN adapter fails without dropping its power to the MAU, if electrical interference in the cable distorts signals, and in other similar situations. A simple protocol analyzer can usually tell you where in the ring a break has occurred.

With Type 1 and 2 shielded twisted-pair (STP) cabling, Token Ring supports up to 260 devices, including MAUs and repeaters, although in practice, going much over 100 will cause problems.

Cable lengths from the workstation to MAU can be 300 meters (975 feet) if there is only one MAU, or 100 meters (325 feet) if there are multiple MAUs. MAUs can be up to 200 meters (650 feet) apart. It is wise to keep cable lengths under 100 meters to allow for expansion to multiple MAUs. Both 4 and 16 Mbps Token Ring can run on Type 1 and Type 2 cable.

Type 3 cabling (UTP) supports 96 devices maximum per ring. Type 3 supports station-to-MAU cable lengths of 100 meters for single-MAU systems and 45 meters (145 feet) for multiple-MAU systems, with up to 120 meters (390 feet) between MAUs. Type 6 cable is more flexible, and is generally used only for connections from the workstation to a wall jack, or in situations where the cable must be routed around tight obstructions.

Table 4.2 summarizes the Token Ring cabling requirements.

LocalTalk

Apple was the first personal computer manufacturer to include built-in networking capabilities. This networking protocol, LocalTalk, is easy to set up, relatively fault-tolerant, and inexpensive. However, by modern standards, it is very slow at 230 Kbps, and under normal conditions, as low as 90 Kbps. For networks of more than a few Macs and a printer, this isn't very useful. To meet the

TABLE 4.2 Token Ring Cabling Requirements	**REQUIREMENT**	**TYPE 1 AND 2 (COAXIAL CABLE)**	**TYPE 3 (UTP CABLE)**
	Maximum number of devices (including MAUs)	260	96
	Maximum cable length (1 MAU), station to MAU	300 meters/975 feet	100 meters/325 feet
	Maximum cable length (multiple MAUs), station to MAU	100 meters/325 feet	45 meters/145 feet
	Maximum distance between MAUs	200 meters/650 feet	120 meters/390 feet

needs of modern networks, versions of AppleTalk that run over Ethernet or Token Ring were developed.

Before EtherTalk over 10BaseT Ethernet became common, a number of companies implemented UTP Ethernet on their own. LatticeNet is one of the most common of these. LatticeNet is similar to 10BaseT, but not completely compatible. You must either make sure that all your Macs use the same one of the two standards or get a concentrator that can handle both types.

The theoretical maximum for LocalTalk is about 300 meters (1000 feet) total cabling distance and 32 stations per network. However, if you are anywhere close to this number, you should upgrade to EtherTalk or TokenTalk. Cabling specifications and lengths are the same as for Ethernet and Token Ring, as explained in the earlier sections on those standards.

ARCnet

Attached Resource Computer Network (ARCnet) is a standard that actually goes back farther than Ethernet. It is not an IEEE standard, as Token Ring, Ethernet, and FDDI are, but it is widely supported in the industry. Its rated throughput is 2.5 Mbps, and it is a star topology, with a token-passing protocol.

One advantage to ARCnet is that, unlike Ethernet, it doesn't require repeaters or relatively expensive concentrators. For larger networks, ARCnet uses a combination of inexpensive passive hubs and active hubs, which are less expensive than similar Ethernet concentrators. Small networks require only the passive hubs. The main difference between active and passive hubs is the length of cable they support.

ARCnet requires RG-62 93 ohm coaxial cable, which is cheaper than the RG-58 cable used for thin Ethernet. It allows 256 stations per LAN, a maximum length of 600 meters (2000 feet) between stations or from station to active hub, and 30 meters (100 feet) between stations and passive hubs. The hub-to-hub distance is 30 meters for passive hub to active hub, 600 meters for active hub to active hub, and up to 6000 meters (20,000 feet) in a segment. Passive hubs can't be connected to other passive hubs.

A new ARCnet specification has been developed that allows 20 Mbps. This specification allows ARCnet installations to be upgraded to provide throughput on par with Ethernet or 16 Mbps Token Ring. It retains existing wiring but requires new NICs. ARCnet over UTP cable is also possible, but allows only 10 stations per ring, with a maximum distance between them of less than 2 meters (6 feet). This gives 80 stations on an 8-port active hub, with a total maximum wiring length of 120 meters (400 feet).

Here are some tips for ARCnet setups:

- Set the server to station address 255.

- Always terminate unused ports in a passive hub.

- Make sure that a segment doesn't loop back on itself (don't connect hubs in a circle).

- Make sure that no two stations use the same station address.

Table 4.3 summarizes ARCnet cabling requirements.

Tracking Down Cabling Plant Problems

CABLING FOR A NEW NETWORK should be installed by professionals. For anything larger than a few workstations, this is almost a necessity. Pulling the wire through the walls; crimping connectors; testing circuits; installing concentrators, patch panels, and punch-down blocks; and so on are all highly specialized tasks best left to experienced professionals.

TABLE 4.3 ARCnet Cabling Requirements	REQUIREMENT	COAXIAL RG-62 (93 OHM)	UTP CABLE
	Maximum overall length	6000 meters/20,000 feet	120 meters/400 feet
	Maximum number of stations	256	10 per ring; 80 per 8-port active hub
	Maximum distance between stations and active hubs	600 meters/2000 feet	6 feet between stations
	Maximum distance between stations and passive hubs	30 meters/100 feet	NA
	Maximum hub-to-hub spacing	Active-to-active: 600 meters/2000 feet. Active-to-passive: 30 meters/100 feet	NA

In fact, when you are planning the network, it is best to get bids and input from several vendors. They may even suggest a better way of networking your workstations. If you want to do it yourself, be very sure that you understand fully the limitations on cable lengths for each type of cable you're using, proper methods of termination and grounding, and the setup and configuration of any networking hardware you will be using.

Generally, the company that installs the new cabling will test all the segments for continuity and polarity. They will often warranty their work for 30 to 90 days. In a new installation, the cabling itself is unlikely to cause problems if it is installed correctly. You should check other, more probable causes first. However, if the more likely problems have been eliminated, a basic understanding of your cabling plant will allow you to isolate problems without too much difficulty.

Often, the administrator may have responsibility for all of the hardware that makes up the network, except for the cabling plant. That part of the network may "belong" to facilities, or to corporate MIS. This sort of division of responsibility can make things difficult to resolve. Even when this is not the case, the actual wiring is usually in the walls and cannot be visually inspected.

In this sense, the cabling plant is the most obscure part of your network. However, you can usually isolate the problem to one of a very few possibilities without specialized equipment, simply by understanding the topology of your network, analyzing its fault point chain, and checking the break points.

Aside from mice chewing through the cabling, it isn't likely that the cable itself will fail. The most likely cause of a failure in the physical plant is that someone has removed, changed, or broken some part of the cabling plant, or that an electronic part of the plant has failed. Some examples of what can go wrong include:

- Construction workers inadvertently cut cabling.

- Users remove or change connectors without realizing the consequences.

- Someone changes the settings in a router without being sure of all the ramifications.

- There is a hardware failure in a repeater or concentrator.

- The software in a router freezes up.

Check for these sorts of problems first, before you run continuity checks on all the wiring. Another thing to check is a new source of electromagnetic interference, such as a fluorescent light ballast or an electric motor near a cabling run. This, in particular, is a situation where a map of the physical cabling plant is very useful. See the "Documenting the Cabling Plant" section later in this chapter for details.

Cabling: Lengths, Termination, Grounds, Connectors, and Type

It's been said that 90 percent of all network problems are problems with cabling, particularly with existing networks where nothing has been changed (well, nothing has been changed intentionally). There are three basic things that can give you an edge in tracking down and fixing such problems: a good understanding of your cabling setup, ensuring correct installation of the network hardware, and using quality components such as connectors.

The first is a good understanding of your cabling setup, both physical and logical. This includes the protocol (Ethernet, ARCnet, or Token Ring, for example) and the physical and logical topology (how the signals are routed throughout the network). What are the possible effects of breaking the line?

Could a bad network adapter bring down the whole network? You should understand not only how the wires are routed through the walls, but where a packet must travel to reach the server. Does it need to be passed on through several intermediate workstations? Does the connection in the office wall go to the server directly, or does it go to a repeater in a broom closet somewhere?

A recent study suggests that bit errors caused by electromagnetic interference or faulty wiring can cause many thousands of times the performance drain that collisions do. Make sure that twisted-pair cabling has the correct number of twists, that connectors are solidly crimped, that network wiring doesn't run close to other electrical equipment, that the wiring is well grounded, and so on.

As connectors age, their ability to provide a solid connection may decrease, especially if inexpensive connectors were used in the first place. Be sure to specify high-quality parts, especially in networks where connections might be changed frequently.

Check for the correct types and lengths of cabling. For example, RG-58 may have been switched with RG-62 (the two types of cable are usually marked with their designation along the length of the cable), or RJ-11 (4-pin phone) plugs may have been placed in RJ-45 (8-pin 10BaseT) jacks. Silver-satin phone cable may have been used for NIC-to-jack connections, instead of Ethernet-rated UTP cable. Are connectors crimped neatly? Are the terminating resistors of the correct ohmage? Make sure that lengths are not over the rated maximums—it's easy to keep adding "just one more" node until you're past the maximum length. Any of these items can contribute to intermittent problems on your network.

Another issue that is becoming a major problem as networks are upgraded is the category of UTP Ethernet cabling. Much of the installed Ethernet UTP cabling is what is known as Category 3 (phone grade). This is not usually a problem for 10BaseT. However, for sites migrating to a 100 Mbps standard, the required specification is Category 5. This is a much more stringent specification, which covers the type of cabling, how often the wires are twisted, what connectors are installed, how connectors are installed, and what types of network equipment (such as hubs) are installed. The slightest variations can cause large drops in performance, from the theoretical 100 Mbps down to 20 Mbps or less. Since this largely negates the expensive migration, it is critical to make sure that the cable installations are done correctly.

Fiber-optic cabling is starting to be seen in even small networks, especially in high-traffic situations or as a "backbone." Troubleshooting tools for optical fiber are not especially complicated, but you need to learn how to use them. A light meter that will read a light source at the other end of a cable and tell you what the transmission efficiency is, and a simple device to ensure that connectors are properly installed are all you will usually need.

One advantage to fiber-optic cable is that once it's configured, it is immune to the electromagnetic interference that can plague copper wire, especially high-performance copper wire. It also tends to be binary in nature; that is, it either works or it doesn't, rather than experiencing some level of performance degradation due to improper installation.

Patch Panels, Repeaters, and Concentrators

Networking hardware should be in a secure area—not just locked up where no one can play with it, but mounted securely and protected from anyone accidentally moving a switch and cutting off 20 users. Don't just put a repeater under a desk and forget about it.

The most important things you can do with a patch panel or punch-down block is to keep it neat and well-documented. It makes it easier to trace or move connections, as well as easier to spot a poorly connected jack.

Repeaters can be thought of as extension cords for networks. If you have, say, 60 workstations on thin Ethernet, spread out over a fairly large area, most cabling cannot connect all of them in one chain—it's simply too many feet of cable, especially if it's run through the walls and up to the ceiling between each office or cube. With a repeater, you can divide the network into several segments, each of which can be 180 meters (600 feet) long. This also gives you some fault tolerance; if one of the segments is broken, it takes down only the workstations on that loop, and the other ports on the repeater aren't affected.

Concentrators, or hubs, come in many varieties and sizes, from a small four-port 10BaseT hub to a $50,000 concentrator that will accept fiber-optic lines to a backbone, provide several hundred 10BaseT ports, and allow remote management through Simple Network Management Protocol (SNMP). With the latter, you can use management software and find out what port on the concentrator has lost its connection or is receiving bad packets, without ever leaving your desk.

The latest developments in Ethernet utilize hubs that are known as switching hubs. They essentially behave as if each PC connected to the hub had its own individual router and the traffic from that PC was sent to only the intended recipient. This greatly reduces the number of packets received by most workstations on the network and increases the total amount of traffic that can be supported on the same network segment. Switching hubs are not cheap, but the performance benefits are great enough that they are rapidly becoming common.

Routers, Bridges, and Gateways

A *bridge* looks at the intended destination of a.packet and sends it by the most direct route, using the software or network layer address. A *router* can route packets for different protocols. A *gateway* converts from one protocol to another. Many of the products on the market today combine parts of all of these functions.

The Novell Multi-Protocol Router allows routing between any protocol supported by NetWare, which is just about everything you might find out there. It can replace dedicated boxes that do only one thing well, and do other things in addition, such as hub management and backups.

All of these devices are fault points in your network. If you find that traffic on one LAN is normal but users can't access services on another LAN, check the router, bridge, or gateway. Remember that a server with two LAN cards is acting as a router between the two LAN segments.

Documenting the Cabling Plant

THE CABLING COMPANY SHOULD PROVIDE you with a physical map of the wiring the workers have installed, as well as locations of punch-down blocks, repeaters, concentrators, and so on. Familiarize yourself with the locations of all the hardware, and identify the workstations/users on each segment of your network. Doing so will make it much easier to isolate faults. For example, if a certain four users who are all on the same loop complain of network trouble, you immediately know where to start looking.

You should also take the time to make a logical map of your network. Identify how a packet actually is routed to get from a workstation to the server and back. Does it need to pass through each workstation on a loop? Which workstations does it pass through, or is that different, depending on which stations entered the network first?

There are many software package and software/hardware combinations being marketed to manage your network. Some of them will create and automatically update a logical map of your network. They can tell you when stations go online or offline, if network devices fail, and when and where failures occur. If you have a complex LAN or WAN to look after, these packages can save you many, many hours of time tracing down faults, and they will also greatly increase your response time when failures occur. Not only will they help you find problems, they will usually alert you when a problem occurs, sometimes long before the users become aware of it. See the sections in Chapter 8 on network management and diagnostic tools and Appendix B for more information about these packages.

Real-Life Stories

WE RETURN TO THE TWO FICTIONAL COMPANIES and their administrators introduced in Chapter 1 to illustrate typical problems with network connections and the process a troubleshooter goes through to isolate and correct those problems.

Scenario One: A New Cabling System

The system administrator encounters some problems typical of a newly installed cabling system and demonstrates some techniques for fault isolation without specialized equipment.

Snapshot—Scenario One

Is this a new network?

- How many nodes are affected? Do some of the workstations on the ring or segment work?

- Is it only one workstation that can't connect?

John, the system administrator for Itsy-Bitsy, Inc., is halfway through a long working weekend. The Marketing department has just moved to a new area, and the cabling contractor finished installing and testing the wiring yesterday. John has gotten the server up and running and is unpacking and connecting the workstations. The network is 10BaseT Ethernet, with a concentrator in a wiring closet and jacks in each work area.

The first few workstations are unpacked and connected to the network with no problems, and they connect to the server without errors. Then John puts his supervisor's PC back together and plugs it in. It boots without error messages, but won't attach to the network. John makes sure that the interrupts are set correctly on the NIC, and then changes the cable from the PC to the wall jack. Still nothing. He goes to the wiring closet and makes sure that the jack for his supervisor's office is active. The connection light is on for that jack. He tries changing the cable to another port, with no improvement. He thinks about changing the jack to another port on the concentrator, but he doesn't have the punch-down tools.

To get some diagnostics, he tries another PC in his supervisor's office, one that was able to connect to the network from another jack. It can't see the server either. He is pretty sure now that there is something wrong, either with the jack, the wiring to the punch-down panel, or that port on the concentrator. He observes that other ports on the same card on the concentrator are working—it's unlikely to be a hardware failure in the concentrator. Next, he gets an Ethernet adapter with an AUI (thick) connector, and a transceiver to 10BaseT. The transceiver has monitor lights for connection, transmit, receive, SQE (heartbeat), and collision. When it's installed and the PC is booted, the connection and SQE come on, and the transmit and receive lights blink on and off, indicating that data is being sent to and from the PC. However, the connection still doesn't work.

There is an electrical connection to the concentrator, and data is being transmitted back and forth. The most likely problem seems to be that the data is being sent but that it's being scrambled somehow. The collision light isn't coming on, and no one is using the network, so traffic is unlikely to be the problem. John concludes that the problem is most likely in the installation of the jack or the punch-down block. He calls the cabling contractor and asks him to come back and recheck this connection, then moves on to the rest of the workstations.

The cabling installer arrives in a couple of hours, grumbling about being called back in. John explains what he has tried, and the installer checks the jack and wiring with a specialized test device. He discovers that two of the wires to the jack have been reversed. He reconnects the wiring to the jack, and then tries the PC. It connects to the server with no problem.

Lessons Learned—Scenario One

- If you aren't familiar with the cabling company doing the installation, you may want to have the work double-checked. Don't assume that what the installers say they've checked is perfect—it's very easy to miss a small thing like a polarity error.

- You can isolate seemingly impenetrable problems by taking them step-by-step and eliminating fault points until you have only one or two left.

- There are some areas that can't be resolved without test equipment. However, if the cabling company hadn't been able to resolve this for John, he could have compared the order of colors of the wiring on both ends of the connection to find or eliminate the issue of the cross-connected wires, and he could have punched down the connection on the block again, or replaced the jack, with inexpensive tools. If in doubt, redo it.

The Fault Point Chain—Scenario One

- The driver software in the PC.

- The Ethernet transceiver in the PC.

- The 10BaseT cable to the wall jack.

- The wall jack and its connection.

- The cabling from the wall jack to the punch-down panel and its connection.

- The wiring from the punch-down panel to the PC's port on the concentrator.

- The concentrator.

- The wiring from the server's port on the concentrator to the punch-down panel.

- The connection at the punch-down block and the cabling from the punch-down panel to the wall jack in the server room.

- The wall jack in the server room and its connection.

- The cabling from the wall jack to the Ethernet card in the server.

- The Ethernet card in the server.

- The Ethernet driver software installed in the server operating system.

A few minor points, such as the solidity of the connector in the wall jack, could also be included. Many of these can be eliminated immediately. For instance, since other PCs can connect to the server, the last seven items can be disregarded. Furthermore, since the PC can connect from another jack, the first two can be eliminated. Trying another cable eliminates the third item. That only leaves three items, a much easier list to test. Traffic lights on the concentrator and the transceiver show that data is being passed through the cable, which leaves only the connections at the jack and the punch-down block.

Scenario Two: Part of an Existing Network Fails

A portion of an existing network goes down. The administrator follows the process of isolating the problem, determining the cause, and fixing it.

Snapshot—Scenario Two

Is this an existing network?

- How many nodes are affected? Do some of the workstations on the ring or segment work?

Fran, the system administrator for Great Big, Inc., gets a number of calls from users in the Engineering department saying that they aren't able to connect to the server. She checks the server to make sure that it is running. Most of the workstations in the department are still able to connect to the server. The workstations are connected with thin Ethernet, in four segments, or legs, to a multiport repeater, which is in turn connected to the server. Fran looks at the wiring diagram for the department and notices that all the affected workstations are on the same loop. The problem could be either of two things: a break in the loop or a problem with the repeater. Figure 4.4 illustrates this situation.

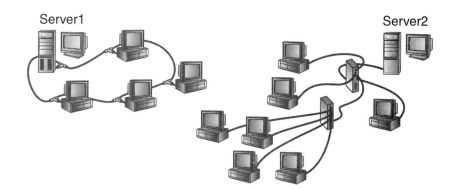

Fran checks the repeater first, since it is simpler to check than tracing the entire path of the loop, looking for breaks. She finds that the switch that controls the loop in question is turned on. Having found segments switched off by accident before, she had hoped it would be that simple this time, but it isn't. She sighs, then begins tracing the path of the loop, using her network map. The first few connections are all solid and look okay. Then she finds a pair of thin Ethernet cables in an unused cubicle, with no connector connecting them. She finds a spare T-connector, reconnects the two cables, and discovers that the workstations in the loop are back online.

Further research uncovers a user who borrowed the connector, reasoning that since the cube wasn't in use, the connector wasn't doing anything. Fran refrains from strangling him, but sends out a carefully worded cautionary note to all the users on her networks, emphasizing that users who need networking work done should go through her.

Lessons Learned—Scenario Two

- Check the simple things first, but don't be afraid to do some legwork. Even the most daunting task can be handled with a calm and methodical approach.

- Break the problem down by isolating the affected elements. In this case, Fran had a network map and was easily able to determine that all the affected users were on the same leg of the repeater. If she hadn't been able to determine that, her job would have been much harder, since there would have been many more elements to eliminate before the fault point was isolated. This is a perfect example of why documenting your network is a necessity, not a luxury.

■ Never underestimate the users' ability to make your life difficult.

■ This is a case where a network monitor would have made troubleshooting easier. Some monitors available now would have sent an alarm as soon as the T-connector was removed, identifying the problem and the most probable location of the break.

The Fault Point Chain—Scenario Two

Since a number of workstations were affected, we can eliminate most points of the chain that are unique to individual workstations, such as the network driver and Ethernet adapter. But we can't eliminate the T-connector connecting each card to the cable, because each one has the potential to affect the entire loop. The fault chain from the server to all workstations could also be eliminated, because if the server's network driver, its Ethernet card, the cable to the repeater, or the repeater as a whole had been damaged, none of the workstations on the rest of the network would have been able to log in, either. The remaining fault points are:

■ The T-connectors on each workstation.

■ The cabling.

■ The port on the repeater to which the loop is connected.

■ The termination on each end of the loop.

■ The grounding of the loop.

Scenario Three: An Existing Token Ring Network

The administrator encounters a problem typical of a Token Ring network. Again, she follows the process of isolating the fault and fixing the problem.

Snapshot—Scenario Three

Is this an existing network?

■ How many nodes are affected? Do some of the workstations on the ring or segment work?

The Sales department of Great Big uses Token Ring workstations that access their mainframe through NetWare for SAA. One day, Fran gets a call reporting that no one in the Sales department can access the network. Fran knows that with Token Ring, one workstation can bring down the network if its card fails to pass the token along properly. She checks the server to make sure that nothing is apparently wrong there, then begins checking the workstations. All the workstations reboot without errors and load the Token Ring driver without error messages about the card's configurations. The network doesn't begin to function when any one of the workstations is offline, which tells Fran that none of the workstations is failing to pass the token along; otherwise, the network would function when that workstation was disconnected from the network.

Fran then checks the wiring closet where the MAUs are located. She discovers that the cable leading from the ring-in port on one of the MAUs to the ring-out port on the next MAU is disconnected. She reinserts the connector into the ring-in port, and then checks the network. Everything is running again. Fran asks around to find out if anyone on her staff disconnected the port on purpose, but no one has (or will admit to it).

Lessons Learned—Scenario Three

- Even though Token Ring has a physical star topology, it is logically a ring, which means that one card that doesn't function properly may bring the whole network down. If the PC with the faulty card is powered down, it should remove that station from the network, which will then begin functioning properly again.

- When you have a single device in your cabling system that can affect the entire network—a repeater, concentrator, or MAU—you should check it before initiating a time-consuming process such as checking every workstation on the network.

- Leave checking the continuity of the wiring in the walls for last, but check connections that users (or janitors) can affect first.

- Like the scenario described in the previous section, this is a situation where a network analyzer would have helped. It could have told Fran where the connection was broken and which PCs were acting properly, thus pointing her in the direction of the lost connection between the two MAUs.

The Fault Point Chain—Scenario Three

With Token Ring, a card that goes dead should remove itself from the network. However, a card that remains electrically active but isn't passing the token along properly will halt the entire network. The relevant fault points are these:

- Each card and driver on the ring.

- The server, and its card and driver.

- The MAU, and the connection between each MAU.

The wiring and the connections (at each card, the wall jack, and on the MAU) were not as a whole really a factor here. If a link between one PC and the MAU had been broken, either by a faulty connection or a broken wire, it would have deactivated that port on the MAU, and the rest of the network would have been running.

Another possibility in this situation is a source of electromagnetic interference near one cable that garbled the token as it passed through. This could have caused the same sort of problem.

Scenario Four: Caring for a Growing Network

This scenario addresses the problems typical of a network that has been added to, or which has evolved from several small networks. Some basic recommendations are given for revamping such systems and working within a budget.

Snapshot—Scenario Four

Is this an existing network?

- How many nodes are affected? Do some of the workstations on the ring or segment work?

- Is it only one workstation that can't connect?

- Is the network experiencing intermittent faults and performance problems?

Fran has some free time, and since reviews are coming up, she picks an item from her to-do list instead of playing Tetris. The Marketing lab workers have been complaining about the performance of the network in their demo room. It is often slow, and some workstations experience intermittent failures.

Fran begins by inventorying the equipment in the demo room. There are two NetWare servers and about fifty workstations, including PCs, Macs, and UNIX workstations, all attached by thin Ethernet or 10BaseT (twisted-pair) Ethernet. The network and servers were all set up by the Marketing people and their system engineer, who quit several months ago and hasn't been replaced. Since then, one of the Marketing staff, who has a fair amount of experience with NetWare and Macs, but almost none with hardware, has been maintaining the network.

After looking at the workstations, Fran inspects the cabling. Some of the workstations have 10BaseT Ethernet adapter cards and are attached to an eight-port 10BaseT mini-hub, which is then attached to another mini-hub, which the server is attached to. Others have a thick Ethernet card (AUI) card, which is then connected to a transceiver that is in turn connected to a 10BaseT cable running to one of the mini-hubs. Others are connected by thin Ethernet to one large segment with about 15 workstations and the other server on it. This situation is illustrated in Figure 4.5.

The thin Ethernet loop is not properly grounded, many of the T-connectors in use are old and obviously low-quality, and some of the cables are ARCnet specification (RG-62, 93 ohm cable) instead of the RG-58A 50 ohm cable required for thin Ethernet. Finally, Fran notices that one of the extra terminators in the box of networking hardware in the room is a 75-ohm terminator, rather than the 50 ohms required for thin Ethernet.

Fran talks with the director of the Marketing department and recommends that they install an all-10BaseT network using two 40-port concentrators. This will let them move connections from one server to the other, allowing for easy reconfiguration of the network as necessary, and it will keep everything in the same topology. She shows the manager how easy it is for things to get out of whack with the current setup, and explains how all the things she found can contribute to poor performance. She adds that the two concentrators would give the lab a much more professional appearance than the haphazard look of the current setup.

The director is unwilling to make the investment, so Fran retreats to her prepared fallback plan: some more 8 or 12-port mini-hubs and the cards or transceivers necessary to get all the workstations running 10BaseT. Even the much more moderate expense represented by three mini-hubs and some new Ethernet adapters is more than the director wants to spend. Finally, Fran

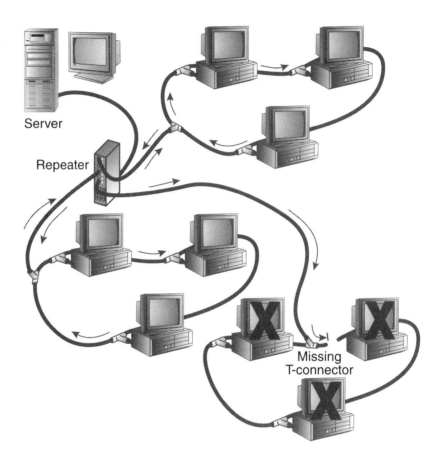

FIGURE 4.5
The Marketing
lab topology

shows the director the bottom-dollar plan: upgrade the existing thin Ethernet cable and T-connectors to new, high-quality ones, including extras for recon-figuring the network as necessary, proper grounding, proper terminators, and a few new transceivers and LAN adapters. And one more item—a half-day training course for the lab administrator in proper cabling techniques and troubleshooting.

The director is happy with the low-cost alternative. After a few hours of work the next evening, aided by the newly educated administrator, Fran replaces the thin Ethernet cabling and T-connectors with high-quality ones, grounds the segment, throws away the old stuff to make sure no one will inad-vertently add it to the network, and upgrades some of the transceivers and LAN cards on the 10BaseT network. She goes over the procedures for adding workstations to either network with the administrator, and makes sure they have sufficient additional high-quality cable, connectors, and transceivers to allow for normal reconfigurations.

They also make sure that all the workstations are using the same network driver software, and that the Macs are using the same system version and printer driver software. A few days later, Fran checks back with the administrator. Everyone is amazed at the increase in network performance, and the Marketing director is happy with the minimal expense required.

Lessons Learned—Scenario Four

- Don't try to save 25 cents on a connector or a dollar on a cable. It won't be worth it in the long run. This is especially true of the T-connectors used with thin Ethernet. Cheap ones will often become very hard to attach or detach with time, and they can cause nasty intermittent problems.

- Try to avoid letting users set up their own networks. In this case, the systems engineer that did the initial setup knew what he was doing, and the setup was fine, until the administration was handed over to someone who wasn't familiar with cabling.

- Watch out for mismatched equipment. Many connectors and cables look similar and will physically interchange with each other, but impedances and other factors can cause big problems.

- In a lab environment, the simplest solution is the best. In this case, the Marketing personnel sometimes needed to reconfigure the network when the administrator wasn't around. Converting everything to 10BaseT would have substantially reduced the chances of an inexperienced user leaving the ring open or making a connection that didn't completely lock.

- When presenting a plan for an installation to management, try to have more than one scenario: "Plan A will cost more, but will also have the following benefits:.... Plan B will sacrifice the following benefits, but reduce costs by this much…"

The Fault Point Chain—Scenario Four

- The network card and network software in each workstation.

- The connection from the card to the cable or transceiver.

- The transceiver (if applicable).

- The connection from the transceiver to the network cable.

- The network cable.

- The concentrator (if applicable).

- The connection from the concentrator to the server.

- The connection at the server on the thin Ethernet ring.

- The LAN adapters and driver software in the servers.

Scenario Five: Fun with AppleTalk

This scenario describes a deceptive problem on an AppleTalk network, and how the solution is discovered through observation and deduction.

Snapshot—Scenario Five

Is this an existing network?

- How many nodes are affected? Do some of the workstations on the ring or segment work?

- Is it only one workstation that can't connect?

- Is the network experiencing intermittent faults and performance problems?

Jethro has one of the toughest assignments possible: someone in the Art department is having problems, maybe with a virus. The user's Mac has been intermittently freezing during startup. He grabs his Mac tool kit and starts tracking down the problem. The virus checker on the affected machine is the latest version, and it doesn't report any problems. The user says the problem doesn't seem to occur during any particular type of operation, or when a certain application is open. There aren't any Inits, Control Panels, or Startup documents that Jethro doesn't recognize, but he tries removing all the extraneous extensions. The system still freezes up occasionally. He then tries reinstalling the System folder. There are still intermittent problems.

Another person in the department wanders by and mentions that she is having the same problem. Jethro realizes that the problem must be network-related if it's affecting more than one Mac. He checks, and most of the people in the department had been having problems but hadn't realized they weren't alone.

He begins the tedious process of trying to isolate the common elements of the affected Macs. They aren't all running the same version of the EtherTalk driver, don't all have the same EtherTalk card, and don't even all use the same System version. Then one of the users asks Jethro to take a look at their printer while he's there—it's been jamming. Jethro figures he might as well take a break from thinking about the other problem, so he shuts down the printer and begins cleaning it thoroughly. After he's been working on the printer for about 20 minutes, one of the users comes over and compliments him on having fixed the problem with her Mac freezing.

A light dawns. He finishes cleaning the printer, then turns it back on. Checking with the affected Macs, he discovers that they are freezing again. It must be the printer. He calls the manufacturer to see if the company know about this. After climbing up the tech support ladder for a while, Jethro is told that yes, they have seen this behavior on some networks, and they'll have a BIOS upgrade that should fix it within a week or two. Jethro arranges to swap the printer with another PostScript printer currently attached to a parallel port on a PC, which shouldn't be affected by the AppleTalk problem, and takes the offending printer offline. The other PostScript printer is a different brand and works fine.

A couple of months later, the new BIOS arrives, and Jethro upgrades the problem printer. He reattaches it to the network and holds his breath. As each day passes without freezes, he breathes a little easier.

Lessons Learned—Scenario Five

- Don't assume that a problem is unique to a user who complains. Check around to see if any others are affected. You won't always hear from some users when they have a problem; there is a certain tendency to take some problems for granted. If Jethro had known from the start that more than one user was affected, he could have saved quite a bit of time working on the system and Inits on the individual Mac. A virus would still have been a possibility, of course.

- This is yet another case where a network analyzer would have been very handy. Jethro would most likely have found that some device on the network was sending out bad AppleTalk packets, and he could have at least isolated the cause to AppleTalk hardware or software, and possibly even determined the device causing the problem.

- Don't assume that the computers on your LAN are the only devices that can cause problems. It is becoming more common for printers to have networking interfaces built in—not just AppleTalk, but Ethernet as well. Each of these is potentially a problem, too.

- Never assume that the manufacturer of a device did everything right. It is common for PCs to arrive from the factory with configuration errors, devices installed incorrectly, and of course, occasionally with faulty components. If Jethro had continued with his fault-point analysis, he would eventually have discovered that what all the Macs had in common was the AppleTalk zone that they were on. That would have led to looking at the other devices on that zone: the server and the printer. He might have spent considerable time trying to determine a problem with the server, assuming that it was a result of a configuration error or old driver version, and possibly never even looked at the printer, assuming that it couldn't be causing the problem.

- Never assume that the manufacturer will notify you if something you bought needs to be updated or might cause problems under certain conditions. The best place to hear about this sort of thing is on the forums on CompuServe or at user-group or CNEPA meetings.

- If he hadn't been lucky, the next step for Jethro should have been to try asking around, either within his department or at some of the sources listed in the previous paragraph. He might have found someone else who already had the same problem.

The Fault Point Chain—Scenario Five

Jethro's initial assumption was that the user's problem was unique to that Mac. That was, of course, incorrect. If Jethro hadn't happened to find out that the problem was actually the fault of the printer, he might have replaced every part of the Macintosh, reinstalling its operating system and all the applications. Eventually, with the whole system replaced and the problem still occurring, he would have needed to look at the other factors in the environment that could possibly affect a workstation: the power, electromagnetic interference, and any connection coming into the Mac. The connections might include the keyboard, the printer (network) connection, a serial connection for a modem, and the SCSI port.

Jethro would then have replaced the keyboard and disconnected anything else connected to the Mac. At that point, he would have discovered that the Mac didn't have the problem when not connected to the network. He would then have known that the problem must be caused by something coming from the network rather than anything in the Mac. The fault points are:

- The Mac hardware—motherboard, memory, power supply, disk controller, disks, and ports.

- The Mac operating system.

- The Apple extensions, such as the EtherTalk driver.

- The non-Apple extensions.

- Any applications running when the problem occurred.

- Other devices on the AppleTalk network—the network driver software for each device on the network. This includes the BIOS in the printer, which was of course the actual problem, and the server.

- The network hardware for each network device.

- The cabling. This could include problems such as lines that run past transformers or fluorescent light ballasts.

- Any other factors in the environment that might interfere with the electronics in the workstation. This could include magnets, power cords that run too close to the CPU, a second workstation, and similar sources of interference.

Troubleshooting
Network Printing

Snapshot: Troubleshooting Network Printing

IS THIS A NEW PRINTER SETUP?

Can you print from any workstations?

If you can print from some workstations, go to the next item. If you can't print from any workstations to a particular printer, try other printers, on other servers if available.

Can you put print jobs directly into the queue with **PCONSOLE?** Do they print?

If not, go to the next item. If inserting the jobs directly into the queue works, then your problem is likely to be with the capture setup on the workstations, with the print job setup, or with the connection to the server. See the section on the printing process, starting on page 169, or the print server section, on page 173.

Is the queue connected to PSERVER?

Use PCONSOLE to see if the queue is attached to PSERVER (the print server software). If it is, make sure that the print server running PSERVER is up and running. See the section on the printing process, starting on page 169, or the PSERVER section, on page 173. If the print server is running, go to the next item. Otherwise, see Chapter 3 for information about troubleshooting workstations.

Can you print from DOS on the print server?

Try printing from DOS on the print server. If the file server is also the print server, you'll need to take the server down first—exiting from NetWare to DOS. Then try printing a DOS file with the command:

```
PRINT FILE.TXT > LPT1:
```

or

```
DIR C: > LPT1: (or whatever port the printer is on)
```

If the printer doesn't respond, you have a problem with the printer itself, or with the workstation configuration. If the printer will print from DOS, then PSERVER or some of the associated software is configured incorrectly. See the section on PSERVER, on page 173.

Is printing affected on only one workstation or a few workstations?

If the problem is with one or a few workstations, but others can print, then you know that the printer itself, the print server, the queues, and so on are operational. Check the workstations that can't print for common items. Are all the workstations that can print using the same print queue or the same print job? Can you print if you log in as a different user? See the sections on print queues, on page 172; on CAPTURE, on page 171; and on print jobs, on page 171.

Can you print from DOS on the workstation?

Try printing from DOS on the affected workstation. If you can't print from DOS, check the network connection to make sure you have a connection to the server and try printing a DOS text file from PCONSOLE. If that works, the workstation itself is probably causing the problem, rather than the print setup. See Chapter 3 for information about troubleshooting workstations. Pay particular attention to the printer port configuration, interrupt conflicts, DOS, and the NetWare shell software. Make sure that the print job or capture setup works on other workstations.

If you can print from DOS, it's probably the application. Try printing from other applications. Make sure that the application is set up to print to the proper printer port or queue. If the program is attempting to print to a NetWare queue directly, and you can't find anything wrong, try printing to the LPT1 port and using CAPTURE to redirect the output to the printer. See the section on CAPTURE, beginning on page 171, and Chapter 10, which covers network applications.

IS THIS AN EXISTING PRINTER SETUP?

Is the printer operational?

With an existing setup, you can have two major things go wrong: a user becomes unable to print, or no one can access a printer or queue. Isolating the people affected will give you your first clues. One of the first places to check is the printer itself. Printers, more than any other equipment on your network, require maintenance. A large percentage of "printing problems" can be fixed by resetting the printer, cleaning it, installing a new toner cartridge, or adding paper.

If the printer is apparently running, has paper, and is online, go to the next item. If not, see your printer's manual for details on your printer. Check power, cables, connections, and other items that users can get to first. Don't forget to check the paper tray and make sure the cover is closed. See the section about the printer's role in the printing process, on page 169.

Is the print server operational?

Next, make sure that the print server, if you are using one, is running properly. Some versions of PSERVER.EXE and RPRINTER.EXE are more likely than others to lock up the print server, especially with PostScript printers. See the section on PostScript printers and their special requirements, starting on page 177.

Check the print server for operation—power on, keyboard responsive, and so on. If the print server is running, go to the next item. If not, troubleshoot the print server as a workstation, as described in Chapter 3.

Can you print from some workstations?

If you can print from some workstations, go to the next item. If you can't print from any workstations, try other printers, on other servers if available. If you can print to another printer, queue, or server, the problem is most likely with the setup of the queue, PSERVER, or the print server you were attempting to print to, rather than the workstation. See the section on the printing process, on page 173.

Can you put print jobs directly into the queue with PCONSOLE? Do they print?

If not, go to the next item. If inserting print jobs directly into the queue works, then your problem is likely to be with the capture setup on the workstations, with the print job setup, or with the connection to the server. See the section on CAPTURE and print jobs, on page 171.

Is the queue connected to PSERVER?

Use PCONSOLE to see if the queue is attached to PSERVER. If it is, make sure that the print server running PSERVER is up and running. If the print server is running, go to the next item. Otherwise, see Chapter 3 for information about troubleshooting workstations.

Can you print from DOS on the print server?

Try printing from DOS on the print server. If this is the server, you'll need to take down the server first, exiting from NetWare to DOS. Then try printing a DOS file with either of these commands:

```
PRINT FILE.TXT > LPT1: (or whatever port the printer is on)
DIR C: > LPT1: (or whatever port the printer is on)
```

If the printer doesn't respond, you have a problem with the printer itself, or with the workstation configuration. If the printer will print from DOS, then PSERVER or some other part of the print software is incorrectly configured. See the section on PSERVER, on page 173.

Is printing affected on only one workstation or a few workstations?

If the problem is with one or a few workstations, but others can print, then you know that the printer itself, the print server, the queues, and so on are operational. Check the workstations that can't print for common items. Are all the workstations that can print using the same print queue or the same print job? Can you print if you log in as a different user? See the sections on print queues, on page 172, and print jobs, on page 171.

Can you print from DOS on the workstation?

Try printing from DOS on the affected workstation. If you can't print from DOS, check the network connection to make sure you have a connection to the server and try printing a DOS text file from PCONSOLE. If that works, the workstation itself, rather than the print setup, is probably causing the problem. See Chapter 3 for information about troubleshooting workstations. The items to pay particular attention to are the printer port configuration, interrupt conflicts, DOS, and the NetWare shell software. Make sure that the print job or capture setup works on other workstations.

If you can print from DOS, it's probably the application. Try printing from other applications. Make sure that the application is set up to print to the proper printer port or queue. If the program is attempting to print to a NetWare queue directly, and you can't find anything wrong, try printing to the LPT1 port and using CAPTURE to redirect the output to the printer. See the section on CAPTURE, beginning on page 171, and Chapter 10, which covers network applications.

IS THIS A MACINTOSH PRINTER SETUP?

Is the printer operational?

Make sure that the printer itself is operational, has paper and toner, and isn't jammed. Also check to see whether it's only one user that is having a problem printing, or whether several users are having problems. See the section about the printer's role in the printing process, on page 175.

Is the printer connected to the network?

With a printer that has been working on a LocalTalk or EtherTalk network, make sure that the connection is firmly seated. If it is, try resetting the printer. If the printer is connected through NetWare for Macintosh and the problem is with the printer, you should see a printer error message in the NetWare for Macintosh screen on the console of the server. The message should give you clues on how to proceed.

Does the printer show up in the correct AppleTalk zone?

If the printer is not showing up in the correct AppleTalk zone, it is a configuration problem, either in the configuration of the printer itself if it is attached to an AppleTalk network, or in NetWare for Macintosh. Make sure the zone name is spelled correctly and remember that the spellings are case-sensitive. See the section on printing with NetWare for Macintosh, on page 178.

Can you print from some workstations?

If you can print from some workstations, make sure that the others are in the same AppleTalk zone. If they are, then see if the ones that can't print are on the same network segment. See Chapter 4 for more information about troubleshooting the physical network. If only one Macintosh can't print, check the network connection. If the connection is solid, try reinstalling the network driver software.

PRINTING FROM MANY WORKSTATIONS to one printer was one of the first uses for PC networks, and printing is still among the most important functions of a network. Network printing services can range from a small piece of hardware that lets a few users share a dot-matrix printer; to a PostScript print server that can service print jobs from DOS, Windows, Macintoshes, or UNIX; to a queue that stores a thousand-page print job and prints it in the middle of the night when no one else needs the printer. These printing services all perform similar functions, but they vary widely in cost and complexity.

Printing usually seems to be more maintenance-intensive than other aspects of network technology. NetWare offers a wealth of features, but with those features comes an attendant complexity that many administrators (and users) find daunting. This need not be the case. If you approach setting up and troubleshooting print services in a systematic manner, and with a basic understanding of the process involved, you will find that problems can be resolved in the same manner as any other problems with the network.

Setting up a printer, its queue, its job configuration, the print server, and print server software can be a very complex process. It gets more complicated if you consider PostScript printing, printing to AppleTalk printers, printing to UNIX print queues, and other possible variations. This chapter is not intended to lead you through the process of creating your printer setup. The NetWare manuals cover the initial setup process well, including some useful troubleshooting hints.

This chapter provides a summary of the printing process and points out where problems may occur. It also offers some specific suggestions for troubleshooting PostScript, Macintosh, and UNIX printing. At the end of the chapter, you'll find a "Real-Life Stories" section, with tales of how common networking problems can be resolved.

Fault Points for Network Printing

C HAPTER 1 INTRODUCED THE CONCEPT of a chain of fault points as a guide to troubleshooting networks and network components. Within any combination of different types of workstations, NICs, LAN topologies, servers, cabling, software, and so on, there are a limited number of points where problems can occur.

Because a conventional flowchart cannot cover all the possibilities inherent in a network, it makes more sense to look only at those places where things can go wrong. Figure 5.1 illustrates a typical fault point chain for network printing.

FIGURE 5.1

The fault point chain for network printing

Each of the items in the chain in Figure 5.1 is linked to the preceding and following items. Any one of them can cause the printing process to fail, and if you can determine that the chain works up to any point, all the points before that point are working and can be excluded from the list of potential causes of the problem.

The printer must have power and a solid connection to the cable, and it must be configured to use the correct interface in the correct manner. It must also have toner (or a good ribbon), a supply of paper, and a clear paper path.

The printer cable must be correctly set up to switch the necessary pins to allow both the workstation and the printer to communicate correctly. The cable should also be within the maximum length limits and well insulated, with properly installed connectors. Of course, the connectors should be screwed snugly into the printer port on the PC and the appropriate port on the printer, if the printer is connected to a workstation.

There are four ways a printer can be made accessible to the network:

- Attached to the server directly

- Attached to a PC acting as a dedicated print server

- Attached to an individual's workstation

- Attached directly to the network through an internal or external print server device

RPRINTER.EXE or NPRINTER.EXE will be running only if the printer is attached to someone's personal workstation, rather than to a dedicated print server or the NetWare server. RPRINTER must be properly configured for the right port on the workstation, and it must be associated with a print queue.

The print server must be properly configured as a workstation to access its drives and NIC. It should also be set up to access the port the printer is attached to, either parallel or serial.

The print server software (PSERVER) provides the connection between print queues and the print server. It must be connected to the print queues with PCONSOLE, and also to the proper print server. PSERVER.EXE can also crash, breaking the connection.

The print queue must be set up and attached to a PSERVER. It must also be able to access the directory on the SYS: volume that actually holds the print jobs until they can be printed.

NetWare must be running properly and must support the PSERVER VAP or NLM. If the printer is set up to print to a PostScript printer or provide print services to Macintosh, UNIX, or other operating systems, you will also need to have those services set up properly.

The network connection to the user's workstation must be working correctly and allow the shell to provide the normal NetWare workstation services.

The printer port on the user's workstation can also affect the NetWare printing process. The port doesn't necessarily need to be turned on in the PC's configuration, but if a job is printed to the wrong printer port, NetWare won't properly redirect it to the queue.

CAPTURE.EXE must be set up to print to the proper print queue and use the proper print job. This is one of the easiest places for problems to occur in an existing setup, because it is one of the few parts that the user interacts with.

DOS must be working for the workstation to be able to load the NetWare shell, attach to the network, and access NetWare print services. If the DOS MODE command has been used to change the settings on a serial port and CAPTURE is set to capture from that port, it may affect the capture process.

Some applications access NetWare print services directly, rather than attempting to send the print job to a port, which is then intercepted and sent to the NetWare queue. Whether the application does this or not, it can affect the print process if it is configured for the wrong type of printer, or if the print menu misleads the user.

The user is the last (and first) link in the printing process, and not one to be forgotten. Users will tell you that the printer is broken when their CAPTURE statement is sending the job to the wrong printer, or tell you that the print server is down when the printer is out of paper.

Users may tell you that the printer doesn't work, or that they can't print, when the only problem is that the printer is out of paper. A system administrator recently reported in a computer publication how he investigated the case of a user who said he couldn't print anymore. After checking a number of possibilities, the administrator discovered that the user couldn't print because the part of the menu that allowed printing wasn't visible on the monitor. After adjusting the display, everything was fine.

The Printing Process

THE PROCESS DESCRIBED HERE assumes a very basic setup: a DOS-based print server and a NetWare 3.*x* server. Using Windows 95, UNIX, or NetWare 4.*x* complicates things somewhat. However, the process is the same conceptually, and if you understand the process, you will be able to follow it through on your system and identify the correct fault point.

Also, in the process described here, the print server may be either a workstation running RPRINTER, NPRINTER.EXE, or PSERVER.EXE, or the server itself. It makes no difference in the troubleshooting process. For clarity, this chapter will always refer to the print server software as *PSERVER*, and the physical workstation to which the printer is connected as the *print server*.

The printing process begins on the workstation, just as it would with a stand-alone PC. The user prints, either from DOS or from an application. Instead of the job being sent to the port the printer is on (LPT1, 2, or 3 or COM1 or 2), it is redirected by the NetWare shell to a file in a queue directory on the file server. PSERVER checks the queue directory and sends the job to the printer.

PSERVER may reside on the server as PSERVER.NLM, on a dedicated print server workstation as PSERVER.EXE, or on a router or NetWare 2.*x* server as PSERVER.VAP. RPRINTER.EXE is not a software print server; it allows PSERVER to access a printer connected to a user's workstation as if that printer were attached to the PC on which PSERVER is running. Wherever PSERVER is located, it looks in the appropriate directory (the print queue) in the file server's SYS:/SYSTEM directory. When a file is placed in the print queue directory, PSERVER prints it to the assigned printer.

NetWare 4.*x* uses a different system. PSERVER.NLM handles routing print jobs to a server running NPRINTER.NLM (which can be the same server running PSERVER.NLM). NPRINTER.NLM runs on the server and supports up to 256 printers. NPRINTER.EXE runs on a workstation and allows network users to print to the local PC, replacing RPRINTER. There is no software for configuring a dedicated print server workstation, although you can run NPRINTER.EXE on a workstation that is used only as a print server.

The Shell—Printer Redirection

IPX.COM and NETx.COM, the ODI network drivers, or the VLMs are the first step in the NetWare printing process. When an application attempts to send output to the printer port (LPT1, 2, or 3), the shell intercepts it and sends it as a file to the queue directory on the server instead. This is the same process used to allow users to access drives on the server as if they were local.

If the application is aware of network print queues, but printing doesn't work when the application tries to insert a print job directly into the queue, try printing to the parallel port (LPT1) and using NetWare's redirection capability instead.

SHELL.CFG is a file in the same directory as NETx.COM (or whatever NetWare shell is loaded) that controls to a degree how the workstation shell is configured. Think of it as the CONFIG.SYS file for the shell. On workstations running RPRINTER, use NET.CFG. There are a number of settings that should be used when configuring printing:

`LOCAL PRINTERS = 0`	This will keep the workstation from hanging if no ports are captured and the user presses Shift-PrintScreen.
`PRINT HEADER = 255`	This will make sure PostScript jobs have enough header space to correctly configure the printer.
`PRINT TAIL = 255`	This will make sure NetWare has enough space in the trailer to the print job to send reset codes to the printer after the job is finished. Use this setting if the printer is being left incorrectly configured after a user finishes printing.
`SPX CONNECTIONS = 60`	This should be used on dedicated print servers running PSERVER.EXE. It is not necessary on workstations running RPRINTER.

CAPTURE.EXE and Print Jobs—Printing Options

The CAPTURE program allows you to specify many options when printing a document. For example, to print a PostScript document to a queue called LaserWriterI, your capture statement might be:

```
CAPTURE LPT1 s=Marketing q=LaserWriterI /NB /NT /NFF
```

This captures any text sent to LPT1 and prints it to the queue LaserWriterI on the server Marketing, with no banner page, no tabs, and no form feed. The no-tabs setting is standard when printing from an application that (like most) handles the print formatting, and the no-form-feed option prevents the printer from printing a blank page at the end of a document. The only time you need to add a form feed is if the last page of a print job doesn't print when printing from some applications.

You can also specify these parameters with NPRINT, or by setting up a print job with PRINTCON (or with the NetWare Administrator program in NetWare 4.*x*). Using a print job is a much easier way to set the parameters for complex printing, because it allows you to make choices from menus rather than requiring you to enter the exact spelling and syntax for each setting, as with CAPTURE. PRINTCON allows you to designate a default print job and to set up queues associated with each job. This means that you can switch from printing forms on a line printer, to PostScript on a LaserWriter, and then to text on a Hewlett-Packard printer, with the following simple statements:

```
CAPTURE  j=line
CAPTURE  j=PS
CAPTURE  j=HP
```

Or you can use PRINTCON to change your default print job. Using print jobs makes it much easier for the user to print and for you to troubleshoot the setup.

The Print Queue

The print queue is actually a directory located in SYS:/SYSTEM with an eight-digit file name that consists of hexadecimal characters (0–9, plus A–F), such as 400000BF. This directory contains any files that have been placed in the queue.

If jobs are being placed in the queue without error messages, and the PCON-SOLE Print Queue Status window shows that they are being sent to the printer, but they never print, you should look in the queue directories to see if the files are still there. This will tell you whether the problem is with PSERVER or with the printer:

- If the files are still in the print queue directory, they aren't actually being sent to the printer, and the problem is likely to be with the software.

- If the files are gone, then they are being sent to the printer and aren't printing out, perhaps because of a configuration problem with the print server or the printer.

You should also make sure that when a print queue is selected in the Print Queue Information window of PCONSOLE, the Queue Servers list has at least one PSERVER attached.

The name of the queue in SYS:/SYSTEM usually matches the Print Queue ID entry you will see in PCONSOLE. Under NetWare 4.*x*, this may not be the case if you create the queue in a different container than the one that contains the server running NPRINTER.NLM or PSERVER.NLM.

PSERVER—Printing Controls

PSERVER.NLM, .EXE, or .VAP is the software that controls how the print file is sent from the queue on the server, and to which printer. PSERVER.NLM runs on the server. PSERVER.VAP may run on a 2.*x* server or on a router. In NetWare 2.*x* and 3.*x*, PSERVER.EXE runs on a dedicated print server workstation.

The version of PSERVER.NLM shipped with NetWare 3.11 has a bug that can cause garbage to be printed if you are using a fast printer and the print server workstation has a small buffer. If the buffer overflows, the job is killed. This can be fixed by upgrading to the latest version of PSERVER.NLM, which can be found on NetWire.

PSERVER.EXE gives you the advantage of off-loading the PSERVER process from the server to a dedicated workstation. The downside is that it requires an additional dedicated workstation. This does have another additional benefit, though. It allows you to lock up your server and still give users easy access to the printers.

Because NPRINTER.NLM supports up to 256 printers, you can offload the print server process from some servers if necessary. This is simpler if the servers are all in the same container. Run PSERVER.NLM on only one server, and NPRINTER.EXE on the workstations with printers attached.

PSERVER creates a directory in SYS:/SYSTEM with a name based on the Print Server ID number assigned to the printer server when it is created (an eight-digit hex number, such as 000A31B4).

The Print Server

The print server can be any of the following:

- A workstation running PSERVER.EXE

- A file server running PSERVER.NLM

- A NetWare 4.*x* server running NPRINTER.NLM and PSERVER.NLM

- A NetWare 4.*x* file server running just NPRINTER.NLM, serving a queue on another 4.*x* server running PSERVER.NLM

In any case, the process of troubleshooting is the same, although it may be easier if the file server and print server are separate workstations. The print server itself can usually be treated as an ordinary workstation. See Chapter 3 for information about troubleshooting workstations.

Configuration Files or Attributes

Several files (under NetWare 3.*x*) or attributes (under NetWare 4.*x*) can be useful in debugging printing problems:

- The PRINT.XXX file is stored in the Print Server directory in SYS:/SYSTEM (for instance, SYS:/SYSTEM/A101B24C) and contains the same information as the Printer Configuration attribute: all the information defined under PCONSOLE in the Printers option.

- The QUEUE.XXX file is also in the Print Server directory in SYS:/SYSTEM and contains the same information as the Queue attribute: the queue name and priority.

- The NOTIFY.XXX file or Notify attribute lists the user(s) or group specified to be notified when there are problems with print jobs. It's also located in the SYS:/SYSTEM Print Server directory.

Serial and Parallel Interfaces

PC serial interfaces use the RS-232 interface. This specification is intended to allow a PC to talk to a modem—Data Terminal Equipment (DTE) to Data Communications Equipment (DCE). In the context of printing, however, both the PC and the printer consider themselves to be DTE devices. The means of fixing this problem is to use a special serial cable that "fools" both the printer and PC into thinking that the device on the other end is a DCE. Unfortunately, the way this technique is implemented varies from printer to printer.

The best way to avoid interface problems is to use a parallel connection, if at all possible, because these connections are faster and easier to configure. There may be reasons to use a serial printer, such as a requirement for a longer cable than a parallel connection allows or a printer that has only a serial interface. In that case, you should use a serial cable made as shown in Figure 5.2, rather than a straight-through cable.

Serial cables are commercially available. The diagram in Figure 5.2 is just to show you how the signals are switched from PC to printer. This is a sample configuration that will work for many printers; your printer may use different pins. See your printer manual for details, or contact the manufacturer to purchase the necessary cable.

If you use a parallel interface, you may have a problem with interrupts. To avoid interrupt conflicts, you can use a setting when you are configuring the printer in PCONSOLE. Set Use Interrupts to No in the Printer Configuration section of the Print Server Configuration menu of PCONSOLE's Print Server Information.

FIGURE 5.2

Serial cable pinouts

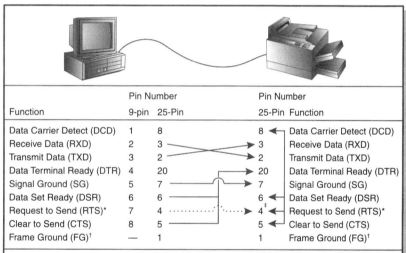

Function	Pin Number 9-pin	25-Pin	25-Pin	Function
Data Carrier Detect (DCD)	1	8	8	Data Carrier Detect (DCD)
Receive Data (RXD)	2	3	3	Receive Data (RXD)
Transmit Data (TXD)	3	2	2	Transmit Data (TXD)
Data Terminal Ready (DTR)	4	20	20	Data Terminal Ready (DTR)
Signal Ground (SG)	5	7	7	Signal Ground (SG)
Data Set Ready (DSR)	6	6	6	Data Set Ready (DSR)
Request to Send (RTS)*	7	4	4 ‡	Request to Send (RTS)*
Clear to Send (CTS)	8	5	5	Clear to Send (CTS)
Frame Ground (FG)†	—	1	1	Frame Ground (FG)†

* NetWare Services keeps this pin high. Don't use it unles your printer requires it to enable input.
† Use of pin 1 on 25-pin connectors is not necessary, and may cause ground loop problems if PC and printer are on separate power sources.
‡ For most printers, pins 4, 5, 6, and 8 should be be bridged together.

The Printer

There is a huge variety of printers available today, ranging from simple dot-matrix printers that haven't changed much in the last 15 years, to laser printers, to dye-sublimation color printers that produce results barely distinguishable from color photographs. In addition to the printers themselves and their hardware interfaces, there is also a control language for each printer. These languages range from relatively simple dot-matrix control codes to the PostScript language, which is as complex and capable as most programming environments. Both the hardware and software aspects of a printer must be taken into account when connecting it to a network.

Printer Hardware

The hardware aspect of the connection to the print server has largely been covered earlier in his chapter. However, you should be aware that most printers have a hardware configuration, which may be set using utility software, with DIP switches inside the printer, or from a front panel display. These will tell the printer what type of connection it has, what protocol and speed to expect over the connection, and so on. See your printer's manual for details. If your print server cannot print at all, even from DOS, it is likely to be a problem with the printer's configuration or its connection.

Printer Software

The other aspect of the printer is the software used to control the printer's actions while printing. In the simplest case, an ASCII-only printer (a daisy-wheel or ball printer) can print only ASCII characters. It may have a few escape codes (so called because they all start with the ASCII character for Esc) to allow bold, italic, and underlined characters. PostScript, at the other end of the spectrum, not only allows any aspect of text to be changed, but prints exceedingly complex graphics as well.

The application from which the user is printing must understand the language of the printer. In addition, the print job or CAPTURE statement must take into account the special requirements of controlling the printer. This is particularly true when printing graphics or PostScript. The flow to the printer must be set to Byte Stream, rather than to Text, when you configure the print job in PRINTCON. This allows the special characters used to control the printer to be sent without being interpreted or removed. The next section offers some tips for troubleshooting PostScript printing.

Troubleshooting PostScript Printers

OSTSCRIPT IS AN EXTREMELY VERSATILE printer control language developed by Adobe Systems. It allows text to be printed in any size, any weight, any angle, any color, and more. It is also very good at producing graphics. The drawback to this flexibility is the resulting complexity.

If you are interested, try printing a word processing file or art file to disk as a PostScript file, and then open it with a text editor. You will see pages and pages of code describing that document. The PostScript file is actually a program that runs on the controller of a PostScript printer, and tells it how to draw the page. It is not uncommon for a 15 KB word processing document to produce a 100 KB or larger PostScript file.

PostScript printers have also been associated from the first with the Macintosh computer from Apple. Today, most PostScript printers have parallel and serial ports in addition to AppleTalk ports, and you may wish to connect your printer via these ports, even in an all-Macintosh department. A PostScript printer attached to a print server by a parallel port may prove to be quite a bit faster than one connected via AppleTalk, especially if the Macs are using EtherTalk cards.

When printing to a PostScript printer, you should make sure that the following configuration items have been set:

- Set the print job to Byte Stream Mode with PRINTCON or use the /NT (no tabs) option in your CAPTURE statement.

- Other CAPTURE options you should use are /NFF (no form feeds) and /NB (no banner).

- Set PRINT HEADER = 255 in your SHELL.CFG or NET.CFG file.

- Set PRINT TAIL = 255 in your SHELL.CFG or NET.CFG file if your printer tends to hang after printing a job.

Troubleshooting NetWare for Macintosh Printing

THERE ARE A COUPLE OF PLACES to check your configuration of NetWare for Macintosh if you have printing problems:

If a printer isn't showing up in the EtherTalk zone, or if the AppleTalk screen on the server has error messages like "Can't connect to printer Laser-Writer," make sure that the printer name specified in ATPS.CFG has the name spelled exactly as it appears in the LocalTalk zone, including uppercase and lowercase. If the name seems to be spelled correctly, make sure that there are no leading or trailing spaces in either the configuration file or the name that was given to the printer with the LaserWriter utility.

- If devices are disappearing from zones, or lots of error messages are appearing in the system error log, or if performance is just very slow, make sure that each LocalTalk and EtherTalk zone has a unique zone number. Zone number conflicts can cause many types of intermittent conflicts and really slow down AppleTalk performance.

- If you have set up a print job with PRINTCON to print from the PC to an AppleTalk printer, make sure that Mode is *not* set to Reinitialize. This will cause jobs to fail to print.

Troubleshooting UNIX Printing

NETWARE NFS VERSION 1.2B supports bidirectional printing for UNIX printers. This means that PC workstations attached to a NetWare server can print to a printer attached to a UNIX workstation, and the UNIX workstations can print to the NetWare queues. Getting this process to work is more complicated than a standard print server; but approached methodically, it is not any more difficult. The complication is added by the basic difference between the methods of printing on PCs and UNIX workstations.

With PCs, the PRINT command in DOS simply sends a stream of data to the parallel or serial port, which is intercepted by NetWare and redirected to a NetWare queue. UNIX workstations use a program (called a *daemon*), LPD, to print. LPD is a command that is part of the system software in UNIX. It is much more capable than the PRINT command in DOS. It knows what kind of printer it is printing to (for instance, text or PostScript) and where that printer is located, whether on the workstation's printer port or on another workstation. It also knows the name of the queue that it is printing to and where that queue is located. This configuration information is stored in a file called printcap, usually located in the /etc directory.

To set up a UNIX workstation to print to a NetWare queue, the printcap file must contain the IP address or hostname of the server and the information on the name of the queue. The manual for NetWare NFS discusses these requirements in detail. For troubleshooting UNIX-to-NetWare printing, you should be aware that the following fault points are added to the normal ones for NetWare:

- The LPD daemon. Is it running?

- The printcap file on the UNIX side. Is the information about the NetWare server and the queue to print to correct?

- The TCP/IP connection to the server. Can you ping the NetWare server?

- The configuration of NetWare NFS. Is the queue exported? Is it configured correctly?

- The PLPD NLM. Is it loaded and configured properly?

For printing from a NetWare client to a printer on a UNIX workstation, the fault chain has the same items, but in reverse order, since the job is going from the NetWare queue to the LPD daemon on the UNIX workstation. Additionally, there is a print gateway on the NetWare server that modifies the file after it reaches the print queue, then sends it to the LPD daemon on the UNIX host. Of course, in both cases, the normal NetWare printing fault chain also applies, including the workstation-to-printer connection. In the case of NetWare-to-UNIX printing, it's a UNIX workstation, but you still need to verify that you can print from the workstation to the printer.

Real-Life Stories

THIS SECTION DESCRIBES typical network printing problems and how a troubleshooter would go through the process of isolating the fault and fixing it. The two fictional companies introduced in Chapter 1 and their administrators are again used as examples. They combine the equipment and experience of a number of actual businesses. These four scenarios show some representative problems often encountered when setting up or troubleshooting printers and printing operations. While you may never see these particular problems, they should give you a feel for the process by which an experienced troubleshooter isolates a problem, determines the solution, and fixes the problem.

Scenario One: A New PostScript Printer

The administrators are setting up a new PostScript printer that will be accessible to both Macs and PCs in the marketing department. They'll be attaching it to a dedicated print server.

Snapshot—Scenario One

Is this a new printer setup?

- Can you print from any workstations?

- Can you put print jobs directly into the queue with PCONSOLE? Do they print?

- Is the queue connected to PSERVER?

- Can you print from DOS on the print server?

- Is printing affected only on one workstation or a few workstations?

- Can you print from DOS on the workstation?

Fran and Jethro are setting up a new PostScript printer for the Marketing department at Great Big, Inc. The printer must be accessible to both Macs and PCs. The server is not physically accessible to the users, so they will be using a PC as a print server. The server is running NetWare 3.12 and NetWare for Macintosh. In earlier versions of NetWare, they would have needed to set the printer up as an AppleTalk printer, and then set up a queue that PCs could use to print to the AppleTalk printer. With this version of NetWare for Macintosh, they can do it the other way: set up a queue and allow Macintoshes to print to the PC print queue. This allows the print server to be a PC with a 16-bit Ethernet card and a parallel interface, which is faster than using the AppleTalk interface.

They set up the workstation that will be the print server. Since it is a dedicated workstation that won't be used for anything else, they use an ancient 286 AT clone that has been sitting around. It has a 20 MB hard disk and a Hercules monochrome setup, which is fine—it doesn't need color or much disk space to run PSERVER. The only card in the AT is a NIC. The laser printer is attached to the parallel port. The printer is supposed to automatically take input from its serial or parallel port, so there's nothing to configure on the printer.

Before connecting the print server to the network, Fran and Jethro want to check the printer setup on the PC for proper functioning. You can't print from DOS to a PostScript printer, so they load an application that will print Post-Script to check the printer. Nothing comes out—the printer's data light doesn't even start blinking. After a while, the application shows a message "Printer unavailable."

Since the application is set to print to LPT1, the problem must be between the application and the printer. The possible fault points are the port, the cable, and the software on both ends to enable the ports. The printer is supposed to determine which port is being used, and the cable is the one that came with the printer, so they check the software on the AT first. After they locate and run SETUP, they discover that the parallel port has been disabled. After they enable it, the application is able to print to the printer.

Fran and Jethro leave the application on the disk in case any future debugging is required, then take these steps:

- Save the existing AUTOEXEC.BAT and CONFIG.SYS files to .BAK extensions.

- Update the DOS version to the latest.

- Add the latest versions of LSL, NIC driver, IPXODI, and NETX.EXE or VLMs.

- Create a SHELL.CFG or NET.CFG file with the preferred server specified and an SPX CONNECTIONS = 60 entry.

- Load the latest version of PSERVER.EXE onto the disk.

- Set up the AUTOEXEC.BAT file so that it loads IPXODI and NETX or VLMs, then logs into the network as a user they've created for printing, then loads PSERVER.

This AUTOEXEC.BAT file setup creates a security loophole in that a user could reboot the print server and interrupt the AUTOEXEC.BAT with Ctrl-C after it's logged in, but they've carefully restricted the access for the user. They want the print server to connect automatically to the network so that it can be rebooted or come back up after a power outage, without one of them needing to be there to enter a password. This way, any user can specify the PSERVER to load (they've printed instructions and taped them to the printer). The next step is to set up a print server account and queues, using PCONSOLE and PRINTCON.

Fran and Jethro use PCONSOLE to define a print server. They configure the printer as a remote printer, since it is not on the file server. Then they set up a queue, using the AppleTalk Print Services (ATPS) NLM and configure it to use the printer they've defined. Then they use PRINTCON to set up two print jobs: one for printing PostScript from PCs and one for printing text from PCs (PostScript printers won't handle text files as HP-compatible printers do). Finally, they reboot the print server, load PSERVER, and start printing test files from several workstations. None of the jobs printed from PCs or Macs come out. Fran and Jethro begin rechecking the configuration.

Oops! "Remote printer" means a printer on a user's workstation attached with RPRINTER. They change the configuration to a local printer on LPT1 and reboot the print server. The jobs that were in the queue begin printing. After the second job prints, the print server hangs. They restart the printer, but the print server still thinks it's offline. They reboot the print server and another job prints, then it hangs again. They look at the configuration of the print server. The Use Interrupts option is set to ON, with interrupt 7 specified. That's the correct interrupt, but they decide to try Use Interrupts set to OFF. This fixes the problem.

The next job in the queue is a Macintosh job. It prints, but the fonts are all Courier instead of what they should have been. They reread the NetWare for Macintosh documentation and discover that they need to specify a font list for the printer, since it isn't on AppleTalk. They change the configuration of ATPS to look for the font list for the printer in a file instead of through AppleTalk and to download the LaserPrep initialization file with each Macintosh print job, and then reload ATPS. Now the Macintosh jobs are printing with the fonts specified in the document.

Lessons Learned—Scenario One

- Make sure the print server is properly configured with SETUP for the printer. This includes setting the speed, parity, and stop bit if using a serial connection.

- Follow the configuration instructions in the manuals explicitly. Make sure to check the NetWare for Macintosh manual and supplement, if necessary, as well as the Print Server manual.

- If the print server freezes or you have intermittent problems when jobs are printed to a printer on the parallel port, try setting Use Interrupts to OFF.

- If you set up a Macintosh queue to print to a printer that isn't on Apple-Talk, you must set up a list that contains the fonts native to the printer. NetWare for Macintosh 3.01 comes with default font lists for the Laser-Writer, LaserWriter Plus, LaserWriter II NT, LaserWriter II NTX, and HP LaserJet with PostScript cartridge. If you have additional fonts, either installed in the printer's ROM or on a hard disk, you can modify the .FNT file to include them. You must also add a -l option to the queue configuration line in the ATPS.CFG file to download LaserPrep with each Mac job.

The Fault Point Chain—Scenario One

The fault point chain in this case begins with the users, their applications, and the workstation configurations and connections, but these aren't relevant, because in the first step, none of the workstations can print, indicating a problem with the PSERVER or printer configuration. Although they are part of the overall fault chain, if the connections from server to workstation, the NIC in the workstation, or the workstation itself aren't working, they should be addressed as discussed in the previous chapters. Therefore, the fault point chain we consider here is as follows:

- The queue. In this case the queue is set up by the ATPS NLM. A standard queue in a PC-only department wouldn't really be any different; it would just be configured with PCONSOLE instead of the INSTALL NLM.

- The print server attached to the queue. This is a software print server that is configured in PCONSOLE and controls the configuration of the PSERVER version running on the server, a bridge, or the print server workstation.

- The copy of PSERVER. It needs to be loaded and attached to a print server that has been configured with PCONSOLE.

- The physical print server. This may be the file server, a bridge, or a workstation. In this context, it doesn't matter. If the workstation is running properly, the only aspects to look at in this context are whether it is configured for the port the printer is on and whether the DOS and NetWare configuration files are set up properly.

- The connection to the printer. The cable should be appropriate for the type of printer attached, should have solid connections, and so on.

- The printer. It should be properly configured for the type of connection. It should also have paper and a ribbon or toner cartridge, be plugged in, and so on.

Scenario Two: A Router as Print Server

In this scenario, the administrator sets up a router (known as a bridge in previous versions of NetWare) to act as a print server. This will allow two physically separated groups to use the same file server and both groups to also have a local printer.

Snapshot—Scenario Two

Is this a new printer setup?

- Can you print from any workstations?

- Can you put print jobs directly into the queue with PCONSOLE? Do they print?

- Is the queue connected to PSERVER?

- Can you print from DOS on the print server?

- Is printing affected on only one workstation or a few workstations?

- Can you print from DOS on the workstation?

John, the administrator for Itsy-Bitsy, has a department that is splitting in two. The Sales department is splitting into Order Entry and Shipping, and the two departments will be in separate locations. The Shipping department needs to take the line printer to print shipping forms, and the Order Entry department is getting a laser printer. The two departments will be separated by several hundred feet, which exceeds the limit for the type of cabling in use for the network. John will either need to add a second server for the Shipping department and move the department's accounts, or put in a bridge, router, or repeater to extend the network.

John decides to locate a router in the Shipping department's new location to handle printing and extend the possible distance from the Sales server by allowing two network segments: one to attach to the server and one for the users in Shipping. This extends the possible distance from the server to the maximum for the type of cabling, since the only things on that segment are the router and the server. It does, of course, also require a second NIC in the server as well as the router, to allow the maximum possible distance between the two machines. Figure 5.3 illustrates this situation.

The server is running NetWare 3.12. The router will utilize an old 2.15 server set up to run PSERVER.VAP. The server will run PSERVER NLM. Alternatively, John could add a second server for the Order Entry department,

FIGURE 5.3
A network connection with two segments and a router

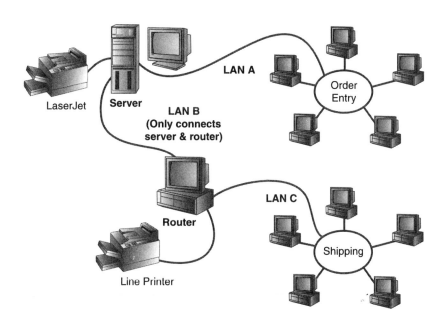

and use a second NIC in both servers to connect the two LANs, but since he already has the old server, he'll use that.

John adds a second NIC to the server to allow the maximum distance between the router and the server, sets up the router, connects the Shipping department's workstations to it, and tests the expanded network. When everything is working, he uses PCONSOLE to set up an additional print queue and print server. He reconfigures the existing queue and print server to use the line printer on the router and sets up new ones for the laser printer on the server.

When the configuration is done, he configures the router with PSERVER.VAP and attaches the printer, then starts PSERVER and tries printing from a workstation in the Shipping department. Nothing comes out of the line printer.

John begins tracing the problem with the CAPTURE statement on the PC he is trying to print from. It's set in the user's AUTOEXEC.BAT file to the old queue. (Nothing came out on that printer either.) He resets CAPTURE to the new print server and queue and tries printing again. Still nothing. Next, he tries inserting a job directly into the queue. Nothing comes out of the printer. He reboots the PC running PSERVER as a workstation and tries to print a DOS file to the COM1 port. Nothing.

He uses the SETUP program to see if the PC is configured to use COM1. It is. The only remaining item is the cable. The line printer is serial-only, and the server uses a 25-pin serial cable; the new router has a 9-pin serial port, so John had picked up a new serial cable at the local computer store. On investigation, it turns out that they have sold him a straight-through, or modem cable. He gets a serial printer cable and hooks the printer back up.

He can print from DOS to the printer. He loads PSERVER and tries printing to the line printer from one of the Shipping department workstations. Success! John knows that the print job configuration is stored in a file in the user's SYS:MAIL/ID# directory, so rather than use PRINTCON to copy the print jobs to every user, he creates the new set of print jobs for one user and copies the file to everyone's mail directory. Then he creates two groups, one for Order Entry and one for Shipping, and adds an entry to the system login script:

```
IF MEMBER OF SHIPPING THEN CAPTURE J=LINE
```

for each group. This sets the default job correctly for each group.

Then he changes the printer configuration for the Order Entry department's print server to match the new laser printer. He leaves the queue alone—there shouldn't be any problem there. Testing the printer, he finds no problems from any of several workstations.

Lessons Learned—Scenario Two

- Most of the printing problems you will encounter are the results of incorrect setup of the printer, workstation, print server, or queue. Double-check all configuration items before you go to the next step.

- Make sure that cabling, interrupts, and printer configurations are correctly set and match the corresponding settings in the workstation.

- Take the troubleshooting process systematically; it's complex, but can be resolved if you take it one step at a time.

The Fault Point Chain—Scenario Two

- The workstation shell and CAPTURE setup.

- The queue on the server.

- The print server attached to the queue.

- The server or router on which PSERVER is running.

- The configuration of the PC.

- The connection to the printer.

- The printer's configuration.

- The printer hardware.

Scenario Three: Remote Printing with NetWare 4.x

This scenario is similar to the one described in the previous section, but the administrator sets up a printer on a hardware printer server and plans to make the printer available in two different containers under NetWare 4.x. This will allow different groups to use the same printer. In fact, one of the groups has people in two locations, one out of state. They will still be able to print to this printer, which will usually be cheaper and faster than faxing.

Snapshot—Scenario Three

Is this a new printer setup?

- Can you print from any workstations?

- Can you put print jobs directly into the queue with PCONSOLE? Do they print?

- Is the queue connected to PSERVER?

- Can you print a test page on the print server?

- Is printing affected on only one workstation or a few workstations?

- Can you print from DOS on the workstation?

John, the administrator for Itsy-Bitsy, has two departments using NetWare 4.01. They both need the use of a high-speed laser printer, but neither can really justify it by themselves. They decide to pool resources, since they are not far apart physically. John will attach the printer to a direct-connect Ethernet print server and put the print queue in both containers. The out-of-state users will also be able to print to the printer, since they're in the same departmental container as one of the local groups.

John sets up and configures the printer and the Ethernet print server box. He loads the printer server installation software on a convenient PC and sets up the print server. The print server can be printed to directly, without requiring a queue on the server, which reduces overhead on the server. He prints a test job to the printer, and it works. He then makes the printer available to the two containers, checks the permissions, and goes home, feeling the satisfaction of a job well done.

The next day when he comes in, one of the department supervisors comments that they had expected to be able to print to the printer, since it was all set up. He feels that old familiar sinking feeling—they should be able to. He looks on their PC first. The printer doesn't show up in the list of available printers. They are using Windows 95 and the new Microsoft 32-bit client with NDS support, but when he browses both containers, the printer doesn't show up. He checks on another PC, and it's not there either. He retreats to his office and brings up NWADMIN, thinking that it may be a permissions problem.

The printer shows up from his system, which is to be expected, since he is the user ADMIN, with rights to everything. He logs in as his test user, with fairly limited rights. He can still see the printer, so he tries printing to it. No problem. He goes back to the PC he configured the print server from and checks the print server configuration. He can't see anything wrong there.

Then it hits him: both his office PC and the one he used to configure the print server are running Windows for Workgroups 3.11, and the two that can't see the printer are running Windows 95 (against his advice, of course). He goes back to the documentation to see if there are any considerations when running Windows 95. He is chagrined to find that neither the printed documentation nor the Help files on the installation disks mention Windows 95! The latest dates on the files on the disks are from December 1995.

He goes back to his office and logs onto the print server manufacturer's Web page. Sure enough, there are specific printer drivers that need to be loaded to support the print server. He downloads them and installs them on one of the Windows 95 PCs. No problems. He then installs the drivers on the rest of the Windows 95 PCs, and everyone is happy.

Lessons Learned—Scenario Three

- Don't assume that because it works on one PC that it will work on all PCs, especially if they're running different operating systems.

- Don't assume that because you just bought the thing, and the system you want to run it on has been out for months, that it's supported. It could be an old copy of the software that's been sitting in a warehouse for months, or it might be that the vendor hasn't gotten around to the update yet.

- Remember that bulletin boards, CompuServe forums, and Web pages are great resources for not only finding problems, but getting the updated drivers necessary to fix some of them, and the experiences of others who have already done it.

The Fault Point Chain—Scenario Three

- The application being printed from.

- The operating system printing setup. This could be anything from CAPTURE on a DOS 3.3 system to Windows 95, OS/2, or UNIX printer drivers.

- The configuration of the print server.

- The connection to the printer.

- The printer's configuration.

- The printer hardware.

Scenario Four: A Single Workstation That Can't Print

The administrator encounters a problem with a user who can't print any more. She isolates the problem to a single workstation, then finds the problem on that workstation and fixes it.

Snapshot—Scenario Four

Is this an existing printer setup?

- Is the printer operational?

- Is the print server operational?

- Can you print from some workstations?

- Can you put print jobs directly into the queue with PCONSOLE? Do they print?

- Is the queue connected to PSERVER?

- Can you print from DOS on the print server?

- Is printing affected on only one workstation or a few workstations?

- Can you print from DOS on the workstation?

Fran receives a call that one of the printers in Great Big's Marketing department is not working. When she arrives, she checks with the user first to find out exactly what the problem is. The user says that an application won't print to the PostScript printer anymore. Fran begins by checking the printer and print server. The printer is online and has paper, and the print server is operational. She checks around and finds that other people on the network can print, both from DOS and from the application the user is trying to print from. Fran tries inserting a print job with PCONSOLE. It prints fine. She then tries printing from DOS. The job prints to the other printer in the department.

A light dawns. She types CAPTURE and finds that the default capture is to the wrong printer. The system login script is set up so that the default printer is the text printer. If the user is using a program that needs PostScript, she puts them in a group called PostScript, which uses a line in the system login script like the following:

```
IF MEMBER OF GROUP POSTSCRIPT THEN CAPTURE
    J=LASERWRITER
```

However, this user has a line in their AUTOEXEC.BAT file that sets CAPTURE J=HP (for the Hewlett-Packard LaserJet), which executes after the user logs in to the network. She looks at the date on the AUTOEXEC.BAT and finds it is more than two years old, dating back to before they had a PostScript printer.

Further research shows that the user had been playing with his AUTOEXEC .BAT and accidentally deleted it, then copied an old version off a backup floppy they had kept from long ago. Fran copies the standard AUTOEXEC .BAT file she has created and stored in the SYS:PUBLIC directory onto the PC, and then modifies it slightly for that particular user. She reboots the PC, and everything works as it should.

Lessons Learned—Scenario Four

- Ask the user if he or she changed anything on the system recently. Fran might have been able to save herself some time by discovering first that the user had changed his AUTOEXEC.BAT file. Again, if you don't need to count on the user for information, your life will be easier. If Fran had a configuration worksheet for the user's workstation, she might have noticed right away that the date and size of the AUTOEXEC.BAT file didn't match the standard.

- No matter how much time and effort you spend making sure that every user is set up properly, there will always be some way the user can mess things up. Be on the lookout for the things that the user can affect, including a personal login script, the configuration files on a PC, the default print job as set in PRINTCON, and so on.

- If you have a standard operating system, set of network drivers, configuration files, and so on, you can make your life easier. For example, in this case, Fran noticed that the AUTOEXEC.BAT file had a date that was older than it should have been. If she hadn't been aware of this, she would have needed to reboot the PC and look at the messages on the screen as it booted and the user logged in, or opened the file with a text editor to find the problem.

The Fault Point Chain—Scenario Four

- The workstation shell and CAPTURE setup.

- The queue on the server.

- The print server attached to the queue.

- The server or router PSERVER is running on.

- The configuration of the PC.

- The connection to the printer.

- The printer's configuration.

- The printer hardware.

Scenario Five: Macintosh Printing Problems

The administrator deals with a problem typical of AppleTalk networks, especially ones with a mixed LocalTalk and EtherTalk environment.

Snapshot—Scenario Five

Is this an existing printer setup?

- Is the printer operational?

- Is the printer connected to the network?

- Does the printer show up in the correct AppleTalk zone?

- Can you print from some workstations?

Jethro receives a call that one of the Mac users can't see their printer in the Chooser any more. He arrives, and after assuring himself that the Chooser is set to the correct EtherTalk zone, begins to track down the problem. The Mac's Chooser does list the correct number of zones and shows the server under File Sharing, so Jethro assumes that the Mac's connection to the network is working. He checks on another Mac, and the printer isn't visible there, either. Since the printer is supposed to be available (although, if you wish, you can hide the actual printer from the Chooser and make only the NetWare queue available), Jethro assumes that the problem isn't related to the queue or printer server.

He then takes a quick look at the printer itself. It's turned on and seems to be working correctly—no error lights, the cover is closed, and so on. Jethro resets the printer just to make sure, and rechecks the Chooser. Still nothing. Then he remembers that the Macs are all connected with EtherTalk, not Local-Talk. That means that the LaserWriter must either be connected to the server with an EtherTalk card or have a LocalTalk-to-EtherTalk bridge.

He finds a bridge in the morass of wiring under the printer. He powers it off and on again, hoping to reset its configuration, but when he checks the Chooser, there is still no printer showing. Then he digs up the control software for the bridge, downloads a new control file, and restarts it. When the restart finishes, the printer is showing in the Chooser again.

Lessons Learned—Scenario Five

- Macintosh networks are no longer the simple creatures they once were. In search of higher performance, many networks now use EtherTalk rather than AppleTalk. If your network is set up this way, don't forget that any AppleTalk device, including the printers, must have some device that makes it available to the EtherTalk network. This may be an AppleTalk card in the server or Mac, an AppleTalk-to-EtherTalk bridge, the built-in EtherTalk interface in a LaserWriter IIf or IIg, or a specialized bridge intended only for use with printers. Each of these devices must also have the correct software to enable it to run properly.

- Just because the lights are on doesn't mean a device is functioning correctly. It is very difficult to tell the status of a laser printer, especially with LaserWriters, which do not have a status panel (many other laser printers do have a status panel).

- With printing problems, one of the first things you should do is find out how many users are affected. This will keep you from wasting time checking a workstation's connections and networking software when the problem is actually with the printer or print server. Another way to approach this is to see if the workstation's network connection is still working. Is the file server still available? If it is, then the problem is not likely to be related to the connection.

The Fault Point Chain—Scenario Five

- The Macintosh AppleTalk and EtherTalk software.

- The Mac's connection to the network, including NIC and connections.

- The bridge from the print server to the LocalTalk printer.

- The printer.

In this case, the queue and print server are not part of the fault chain, because the Macintoshes were printing directly to the LaserWriter rather than to the queue. If NetWare for Macintosh had been set up so that only the queue was available in the Chooser, and the printer itself hidden, then it would have been necessary to include the queue and printer server in the troubleshooting process, as it would have been if a similar problem had occurred with PCs.

Disasters: Before and After

A Pound of Prevention

A S ADMINISTRATOR OF EVEN A SMALL NETWORK, you can spend most of your time putting out fires—reacting to problems rather than planning for them. Prevention is a difficult area for most administrators. The time and expense involved are difficult to justify, because if you do it correctly, the problems you prevent will never show up; and it can be hard to convince your supervisors to spend money on something that might never occur.

Some preventive measures are becoming easier to justify. For example, when PC-based networks first began cropping up, backup systems were not always included as a matter of course. Now, it would (or at least should) be highly unusual to see more than three or four PCs networked without some type of backup system in place. UPSs (uninterruptible power supplies) are becoming equally common, at least on servers.

Other types of prevention and preventive maintenance will be more difficult to justify. One plan of attack is to begin small and document the results. The difference between a network with no downtime during business hours in the course of a year and one in which several failures interrupt business for hours or even days is not hard to quantify. If you can improve your uptime by some quantifiable amount, and show where other preventive measures would have reduced or eliminated downtime, you will have less trouble justifying future requests.

Another area to look at is tracking the growth of your LAN, and planning for the future. It may seem that the new high-powered server you just installed should last for a good while, but suppose the department has also grown by 20 workstations, and that the average load per workstation has increased by a factor of four as users begin to be accustomed to their new PCs. Tracking this sort of growth will enable you to justify and install upgrades or additional equipment as necessary to meet the growing needs of your users.

Finally, you should plan for problems beyond the scope of a disk drive crash or lost files disasters. If you don't plan for disaster, and it occurs, it isn't just a question of interruption of business. Of all the businesses whose networks were struck by disasters such as floods, thefts, lightning, earthquakes, or viruses wiping out their data, most of those that had disaster-recovery plans are still in business. More than 90 percent of those who didn't have plans were out of business within two years.

This chapter will cover the following topics:

- Backup systems

- Protection against power failures

- Equipment quality

- Preventive maintenance and other precautions

- Fault tolerance

- Network plans and logs

- Network baselining

- User training

- Virus protection

- Security measures

- Disaster recovery—in advance

Managing Backup Systems

E VERY NETWORK that does more than allow printer sharing should have a backup system. You will need backups. Eventually, any LAN administrator who doesn't have a verified backup plan working will regret it. Even mirroring disks is not a substitute for a good backup procedure.

Backups are not only for restoring a drive that breaks. You'll find that users will occasionally delete files that are still needed. If a server's drive is close to full, the NetWare SALVAGE utility, or similar utilities from other vendors, may not be able to recover a deleted file, depending on how long it's been since the file was deleted.

Every server, no matter how small or how little data it stores, should be backed up. Backup drives are available in a price range from a couple of hundred dollars to many thousands. Even a server being used solely as a print server, with little or no data on it, should be backed up. For one thing, there are probably also mail directories on the server that users would be very unhappy about losing; and for another, restoring from an inexpensive 60 MB tape is a lot faster than reinstalling NetWare from scratch.

If you don't have backups of your server, you will wish you had. Eventually, you will need a backup, either to restore the server after a disaster, or to recover files that a user has inadvertently deleted. Fast, reliable, and convenient backups are available in capacities from 20 MB to 10 GB and more, and in price ranges from a few hundred dollars to many thousands. There is no excuse for not having backups. The cost is much less than the cost of reconstructing the data on even a small hard disk.

Back up your server. Back up your server. Back up your server. This can't be stressed enough. There is nothing more important to surviving a disaster than having backups. Once you have them, test them.

Be sure of the integrity of your backups. Many backup programs do not adequately warn you if a backup didn't completely finish, or if there were bad blocks on your tape. At a minimum, you should back up your entire system and then restore at least some of the files to test the backup when you install the server and backup device, and also whenever you make major changes in the server, such as upgrades. Depending on the nature of the data on your server, you may need to do full backups every night, or incremental backups may fill your needs.

Thanks to the growing awareness that backups are not a luxury but a necessity, there are numerous systems available from many manufacturers. There are several varieties, including ½-inch tape in several cassettes, 8mm and 4mm (DAT), and even systems that use video cassettes. Usually, only a few companies make the actual mechanisms, which are then packaged with different software and sold under brand names. The software is a major part of the difference between different brands, and much more important than a slight difference in speed or transfer rate.

Evaluating Backup Systems

The PC and LAN magazines probably publish half a dozen backup-unit evaluations a year. Read the latest articles to gain an idea of what's available. You will usually also learn which units to avoid, and why, and which variety of tape is currently considered the best.

When evaluating a backup system, there are a number of factors to consider:

- Capacity

- Speed

- Software

- Cost of the media

- Cost of the unit

- Reliability of the drive

- Operating systems supported

- Support from the manufacturer

- NDS backups (for NetWare 4.*x*)

- Support for other file systems

These factors are described in the following sections.

Backup System Capacity

What is the capacity of the tape drive? It should be enough to support your current configuration, and at least double your current disk drive capacity. Don't buy a 1 GB tape system if you have a 1 GB hard drive—in a year you will probably have 4 GB of hard disk space. Besides, the difference in price between a 1 GB tape drive and an 8 GB tape drive is relatively small.

If your backup capacity is limited, back up data first, applications second. Applications, and the NetWare directories, which can be reinstalled and usually don't change after installation, can be backed up once in a while, when new versions are installed. Data, on the other hand, should be backed up regularly—nightly if possible. If backup capacity is an issue, nightly incremental backups of data are better than weekly full backups.

Backup System Speed

Speed is an issue not because you will be sitting and watching the backup (the software should allow unattended backups), but because you need to schedule the backup for a time of day when nobody will be using the network, and that time may be limited.

If you designate 2:00 AM to 6:00 AM as the time when no one will be using the system, your tape drive should be able to back up your system in less than four hours. You can estimate this by dividing the number of megabytes on the server by the rated speed of the tape drive (for example, 500 MB, divided by 10 MB/minute, equals 50 minutes).

Backup Software

The most important thing to evaluate in choosing a tape drive is the software provided with it. This may range from no software at all to a versatile suite of programs that will not only do your backups at 2:00 AM for you, but verify the tape and inform you of any errors.

This software may seem expensive, and it can cost a good bit more than the tape drive. Some versions cost more depending on how many clients your version of NetWare supports. But keep in mind that if the software provides consistent, reliable backups and works with everything on your network, it's worth the expense—how much is your data worth?

Cost of the Backup Media

The cost of the media your backup system uses will be more important in the long run than the cost of the drive. If you use 20 tapes for your incremental backups, and 2 tapes a month for full backups that are then stored off site, you will use about 50 tapes a year. In two years, this expense could be more than the cost of the drive.

In some cases, lower-cost alternatives exist. For example, in an 8 mm tape drive, you can use 8 mm video tape instead of data-certified tapes, reducing your costs by about half. However, unless your software verifies the backup every time it is made, and is capable of bypassing a bad block on the tape, you may get backups that can't be restored from and not know this until you need to restore that backup. The few hundred dollars a year you save aren't worth it if you can't restore from the tapes.

Cost of the Backup Unit

Tape backup units range in price from a couple of hundred dollars for an 800 MB unit to thousands of dollars for a unit that will do a month's worth of unattended backups on a multi-gigabyte system. Within any standard (such as 4 mm DAT), the mechanisms are often similar or the same. What you'll pay for is the software and support. Determine what capacity you need, double it, and then buy the best software you can afford. Remember, your server's disk contains hundreds or thousands of hours of work, at many dollars an hour. Don't skimp on the backup system.

Backup System Reliability

It does no good to have an extensive backup system in place, and then discover that the tape drive has failed or that the software didn't inform you that the backup tapes had bad blocks and your backups can't be used. Read the magazines for impressions of the internal mechanisms and the various companies that package them. Before you buy a unit, you might also want to ask about it on CompuServe, the NetWare news group on the Internet, or at your local CNEPA chapter or Novell user group meeting.

Make sure to test whatever backup system you have in place. After the hard disk has disintegrated is no time to discover that those backup tapes you've been making for the last year can only produce an "Error reading from tape" message.

Backup System Support

Support for your backup system can be difficult to evaluate in advance, except by learning what experiences others have had with the company. Ask the company for names of users in your area. Read the reviews to see if the reviewers tried to access the tech support or had hardware or setup problems. Check the forums on CompuServe or your local user group meetings.

You might also try placing a test call to the backup system manufacturer's support line, to see how easy or difficult it may be to get help when you actually need it, and to get first-hand experience of the support process for the device.

NDS Backups

If you are running NetWare 4.*x*, your backup software should be able to back up and restore the NetWare Directory Services database. This can be critical, because if your Directory database is corrupted, not merely the one server, but all services on your entire network could be inaccessible.

Backups for Other File Systems

If you have clients other than DOS/Windows 3.*x*, you will need to consider the backup software's support for other name spaces. This includes Windows 95 and OS/2, Macintosh, and NFS (UNIX) systems, which support longer file names and have different permission structures than DOS. For example, although NetWare supports the name spaces on the server's hard disks, if the backup software doesn't support them, when you restore files, you'll get file names truncated to DOS's standard eight-character plus three-character extension.

Developing a Backup Plan

Your backup strategy will depend on your users' needs. There are many possible strategies, ranging from a full backup of all files daily to an incremental backup that only adds files that have changed since the last backup. Each strategy has advantages and disadvantages. A daily full backup provides the maximum possible level of recoverability, but uses a very large number of tapes; the incremental systems use fewer tapes, but take more effort to recover complete file systems.

If you don't want to do a full backup nightly, I recommend that you do an incremental backup nightly, and a full backup either weekly or monthly. The full backups should be stored in a secure area on site or off site, for at least a year. This gives you insurance against accidentally deleted files that aren't noticed for a while, as well as against a virus infecting your recent backups.

If you are using incremental backups, be sure that you know the order in which the tapes were made. You will usually restore first from the last full backup, and then from each incremental tape. If you get one of the incremental tapes out of order, you can overwrite recent files with older versions. Label the tapes clearly, both on the case and the tape cartridge itself. It is a very good idea to have your backup schedule documented and posted. This can ease the headache if a problem occurs when you are off site. Do you want to fly back a week early from your first vacation in two years to restore some data? Print a schedule that shows the rotation of the numbered incremental tapes, and what dates they will be used.

You may also wish to use an off-site storage service for some or all of your backups. This is a typical part of most disaster-recovery plans. It allows a business to restore working files to new servers after fire, earthquake, theft, or other disasters that could affect any backups stored near the original server.

Backing Up Workstation Data

I strongly recommend that you confine the data on workstations to the operating system and applications. Instruct your users to store their data on the file server. This will ensure that the data is included in the regularly scheduled backups. In almost every case, if the application is on the local drive and the data is on the server, users will not notice any degradation in performance.

Unfortunately, with most operating systems, there is no way to prevent the user from storing data on the local hard drive (UNIX is a notable exception). The only way to deal with this problem is education and continuing reminders.

If your users absolutely must store data on their workstations, you might want to install a backup tape device in each workstation, and automatically back up each machine every night. Internal tape units for PCs are quite inexpensive.

There are several other solutions to the problem of backing up workstations. You can create a backup volume on a server, and create batch files that log in and copy everything on the workstation hard drive to that area. For example, if you have 20 users on your network, each with a hard disk of 400 MB, this system would back up every workstation once every 20 days and use 400 MB of disk space on the server. Each day's backup can be deleted from the server after the volume has been backed up to tape, to make room for the next workstation backup.

Another approach is to get a small portable tape drive that attaches to a workstation's parallel port (or a Mac's SCSI port). You can then back up each workstation in rotation with this device. If, as suggested, the workstation has only the operating system and applications, this sort of backup will be necessary only when a system is first configured, and then when significant changes have been made, such as the installation or upgrading of applications or the operating system.

There is also software available that allows workstations to back up to a networked tape drive. This system uses a TSR program that runs on each workstation and sends the files to be backed up to a network backup server. This is a fairly inexpensive way to back up workstations, but there are a couple of caveats: all workstations must be left on, and you need to buy and set up a network backup server. Also, if you back up all the data on each workstation, it can take quite a long time. If you back up only specified directories, anything the user puts anywhere else won't be backed up. Some software will let you back up everything except specified directories.

Managing Power Protection

GIVEN THE NUMBER OF PROBLEMS that can follow power loss or fluctuation, a good UPS, SPS (standby power supply), or at least a surge protector is a very cheap investment. It doesn't take a lightning storm to damage computer equipment; the spikes caused by some appliances being turned on or off, static discharges from a variety of sources (including users), and older power company equipment may cause enough variation in power to damage systems.

Evaluating Power Protection Systems

There are several levels of protection against faulty power. The first level is a surge protector, which will screen out harmful over-voltages, surges, and spikes. It will not protect your system if the power goes off. The second level of protection is an SPS. It switches to a battery-powered power supply if it detects problems with your power. It will provide protection against brownouts and power outages. The third level of protection is a UPS. This type of protection is the ultimate—your computer is always powered by the battery-powered power supply, which is constantly being recharged by your normal AC power. This means that there is no direct connection between your power line and the computer. There is also no switchover time as with an SPS.

There are several items to check before buying power protection:

- Look at the manufacturer's warranty. Some manufacturers will replace any equipment damaged by power variations while connected to their system.

- Check carefully whether a battery-powered unit is an SPS or a true UPS. UPSs tend to be a little more expensive, although both types are much less expensive than they were a few years ago.

- See if the power supplied from the battery is true sine wave. Some units simulate sine wave power, which can provide slightly different results that very sensitive equipment might not like.

Both the simulated sine wave power supplies and SPS devices have come a long way in the last few years. It is now difficult to say that a UPS is distinctly better than an SPS, or that true sine wave is better than simulated. However, with prices on even the best units dropping as they are, UPSs, true sine wave power supplies, and the premium surge protection systems are the best bets. See the latest reviews in your favorite PC and LAN magazines.

Another issue for the server is the UPS interface. Most UPS and SPS devices provide a serial connection or a card for the server that will allow the server to detect a power outage and shut down properly if necessary before the battery power runs down. This prevents disk corruption due to powering off the server without taking it down first. This type of interface is highly recommended for server UPS systems.

A reasonable balance of protection and cost is to put a surge protector on every computer and a UPS on each server. Modems and fax machines should also be protected. Phone lines can also transmit potentially harmful variations in current, and surge protectors with phone line filtering capability are available. If cost is not a large factor, or if some workstations are mission-critical, consider using UPSs on workstations as well.

Evaluating System Power Requirements

Evaluating the power requirements of your computer system is fairly simple. Look on the power supply of each unit that will be attached (system unit, monitor, external disk drive, and so on). Each power supply should have a rated capacity in amps. Usual figures are in the neighborhood of 5 to 7 amps for the CPU, 1.5 to 2 for small monitors, 5 to 10 for large monitors, 2 for external hard disks, and the like. If the total is 10, multiply that by the voltage of your system (110 in the U.S.). The total figure, 1100, is the maximum number of volt-amps (VA) your system can use.

For a workstation with a small (14-inch) monochrome monitor, a 400 VA power supply will probably provide 10 to 20 minutes of backup. For a workstation with a large screen monitor, you might need 600 to 800 VA. A server with a couple of external hard drive subsystems should probably have 800 to 1200 VA for a reasonably long duration if the power goes off.

The Quality of Your Equipment

THE DIFFERENCE IN PRICE between an inexpensive clone server and a high-performance, brand-name server can be double or more. However, eight hours of downtime for a department of 20 users can cause a loss of more money than what you saved on a lower-cost server—not counting the possibility of deadlines missed, extra costs to rush jobs through, overtime, repairs to the downed equipment, and so on.

This is not to say that even the most expensive equipment will not break down occasionally, but it should be less likely to do so. The service providers should be more responsive as well, and it's easier to find replacement parts for brand-name equipment. But keep in mind that some major brands tend to use proprietary parts, which can mean that replacements can be obtained only from the original vendor, at rather high prices.

Many computer manufacturers and retailers are sensitive to the special requirements of servers. In addition to bigger PCs with extra-high-speed interfaces and more drive slots, they may offer both added features to make their equipment more reliable and service programs that guarantee repair or replacement of defective parts within a matter of hours. The added features may include redundant power supplies or special bus slots that allow swapping cards in and out with the PC still running.

Again, even the most expensive, best-rated equipment can break down. In the case of mission-critical equipment, it's not a bad idea to have a replacement machine, fully configured, ready to replace an existing machine if necessary. The investment can readily be recouped by avoiding the delay necessary to buy new equipment if the existing setup goes down, especially in cases where equipment orders must be processed by another part of the company, such as a purchasing department. In a large WAN, having a standard server configuration can make it much easier to provide parts, and of course will also make it easier for the corporate MIS department to support the platform. Fault tolerance systems provide another way to protect your server, as discussed later in this chapter.

Preventive Maintenance and Other Precautions

REGULAR MAINTENANCE IS OFTEN OMITTED, either because it isn't seen as a high enough priority to justify the time spent or simply because it can be a chore. However, preventive maintenance can save the administrator considerable trouble. It is much easier to fix something before it becomes a problem than to wait until it interferes with a user's work, requires the administrator's time for emergency repairs, and costs money to replace parts that might have lasted much longer with good maintenance.

Getting Rid of Dust and Other Contaminants

It is impossible to prevent dust from getting into equipment, and too much dust may have unfortunate consequences. To minimize dust, make sure that slot covers are replaced if cards are removed from a PC, and that the case is completely closed. This can also prevent bugs in the machinery—literally! Insects of many types and even mice have been known to take up lodgings inside computers, often with very strange results. In commercial settings, the normal dust can have a fairly high metallic content, and too thick an accumulation can cause electrical shorts. It can also interfere with ventilation, causing overheating and shortening the life of equipment as well as causing failures. Regular vacuuming and adequate ventilation can extend the life of equipment.

Keyboards are also susceptible to dust and many other forms of contamination, from food to eraser shavings. Again, regular vacuuming is a simple way to prevent failures. Keeping monitor screens clean may not increase the life of the monitor, but it will definitely reduce eyestrain among users. The static charge that normally builds up on most monitors collects dust and other airborne particles like a magnet. Mouse devices will also last longer and function better if they are cleaned regularly.

Checking Connections

There are no perfect connections. It is a good idea to schedule some time every six months or so to check all the computers on a LAN for loose connections. Take a look at the power cords, monitor, network, serial, and parallel cables and the cards.

A power cord that is loose in the receptacle in the power supply can cause arcing, which can not only cause the eventual failure of the power supply, but can generate interference with the electronics in the PC. Likewise, a network connection that is not fully seated may not simply fail, but may produce intermittent problems that are difficult to trace. Make sure that all fasteners are screwed down snugly and that everything is seated properly. At the very least, check all the connections whenever you have occasion to work on a PC.

Taking Anti-Static Precautions

Walking across a carpeted room can build up a 50,000 volt charge in your body. Discharging this voltage into electronic equipment designed to deal with a maximum of 12 volts can destroy it. Newer electronics, with their tighter tolerances and lower power requirements, are even more susceptible to static than older equipment. An anti-static mat and professional-quality grounding strap are quite inexpensive—some hardware maintenance courses include a set as part of the cost of the course. In any case, the investment is much less than almost any circuit board.

Not following anti-static precautions may not result in dead equipment but can still incur high costs. Static can cause cumulative, nonfatal damage that has the effect of drastically shortening the life of electronics.

You can kill electronic parts by holding them in your hand and walking across a carpet floor. Be sure that the parts are protected in an anti-static bag, or that you are grounded before touching them.

When working on a PC, you should always have a grounding strap attached to a good ground before you open the PC. That said, however, you can ensure generally adequate protection of the PC's components by leaving it plugged in and touching the power supply or frame before handling any components. This field expedient is much better than nothing.

If you remove parts from a PC, you should always transport them in a static-safe bag. Just walking across a room holding a PC board could damage the board. Be sure the bag is an anti-static bag (the silvery mylar type) rather than a plain plastic bag—some plastic bags can generate enough static to damage the cards by themselves. Save the anti-static bags that most cards come in and reuse them when you need to transport parts.

Following Manufacturer's Directions

Another type of precaution you should take is to follow the manufacturer's directions when dealing with hardware or software. For example, most programs should be exited before the workstation is turned off. This is also true of most operating systems these days—Windows 95, OS/2, the Macintosh OS, most varieties of UNIX, and, of course NetWare, should all be shut down before powering off the system.

Make sure that an SVGA monitor and the graphics card it's attached to both support the same resolutions; you can damage a monitor by trying to run it at too high a refresh rate or resolution.

If you're dealing with a Macintosh, it is recommended that you wait five minutes after it has been turned off before removing or adding cards.

Maintaining a Return Path

Another precaution that takes a little extra trouble, but can make the administrator's life much easier, is to provide a simple return path to the old version of anything being changed or upgraded. Rename AUTOEXEC.BAT files to AUTOEXEC.OLD, and save old versions of applications, drivers, and so on.

Under Windows 95, export the registry to a text file. If the registry and its backup copy both become corrupted (an unfortunately common occurrence), you can import the text file back into the registry and reboot. Use the Registry Editor (REGEDIT.EXE) to export the registry. Be sure to export the entire registry, not just one branch.

It's much easier to make sure that you have a good copy of a setup that works than to try to re-create a configuration from memory or track down and reload an application, its updates, new version of printer drivers, and the like, all of which may be in different locations.

Similarly, when upgrading hardware, don't rush to throw the old equipment out. For example, if a new video card fails, it's much better to be able to get a workstation running again with a monochrome monitor and have at least partial functionality than to rush out and buy another VGA card or waiting for the purchasing department to buy one and forward it to you.

Maintaining Fault Tolerance

N THE OLD DAYS OF MAINFRAME AND TERMINALS, everything had a backup. There was a generator that took over if power failed, and most parts that might fail in the mainframe had a backup part that took over without interrupting service. As PC networks have begun to be used for the same sorts of things that mainframes were used for—namely, applications in which a few hours without service could literally ruin a company—manufacturers have begun to provide the same sorts of redundancy and fault tolerance. Novell has led the way in providing System Fault Tolerance (SFT) as a part of NetWare. Chapter 2, which covers troubleshooting servers, describes in detail the SFT levels and how they work. Here is a brief review of SFT functions and their benefits.

The first level of SFT provides for protection from disk drive failure in several ways. First, it performs read-after-write verification. Data written to disk is read immediately and compared with the data still in memory. If there is a difference, the block on the disk that was written to is marked as bad. The Hot Fix Redirection area is that part of the disk that is used to provide substitute blocks for any blocks on the disk that fail. If your Hot Fix Redirection area starts getting full, it is a sign that the disk is failing.

Next, SFT allows duplexed and mirrored drives. With both techniques, each logical drive is actually two physical drives—data written to a drive is actually written to two different mirrored drives. This has two benefits: it is a highly effective precaution against drive failure, and it effectively reduces the access time of any physical drive by 50 percent. Technically, the difference between these methods is that a mirrored drive may have two drives connected to the same controller and power supply; a duplexed drive has separate power supplies and controllers, so that no one failure will result in a loss of data or access to data.

Mirroring doubles the cost of data storage, but in mission-critical areas, it can prevent a much more costly loss of time, productivity, and data. If a drive fails in a mirrored system, the users don't even notice. The administrator is notified and can replace the defective drive when it won't disrupt the network.

The next level, SFT III, provides complete protection against any failure of any component in a server—the whole server is duplicated. All functions of the main server are duplicated on the mirror server. If anything happens to the first server, the second server takes over and service is not interrupted. The servers can even monitor each other for hardware problems and take over if a fault is causing a slowdown in networking capability.

The cost involved will be double that of a single server, but in mission-critical circumstances, this technique will ensure that no single equipment failure can bring down the network. Moreover, because the two servers don't need to be right next to each other, it can also provide insurance against theft, fire, or other catastrophes that can destroy all networking capability.

In addition to the SFT III package offered by Novell, there are other alternatives offered by other vendors. These may offer advantages such as not requiring the high-performance (expensive) connections between servers that SFT III does, or not requiring that both servers be identically configured. As with other network components, your best sources of information about the other fault-tolerance system products are magazine reviews, online sources, and user groups. See Appendix A for more information about resources.

Keeping Network Plans and Logs

K EEP A RECORD of existing configurations. This not only makes it easier to plan upgrades and determine possible causes without opening PCs, it provides a place to return to if an upgrade or new configuration doesn't work. If you include serial numbers in your log, it will make dealing with most technical support departments much easier. Instead of needing to trot down the aisle, open a PC, and pull a card to get the serial number, you will have it on record, easily accessible when calling tech support.

Documenting the Network

The level of documentation that you have for your network will directly affect the time it takes to recover from a disaster. Ideally, you should document all of the following:

- Each server and workstation's hardware configuration. This includes processor, memory, floppy and hard disk types, installed cards and their settings, and any other hardware additions.

- The software configuration of each workstation. This includes the operating system version; printouts and/or backup copies of configuration files such as AUTOEXEC.BAT, CONFIG.SYS, SHELL.CFG, WIN.INI, and SYSTEM.INI; a printout of the directory structure; a list of applications, including version, license number (if applicable), and any other specialized software such as device drivers.

- The software configuration for the server. You do have printouts of your AUTOEXEC.NCF and STARTUP.NCF files, don't you? How long would it take you to re-create them if they were lost? Even if you have good backups, you may wish you had a map of the directory structure on all volumes of your server, and copies of NET$OS.EXE or SERVER.EXE, the other .DSK and .LAN drivers necessary to boot the server, and any other configuration files or drivers stored in the DOS partition of the boot drive.

- Maps of the physical and the logical structure of your LAN. The physical map will help you with problems in the cabling plant, and the logical map will help you to conceptually isolate the fault points involved in any particular problem.

- The backup plan. What tapes are used in what rotation? How often are full backups made, and where are they stored? Remember, your assistant might be the one guessing which tape to restore from.

- Procedures to follow in case you aren't there. What do the users do if a print server hangs the day after you leave for a two-week training seminar? (You may also need a quick reminder yourself if it's something you haven't dealt with for a while.)

After backups, the next most important thing you can do to survive a disaster is to document everything, and keep a copy of the documentation and backups off site.

All this information can be collected manually, and should be, if there's no other alternative. Appendix C has forms that you can use to collect the data. However, there are programs that will do all the data collection for you, nicely format the reports, and update the information automatically each time a workstation is logged onto the network. See Appendix B for information about some of the products available.

Using a network analyzer or a statistics program such as FCONSOLE or MONITOR to get an idea of normal traffic on your network will make it much easier to isolate problems caused by abnormal traffic. See the next section for information about baselining your network.

Logging Network Events

Keeping a log or diary of changes to the LAN, as well as problems that have come up and the solutions, will also save you a good deal of time. Re-creating a solution that took 20 hours of work to discover the first time doesn't make sense, especially when a few minutes spent logging the problem and solution can prevent the necessity.

A log can also be useful in other ways. It can allow you to establish trends with problem equipment, situations, or users. It is much easier to justify a more reliable (and more expensive) server if you have documented how many times the current model has failed in the last year. A log can also provide documentation of how you spend your time. Many managers want regular status reports; a well-kept log can provide the basis for your reports, or may even be copied and pasted into a template status report. Even if a regular status report is not required, a log can make justifying a promotion or getting additional personnel much easier.

Baselining Your Network

BASELINE INFORMATION ABOUT YOUR NETWORK can be invaluable when odd things begin happening. Depending on the level of resources available to you, baselining your network could mean anything from knowing how often collisions show on a transceiver to maintaining a complete network traffic history automatically created and updated by a sophisticated network analysis package. Such a package can not only show network traffic patterns over an extended period of time, but can be set to warn you if limits are exceeded or if any of dozens of types of events occur.

Baselining means knowing how your network should be performing. You should know what your average server utilization is, what the average number of packets sent and received by your server is, as well as the usual number of bad packets of each type. You should be able to tell if any part of your network changes dramatically, or if there is a trend upwards or downwards in any characteristic. The number of characteristics you will be able to monitor will depend on the software you have to monitor your network with.

Baselining is also essential to being prepared for future growth. Without some idea of how much traffic is increasing over time on your network, you won't be able to spot approaching overloads of servers or LAN segments until it is too late and LAN performance has suffered.

Monitoring the Server

You should use the tools built into NetWare to become aware of the normal state of your network. Keep records of at least the average server utilization and number of packets received. Following the history of certain items can let you know when it's time to add more memory to your server or if a hard disk is beginning to fail.

As explained in Chapter 2, when an existing server begins having problems servicing users, the most common reason is memory. Often, the initial amount of RAM in the server and the settings for memory allocation seem sufficient but prove otherwise after a period of growth or as users begin to really make use of the network. The second biggest problem of this nature is disk space. Users will expand their disk usage to fill any possible amount of disk space. You can either monitor them and ask heavy users to cut back or resolve to allow for regular increases in the size of your server's disk space.

NetWare uses as much memory as it can get for cache buffers. When NetWare receives a request for information on one of its disks, it copies the whole block into memory. Then, every time it receives a request for that data, it reads from memory rather than from the disk. This speeds access to the data by many thousands of times. As new disk requests come in, the oldest requests are flushed from memory to make room for the new ones. Thus, the larger the pool of memory allocated for cache buffers, the more likely that a disk request can be serviced from memory, rather than from the disk. Any memory not necessary for other services is used for cache buffers. Adding RAM for caching is often the cheapest improvement you can make in your server.

Monitoring a NetWare 2.x Server

To monitor memory usage on a NetWare 2.x server, use FCONSOLE to check the Disk Request Serviced From Cache line in the File Server Statistics Summary, and Dynamic Memory Pool Statistics Peak Usage. If less than 93 percent or so of the disk requests are being serviced from disk instead of memory, or if the peak usage is at or near the maximum, add more memory. You should be able to watch these numbers approach the recommended maximum as network utilization increases.

Also check the I/O Error Count under Hot Fix with FCONSOLE. If the error count is not zero, the hard disk is experiencing failures. You should monitor it carefully. One failure may not indicate a hard disk about to fail catastrophically, but a series of errors in a short period, or a small but steady number of errors over time, indicate that the drive should be completely backed up and then replaced as soon as possible.

Monitoring a NetWare 3.x Server

NetWare 3.*x* is capable of dynamically reallocating memory. It will use all available memory not being used for other things (such as NLMs) for disk cache buffers. Therefore, MONITOR's best indicator of your total memory utilization is the Available Cache Buffers line. The following statistics will help you monitor the performance of your server.

AVAILABLE CACHE BUFFERS If the total number of available cache buffers gets too low, it's a signal that almost all the server's memory is in use. Also, the number of disk requests that must be read from disk (rather than from the cache buffers) in memory will increase, slowing the performance of the server. If the available cache buffers number drops below 20 percent, you could experience data loss under some circumstances. This would mean that in a server with 16 MB of RAM, only 3 MB would be available for cache buffers. You should start planning to increase memory if the Available Cache Buffers percentage drops below 50.

PERCENTAGE OF UTILIZATION This statistic shows how much of the total processing power of the CPU is in use. It thus gives you a basic indication of the load on the server. If this number is above 75 percent or so on a regular basis, you should consider upgrading to a faster processor.

ALLOC SHORT TERM MEMORY The default size of the pool of Alloc Short Term Memory is 2 MB. As the amount in use gets close to 2 MB, you should increase the size of the pool with the SET command. Also, you should monitor the resource tags for this memory pool. If you see a module (usually an NLM) using an ever-increasing amount of memory, it's likely there's a problem with that NLM. If unloading and reloading the NLM doesn't fix the problem, see if there's an update or bug fix for the NLM.

SERVICE PROCESSES The number of service processes indicates outstanding read requests. If an application issues a read request to the server and the disk can't be accessed immediately, a service process is created that will fulfill the read request as soon as possible. If there aren't enough cache buffers, the number of service requests will go up, since more requests will need to be serviced from the slower disk instead of memory. Furthermore, the disk can be accessed by only one request at a time, whereas more than one cache buffer can be accessed at once.

If you have enough memory and are still getting service processes, you have a problem either with disk I/O or with packet receive buffers. You might consider upgrading to an EISA or PCI system and bus-mastering controllers for the hard disks, a faster CPU, or spreading disk usage out by using multiple hard disk adapters or spanning volumes across multiple disks.

PACKET RECEIVE BUFFERS Packet receive buffers hold packets from workstations until the server can process them and initiate service requests. The default number of buffers is 100. If the number of allocated buffers gets close to 100, increase the number of buffers with this command in STARTUP.NCF:

```
SET PACKET RECEIVE BUFFERS=xx
```

If you have a large number of packet receive buffers allocated (it could be up to one for every ISA workstation attached to the server or up to 41 per EISA workstation), the requests to the server from the workstations aren't being serviced fast enough.

You can address this problem by increasing the number of service processes, and by increasing disk I/O, either with faster controllers and disks or by increasing the memory available for cache buffering.

DISK-FULL EARLY WARNING You can have NetWare warn you if the available disk space on any volume drops too low by setting the Volume Low Warning Threshold and the Volume Low Warning Reset Threshold. These parameters are specified with the SET command or in STARTUP.NCF. Specify the number of blocks. The default is 256 blocks; with 4 KB blocks, the default will warn you when the available space drops below 1 MB. You may want to set this to a larger number—1 MB of space isn't much any more.

Monitoring a NetWare 4.x Server

NetWare 4.x adds a number of new tools for monitoring the server. In general, the items listed for NetWare 3.x apply to 4.x as well. In addition, NetWare 4.x allows you to monitor the percentage of disk requests that are serviced from cache buffers rather than from the disk. It can also show you the processes currently running and how much of the available processing power they are using, and it can provide early warnings in the event of insufficient memory for cache buffers or full disks. The following are some NetWare 4.*x* settings to monitor.

CACHE BUFFER HITS Rather than simply telling you what percentage of the total server memory is available for cache buffers, NetWare 4.*x* will allow you to specifically monitor the percentage of disk requests that have been serviced from memory instead of from disk. MONITOR displays the Percentage of Long Term Cache Hits. Keeping the percentage above 90 will result in optimum performance.

PROCESSOR UTILIZATION NetWare 3.*x* displays processor utilization in its main MONITOR display. In addition to this, NetWare 4.*x* has a new menu item in MONITOR, Processor Utilization, that will allow you to track the processes and interrupts (I/O—both disk and LAN cards) that are running on the server and how much of the available processing power they are using.

CACHE BUFFER EARLY WARNING You can use SERVMAN to set NetWare 4.*x* to warn you if the number of available cache buffers drops too low. To do so, set the Minimum File Cache Buffer Report Threshold option to 100. This parameter is set in the File Caching submenu of the Console Set Commands menu. It can also be set directly in the STARTUP.NCF file.

DISK-FULL EARLY WARNING You can use SERVMAN to set NetWare 4.*x* to warn you if the available disk space on any volume drops too low by setting the Volume Low Warning Threshold and the Volume Low Warning Reset Threshold options. These parameters are set in the File System submenu of the Console Set Commands menu. They can also be set directly in STARTUP.NCF. Specify the number of blocks. The default is 256 blocks; with 4 KB blocks, this setting will warn you when the available space drops below 1 MB. You may want to set this to a larger amount, since 1 MB of space isn't much any more.

Using Utilities for Baseline Information

Baselining your network can be done with FCONSOLE or MONITOR, although it isn't easy. There are many utilities that will perform monitoring of your network and server. These range from freeware and shareware products available on CompuServe to $20,000+ network monitoring systems that run on UNIX workstations and will provide full documentation and tracking of every element of a complex, company-wide WAN.

The range and scope of utilities available is enormous. You may not need a high-end system that will provide a complete map of your network, an inventory of the software on every workstation on that network (including operating system and network driver version), and immediate warnings if any of hundreds of problems occur. You may also not have the thousands of dollars in your budget. On the other hand, the administrator of even a small LAN might find it hard to resist a utility that will record and print the configuration of your server, including all the bindery or NDS information, printer setups, and so on, especially if it's free.

The best sources for discovering and evaluating these utilities are the LAN magazines, your local user groups, and the online services. You can download many utilities (freeware and shareware) from CompuServe or Novell's Web page.

As always, if you find a shareware utility useful, please send a check to the programmer. If the program saves you hours of work, the small fee is more than justified. Besides making you feel good, it will help finance updates and bug fixes on the utility and will increase your chances of receiving updates.

Baselining and documentation of your network can be a chore, but it could save your hide in a crisis. Find out what utilities are available (see Appendices A and B) and use them, or record your configurations manually with the forms in Appendix C. Use NetWare's built-in utilities and simple devices like the PC transceiver's collision light. Whatever system you use, get a feel for what's normal and what things should look like, *before* something goes wrong.

Training the Users

MUCH OF YOUR TIME as an administrator will probably be used to support users. Most of the problems your users have will not be related to hardware or software failure, but to failures in understanding. From the user who can't find the "Any" key ("Press any key to continue") to the one whose document won't print because there's no paper in the printer, these people have problems that they could probably solve themselves with a bit of encouragement and a little training.

There are several methods you can use to train your users and to encourage them to acquire training on their own, without being perceived as unresponsive or condescending. For example, try to put a little time between a user's request for help and your response. Don't delay obviously, just finish what you're working on first. Not only does this improve your chances of completing your regular tasks, but it increases the chances that your help won't be needed; users left to themselves for a while will sometimes be able to solve the problem on their own. If your users get accustomed to your leading them by the hand through every unfamiliar process (and some familiar ones), they will always expect these things of you. As a result, you will spend more and more time in these tasks instead of administering your network, let alone planning for the coming requirements for your organization.

Without making users feel stupid, you can also encourage them to read the manual. Rather than jumping up from the dead PC you're working on and showing someone how to print from within his application, tell him you can't get away right now, but the information he needs is in the manual.

The biggest hurdle you may face in training your users and getting them to be more self-sufficient will be in obtaining support from management. The best approach to take with your supervisor is to document how you spend your time, what support requests you receive, and your proposed future projects. Let your bosses tell you that they would rather have you working on optimizing network performance than reading an application's manual to a user.

You might wish to institute regular training sessions, either formally or informally, depending on your group's needs and political structure.

Protecting Your Network against Viruses

YOU'VE DOCUMENTED EVERYTHING IN SIGHT, you have a UPS on every workstation, you've just finished mirroring the server with SFT III, and you have a thoroughly tested backup system and the best equipment available. Then, one day, a user brings in a disk from home, loads a program onto their PC, and a short while later, your entire network is out of commission. And, since the virus was replicated in several days of backups, it turns out that you've permanently lost 10 days of work. Sound far-fetched? It has happened. It put a flourishing British investment firm into receivership. Don't take chances. Use a network virus-scanning system on your server, and equip every workstation with scanning software.

There are virus checkers that check for more than 2000 viruses. Some virus scanners run as NLMs, some as TSRs on workstations, and others as stand-alone programs that will scan local and network drives. Many are free or low cost; and all are less expensive than re-creating all your data and reinstalling all your applications, to say nothing of trying to figure out what has been scrambled and what hasn't, and what to do about that.

Keep the scanners updated. With the rate at which nasty people are creating new viruses, a current version of virus software probably won't be providing good protection for more than a month or two.

I had a user bypass the virus-scanning system on a PC and infect my network. Her reason? The virus scanner on her PC in the other building had "passed" the disk, and she knew therefore that the disk couldn't be infected. It turned out that her scanning software was over a year old!

Software developers are constantly making advances in virus detection and prevention. There are NLMs that monitor suspicious activity on the network and new hardware add-ons that should prevent viruses from gaining access to the PC. However, the only constant in virus detection is that the virus creators will eventually figure out a way to bypass anything that comes along on the preventive side. Stay abreast of the technology. See Appendices A and B for some suppliers of virus-detection software and resources for learning more about virus detectors. If your system has already been infected with a virus and you're wondering what to do, see the section about recovering from viruses in Chapter 7.

Elements of Network Security

AS IN THE CASE OF having a virus infect your well-protected network, it does no good to protect your network against every sort of problem you can imagine, only to have a disgruntled employee or hacker reformat your hard disk or worse. There are several elements to security, including physical security, login security, user access rights, and dial-in access.

Physical Security

Your server should be physically secured. This can be difficult, especially if it is used as a print server and has printers directly connected to it. At least, lock the console on NetWare 3.*x* and 4.*x* servers, and use the dedicated mode only for 2.*x* servers and routers. You may want to use the SECURE CONSOLE command on 3.*x* and 4.*x* servers, as well. This prevents the loading of unauthorized NLMs designed to bypass security, and it unloads DOS, so that no one can take the server down and run a DOS program to alter data or bypass security. Once DOS is unloaded, the server must be powered down and back up to reload DOS.

It is still possible to reboot a server from a floppy and load SERVER.EXE or a DOS program designed to bypass NetWare security, then access the server. If this kind of access is a concern, you can disable the floppy drives, or you can install a hardware password, if your server's BIOS permits it. Most PCs allow this.

Another aspect to physical security involves every workstation on your network. A hacker, given access to users' PCs and desks, can often break into their accounts, or even the supervisor account. You can limit the workstations from which the supervisor can log in to yours, and lock it up. But the best idea is to arrange for a guard to walk through the building, and make sure all users monitor unauthorized access to other PCs in their area. Other physical security techniques are anti-theft registration stickers, cables that secure the server to something immobile, and video surveillance.

Password and Login Security

Companies that hire outside consultants to check their security are often astounded at the ease with which the consultants acquire access to their networks. Many users choose passwords that can be guessed easily, or even write the passwords down and "hide" them on the bottoms of drawers and similar obvious places. When you set up a user's account, you can set the password and keep the user from changing it, set a minimum password length, or force password changes at specified intervals and require that new passwords be unique, which prevents users from using the same password they had before.

Other programs will produce passwords that are not in any dictionary, yet are easy to remember. If this kind of security is a serious consideration for you, you might consider using this sort of program to issue passwords, and lock the passwords so the users can't change them.

The supervisor password should be known only to you and a designated backup person as may be required by company policy. If other users need to have access to supervisor privileges, create a supervisor-equivalent account. This prevents someone else from logging in as supervisor and changing the supervisor password. If someone changes the password on the supervisor-equivalent account, you can fix that by logging in as supervisor and changing the password or even deleting the account. Just remember that there's only one supervisor account, and if you're locked out of it, regaining access to the server can be a major problem.

If you do have the misfortune of being locked out of the supervisor account, you can some-times fix it, but it will generally require taking down the server and playing games with the binderies or the NDS database —not for the faint of heart. There is always the possibility that you will need to re-create the binderies or NDS database by hand from your docu-mentation if something goes wrong, too… You do have your bindery or NDS database information documented by now, don't you?

Many users have their login name in their AUTOEXEC.BAT file, as in:

```
LOGIN SERVERNAME\LOGINNAME
```

This means they don't need to type their login name at the login prompt, but it also provides a would-be break-in artist with half of the combination to their workstation. If security is a major consideration for you, you may wish to leave this line out of the AUTOEXEC.BAT file.

Trustee and File Rights

If someone bypasses the physical security and the login security, and is able to log in as a user, you can still limit his or her ability to wreak havoc on the network by setting trustee and file rights correctly. Trustee rights apply to individual users and define their access to directories and files; file rights apply to the files or directories themselves and define all users' access to those files. These two types of rights can aid you in preventing unauthorized modification or deletion of critical files.

For instance, the files in SYS:PUBLIC and SYS:SYSTEM are normally set read-only, so no one can change or delete them. When updating some files in these directories, some administrators simply change all files in the directory to read/write. Failure to change them back to read-only afterwards allows anyone to delete or modify the files.

You should also set rights carefully on applications and data files on the server. Most applications require only read rights to use them. However, some applications require that users be able to modify some files. You can often have separate copies of these files in each user's directory. At least make sure that all the other files in the application's directory are write-protected.

Dial-in Access Security

As telecommuting becomes a reality for more workers, network administrators are increasingly faced with security problems related to dial-in access. Having an access server on your network is equivalent to having a workstation plugged in at a park bench somewhere, where absolutely anyone in the world can attempt to log in.

To provide dial-in access security, you can restrict the number of login attempts allowed during any dial-in session. This prevents hackers from dialing in and trying thousands of logins or passwords. You can also use dial-back systems. These range from a (not very secure) system that calls the user back at a number entered during the login attempt, to a system with a separate line for dialing in and dialing out, which won't even allow dialing in on the lines that dial users back.

In addition to the access server, you may have some users with modems on their workstations. If they routinely leave these on, a hacker could gain access to the PC, load a remote control program onto the PC, and use that to attempt to log in to the server. You can address this by preventing logins from that workstation during off hours (of course, this won't work if the user needs to be able to access the network during those hours). At least, you should make sure that the workstation's AUTOEXEC.BAT file doesn't include the user's login name or password. The important thing is to be aware of the potential hole in your security.

Other Access Security

There are other possibilities that a hacker could use to gain access to your system. For instance, if you have NFS support on your server, a user with a UNIX workstation could mount the drives on your server that have been exported, and possibly bypass your security. You can fix this by setting the NFS NLM up correctly. Keep in mind that some add-ons may cause potential holes in your system, so you need to look for them and find ways to prevent them.

The only constant in security systems is that anything that someone creates as the ultimate, undefeatable security system, someone else will eventually circumvent. You should make a regular effort to learn about new advances in security (and virus detection), and keep your system updated.

Recovering from Disaster—In Advance

THE PREVENTIVE MEASURES DISCUSSED in this chapter can save you from many kinds of problems. However, you should be prepared to recover from fires, floods, and other kinds of disasters that you cannot avoid. Having a plan gives you a sense of direction after a problem occurs. Creating the plan forces you to consider possible problems and prepare for them, which can prevent serious losses after disaster strikes.

The Recovery Plan

Most areas of the country have their regional disasters. Earthquakes, cyclones or hurricanes, floods, blizzards—they all have potential ramifications to your network. Although you can't constantly worry about what might happen, you should consider the possibilities and how you would deal with them.

Your plan may be as simple as storing your backup tapes and copies of your network documentation in a different room from the server, or as extensive as detailed lists of what steps you would take, who you would talk to (with their phone numbers and addresses), what services or equipment you would request, and what these items would cost. The scope of your recovery plan will depend on the complexity of your network and on how soon it must be working after a problem. See Chapter 7 for more details on how to develop a disaster-recovery plan.

Data Recovery in Advance

There are programs available for both PCs and Macs that will (sometimes) recover deleted files or data from drives that crash or are accidentally formatted. Most of these programs have a utility that should be loaded on the workstation ahead of time. This utility will keep track of files after they have been deleted, significantly improving the recovery program's chances of getting your data back. You should consider a utility of this type for all your network workstations. See Chapter 7 for more information about data-recovery software.

Recovery Services in Advance

Many companies offer troubleshooting and disaster-recovery services. These companies range from large national organizations, such as TRW and Wang, to local businesses, to freelancers, to companies that specialize in recovering as much as possible from fire or flood-damaged systems. The services they provide range from network analysis using LANalyzer or another protocol analyzer to hard disk recovery.

You should develop a disaster-recovery plan and set up relationships with these services in advance. It will not make things easier for you if you must spend two days after the disaster setting up an account and authorizing payment before the service will begin fixing your problems.

No matter how prepared you think you are for disaster, coping with one that actually occurs is a true test for the network administrator. The next chapter provides some suggestions to help you get your network through a crisis and up and running again.

Coping with Disaster

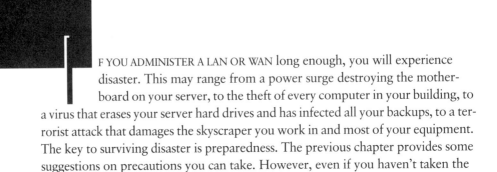

F YOU ADMINISTER A LAN OR WAN long enough, you will experience disaster. This may range from a power surge destroying the motherboard on your server, to the theft of every computer in your building, to a virus that erases your server hard drives and has infected all your backups, to a terrorist attack that damages the skyscraper you work in and most of your equipment. The key to surviving disaster is preparedness. The previous chapter provides some suggestions on precautions you can take. However, even if you haven't taken the right precautions, there may still be hope, depending on the problem.

The most important part of your network is not the computers, the networking hardware, or the server. It's the data. Obviously, if you have had all your computers stolen or destroyed in a fire or earthquake, you can't do much with the computers. However, if you have good backups and logs of what equipment you had and how it was configured, you may be able to get your business back online. Backups are the single most important precaution you can take against disaster. There is no justification for not regularly backing up your server.

If the server's hard drive has failed, and your backups to the new drive don't work, there may still be options. There are data-recovery services that specialize in recovering data from drives that have gone bad. Depending on why the drive failed, it may be possible to get some or all of the data back.

Sometimes it will prove impossible to recover your data. In that case, you will need to reconstruct the system or data. The more documentation you have, the easier this will be. The most expensive part of this, of course, will be the labor. Even a large network is not expensive compared with the cost of re-creating thousands or millions of pages of data.

This chapter will cover how to recover from a wide range of network failures, including mechanical failures and software problems. After you've read about the various recovery and reconstruction methods, you can use this information to plan how you will cope with your own network disasters. The final sections describe how you can develop and document your disaster-recovery plan.

Attitude: Keeping Your Head

THE MOST IMPORTANT THING TO REMEMBER in a disaster, however large or small, is to keep your head. Any problem can be broken down into small chunks that can be solved. Looking at a widespread disaster, throwing your hands up, and quitting will not solve any problems. It probably won't even make you feel any better. You need to look at the problem realistically, determine its full scope, break it down into tasks you can accomplish, and then forge ahead.

Another important thing to remember is that there are always options. If getting a mission-critical server back online is your goal, for instance, you need to evaluate all possible options. You may need to replace the server with another workstation (your least critical user's workstation, if necessary). If necessary, you can call in outside—and probably expensive—consultants in data recovery, PC hardware, or NetWare configuration.

Don't be afraid that you will look bad if you admit that a problem is beyond you, or that you can't solve it quickly without help. Your boss and colleagues should respect the priority of getting the server back up quickly. A good way to present this is to say, "I can get this done, but it may take several days or a week. Mr. Jones from Harem Guard Consulting says he can have it fixed this afternoon for $1,000. That is much less than what we will lose by being offline for a few days."

Similarly, don't hesitate to ask for help from within your organization. Is there someone else who knows the system well? Can some of the users who are sitting on their hands waiting for the server to come back online take some tasks off your hands? Don't get trapped into thinking that you must accomplish everything yourself. Asking others for help during an emergency will not only off-load some tasks, but possibly even keep users from continually asking you when things will be operational again.

Recovering from Mechanical Failure or Destruction

I F YOUR BUSINESS DEPENDS on your network, you should have some level of fault tolerance in place. This might be anything from a UPS and a duplexed hard drive to a mirrored server under SFT III. Fault tolerance is discussed in detail in Chapters 2 and 6.

Your solution to damaged or destroyed equipment will depend on your resources. You may be able to replace the equipment with a spare system, or you might need to rent a replacement until your system can be repaired or replaced.

The important thing is to preserve your data. If your server is damaged, for instance, the first step would be to move the hard disks to another PC and see if they work. If the drives don't function, then you can set up a new server and restore from tape. If neither step works, don't panic. There is probably a data-recovery service near you that may be able to restore the data on your hard drive. The technicians can sometimes restore data from fire- or water-damaged disks, or disks that have been hit by a power surge. They may even be able to recover some of the data if the heads have crashed. Another consultant might be able to fix the problem with your backups and get your data restored properly. These services can be expensive, but not nearly as expensive as re-creating your data.

Your Emergency Kit

Your emergency response kit should consist of at least the following:

- A workstation boot diskette for each type of operating system and each NIC used on your network

- A server boot diskette for each type of server (with NET$OS.EXE or SERVER.EXE)

- A spare NIC, and if possible, a set of the standard cards—disk controller, display adapter, and so on

- Tools for opening and working on PCs

- An anti-static strap and mat

- A can of compressed air for dusting off equipment, or a vacuum

- A configuration worksheet for each workstation and server

- A text editor for changing configuration files

- A directory on your server that contains copies of DOS, Windows, or whatever operating system you use, standard configuration files, and any other files, programs, or applications you need to set up a workstation (make sure you have licensed copies corresponding to everything you download)

What to Try First

Your biggest disasters will generally involve hard disks, especially your server's hard disk. As stated earlier, your data is the most critical part of your network. You can replace workstations and even the server, but your data is much harder to replace. If your server is stolen, or melted into slag in a fire, or crushed by the floor above during an earthquake, you won't be able to recover the data on the drive. Of course, if your backup tapes are lying next to the server, you may not be able to restore from them, either. This is the main reason for off-site storage of backups (see the section on disaster planning, later in this chapter). Fortunately, such disasters are rare. The typical problems you are much more likely to face will generally involve malfunctions. For example, your server may stop working; or it may be working, but the hard disk won't be responding, will be corrupted, or will be missing files or directories.

Don't panic, and don't take steps you can't back down from. If you try undeleting and it doesn't work, you may not be able to try any other steps. Check for little things first, and then try progressively more drastic measures.

The first thing to remember when faced with disaster is not to panic, and to never make your first step something that you can't recover from. Make sure that the malfunction is actually in the hard drive. Check the rest of the server or workstation to make sure that the other parts are all okay. If your disk is mirrored, make sure that when you re-mirror the disks, the good disk is mounted. Try running BINDFIX or VREPAIR on a server's hard drive (maybe several times), rather than reformatting or repartitioning the drive and restoring from backup. Try using a disk recovery program or running CHKDSK on a PC's disk before reformatting and reinstalling all the software. The important thing is to consider the results of what you're trying. If you get a warning like "Warning! All Data Will Be Erased!" try other things first.

Physical Recovery

The first thing to do is to get the hardware functioning again. This may be as simple as replacing a hard disk controller card, or it may be much more involved. Your disaster-recovery plan should include vendors to replace nonfunctioning machines and recovery services to get damaged machines back online. This may include a local service that can remove fire by-products, a service that can get hard drives working again, and specialists in recovery from whatever regional disaster is most likely for your area. In every case, the more planning you do in advance, the less trouble you will have when disaster occurs.

Server Recovery

The server can be broken down into two basic areas. The first is the basic workstation hardware. This hardware is easily replaced. Almost any PC clone company can provide you with a PC that will do in a pinch. It doesn't need to be the latest model, just something that will function until you can get a permanent replacement.

The second server area is your data storage: the hard drives and associated equipment. This may include SCSI adapters, subsystems to hold the drives, and the like. Again, the basic parts are commodities, easily replaceable. Many companies keep complete backup servers, preconfigured and ready to replace malfunctioning equipment.

Workstation Recovery

As with servers, you may want to keep a supply of the basic parts (power supply, extra RAM, video adapter, NIC, and so on) or simply a spare workstation that you can swap. As the system administrator, you may find it necessary to cannibalize your personal PC for working parts to get another system back online.

Data Recovery

After you have the hardware functioning again, the next step is to get the data back. Even if you have not had a hardware problem, some or all of the data on your hard drive may become inaccessible. Your ability to get it back will depend on the severity of the problem and the resources available.

The thing that gives a hard disk its structure is the file allocation table (FAT). This is a data table at the start of the disk that keeps track of what files are on the disk and where they are. NetWare adds additional information in other data tables. It stores information on rights to the files and ownership in a database known as the binderies or the NDS, and additional characteristics such as the longer file names used by the Macintosh and other file systems (created when you add name space support to a volume) in other data tables. If the FAT is corrupted, NetWare has other copies stashed on the disk to check. In some cases, NetWare can recover automatically or with the use of VREPAIR.

Server Data

The basic tools for data recovery on the server are VREPAIR, BINDFIX, and DSREPAIR. Read the manual carefully before using these utilities, to make sure you understand what questions they will ask and what you should do. VREPAIR can fix problems with the FAT, partition information, and name space information BINDFIX will (sometimes) repair the binderies, and DSREPAIR will repair problems with the NDS database. These utilities may need to be run more than once to fix the problem completely. Often, when they fix one problem, they will leave others unresolved. Run them until they report no errors.

Workstation Data

Workstations are simpler to recover data on, because they don't have the extended attributes that NetWare does. On the other hand, workstations are seldom protected with mirrored drives, they don't generally have data-recovery software built into the operating system, and they aren't often backed up. Some data-recovery tools build a duplicate copy of the FAT and can use this to recover from many disk errors. I highly recommend using one of these utilities. See Appendix A for some sources that you can use to learn more about these programs.

Backups are a stickier issue. I strongly encourage you to limit workstation disks to system software and applications. Train users to store all data on the server, which should be backed up. With a good log, you will know what operating system, configuration files, applications, and so on are on the workstation, and you'll be able to restore these fairly easily.

If the data is scrambled and you don't have backups, you may want to send it out to a data-recovery specialist as your first step. Anything you try to recover the data could prevent any recovery at all if it doesn't work.

If your data-recovery tools can't help, you have exhausted the first level of recovery tools. The next level involves restoring from backups. The third level of recovery involves refurbishing the hard drive, and the last level is the recreation of your data from scratch. These are discussed in the next sections.

Restoring from Backups

Your server should be backed up with a documented schedule of tape rotation, and you should consider either a fireproof secure storage area on site or off-site storage of the tapes. Chapter 6 stressed the importance of backing up data and applications and discussed backup strategies in some detail. Here, we'll focus on what happens when you actually need to restore what you've backed up.

If you weren't able to get the data on your drive back, or if the drive itself can't be repaired, you will need to restore from backups. This may be as simple as restoring a server's drive from the full backup tape made the night before, or as complex as booting from a floppy and downloading a new operating system from the server, reconstructing the user's configuration from your log files, and reinstalling all the user's applications.

Restoring the Server

A complete restoration of the server will involve three basic components:

- The NetWare operating system, NetWare partitions, and additional NLMs and configuration files

- The binderies or NDS database, which contain all the information about which users are able to use the server, what files they own or have rights to, and so on

- Your data files, including your users' files, applications, and work directories

Most backup software gives you the option to back up and restore the binderies or NDS database as well as the operating system and data.

Three things to watch out for when you are restoring the server are:

- Restoring to different drives than were originally on the server

- Restoring to a drive that hasn't been formatted with NetWare yet

- Restoring drives that had name space support for other operating systems besides DOS

If your server's hard drive has failed and you think this is a great time to increase the size of the drive, since it was 98 percent full anyway, be aware that restoring the partition information will result in errors, because the partition information is based on the size of the drive and its configuration in terms of number of blocks, tracks, and sectors. If you wish to change drive sizes, you will need to reinstall NetWare from the diskettes, create new partitions, and then restore the binderies or NDS database and data.

If the drive you are restoring to is new and hasn't been formatted with NetWare yet, most backup software will be able to create the NetWare partition during the restoration process. You may, however, need to create the partition first with some backup software. Make sure that you have the latest version of the backup software, and of course, that you've read the manufacturer's documentation carefully.

If you have name space support for another operating system, such as the Macintosh OS, Windows 95, OS/2, or UNIX, you should be sure in advance that your backup software will handle the name space support. If it doesn't, you may get the files back, but with names truncated to eight characters and a three-character extension.

Restoring Workstation Data

As discussed in Chapter 6, you should attempt to confine the data on workstations to the operating system and applications. If the user's data is on the server, then restoring the workstation is simply a matter of reinstalling the operating system and applications, as described in the next section. However, if the workstation stored other data, there are some approaches that may help you restore the lost files.

Don't take actions that you can't back out of. Most data-recovery utilities will irreparably change the disk. If you run a utility and it doesn't recover the missing data, what will you do then? The time to plan for this is before you run the utility. If the utility gives you the option of creating a backout disk or file, use it.

If the disk is not completely defunct, you can try using built-in utilities such as UNDELETE or SCANDISK, or separate utilities from companies such as Central Point or Norton to recover data. The results will vary, depending on the degree of damage and the number of files that have been created or erased since the problem occurred. Of course, as discussed earlier, a utility that keeps backup copies of the FAT will give you a much better chance of recovering data from a drive. Some utilities may be able to recover data even if they weren't installed before the problem occurred.

If you can't recover the data with utilities, then you will need to use backups. If backups aren't available, the only remaining option is to send the disk to a data-recovery specialist. If the data on the disk is critical, this might be your first step; anything you try to do to recover the data could scramble it beyond the ability of anything or anyone to get it back. (Of course, if the data is that critical, you should have arranged for backups!)

Restoring Applications and Operating Systems

The easiest way to reinstall applications is simply to have an area on the server with a standard set of applications and the standard operating system. As long as you have an appropriate license for each workstation, it is quite legal to download the actual files from the server. You can also restore from tape, or restore from the server's tape drive to the server and then copy everything back onto the workstation, after reinstalling enough of the operating system to boot and connect to the network. You should have boot diskettes for this purpose for every type of workstation on your network.

If your users' requirements are similar enough that you can standardize on one or two operating systems and a standard suite of applications, this makes restoring a workstation or setting up a new one quite simple. You can just boot from a floppy with a networking driver on it, log in to the server, and install the standard operating system and applications. This is also much faster than installing everything from floppies, and can usually be done as a batch operation.

You can copy the operating system and all the applications with one command, such as:

```
NCOPY G:/SETUP/*.* /S
```

This approach to storing applications and operating systems also makes updates easier. You can simply copy the new version from the network to each users' workstation (observing license requirements, of course). This is a good way of keeping the versions on your network in sync, another practice I recommend. In some cases, as with the Macintosh operating system, having different versions on the network can cause printing problems, network protocol routing conflicts, or file system errors.

Many operating systems today come on CD-ROM. If the workstations have CD-ROMs, or if you have a parallel-port CD-ROM, you can install this way, which is still much faster than using floppies.

Since all your applications are legally acquired and registered copies, if necessary, you can reinstall them from the original disks. I suggest that you have a central repository (perhaps fireproof and lockable) to hold these application disks. It will make your life much simpler than searching for everything in various areas, and discovering that someone from another department has "borrowed" the manuals and disks.

Recovery Services—How Much Is All Your Work Worth?

If your disk is not responding, and backups are not available or aren't working, your next step is a data-recovery company. A good recovery service can repair or replace the electronics on a damaged hard drive, and may be able to open the drive itself in a clean environment and replace damaged components, enabling you to recover some or all of your data. You should have already set up relationships with these services—before any disaster strikes—so that you don't need to worry about establishing an account and authorizing payment before the service will begin working on your problems.

Some companies employ a software-only approach and are experts with data-recovery software. They may be able to get better results than you can, or be able to reassemble scrambled data that is beyond most data-recovery software. Their services may seem expensive, but are likely to be much less than the cost of re-creating all your data from hard copy or from memory.

Recovering from Software Problems and User Errors

THE MOST COMMON PROBLEMS you will have that aren't related to hardware are caused by incorrect software configuration, inadvertent changes in permissions, and user errors. Users setting up their own programs and workstation utilities will often have an incomplete understanding of your network, and they may specify settings that are not correct for use on a network. Unfortunately, even with an effective user-education program, you will often find out about these problems after the fact.

Applications and Network Access

Short of becoming an expert on every application in use on your network, your best option is to become aware of the methods that applications use to directly access the network. These are the most common problems with network applications. Typically, applications access print services or file services. If the application has problems accessing print queues or file permissions directly, set the program to a non-networked mode, and use the standard NetWare redirection utilities to access print and file services.

If a user has problems using data files on the network, the most common reason is permissions. If a file is still there, but it is not opening correctly, check first for things that may be affecting it. For example, if the permissions were altered, a user might be getting messages that imply that the file is damaged, when the problem is actually that the user doesn't have the proper access. Similarly, if a file is shared or being worked on by several users, permissions might be altered by one user. Or if the file is being worked on by one user, it may be locked (perhaps with good reason), so that others are temporarily unable to access the file. Here, again, the application's messages may be misleading.

Restoring Individual Files

Your biggest use for your backups will be restoring files that have been scrambled by programs that were incorrectly terminated or are simply buggy, or for restoring files that were accidentally deleted by users.

If the files were accidentally deleted, you may be able to recover them with SALVAGE, which is much simpler than restoring from a backup. However, you won't be able to use SALVAGE if you don't have much free space on the volume, or you have turned on the Purge Immediately feature. See the System Administration manual for details on SALVAGE and the PURGE options.

Handling Other Hardware Failures

F AILURES IN NETWORKING HARDWARE other than servers can be catastrophic, because they can affect everyone on the LAN, or even everyone on a WAN. The failure will not necessarily be total, and tracking the problem can be very difficult without some sort of network analyzer. For example, a router on a LAN or WAN could become defective and begin sending out extremely large packets, which could cause every server or workstation receiving those packets to freeze or be unable to communicate with the network. With a protocol analyzer, a log of normal traffic, and a table of all network devices and their ID numbers, diagnosing this type of problem is easy. Without such tools, you can only try to isolate your WAN into LANs, find the LAN that still has the problem when cut off from other LANs, and then take devices off the LAN until the problem device is found.

There are a number of routers and other types of networking hardware that allow you to swap boards in and out of the device without powering off or affecting other connections. Many devices also support Simple Network Management Protocol (SNMP), which allows you to remotely diagnose and control them using an SNMP management console. See Chapter 4, which covers the physical network, and Chapter 9, which is about connecting to other systems, for more details on finding and fixing these types of network problems.

As with every other area, planning in advance can make your life easier when problems occur. In the case of a LAN or WAN hardware failure, you can set your network to use alternate routes for data. For instance, if you have one large concentrator or switch and it dies, everyone is out. If you have two that are not completely used, you can move the most critical users onto the remaining one.

You can also set up dual routes from one site to another. For instance, if you have a leased-line connection from one site to another, you can back it up with a dial-up connection, perhaps ISDN. If the main connection fails, the modem will automatically dial up the other site and provide a connection, albeit at a much slower data rate.

Reconstruction—When All Else Fails

YOUR ABILITY TO RECONSTRUCT YOUR NETWORK in the event of physical destruction or unrecoverable data loss depends on the extent of the records you have kept. If you have hard copies of documents, you can probably have them rekeyed, either by in-house staff or by a company that specializes in such work. Replacing, reinstalling, and reconfiguring your network without documentation will take much longer, if it's not impossible. See the "Disaster Planning" section later in this chapter for suggestions on what you should record.

The recurring theme of this chapter applies here, too. The two parts of your network you will need to reconstruct will be the physical network and the data. You may or may not need to reconstruct both parts. Obviously, getting the hardware back in place will be relatively simple—a matter of buying, leasing or renting whatever is necessary. Next, you will need to reinstall the components and software and reconfigure the network. The time involved will be a function of how complex your network was and how well it was documented. Finally, you will need to recover your data. If your backups were lost, too, you will need to reenter everything. You may be able to rekey much of your data from hard copy. If this isn't possible, it will need to be re-created in other ways. One factor here is time. The longer you must wait before people can begin re-creating their work, the less they will remember.

Another approach to reconstructing your data is to find alternate sources. For example, an employee manual could be rekeyed from a copy an employee had at home, accounting records could be reconstructed by contacting your accounting or tax firm, and other records might be obtained by asking the companies you do business with for their records of transactions with your company. The critical thing is to make a list of all the data that was on the network, and then work out methods to recover as much as possible. You may want to have a group meeting of all employees who used the affected network, and brainstorm on both what was there and possible methods for recovery.

Recovering from Viruses

THE THREE IMPORTANT PARTS to dealing with viruses are using virus-detection software, keeping it updated, and using virus-recovery programs if necessary. As discussed in Chapter 6, ideally, you should have virus-scanning software covering every workstation and server on your network. Given the cost versus the potential for damage, there is no excuse for not doing this. Educate your users on the necessity for virus scanning and the importance of not disabling the software to save two seconds when inserting a floppy disk. The one time that you may need to disable virus-checking software is when using some software installation programs.

Also, as stressed in the previous chapter, keeping your virus-scanning software updated is critical. Having a virus checker in place can give you and your users a false sense of security, since people tend to assume that having a virus checker will automatically prevent any viruses from infecting your system. The sad fact is that there are a small number of asocial criminals who are constantly devising new viruses that can bypass existing scanning software.

If you do have workstations or servers that become infected, there are a number of programs that may be able to remove the virus and possibly repair any damage. These programs are definitely a good investment. They will often tell you in an introductory message that you should really delete the infected application and reinstall it. This is usually the best way to recover from a virus. But the program will always tell you whether the virus removal was successful, and if the program runs properly afterwards, you may wish to leave it alone.

The most critical thing on your network to protect from viruses is your server. I whole-heartedly recommend that you get an NLM that will scan your server for infected applications and files and warn you if anyone attempts to place an infected file on the server.

The worst thing about having a server infected with a virus is that it can corrupt your backups, making it difficult or impossible to recover from the damage. If this happens, the key is to determine the latest backup that is not infected and restore from that. If you don't catch the virus in time, you could lose all your recent data. If you can isolate the infected files, you can sometimes restore earlier versions of just those files, and recover everything else.

Disaster Prevention Tools and Techniques: A Recap

THE FOLLOWING ITEMS ARE COVERED in detail in the previous chapter. They are summarized here simply to reiterate the importance of preventive measures. All of them can prevent disaster by shielding your network from the things that can cause problems in the first place.

- UPSs and surge protectors. Power spikes and surges, brownouts and blackouts—these have the potential to cause disaster. Whether the disaster is a motherboard destroyed by a surge or a NetWare volume damaged by powering the server off without taking it down first, a good surge protector or UPS would have prevented the problem.

- Quality equipment. Hardware failures are in general less likely with quality equipment. Many manufacturers also offer on-site service. When purchasing equipment, saving a few hundred dollars may cost you many times that amount later. This may be the case if you can't find compatible hardware for PC repair or if a hardware failure causes an unrecoverable loss of data.

- Preventive maintenance. Proper maintenance techniques can prevent hardware failures from occurring in the first place. Too much dust in a PC can cause shorts on circuit boards, or read or write errors on floppy drives. Dust can also cause filters to clog on hard drives, making them run hotter and reducing their life. Similarly, keeping the disk drive heads clean can prevent floppy drive failures, and keeping connections tight can prevent failures of several kinds.

- Precautions. Not observing anti-static precautions can damage the parts you are inspecting or trying to repair. Your body can hold a static charge of many thousands of volts, more than enough to damage the circuitry in your PCs. Units that aren't properly grounded can be affected by static discharges even when the cases are closed. Other precautions include following the manufacturer's directions when dealing with hardware or software. For example, most programs should be exited before the workstation is turned off. Another example is waiting five minutes after a Mac has been turned off before removing or adding cards.

- Fault tolerance. SFT II or III can protect your network from what would otherwise be disaster. SFT II is disk duplexing or mirroring, which can protect you from hard drive failure. If a mirrored drive fails, users won't even notice. The system will notify you that a drive has failed, and you can take down the server and replace it at your leisure. You won't even need to restore data once a problem is fixed; the servers will automatically re-mirror. SFT III carries fault tolerance to a level unique in the LAN world. It creates a duplicate of your entire server, which can be in another part of the building or at a remote location (as long as a high-speed data link is available). With SFT III, even the total destruction or theft of one server won't bring the network down.

- Baselining. Monitoring your network can not only help you isolate the problems with LANs, it can prevent disaster by allowing you to identify trends in advance and expand the capacity of your network in time to deal with increased demands before they cause your system to shut down. For example, if your percentage of available cache buffers is gradually declining, you can add more memory to your server before it gets to a state where you need to remove services to get it to run at all.

- User training. Educating your users has a number of advantages. It can lighten your workload by reducing the number of requests you receive for support. User training can also reduce or eliminate some types of failures by getting users to observe proper procedures and even do some preventive maintenance on their own equipment.

- Security. Some of the potential disasters that could befall your network can be prevented by proper security. This has a number of levels. For example, in addition to breaking into your building, thieves should also need to defeat the lock on the server room door before they can walk off with your server. Anti-theft registration stickers, cables that secure the server to something immobile, or video surveillance could also deter thieves from walking off with your equipment. Another step to take is to lock software and backups in a cabinet, perhaps in another room.

Disaster Preparedness

I T IS A SAD FACT that more than 95 percent of businesses that experience a disaster and don't have a disaster plan will be out of business within two years. To get a feel for the scope of disaster preparedness, imagine what would happen if your building was bombed and you were unable to even enter your facilities for several months. What would happen to your business? Similar effects could result from fire, earthquake, flood, or simply a virus that isn't caught until it's too late. You only need to look at recent news to find examples of businesses forced into receivership as a result of any of these events.

Disaster Planning

You've just entered the parking lot Monday morning, and there's a hole in the ground where your building used to be. Where do you start? Your disaster plan may include many elements not germane here, such as evacuation plans, a relationship with a real estate broker to get new facilities, and arrangements for employee counseling after the disaster. Here, we'll deal with recommendations for just the areas involving your network. These may be more extensive than you imagine.

Pipes burst, buildings burn, and thieves steal computer equipment. You can't spend all your time worrying about what might happen, but you should take some time to think about the possibilities and what you could do to recover from them.

Sit down, maybe with other members of your staff, and list all the things you would need to do to get your system back online if your building were completely destroyed. Lesser disasters will be a subset of this, but don't skimp here. You may later decide that some measures will be too expensive, but you will at least have an idea of what might be necessary.

If your business couldn't run without your network and the data on it, which is very probable, then you should have backup tapes stored off site. Many disasters will either destroy on-site tapes or render access to them impossible for extended periods of time. For example, some buildings have not reopened for months or even years after fires. And even if your equipment or backup tapes weren't harmed, you might not be able to get to them.

Test your backups before you need them. It is unfortunately all too common to be running a backup program for months or years, only to discover that when you really need to restore files the backups aren't really working properly.

If you can re-create your hardware setup and your data, you can probably survive most disasters. Having a plan is not enough. You should test your plan, at least on a small scale. Rent some space, set up a small network at home (using rented equipment, if necessary), get backup tapes from your off-site storage company, and restore to a test server. You will uncover flaws in your plan and areas you hadn't considered. Modify your plan to accommodate these, and test it again. Finally, document the whole thing, as described in the next section, and make sure that your management is familiar with the plan. Keep copies at home.

Documenting Your Disaster Plan

After you've decided on a disaster-recovery plan and tested it, you should document that plan. This doesn't need to be a formal, 100-page document, but it should be thorough and cover all aspects of your network. Your company as a whole should have a more comprehensive plan that includes every aspect of recovering from disaster, from new buildings to employee counseling, but as the network administrator, your documentation only needs to cover your network.

You should have both soft and hard copies of your network documentation and disaster plan, in several locations. Give a copy to each manager to keep at home. Store a copy with your off-site backup tapes. Now you have a list of what equipment you need to replace (your complete disaster plan will also include other equipment—from office furniture to phones and copiers). You should include in the plan a list of your standard suppliers, your customer representative's name and phone number, and so on. Include copies of all of the following:

- The hardware and software configuration worksheets for your workstations and servers

- The documentation of your network wiring plan and networking hardware

- Your backup plan

- The address, contact name, and authorization code for your off-site storage facility

- The names of your hardware and software suppliers and their customer representative's phone numbers

- The number of your local phone company's networking services representative

Include other information as needed and as time permits (see the "Documenting the Network" section in Chapter 6). It's impossible to make this plan too thorough or complete, although time will be your limiting factor.

The two prevailing themes of this chapter have been "back up, and document everything." Easy to say, but hard to do? Not really. The forms in Appendix C can be used as-is or customized as you wish. Make a copy for each workstation and server on your network. Fill out as much as you can from your own knowledge. Lots of blanks, aren't there? Take the remaining items a few at a time. Do one workstation or server a day until you have them all done. Then you can start updating.

Create a network map, showing every workstation and server on your network and how they're connected. Print a copy of your directory structure. Get network and file server management packages and use them to create complete inventories of what's on every workstation and server on your network. Whether you do it manually or with software, create the documentation, keep it updated, and spread lots of copies around.

Another step that will help you is to keep a diary or log, as suggested in Chapter 6. This task doesn't need to be onerous—use a word processor and keep the file open. Update it with what you're doing during the day, or make it the last thing you do before you go home. Keep copies of this document around, too. Not only can it be helpful in reconstructing your network in case of disaster, but it can show your boss that the user you've been griping about asked for your help with the same problem eight times in the last two months, and it also makes a great place to start when writing up your job description, doing a job review, or showing your boss just why you need an assistant or some new equipment.

Troubleshooting
Techniques for
Large Networks

PART

Troubleshooting
WANs

MANY COMPANIES ARE NO LONGER LIMITED to single LANs, but have multiple LANs connected to form WANs, or internetworks. As you would expect, it is more difficult to isolate problems when internetwork connections are involved. Your system may consist of multiple LANs within a single building or campus, or WANs over multiple sites, which may span a city, a continent, or the entire globe.

In your role as network administrator, you may be called on to troubleshoot a WAN connection. Suppose one of your users is trying to download files from a server in another state. Is the problem one of permissions on the far end? The router? The internet connection service provider? User error? This chapter will help you determine where the problem lies. It will not cover how to set up WANs and every possible variation used to connect LANs. Instead, it provides the basic principles of connecting and troubleshooting WANs; these principles will be applicable no matter which specific hardware or topology you use.

This chapter will discuss how LANs are interconnected, troubleshooting methods and tools, and user services. Here, we will cover the following topics:

- How LANs are connected to form WANs

- Additional fault points of WANs

- WAN-related problems

- Network management and diagnostic tools

- Services across WANs

- NetWare Directory Services (NDS)

How LANs Are Connected to Form WANs

TO HELP YOU UNDERSTAND the process that you are troubleshooting, we will begin with the various methods of connecting LANs. A basic definition of a LAN is a group of workstations connected to a server with a single type of topology. This can be as simple as a few PCs connected by Token Ring to a server, or as complex as PCs running Windows, Windows 95, and OS/2 connecting with IPX/SPX, TCP/IP, NetBIOS, and NetBEUI; Macintoshes using EtherTalk; and UNIX workstations using TCP/IP; all connected by Ethernet to a server. As long as there is only one network number and one server, it is still one LAN.

Another network size classification is metropolitan-area network (MAN). A MAN is a network linking more than one site, but limited to a metropolitan area. (In cases such as Los Angeles or New York, these can, of course, be quite extensive.) Generally, a MAN offers public access and high performance (100 Mbps or greater).

If you need help with creating or maintaining a WAN, you can refer to many good books and other network resources (see Appendix A). If you're not familiar with some of the standards and acronyms used in WAN technology, see the glossary at the end of the book.

The simplest method of connecting two existing NetWare networks is to put two NICs in a single server, and connect each of the existing networks to one of the NICs in the server. In this case, the server with two network cards is acting as a router. From this simple example you can go all the way to multiple LANs connected via high-speed leased lines or even through satellite connections.

Connecting Multiple LANs at One Site

There are several reasons you may have multiple LANs at one site, such as:

- The LANs were created separately and at different times, in response to the varying needs of different departments. Later, they were hooked together to form an internetwork. In fact, this is typical of the development of networking at many companies.

- Different departments are using different types of LANs. For example, the Engineering department might be using Token Ring, the Accounting department Ethernet, and the Marketing and Art departments LocalTalk.

- You needed to reduce network traffic or provide more services than a single server could handle. Too many workstations on a single LAN, or too many users on a single server, can cause the entire network to bog down. Splitting the network into several LANs reduces traffic and server overhead, improving performance for everyone.

Depending on the setup at your site, the LANs may be connected with bridges, routers, or gateways, as explained in the following sections.

Bridges

Bridges are the least complex method of connecting two LANs (although once they are connected, they are actually one LAN, with one network number). A bridge generally connects similar types of networks, such as Token Ring to Token Ring, but it can connect different types of cabling, such as thick Ethernet to 10BaseT. A bridge can be used to divide a LAN with too much traffic into several segments. Because only the packets that are destined for the segment on the other side pass through the bridge, it can substantially reduce traffic on both parts of the LAN.

Versions of NetWare before 3.x called the function built into NetWare a bridge. Actually, the NetWare product has attributes of both a bridge and a router. In later versions of NetWare, it is referred to as a router.

Bridges are designed to handle specific protocols, such as IPX/SPX, Apple-Talk, TCP/IP, and so on. A bridge looks at the hardware address of each packet and sends it to the other side if the address is on that side. Since the hardware address is always in the same place in a packet, the function of a bridge is relatively simple, and bridges are generally the fastest type of connection between two LANs (for a given cost or speed of processor). A bridge generally learns the addresses of all the workstations on either side by occasionally polling them for this information.

Routers

A router differs from a bridge in that it can handle multiple protocols. Also, the network on each side of a router is actually a different LAN, with different network numbers. A router doesn't just read the destination hardware address; it can read the packet to find out its eventual destination, rather than just the next one identified by the destination hardware address. A router can add further information to a packet to enable it to go through a LAN that uses a different hardware standard, such as Ethernet to Token Ring, or take that information off a packet it receives from the other side of such a LAN.

Another difference is that routers don't handle every packet on the LAN. (They aren't "transparent.") Instead, a packet that is to be passed through the router must be addressed to it. NetWare handles this automatically, but some protocols (TCP/IP, for instance) require you to tell a workstation the address of the router to which it should send packets for forwarding.

A router is more capable than a bridge but requires more processing, which, all other things being equal, makes a router either slower or more expensive than a bridge. There is also an in-between class of devices called *brouters*, which combine the functionality of bridges and routers, generally by examining every packet on the LAN (transparency) but only being able to handle some protocols.

Gateways

A gateway is the most complex type of device for connecting LANs, and it is typically very specialized. It doesn't just transfer packets from one LAN or one protocol to another; it usually translates between two dissimilar standards. For example, a gateway might act as a file translator, to allow your Macintoshes to access files on a UNIX server, or as a mail gateway, translating between the Net-Ware mail protocol MHS and another such as X.400.

Gateways are typically complex to configure. You should understand the basics of configuring both sides of the gateway. For instance, for a file and print services gateway that translates between AppleTalk and UNIX (TCP/IP), you should understand how to configure both AppleTalk and TCP/IP.

Connecting LANs between Buildings

LANs in buildings that are close enough together to be linked with a cable or by a beam of light can be connected by either repeaters or bridges, depending on the requirements of the network. Buildings can be connected with wire or fiber-optic cable, or linked with wireless means such as an infrared laser or a pair of radio transceivers.

Repeaters

A repeater is a device that simply passes everything it sees to every segment hooked up to it. It may support several types of cable—for instance, thick, thin, twisted-pair, and fiber-optic Ethernet—and is primarily used to extend the maximum length of cable. The primary disadvantage to a repeater is that it passes everything through; this can make for a very high-traffic load if too many workstations are connected.

There are two basic types of repeaters, single- and multi-port. A single-port repeater is used simply to extend the possible length of cabling for a network segment. A multi-port repeater allows several "legs" on the same segment. A repeater with many ports may also be known as a *hub* or a *concentrator*. Repeaters are relatively inexpensive and easy to set up.

Bridges

A bridge provides the same type of extension as a repeater, with the added benefit of traffic isolation, since only the traffic destined for the other building is passed across. Bridges do cost more and require software configuration, but they are also much more flexible.

Connecting LANs across Long Distances

Once you go beyond the range that can be spanned by physical cabling, your options become much more limited. You can set up a satellite or microwave link, lay your own long-distance cable, or use the facilities provided by your local telephone company.

Telephone Company Services

Transmitting data over a phone line intended for voice has its limitations. Because the line is engineered for voice communications, it will support a maximum data communications rate of only about 33,600 Bps (bits per second), or 115,200 Bps with data compression.

The basic divisions between the types of services are:

- Dial-up connections that can connect to any other phone line versus leased lines that connect two specific sites

- Analog connections versus digital connections, which can allow speeds of up to 622 Mbps (million bits per second) or more

Where there were once no competitors to the phone companies, there are now many. The service of providing a long-distance connection, say between an office in San Francisco and one in New York, can be broken into three parts: the connection from your building to the local branch office of the local phone company at each end, plus the carrier between the two local offices. You may find several companies that can provide the long-distance service—AT&T, MCI, Sprint, MCI, and WillTel to name a few.

It may still be difficult to find more than one local service in many areas, but that will probably change in the near future. The upshot of the competition is that prices are dropping every year, and what was once an economic impossibility is now feasible, and will soon be taken for granted.

Improvements in switched digital circuits, and decreases in connect times (the time required to initiate a connection between sites) are making dial-up digital connections a reasonable alternative for WAN links that don't need to be up all the time. How often do you need to be able to print to a remote site? Is a two-second delay acceptable? Call your local carrier and the long-distance companies if you're not sure what alternatives are feasible in your area.

ANALOG DIAL-UP CONNECTIONS Almost all dial-up connections use analog service, which is slower but offers the flexibility to connect to anyone with a phone. The typical problems associated with analog dial-up connections are:

- The limited speed available through lines intended for voice

- The relatively high levels of line noise

- The rates charged for standard phone service

LEASED ANALOG CONNECTIONS If you are using a dial-up line to connect regularly with another site, you may save money by leasing an analog connection. This won't typically offer higher speed, but it can give you a cleaner, more reliable connection. If the connection is used frequently, a leased line will be less expensive than making standard connections.

DIGITAL DIAL-UP CONNECTIONS As the phone companies convert from equipment intended only for voice transmission to digitally based equipment designed to also handle data and even video, they are making high-speed dial-up connections available. These range in speed from 56 Kbps (thousand bits per second) to 100 Mbps or more.

The typical problems associated with digital dial-up connections are:

- These services are currently available only within metropolitan areas, and then only in some areas.

- A dial-up connection that is used more than a few minutes a day may end up costing more than a higher-speed leased line.

- Digital connections generally require equipment much more expensive than a simple modem, although you can find ISDN (Integrated Services Digital Network) adapters for under a few hundred dollars.

The areas served by all-digital services will expand, and eventually you will be able to get a dial-up digital connection anywhere that you can now reach with a standard phone line. Check with your local phone company for availability. The equipment you will need depends on the type of connection. When contacting vendors such as MCI or your local Bell, ask them what type of equipment they recommend and support.

LEASED DIGITAL CONNECTIONS If you need a connection with a throughput of over 64 Kbps, you will probably need to lease a digital line. Digital services that may be available to you include:

- T-1, which provides 1.544 Mbps. A T-1 connection is a connection from your office to another location—either another of your offices or the phone company's branch office (for Frame Relay). You can usually get any multiple of 64 Kbps within the T-1 speed range; 64 K, 128 K, 256 K, 384 K, and 512 K are the most common connection speeds available.

- T-3, which provides 45 Mbps. A T-3 connection is just like a T-1 connection, but with a higher maximum data rate. You can also get fractional rates with a T-3 connection.

- Leased ISDN at 64 Kbps and up. ISDN is an international standard for telecommunications developed by the CCITT. It can handle voice, video, and data over one digital line. It generally provides 64 or 128 Kbps. Broadband ISDN (B/ISDN), which will soon be available, uses broadband transmission and fiber-optic cables to provide speeds up to 150 Mbps.

- FDDI at 100 Mbps. FDDI (for Fiber-optic Data Distribution Interface) is an ANSI standard for fiber-optic networks.

- ATM, which can provide 622 Mbps or more. ATM (for Asynchronous Transfer Mode) is a protocol designed to send parts of a transmission over different routes as they become available. It works well with mixed video and data transmissions.

CCITT stands for Consultative Committee for International Telephony and Telegraphy. It is an international organization headquartered in Geneva that sets telecommunications standards, including X.25, V.22, V.32, V.42, X.400, and X.500. ANSI stands for American National Standards Institute. It is an American body that sets standards, and is a voting member of ISO (the International Standards Organization, a standards organization with over 75 member countries).

These types of services tend to become more expensive as the distance between sites increases. There are also services called fractional T-1 and fractional T-3, which divide the channel into several subchannels, at a reduced cost and speed. Your local service provider's representatives can quote rates. As with digital dial-up connections, you will need special equipment to access these services.

Where the only option was once to lease a dedicated line from one site to another, there is now an alternative that is expanding very rapidly, due to its relative economy. This alternative is Frame Relay, which provides a structure similar to X.25, but at T-1 or even T-3 speeds. Frame Relay and X.25 are described in the "Connecting LANs Around the World" section.

Other Options

Other options for connecting LANs include satellite communications, microwave relays, and independent providers of services similar to those available from the phone companies.

Satellite services can provide widespread communications for organizations with many sites across a continent. However, the drawback is that satellite communications are more expensive than leased lines for distances of less than a thousand miles or so. They also tend to be slower than land-based communications, at least unless large, expensive antennas are installed rather than the usual 6-foot dish.

Microwave relays can provide high-speed, secure communications between sites, but are generally so expensive that they are reserved for highly specialized applications and those with unlimited budgets (like the government). Some organizations such as railroads, television networks, or cellular phone companies may lease some of their extra capacity. Within limited ranges (three to five miles), inexpensive microwave equipment can provide 1.5 Mbps connectivity to a large number of sites for a one-time investment with no monthly fees. The drawbacks are that the range is limited and all sites to be connected must be in line-of-sight.

Connecting LANs around the World

Beyond WANs and MANs are world-wide networks. Depending on the country you need to connect to, you may find that standard services range from some that are more sophisticated than U.S. services, to some that are barely above the level of carrier pigeons. Western Europe, for example, has large areas already networked with ISDN and ATM, and Eastern Europe has areas in which the line quality is so bad that special modems are required to support any speed over 300 Bps.

Cost can also be a major factor. A leased line that costs $1,200 per month to connect San Francisco to New York could cost $3,600 a month to London, and $5,000 a month to Tokyo.

X.25

X.25 is the CCITT standard for a terminal interfacing with a packet-switching network. It is implemented world-wide in many public and private networks.

Illustrations of X.25 typically show a number of different types of installations, all with lines ending in a cloud in the center of the picture. This is meant to illustrate the wide variety of ways that users can access X.25 services, and the large number of possible routes that the data can take from one end to the other.

X.25 services can be accessed by dial-up lines or leased lines, at speeds from 1200 Bps to 1.544 Mbps or higher. The primary advantage to this type of service is that it is very widespread and widely supported by many vendors. The biggest disadvantage is that it is relatively slow. It is an excellent way of forwarding e-mail between LANs, but would not be appropriate for a regularly used data connection.

Frame Relay

Frame Relay is similar to X.25 in that it is often pictured as a cloud. However, it can provide speeds of T-1 (1.5 Mbps) or T-3 (45 Mbps). Charges are based on the local-access charge at each end, plus a set fee for the long-distance connection. It can provide a very cost-effective method of connecting remote sites. Frame Relay service is expanding rapidly because the overall cost can be much lower than for dedicated lines.

The problem with Frame Relay is that all the traffic from all customers goes through the same public network. This means that unless you pay for guaranteed access speeds, you may experience delays if there are lots of other people using the network, too.

Leased Lines

Typically, any service that can be had across town can be had around the world, but the cost will be much higher. For instance, T-1 lines typically double in cost as distances increase from 500 miles to 2000 miles, so connecting New York to Japan will increase the cost considerably. Where a 1000-mile T-1 (1.544 Mbps) line might cost $10,000 per month, a T-3 (45 Mbps) line would cost $100,000 per month. For longer distances, especially overseas, these prices go up much higher.

Other Options

As distances increase, satellite communications may become more practical. If you have heavy traffic between LANs on different continents, a satellite link can provide reliable, relatively inexpensive high-speed throughput. The initial installation can be expensive, but with enough use, it can save you money over a leased line that continues to cost you money every month.

Additional Fault Points of WANs

As is sometimes the case within buildings, the actual hardware and wiring used to connect your LANs will seldom belong to you or be under your control. The positive side of this is that the service provider is responsible for maintaining, troubleshooting, and upgrading this hardware. The down side is that it can be difficult to get a response from some companies as quickly as you would like in an emergency. Although you won't deal with equipment that is typically outside your jurisdiction, you will need to be able to determine whether it's your equipment or the phone company's that is causing the problem.

Of course, the basic principles of troubleshooting apply to WAN equipment as well. If your problem is with an existing installation, determine what has changed. One item that makes routers and bridges different from most of the equipment you'll deal with is that they add items on their own. They build lists of the equipment and networks they know about. If a workstation with the wrong address comes up on the network, the router could add the address, then become confused about the services it's supposed to provide. You can usually reboot the router and get back to the default routing table.

If it's a new installation, get the most basic configuration possible working first, then add the additional features in. This might mean concentrating on IPX first, then other protocols, or even following the boot process similar to a PC's to see if the router is operating correctly.

Another item to look at is the scope of the problem. Is every group in the building affected? If you can isolate the groups having problems, you can get an idea of what they have in common.

Troubleshooting WAN Hardware

The basic WAN hardware is a device that sends traffic from your LAN to another LAN. This may be as simple as a repeater on either end of a few hundred feet of coaxial cable to link two buildings, or as complex as a T-1 bridge connected to a CSU/DSU, attached to a leased line that connects two sites in different states.

From a troubleshooting standpoint, there is very little difference in the basic approach to either of the extremes. First determine whether traffic is getting to the WAN link device, then whether the device is operating correctly, and finally whether the device is able to read signals coming or going on the link. If these conditions are all met, the problem is probably elsewhere. Of course, determining these items can be difficult, especially without a LAN analyzer or similar equipment. The simplest test is to see whether you can get to any devices on the other end of the connection.

Problems with Repeaters

Repeaters are the simplest type of device used to link LANs. Depending on the distance, you could use a repeater to link two buildings with either thin or thick Ethernet, or with a fiber-optic connection. Thin Ethernet allows a maximum distance of 185 meters (about 600 feet), and thick Ethernet allows 500 meters (more than 1600 feet). A fiber-optic connection can be up to several miles.

It is relatively simple to tell whether most repeaters are operating. If the activity lights on the front are blinking, the device is probably working. Also, if a device on one side of the repeater can see devices on the other side, the connection is working. The additional fault points for this type of setup include the repeater at each end of the long cable and the long cable itself. With a multiport repeater, the separate ports can be isolated, usually with switches. This can make isolating parts of the network for troubleshooting easier, but it can also cause problems if a port is shut off accidentally.

Problems with Bridges

A bridge can be used for something as simple as a few hundred feet of cable linking two buildings or for an application as complex as a T-1 leased line linking a New York office to a Los Angeles office. As with any other network connection device, the elements for troubleshooting are to determine whether the traffic is getting to the bridge, whether the bridge is operational, and whether the traffic is getting from the bridge to the other side of the link.

Bridges, routers, and gateways usually can be accessed through remote management or monitoring software, which means you can make sure that the device is operational without needing to physically go to it and use its console. You should also be able to examine the routing table to determine what network devices the bridge knows about.

A simple way to isolate a bridge as a break point is to try to attach to a server that is on the other side of the bridge. If you know that the server is up (if workstations on that side of the bridge can attach to it), but you can't reach it from the far side of the bridge, you have isolated the break point to the bridge or to the physical connections attached to the bridge.

Problems with Routers

A router may be internal to a server (a server with two NICs that routes between the two LANs), or it may be a stand-alone product, running either proprietary software on proprietary hardware or generic software on a PC platform. Novell has two products, the standard router included with NetWare, and the Multi-Protocol Router (MPR), both of which run on a standard PC platform.

The troubleshooting process described above for bridges applies equally well to routers. The biggest difference is that because routers handle multiple protocols, a router may be routing one protocol (perhaps IPX) correctly, but not another (such as TCP/IP). To isolate such problems, you will need to check each protocol to see if it is being forwarded through the router.

Problems with Gateways

Gateways can be more difficult to troubleshoot because they generally involve a service as well as protocol translation. For instance, a gateway that allows Macintoshes to print to a UNIX printer might seem to be inoperative when the actual problem was that the LPD daemon on the UNIX host wasn't working. To troubleshoot gateways, you must understand the process on both sides of the device. Whether file, print, or mail services, you should be able to determine that the process is functioning properly on both sides of the gateway. The starting point here is to make sure that the service can be used from the near side first.

For instance, if your are trying to determine if a gateway is causing the printing problem in which Macintoshes on one network can't print to a printer on a UNIX system on the other side of a gateway, try printing from the UNIX system first. If that works, try printing from another UNIX system. If that also works, then you can safely assume that the physical process of printing is okay. However, one user might be able to print and another not, depending on how access to the queue is set up. You should be sure that the Macintosh user is set up as a user on the UNIX system, or that the permissions will allow anyone to use the queue. If it all works, then you can move on to testing the gateway.

Problems with Dial-in/Dial-out Servers

With more and more services accessible through modems, dial-in/dial-out servers are allowing users to connect with a network from home or a portable computer, or dial out to a service from their office, without needing to have a modem for each workstation on the LAN. One such server, with up to 16 modems, can serve the needs of dozens of users at a much lower cost than a modem for each work-station. Consolidating the modems on a network in this way can also enhance security and make upgrades to hardware and software much easier. Some network modems also provide fax services. As ISDN becomes more available, servers are beginning to support ISDN modems as well.

TELECOMMUNICATIONS STANDARDS The biggest difficulty in trouble-shooting dial-in and dial-out connections lies in the lack of standardization in the telecommunications world. There are many protocols and standards, such as V.32, V.32bis, V.42, and so on, "Hayes-compatible," and others. The problem is that different manufacturers do not always implement these standards in the same way. Even modems that claim to be Hayes-compatible may have different default command sets than other modems that also claim Hayes compatibility. The modem world very much resembles the PC world before the IBM PC became the dominant standard. There are many manufacturers offering enhanced performance, but their equipment may only work with the same modem on the other end.

There is also no set standard for communication protocols. The simplest protocols specify data bits (7 or 8), parity (odd, even, or none), stop bits (1, 1.5, or 2), and speed (50–57,600 baud). There are also several data-compression schemes, some "standard" and some proprietary. Furthermore, the serial port that connects the modem to the server may be a standard COM port or an enhanced port using the 16550 UART chip or the one offered by the Novell WNIM+ adapter. The only way to ensure that these settings match is to speak with the users on the other end and ascertain what settings they are using.

Baud is the number of transitions per second in a signal on a line. It is commonly, but not always accurately, equated with bits per second. For instance, 9600 baud with compression can produce 19,200 Bps or more.

COMMUNICATIONS SETTINGS Setting up the server itself will not require that you confirm that both sides of a connection are using the same speed, protocol, and so on, but you cannot troubleshoot problems with such connections without understanding the settings. There are several parts to a dial-in/dial-out server. The easy parts are the ones that are the same on any server: the work-station, NIC, COM port or WNIM+ adapter, operating system software, and server software. You may also need to troubleshoot the user's software that is accessing the server. The hard part comes when everything up to the modem is working correctly.

The great number of possible settings makes it imperative that you know exactly what both sides of the connection you are trying to set up expect. Dial-in/dial-out servers include software for the workstation that allows the user to configure the modem for the protocol that is used on the other end. Many modems will negotiate automatically with the modem on the other end until they determine a common setting that they both understand. Unfortunately, this may be much slower than what could be achieved if the modems were both set properly to begin with. This can mean the difference between requiring a few minutes to send a file of several hundred kilobytes or a few hours to send the same file.

LINE QUALITY Another factor in the smooth operation of a dial-in/dial-out server is the line quality. You will probably want to use a line that doesn't pass through your PBX system. Check with your phone company for other options that may be available. You may already have such a line for your fax machine.

ISDN connections are both simpler and harder. The morass of protocols and standards goes away. Getting two ISDN modems to connect to each other is much simpler and faster than with analog modems. The hard part is getting the phone company to connect a line for you, and figuring out what it costs. Also, there are a two basic types of ISDN services. They are Basic Rate Interface (BRI), which provides two 64 Kbps channels plus a control channel, and Primary Rate Interface (PRI), which provides thirteen 64 Kbps channels plus a control channel. You may want a BRI at each remote site, and a PRI at your main office.

Dealing with Telecommunications Service Providers

In general, you will not be able to troubleshoot the problems that originate with your telecommunications service provider. However, you will get faster service if you do your best to eliminate all other possibilities before contacting the provider. If you have a good idea of the topology of your network, you should be able to isolate the problem to one side or the other side of the interface with the telecommunications network.

For example, if the workers in the other office can ping their router, but nothing past it, and you have the same experience, and the routers were working before, you probably have a bad connection. You should try at least this much fault isolation before calling the service provider.

Try to establish a relationship with a particular customer representative. Once you've established mutual trust, you won't need to prove to the telecommunication service company that you know what you're doing every time you call.

Troubleshooting WAN Software

There are two typical problems with software on a WAN:

- Incorrect configuration, which is symptomatic of a lack of planning or management on a WAN. This kind of problem is usually caused by two workstations or servers using the same address or network number, or two servers on the same cable segment not having the same number for that cable. In either case, the ultimate cause is a lack of documentation or standards for that network.

- Corruption of files or software freezes, which can be caused by many different things, such as hardware problems, user errors, bugs in the software, or configuration problems.

Most routers can be upgraded via software, and run proprietary code to route between sites. This code may be updated regularly, and the updates may fix one problem while breaking something else. There are several things you can do about this. One is to retain the old versions; better the devil you know than the one you don't. Also, develop a relationship with the vendor's tech support. If they know you, they'll not only respond better, but may make early releases available or be more honest about problems. Don't jump on a new release right away if what you have is working. Some of this software is so complex that it may seem that there's no way to make everything work—something will always be broken.

Software Planning and Management

At a minimum, you need to coordinate the internal network numbers, IPX numbers, and similar configuration settings for other protocols such as TCP/IP. You may need to coordinate these numbers with an outside agency. TCP/IP, for example, is regulated by the Defense Data Network's Network Information Center. If you have a site that is not connected to the Internet, and never will be, you can use any numbers that are valid. If you want to be able to connect to the rest of the world, you must have an assigned address. The same will shortly be true of IPX addresses.

NETWORK ADDRESSES Management software will quickly compile and show you all the addresses in use on your network. If you don't have such software, use the forms in Appendix C to document your network manually. This not only ensures that you won't have address conflicts, it will also make troubleshooting easier when you receive a message like: "node at 140.11.138.244 has caused a bindery error." Another alternative is to use a service that provides addresses when PCs boot. There are several for TCP/IP, including BOOTP and DHCP.

CONFIGURATION UTILITIES Bridges, routers, and gateways come with some sort of configuration utility. This utility will usually allow you to monitor and troubleshoot the device as well as establish the initial configuration.

If you have a NetWare server that is also acting as a router, you can use NetWare utilities to monitor the router. Utilities such as MONITOR, FCONSOLE, and TCPCON enable you to track packets sent and received and monitor other device information.

With both stand-alone devices and servers, you should have some idea of what the normal traffic looks like and what normal statistics are for the device. If nothing more, occasionally open the device with the configuration utility and look at the information, just to familiarize yourself with what things should look like. Unless you know this, you won't know what is out of whack when you're trying to troubleshoot the device.

Baselining, as discussed throughout this book, is one of the cornerstones of troubleshooting. It is very difficult to know if something is wrong unless you know what it should look like. The items to look for at the most basic level will tell you that traffic is moving in and out of your device. The specifics will vary with the type of device, the protocol, and so on, but you should see information about the number of packets received, number of packets sent, and the number of bad packets (often subdivided into different types of bad packets, depending again on the type of protocol).

For example, if you have been monitoring the packet information and know that you are usually receiving about 10,000 packets a day, and the number drops to 1,000 or jumps to 100,000, you will have a start on finding the problem. If you are receiving a larger number than you are sending, this may also indicate a problem. Of course, large or steadily increasing numbers of bad packets also indicate a problem. The NetWare System Administration manual discusses the statistics that MONITOR tracks, and the manual for your device or monitoring software may also describe which items you should check.

The causes of bad packets, and how to isolate and fix the problem, are the subject of numerous books. LANalyzer for Windows offers a distinct advantage is this area; it has a help facility called the Network Advisor that will tell you not only that bad packets are being received, but also what typically causes that sort of error and where it is coming from. I highly recommend this product or something similar for anyone with a large LAN or multiple LANs. The LANalyzer for Windows package also includes a very good book on the subject, Novell's Guide to NetWare LAN Analysis, *by Laura Chappell, which covers using LAN-alyzer for Windows to diagnose problems on Ethernet.*

Software Configuration

Once you get a configuration that works for a network device, server, or whatever, record it! Keep copies of the information with the machine, in a central area, and at home. It will be useful in reconstructing a device after the configuration is lost, in identifying conflicts with other devices, and in determining the best settings for new devices.

If you have your configurations documented, you can also avoid discovering conflicts after they have caused every server on your network to crash or caused a "Router Configuration Error" message. Solving a conflict problem quickly won't make you look good if you could have avoided it in the first place. Also, since routers may add to their configuration tables automatically, you should have a base configuration that you can return to if there are problems.

Address Conflicts

A major problem with LANs is also one of their benefits. They are not terribly complex (compared with a mainframe) and can be administered by local personnel, rather than requiring a centralized IS department. However, as companies and their networks grow, some level of coordination becomes critical. With two or three servers, the chances that two will use the same internal IPX number seem minuscule, but that's exactly the time to begin coordinating information, not when there are fifty servers.

With an IPX address conflict, you will get a "Router Configuration Error" and an annoying beep on the server's console. With a TCP/IP address conflict, you may have every workstation on your network crash. The only way to avoid address conflicts is to document configurations and coordinate with other administrators.

Network Management Tools

As NETWORKS GROW IN COMPLEXITY, the need for management and diagnostic software becomes greater. With a single LAN, it's relatively easy to determine whether network traffic is getting to a device or not. Once you have several LANs, perhaps running different or multiple protocols, diagnosing problems becomes much more difficult. Fortunately, the software necessary to help you determine and fix problems is becoming less expensive and more capable all the time. For example, the original Novell LANalyzer product retailed for around $15,000. LANalyzer for Windows offers 90 percent of the functionality, plus some great features the original product lacks, and has a street price of under $1,000.

If you have a WAN, or even multiple LANs at a single site, you should have some level of network monitoring capability. You can usually diagnose most WAN problems without such capability—eventually. Given the cost of having dozens or hundreds of users offline for hours while you track down what went wrong, the software will quickly pay for itself.

What's Available

There are network management and/or analysis products ranging in price from less than $100 to about $100,000. The capabilities you need depend on the complexity of your network. The basic, bottom-line capability is to track the packets flowing on your network. How much the program can tell about the packets, and the other diagnostic tools included, will depend on the product.

Most products can cover only one LAN. You will need a basic tool for each LAN segment, or a more capable (and expensive) product that can cover the WAN. Top-of-the-line packages include a workstation (usually a UNIX workstation) and may offer services such as network mapping that will alert you if any configuration on your WAN changes.

It can be difficult to justify spending money on preventive measures and "conveniences." However, you can estimate the cost of downtime per hour on your LAN, and then measure that against the cost of a tool that could save you hours in getting your network fixed and back online. The larger your network or internetwork, the easier it is to justify management and diagnostic tools, and the more you need such tools.

Features to Look For

The following sections describe some of the basic features that you may want in your network management package. You can then use the information resources listed in Appendix A to determine the best program for you. Appendix B lists some of the software available.

Packet Monitoring

You should be able to see information on the various types of packets moving on the network, including numbers of good and bad packets and their sources. Packet-monitoring facilities may also include the ability to look at the header information for each packet, or to decode the packet completely and look at the contents. You will usually be able to set thresholds for certain types of events, and the software will then notify you if the limits you set are exceeded.

Trend Analysis

Some programs allow you to save information about your network's normal traffic and establish trends over time. This can be enormously helpful in both identifying problems and upgrading your network before performance degrades significantly.

Online Help

You can have megabytes of decoded packets, but unless you understand what the information in the packet header means, the data won't do you much good. You can have an alarm that tells you that your token-ring network is beaconing, but unless you know what beaconing is and what the likely source of the problem is, there isn't much you can do with the information. You can learn this information in a class such as the Basic and Advanced LANalyzer classes available through Novell Authorized Education Centers, or you can get a book on the subject and learn the information yourself, or you can get a program that will help you figure it out. (The Network Advisor in LANalyzer for Windows is a great example of how such built-in help should work.)

SNMP Management

The Simple Network Management Protocol (SNMP) is a standard for managing networking devices that many manufacturers incorporate into their software and hardware. If your management software and your network devices support SNMP, you will be able to manage many different devices, from different manufacturers, with one management tool.

Network Mapping

Management programs offer many levels of network mapping. Some produce simple logical maps of your network that tell you how many workstations are on each segment and provide some basic information about them. Other programs can keep track of data on device locations, distance between devices, types of connections, and so on, and can then help you isolate faults caused by changes in the physical network.

Network Inventory

Network inventory programs also span a wide range of functionality. Simpler programs can tell you what kind of workstation is at each network address. Other programs can tell you all the software on every workstation's disk, the operating system version, the contents of the AUTOEXEC.BAT and CONFIG.SYS files, and more. You can even find programs that allow you to track usage of applications and how many valid copies of each you have, and update software remotely on every workstation.

Server Management

NetWare provides some basic tools for managing your server and keeping track of users, and so on, but these tools are limited. There are a number of companies offering extensions to NetWare. These products allow you to print reports of all users and the files and directories they own and have trustee rights to; the setups of printers, print servers, and print queues; the basic configuration files and the ones for any additional NLMs you may have installed; and other aspects of your server. If you have more than one server, or even one that has a lot of disk space or many users, this sort of utility can make your documentation chores much easier. Some programs will even monitor CPU utilization, disk access, and memory usage and alert you if you need to upgrade your processor, NIC, or disk system.

Diagnostic Tools

DIAGNOSTIC TOOLS RANGE from a simple volt-meter or continuity checker to a $100,000 package, preinstalled on a UNIX workstation, that can monitor your entire WAN and alert you if problems arise or are about to arise. The two basic categories are hardware-based products and software-only products. Hardware-based tools are generally faster, and often more capable than software-only tools, and usually more expensive, as well.

Many diagnostic tools include management functions, and some management tools can be used for diagnostic purposes—it depends as much on how you are using the tool as what it is intended for. The two functions should be tightly integrated: if you manage your network well, and document it well, you will often be able to avoid problems before they arise.

The larger your network, the more you should have some kind of diagnostic tools. There are many multi-site networking problems that cannot be diagnosed without the right tools, or at least will take much longer to figure out. Some networking errors are quite deceptive. For example, a bad routing table can produce errors that are similar to other types of problems.

Hardware-Based Products

Most hardware-based tools for WAN troubleshooting include protocol analysis. They may be referred to as sniffers, protocol analyzers, or packet decoders. These are all descriptions of the same basic function: intercepting the packets flowing through your network and gathering information about them. The differences between products lie in how much they will do with the packets and how much information they can collect, sort, generate reports on, and watch over a period of time to establish trends.

If you have a large internetwork or very high levels of traffic, the hardware-based products can still provide an advantage. At the high end of the scale, products are available that provide much more than capturing and decoding packets. They may be able to monitor every device on your network at once, or build both physical and logical maps of your network, or even allow you to simulate different network configurations so you can plan upgrades in advance.

Protocol Analyzers

A protocol analyzer consists of two parts: the hardware that collects the packets that are traveling along the wires of your network, and the software that provides you with information about those packets. The hardware may be a special NIC for your workstation or a complete (sometimes portable) workstation. The need for dedicated hardware is decreasing as LAN adapters grow in power. Many modern LAN adapters include a CPU with more power than PCs had a few years ago, as well as on-board RAM.

There are problems that simply can't be solved without a protocol analyzer, and many others that will take much longer to diagnose without one. For instance, if all the packets from another site are arriving, but have been mangled by the router, all the connection lights will be on, and everything will appear to be working, but you won't be able to communicate. A protocol analyzer is the only way to see a problem like this directly, although you might get a clue from your server showing that all the packets from a certain address are bad.

Hardware-based protocol analyzers range in price from a few hundred dollars to $50,000 or more for some workstation-based integrated network management and analysis tools. The level of capability you will want (or need) will depend on the complexity of your internetwork and its stability. If you seldom or never have new networks or servers added to your network, you may not need much management capability at all. If you have a dynamic, growing internetwork, or are supporting hardware or software development, for instance, you will probably want more capability.

The basic items you should look for in a protocol analyzer include:

- What protocols are supported? Even if you are only using one protocol now, you may want to leave room for expansion or upgrades in the future.

- How much information will the product gather? This may range from simply telling you how many packets of each type are coming through the network to providing specific information such as the original sender of the packet, its intended recipient, the purpose of the data in the packet, and the contents of the data part of the packet. Some products may allow trend analysis over periods from days to years.

- Can it save your network information in a spreadsheet or database format? You should look at what data formats the product will export to.

- Can the product simulate network traffic levels (loads)? One of the problems that you will face in trying to troubleshoot WAN problems is that some of them will occur sporadically or periodically. Some protocol analyzers will also allow you to simulate a number of users producing various levels of traffic to stress the network, hopefully reproducing the conditions that caused your problem.

- Can the product gather information about the networking devices that connect your LANs? Some products are limited to gathering information about the single LAN segment they are attached to.

- Does the product support SNMP or CMIP (Common Management Information Protocol)? If so, you will be able to remotely manage any devices that also support these protocols.

- How portable is the product? Many protocol analyzers can only see the LAN segment they are attached to. If you have to carry the machine from segment to segment, it's nice to have a fairly small package.

- Does the product include time-domain reflectometry (TDR)? This allows you to isolate cable breaks to a particular distance from your location or the nearest node. TDR can be invaluable in tracing cabling problems.

- Does the product include packet filtering? This allows you to select packets that fit certain parameters; for instance, you could select only the packets being sent by a certain workstation or server. You might consider the number of filters a product has, the degree of flexibility in combining filters to provide Boolean searches, and whether it allows you to create your own filters.

Other Hardware Tools

Other types of diagnostic tools serve specialized functions. Some examples are:

- Stand-alone products that perform the TDR function mentioned in the previous section to determine the location of breaks in your cabling

- Continuity testers, which can check cabling for breaks, and in some cases, also check polarity, to make sure that the two wires in a twisted-pair connection haven't been crossed

- Voltage checkers, which can help diagnose a LAN adapter that is defective and unable to maintain the proper voltage

Software-Only Products

The only real difference between hardware-based products and software-only products is that software-only products rely on the standard networking hardware already installed on your workstation to gather the packets off the wire. These products will usually require a special LAN driver for your card, and they may not support all NICs. Software-only products are usually much less expensive than hardware-based products, but may be less capable or slower.

Tools in NetWare

NetWare comes with some basic tools that can be used for diagnosing problems on your networks, and these should not be underestimated. Using MONITOR, FCONSOLE, or TCPCON, you can determine traffic flows for each of the LAN cards in your server, and you can monitor some common problems, such as packets that are outside the normal size or improperly formatted. The only problem with these tools is that they have no data-gathering or reporting features. The numbers are reset every time you bring the server up or down, and there is no easy way of printing the information.

There are a number of inexpensive programs, some created but not supported by Novell, that can provide you with the ability to save these statistics and format them nicely for printed reports. If you can't fit anything more into your budget, I highly recommend that you at least get one of these reporting programs. Most are available as shareware from NetWire. (See Appendix B for a listing of some of the programs available and their sources.)

LANalyzer for Windows

One software product that is highly recommended for anyone managing more than two small LANs is LANalyzer for Windows. This extremely capable package not only has the advantage of being a Novell product, designed to work well with NetWare, but it also includes almost all of the features listed above for hardware-based products, as well as the Network Advisor, a tool that is a highly useful product in itself. It can not only recommend actions for any problem you are likely to run across, it can explain the underlying principles of networking involved and teach you the specialized terminology and concepts you need to know to really understand your network.

Other Software Products

There are many other software-only products available, designed to support various combinations of software platforms and many different LAN adapters, and offering widely varying capabilities. Most of the features in the list for hardware-based products are available, with the possible exceptions of load simulation and TDR. There may even be software-only products with these features coming soon. Use the sources listed in Appendix A to determine what's available and what will suit your needs. Your fellow administrators will generally be happy to tell you about their experiences with products they've used (sometimes in greater detail than you want).

Managing without Diagnostic Equipment

All of the products described so far can make your life easier, greatly speed up the process of finding and resolving problems, and enable you to manage larger networks with fewer network administrators. However, it is very rare that a problem will be unsolvable without such equipment. If you have the problem now and don't have the equipment, you will simply need to follow the basic principles of troubleshooting: identify the fault points, check them one at a time, and approach the problem systematically.

For example, if you have a problem with a network card that has gone bad, it may be *jabbering,* or sending out large numbers of bad packets. This may not only affect network performance in general, it may cause servers or workstations to freeze. In this case, something like LANalyzer for Windows could identify the problem in seconds. However, you could identify and isolate the problem without special tools by following a procedure like this:

- Check the LANs with MONITOR, looking for a large number of bad packets.

- Isolate each LAN until you find the one that is producing the faulty packets.

- Take workstations offline one at a time until you find the one that has the faulty NIC.

You might not be able to identify the NIC as the problem immediately, but you can isolate the problem to the workstation, which will then give you a limited number of fault points to check: the motherboard, the operating system, the LAN driver, the NIC, and the transceiver (if installed).

Services across WANs

L ANS WERE ORIGINALLY CONCEIVED of as a way to share resources, such as files, printers, and modems, within a department. Providing these services to many users across multiple LANs is a growing concern as companies grow or replace mainframes with LANs (commonly known as *downsizing* or *rightsizing*). Setting up, maintaining, and troubleshooting a print queue can be complex on a single LAN with a few dozen users. Trying to give users on other servers or at other sites access to your printer can become an enormous headache. These issues have become enough of a concern that NetWare 4.*x* contains many new features specifically designed to address the needs of users across WANs. These services are known collectively as NetWare Directory Services, or NDS, and are discussed a little later in this chapter.

Printing on WANs

Giving users outside your LAN access to your printer can be relatively simple. Just give the user GUEST and/or the group EVERYONE access to the print queue. However, a user in another state who needs to print a document to your printer (saving considerable time over mailing the printout) will need to know the exact name of your server, how to attach to it, the exact name of the print queue and print job, if any, and how to set up CAPTURE to print to that queue. They may also need other information if the printer is specialized (PostScript, a color printer, or the like).

Things can be further complicated if you need to restrict use of the printer and cannot grant GUEST or EVERYONE access to the queue. In this case, you may need to create a special user with access to the queue.

If you must coordinate the details of WAN printing, the first step is to document your configuration, including the configuration of the printer, print server, and print queue. As I have said many times before, you cannot overdo documentation. In this case, it is especially true. If a user in another state is on the phone, waiting for the information necessary to print to your printer, it will be much faster to open a binder and read the information off, than to log in, run three or more different programs to obtain the configuration information, and try to present it in an orderly manner. If this is a frequent request, you might want to prepare instructions on how to accomplish the process, which would also be very useful as part of a manual for new users on your LAN.

Another thing that will make your life easier is to take the time to set up print jobs and become familiar with the NetWare print utilities (PRINTCON, PCONSOLE, and CAPTURE). Use PRINTCON to define print jobs, rather than depending on long CAPTURE statements. It is much easier to explain (and document) CAPTURE J=LW than CAPTURE Q=PostScript F=1 NB NFF K. Similarly, you can set up a print job as the default job for the GUEST account, letting anyone logging in as GUEST print without further effort.

You can also set up queues on other servers that print to the print server on your LAN. If you have users on other servers who regularly send jobs to your printer, you may want to consider this. Keep in mind that this approach requires coordination between the supervisors of both servers, because you must be SUPERVISOR to create the queues, and SUPERVISOR on the other server to attach the queue to that server's print server.

Managing Multiple Logins

Some of your users may need to attach to more than one server. With NetWare 2.*x* and 3.*x*, you can LOGIN to only one server at a time. If you need to connect to more servers, you must use ATTACH, which does not execute a login script. This means that users attaching to multiple servers must manually execute the additional commands to map drives, set up default print queues, and so on.

NetWare 4.*x* fixes these problems by having one login for the entire network. However, you can make life easier for users by putting a batch file in the login directory that will execute the appropriate MAP and CAPTURE statements.

NetWare Directory Services and WANs

NETWARE 4.0 IS THE FIRST VERSION of NetWare designed specifically with the needs of large company-wide WANs in mind. Its principal new feature is the NDS database, which is the equivalent of a network-wide bindery that encompasses all the servers on your network. You can organize your network by logical groups, since you are no longer confined by the physical structure of your system.

The New Structure of NetWare 4.x

NDS uses a completely new paradigm for network structure. Instead of a group of servers, each with its own bindery, containing information on the users, printers, volumes, and so on for that server only, there is a single distributed Directory, with multiple copies replicated throughout the network, which contains information on all the resources, users, groups, and so on, on that network. Users, resources, and rights to those resources are managed on a network-wide basis, rather than by individual server. Each user has one login, and can log in from any workstation, on any LAN, and have the same access to resources that the user would have on his or her own workstation.

The NDS Tree

A company-wide internetwork is organized in a tree-like structure, as illustrated in Figure 8.1. The root is the total directory that encompasses the entire company. It is divided into *containers*, which are logical units such as divisions, organizations, workgroups, and so on. Containers may contain other containers. Each container contains *leaf* objects, which are entities such as users, printers, print queues, volumes, and so on. Leaf objects do not contain other objects. For example, you might be a user Admin, in a container Engineering (Organization), in a container Explosives (Organizational Unit), in a container Road Runner Traps (Organizational Unit), in a company Acme (Root).

Every container and leaf in the database has properties, which hold the information about the object. These include, for example, login name, phone number,

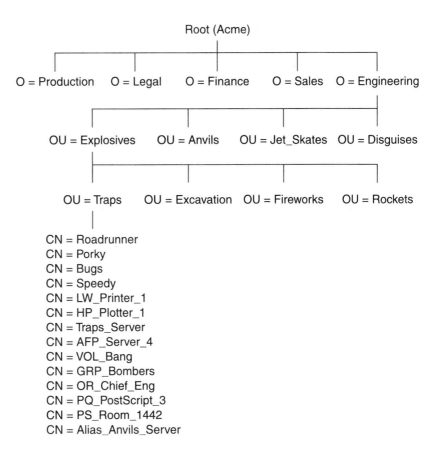

FIGURE 8.1
An example of a
NetWare 4.*x* NDS tree

address, and so on for a user object, and printer type, print queue, Access Control List, and so on for a printer object. An Access Control List is associated with each object, and it lists which users have access to that object.

NDS Objects

Every part of the network, whether container or leaf, is an object. There are essentially three types of objects: the root object, container objects, and leaf objects. There can be only one root object in a tree structure.

If you have two organizations, and make each a separate tree, with its own root, you can have great difficulty later merging the two trees into one. NetWare 4.1 provides a tool for merging trees, but you may find that usernames or other items are duplicated, and you will need to rename resources. It is also painful to change the names of existing Organization (container) objects. For these reasons, you should consider very carefully both your existing organization and possible growth or changes in structure before planning your network. I strongly recommend that you read the April 1993 NetWare Application Notes, Novell's QuickPath to NetWare 4.1 Networks, or the NDS booklet provided with each copy of Net-Ware 4.1 before planning a 4.x network.

There are two types of container objects you will usually see: Organization and Organizational Unit (OU). Each allows you to set defaults for a user, and to set up a login script for every user in that container. Each user can have only one container login script. Thus, you can give every member of a department access to the same resources, whether they are attached to the same server or located in different states.

There are many different leaf objects, organized into user-related objects, server-related objects, printer-related objects, informational objects, and miscellaneous objects. User-related objects include users, groups, organizational roles, and profiles. An organizational role is a set of rights that can be assigned to different users. For instance, if the manager of a group changes, you would disassociate the former manager as a user from the Manager organizational role object, and associate the new manager with that object. A profile is a type of login script that can be associated with a group of users who may not all be in the same Organizational Unit. Login scripts are executed in the following order: container login script (associated with the Organization or Organizational Unit), profile, and then user login script.

Server-related objects include servers, volumes, and directory maps. Servers and volumes are what you would expect. Directory maps can be thought of as aliases for a directory. If you map a search drive to a directory in your user's login scripts, and then later change the name of the directory, you will then need to change each login script. With a directory map, you can map the search drive to the directory map in the login scripts. Then if the name of the directory changes, you can modify the directory map and leave the login scripts as they are.

Printer-related objects include print queues, print servers, and printers. These are handled in the same manner as with previous versions of NetWare, but can be managed through the NDS system as well. Informational objects include AFP servers and computers. AFP servers are separate objects holding information on servers running the AppleTalk Filing Protocol. These may include NetWare servers represented by server objects. They will need a separate AFP server object to describe their AFP-related information. Computer objects store information about the computers on your network. They are not required, but are an easy way to store, maintain, and access the information you should have about the workstations on your network.

Miscellaneous objects include aliases, bindery objects, bindery queues, and unknown objects. Aliases are pointers to other objects in the NDS. They make it appear as if the object referred to is located where the alias is stored. Aliases are a simple way to give users in one container access to resources in another container. Bindery objects and bindery queues are used to provide backward-compatibility with previous versions of NetWare. They represent resources that are to be made available to users with previous versions of NetWare. Unknown objects are objects that cannot be classified as a known type of object.

NWADMIN: The New Management Tool

The most welcome addition to the management tools provided with NetWare in version 4.*x* is NWADMIN. This is a graphic user interface utility that runs under Windows.

NWADMIN can show you the entire network (if you have the rights to view the whole network) and allow you to inspect, modify, create, or delete objects on any part of the network (if you have those rights). It allows you to perform tasks that previously required switching between a half-dozen different programs such as SYSCON, FILER, PCONSOLE, PRINTCON, and PRINTDEF.

Troubleshooting NDS

NetWare 4.*x* can be harder to troubleshoot than older versions of NetWare, simply because it allows a more complex structure to be built. Some things to watch for are:

- Make your directory structure as flat as possible. Try not to have more than three or at most four levels of organization.

- Don't have too many copies of the directory. The directory is updated regularly, and every copy is also updated. If there are too may copies, your network traffic may become unmanageable.

- Remember to think globally. Don't have more than one account per user. Similarly, login scripts from multiple accounts on prior versions of NetWare must be consolidated. Be sure that you resolve any potential conflicts in the new scripts.

- You may find that you will have different EVERYONE groups and GUEST accounts in different partitions. This can happen if you use the server upgrade system to upgrade to NetWare 4.*x*. Each server has a different membership for EVERYONE, and this forces the creation of a new group.

- The biggest problem for users with NDS will be in understanding the new structure, especially contexts. Make certain you understand the contexts on your network completely. I recommend setting the user's context at login to their usual work area. This will allow them to type:

  ```
  login username
  ```

- instead of:

  ```
  login .cn=username.ou=widgets.o=marketing
  ```

In general, the differences between NetWare 4.*x* and NetWare 3.*x* are in the organizational structures allowed rather than in the underlying protocols used. Of course, there will be an adjustment period as vendors upgrade their products to conform to the requirements of the newer versions, but your biggest problems will probably be related to the items listed above.

Connecting to
Other Systems

EW COMPANIES MORE THAN A FEW YEARS OLD have a homogeneous computing and network environment. More typically, some departments were automated with mainframe technology many years ago, and different sorts of PCs, topologies, and network operating systems are in use in different departments throughout the company. Integrating all these services into one network provides a number of benefits, such as easy communication and data exchange between groups, but it requires a much more complex network structure.

A large company might include an office using a mainframe or minicomputer for order entry, connected to another building through high-speed leased lines. The second building might have an IBM AS/400 serving workstations connected via Token Ring, a UNIX server connected to workstations and terminals with Ethernet, Macintoshes connected to a NetWare server with EtherTalk, PC workstations connecting to a NetWare server with IPX and Windows 95, and NT clients attached to a Windows NT server.

These additional capabilities bring with them additional complexity, whether they are implemented within NetWare or with external devices. This chapter will guide you toward understanding the mechanisms involved in an internetwork and troubleshooting it. The primary difficulty from a troubleshooting point of view is that you must understand the basics of both the networks and of whatever hardware or software you are using to translate between them. This chapter outlines the basics of other operating systems and suggests possible problem areas in the interface between the systems.

Methods for Connecting to Other Systems

S AY YOU HAVE TWO NETWORKS, one consisting of PCs running DOS and connecting to a NetWare server, and the other containing UNIX workstations connecting to a UNIX server. There are three ways to allow two different systems to connect:

- On one of the servers, you can run software that allows the other network's workstations to access files on that server. In this case, that would mean running NetWare NFS on the NetWare server or NetWare for UNIX (formerly Portable NetWare) on the UNIX server.

- You can add software to the workstations that allows them to communicate with the other network server. In this case, that would be LAN WorkPlace for DOS or the NetWare UNIX Client.

- You can add a gateway between the two systems that allows them to exchange files. One gateway can be run on a NetWare server. In this case, that would be the NetWare NFS Gateway, which allows DOS and Windows users to access UNIX volumes as if they were native NetWare drives and allows UNIX users to access NetWare volumes.

Each option has advantages and disadvantages. Running software on the server takes advantage of the processing power of the server, and is generally the most transparent to the user.

Software on the workstations allows you to keep the server free for more important tasks if it is already running near capacity, and can be cheaper if there are only a few of one type of workstation.

A gateway doesn't require any software on either servers or workstations and may provide services beyond what the software solutions have. But a gateway will produce a bottleneck that all traffic between the two systems must funnel through, which can become onerous on systems with lots of traffic.

Since a gateway is required between every two systems, a network with three different systems would require three gateways: one from network A to B, one from B to C, and one from A to C. This gateway setup is shown in Figure 9.1.

In a similar setup using NetWare software (assuming that NetWare is one of the three systems), only two packages are required to allow the other two systems to access NetWare services. Figure 9.2 shows three systems connected

FIGURE 9.1
Three LANs connected
with gateways

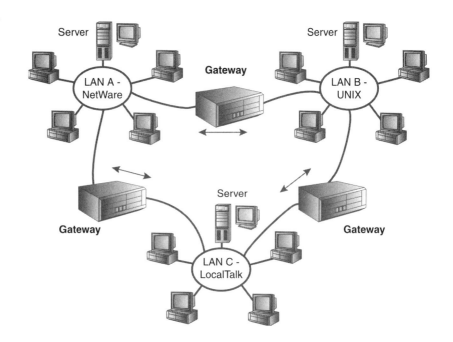

FIGURE 9.2
Three LANs connected
through NetWare

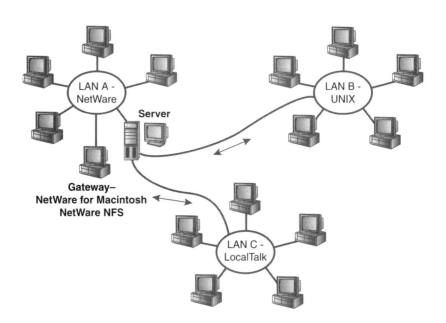

with NetWare packages. This approach is often cheaper than stand-alone gateways. It also offers higher performance and provides more features.

Notice that in the second example, Figure 9.2, there is no direct connection between the Macintosh network and the UNIX network. Users on both LANs can share files by placing them on the NetWare server, or take advantage of the routing capabilities of the server to communicate with the other LAN. For instance, the Mac users could use MacTCP to send files to the UNIX workstations through the server.

NFS for NetWare and NetWare for UNIX are both fairly expensive. If your network has just a few users, you may find it more economical to use a gateway or client software. However, if you have more than ten or so users, or want to allow for expansion, you should consider the server-based solutions, because they'll be less expensive in the long run.

Using a server-based solution also makes upgrades much simpler. Consider that upgrading a gateway will require at least a BIOS replacement, and possibly the whole system will need to be replaced. Workstations, of course, must all be updated individually when a new version is released, unless you are running a software update management package.

Connecting Other PC Operating Systems

THERE ARE MANY OPERATING SYSTEMS other than DOS that run on PC-compatibles. The first that comes to mind is Windows, especially Windows 95 and Windows NT, which do not use DOS. OS/2 is another major PC-based operating system. Several varieties of UNIX, from a number of vendors, run on PCs. These will be covered in a general way in the section "NFS for NetWare Access," later in the chapter. Some versions of PC-based UNIX also provide direct support for IPX and NetWare. Two of these are NeXTStep for PCs and UnixWare.

The client software that you use to allow DOS workstations to connect to another environment depends on which operating systems are running, as explained in the following sections. If you want to be able to access more than one environment at a time from a DOS workstation, you can run the ODI driver. ODI allows you to run IPX and other protocols such as TCP/IP at the same time, providing simultaneous access to both NetWare and other types of servers from the same workstation.

Windows Clients and NT Servers

Connecting Windows workstations to NetWare is discussed in Chapter 3. Here we will address getting Windows NT servers and NetWare servers to work together to provide client services.

NetWare has long been dominant in the network operating system marketplace. It offers more and better services for file and printer sharing, and for allowing different systems to communicate. However, as IS groups move applications that used to run on mainframes down to the client/server world, they have been less than wholly satisfied with NetWare as an applications server. This has led to the adoption of Windows NT for application services. Since NT performs file and print services, too, and since when the Windows 95 and NT clients first came out they didn't support NetWare well, many groups that need applications services have switched over to Windows for Workgroups (WFW), Windows 95, or Windows NT clients running on Windows NT servers.

Of course, companies that are running NDS, or that need to connect to systems not yet supported (or supported well) under Windows NT, are continuing to run NetWare. Some groups have found that NT doesn't provide the same level of performance for basic file and print services, especially for large groups or under heavy loads. The real challenge to someone supporting both a NetWare and Windows NT Server environment is getting users of both servers to be able to share information and services.

Protocols and Installation

By default, Windows clients of NT servers don't have access to NetWare services, and NetWare clients may not be able to access NT servers, depending on how they were set up. This is because the default protocol for Windows clients attaching to a Windows NT server (NetBIOS or TCP/IP, depending on the version) is different from the default for a Windows client attaching to a NetWare server (IPX/SPX). You can load support for both types of servers when installing the clients, or use a different protocol than the default on the servers.

If you know in advance that a Windows client will need to access both NetWare and NT servers, you can install both NetWare and Microsoft networking when you install Windows. This is a simple procedure and it works well. If you need access to NDS services, you will need either the add-on Microsoft driver or the Novell Windows 95 client software, but the installation process in not difficult.

As alternatives to loading both protocols on all clients that need to see both servers, you can use two products from Microsoft:

- File and Print Services for NetWare (FPNW). FPNW allows an NT server to appear to NetWare clients as a NetWare server, making its drives and print queues available through the NetWare shell.

- Gateway Services for NetWare (GSN). GSN lets you attach a NetWare server's drives and print queues to an NT server, and lets its clients access them as if they were on the NT server.

You should be aware of filename differences among systems. If you are using FPNW to make a Windows NT server available to NetWare clients, and the clients are DOS or Windows 3.*x*, they will not be able to see the long filenames used by later versions of Windows. Likewise, if you are using GSN to allow Windows 95 or NT clients to use a NetWare server's drives, those drives must have the OS/2 name space loaded to be able to support long filenames. FPNW is an add-on, extra cost product. It is still in its first generation and doesn't support NDS yet, and there may be other problems.

Security Concerns

Another area that can cause problems is security. The peer-to-peer oriented security of Windows 95 and Windows for Workgroups can allow users to accidentally give access to their workstation drives to others in the group. NT has 27 security privileges in contrast to NetWare's 6 or 7. Describing how these privileges map to each other and how they interoperate is beyond the scope of this book.

If you are supporting this kind of environment, the best you can do is to make sure you fully understand how permissions work on each of the systems you support. Experiment with user accounts to see how permissions cross boundaries. Set up some normal user accounts for this; administrator accounts often will not encounter problems that others may, because administrators usually have access to everything.

OS/2 and NetWare Access

NetWare versions 2.15c and later support access by OS/2 workstations. OS/2 requires additional software to access NetWare services. The OS/2 Requester is supplied with NetWare and is also available on NetWire. OS/2 Warp and Warp Connect come with the OS/2 Requester. OS/2 also requires a directory on the server equivalent to the SYS:\PUBLIC\DOS directory, to supply the OS/2 files corresponding to LOGIN.EXE, SLIST.EXE, SYSCON.EXE, and so on. These files are supplied on the OS/2 Requester disk. If you are running the High Performance File System (HPFS), you must also have OS/2 name space support on the server.

Two things to remember with OS/2 clients are:

- When you log in or attach to another server, that server must also have the OS/2 directory. You must have LOGIN.EXE or ATTACH.EXE on your local drive, as well as any other NetWare utilities you might want to run, such as SLIST, SYSCON, or PCONSOLE.

- You must make sure that the DLLPATH to the NetWare requester files is in the DLLPATH set up for your environment, or edit the AUTOEXEC.BAT file and add the path to the NetWare DLLs to your DLLPATH statement.

NeXTStep and the NetWare UNIX Client

NeXTStep is the first PC-based UNIX operating system to include the NetWare UNIX Client (NUC). It provides direct access to NetWare file servers through the normal login and authentication process. It allows you to print to NetWare queues as well as to standard UNIX queues. NeXTStep must be configured to use the NUC. This can be done during installation or afterwards. Once the NUC is installed, it automatically provides access to any available NetWare servers.

Filenames are automatically translated into the DOS eight.three format when they are moved to a NetWare server. In fact, the filenames are automatically truncated even if the NetWare server supports the NFS name space, unless the server is also running NUC.NLM. Other than file-translation problems and the ubiquitous permission problems that occur when NetWare and UNIX collide (see the section "NetWare and UNIX Permissions," later in this chapter), you are unlikely to encounter problems with this setup. The Ethernet interface and driver software are built-in and supported by the operating system itself.

UnixWare and NetWare Support

UnixWare, being a Novell product, supports NetWare and IPX automatically. In fact, that is the default configuration. To get support for the UNIX standards TCP/IP and NFS, you must add a support package.

Be sure that the installed NIC is supported by UnixWare and that the PC meets the minimum standard for UnixWare, and there shouldn't be problems with this setup. Unless you have NFS name space support and are running NUC.NLM on the server, only DOS eight-character filenames will be supported on the server. Both UNIX and NetWare printers and print queues are fully supported.

Connecting Macintoshes

THERE ARE FOUR BASIC WAYS to connect a Macintosh network with a NetWare PC-based network:

- You can run NetWare for Macintosh on the NetWare server. (Note that there is no equivalent for an AppleShare server; there may not even be a server in the AppleTalk environment.)

- You can run AppleTalk on the PC workstations, which would be expensive. This requires an AppleTalk network adapter in addition to the regular NIC that connects the PC to the NetWare server.

- You can run IPX (the NetWare protocol) on the Macs, as long as they are connected to the network with EtherTalk, rather than AppleTalk. This can be an inexpensive solution, especially if you have a number of NetWare servers and don't want to install NetWare for Macintosh on all of them.

- You can run a gateway that translates between the PCs and Macs.

NetWare for Macintosh on the Server

All versions of NetWare from version 2.1 on support AppleTalk. The method is different for 2.x than for later versions. NetWare 2.x servers use the VAP (Value-Added Process) to add AppleTalk support and allow Macintoshes to access NetWare volumes. The VAPs function as an AppleTalk gateway. That is, AppleTalk is converted to IPX, file or print requests are processed by the server, and the results are converted back to AppleTalk.

Under NetWare 3.*x* and 4.*x*, this functionality is provided by NetWare for Macintosh. This product is a series of NLMs that provides direct support for the AppleTalk Filing Protocol (AFP) and AppleTalk Print Services (ATPS). With NetWare for Macintosh, there is no gateway; the NetWare server is running AFP and ATPS as if it were an AppleShare server.

Servers running NetWare for Macintosh should have a minimum of 5 MB RAM, plus the RAM required for name space support. You can calculate the RAM for name space support by multiplying the number of megabytes on the volume by .032 and dividing the product by the block size (the default is 4 KB blocks—divide by 4). For example, a server with one 660 MB hard drive that has Mac name space support loaded and 4 KB blocks would need (660 x .032) / 4 = 5.28 MB. Add the 5 MB minimum and you have 10.28. The server will probably allow you to install 8 or 16 MB—it would need 16, assuming no other memory requirements, such as other name spaces, other NLMs, or additional protocols.

Configuring AppleTalk Support

Configuring AppleTalk support requires that you understand the basics of AppleTalk networking. AppleTalk is a protocol that can run over LocalTalk, which is the built-in interface provided on every Macintosh. Or it can be run over Ethernet or Token Ring, using EtherTalk or TokenTalk, respectively. An AppleTalk network can theoretically have up to 254 nodes, although 100 nodes is a more practical maximum in real-life conditions.

AppleTalk Phase II provides support for large networks, allowing up to 1024 zones, each with up to 254 nodes. If you run AppleTalk Phase II on your network, every server or router must also be running Phase II; don't mix it with Phase I. This can be done with transition routing, but isn't worth it. Upgrading everything on your network to Phase II requires changing only the software drivers, and is very much worth the trouble.

When configuring your server, remember that the zone name may contain spaces. If you can't get access to a particular zone, try inserting a leading or trailing space in the configuration entry; it's easy to accidentally put a space at the beginning or end of a zone name when you create the name. This also applies to printer names. A simple way to test for spaces is to use ATCON.NLM to do a lookup test in the suspect zone or on the suspect printer. If the lookup fails with the name spelled as it looks, try adding spaces before or after, until the lookup succeeds. If you have control over the zone and printer names, you should change the names to remove the spaces.

If you set up NetWare print queues that print to Macintosh printer, you will see both the NetWare queue and the printer itself in the Macintosh Chooser. You may wish to hide the printer itself, to keep users from printing directly to the printer, which can insert their print jobs ahead of those in the queue. See the NetWare for Macintosh Installation and Maintenance manual for details.

If NetWare for Macintosh is running, you will have an additional status screen on your server. Check this screen occasionally. It will show jobs printed through ATPS and any problems encountered, and will also identify any problems with file services.

The Desktop Files and Volume Access

A fairly common problem is that the directory used to maintain the Macintosh desktop becomes corrupted or out of sync. The Macintosh desktop file holds information on each file on the disk, including what program it was created by. The corresponding directory, DESKTOP.AFP, contains three files:

- ICONINDX.AFP. This links each file to its creator application.

- ICONDATA.AFP. This file holds the bitmap image for each icon.

- APPLDATA.AFP. This has the location of each application so it can be started if the user double-clicks on a document icon.

If the desktop files become corrupted, Mac users may be unable to access files on a volume by double-clicking on them, or they may not be able to access the volume at all. In this case, you should unload AFP.NLM by typing this command at the server console:

```
unload afp
```

Then reload it with the CDT option, which re-creates the three files:

```
load afp cdt
```

Finally, rebuild the Macintosh desktop by first highlighting the server's drive in the Chooser and then holding down the Option and Apple (flower) keys together while clicking on the Open button. Hold down the keys until you see the dialog box that asks "Are you sure you want the desktop rebuilt on the disk rebuilt *diskname*? (This could take a few minutes.)" Rebuild the desktop for each volume that supports the Macintosh name space. This will update the information in the .AFP files to match the files on the disk.

AppleTalk Support on PCs

You can add AppleTalk support to a PC workstation in either of two ways, depending on the type of network:

- With LocalTalk. This requires that you add an NIC to the PC that will allow it to access the LocalTalk network. Then you must add the driver software that allows the PC to access the NIC. Using an AppleTalk board in a PC is usually an either/or situation—you can access the AppleTalk network or whatever network you use to communicate with your NetWare server, but not both at once.

- With EtherTalk. If you have PCs networked with Ethernet, and Macs networked with EtherTalk, you could add an ODI driver on the PCs that would allow you to simultaneously access NetWare services over Ethernet and AppleTalk services over EtherTalk.

IPX for Macs

NetWare on Macintosh uses MacIPX to provide Macintosh users with full access to NetWare services on NetWare servers that aren't running NetWare for Macintosh. If you have only a few Mac users in a large PC group, this can be more cost-effective.

Remember, MacIPX is a one-way link. If you have Macintosh resources such as printers that you want to make accessible to PC users, you will need to use NetWare for Macintosh. If the Macs are running LocalTalk, you will also need a LocalTalk NIC in the server and the gateway NLM provided with MacIPX.

AppleTalk Gateways

You can use gateways between LocalTalk and Ethernet, and between AppleTalk and TCP/IP. The simplest gateways are small devices used to connect Macs or printers that don't support a direct Ethernet interface into an EtherTalk network.

The AppleTalk-to-TCP/IP gateways are useful if you are trying to connect a Mac-only network to a UNIX network, but such networks are beyond the scope of this book. If NetWare is also being used, you will probably find that NetWare for Macintosh plus NetWare NFS gives you greater flexibility and easier upgrades, at roughly the same cost as the gateways.

There are many products that provide Macintoshes with the ability to communicate with other systems. One example is the Apple Coax/Twinax card and software that provides access to IBM 3270 services. These sorts of products are generally not necessary in the NetWare environment. It is simpler to provide an Ethernet connection to the NetWare server, which then provides connectivity to the 3270 host, without the need for a second network adapter. Of course, you will still need the software on the Macintosh that allows the Mac to access the services on the 3270.

TCP/IP and UNIX Connectivity

CP/IP WAS ORIGINALLY DEVELOPED in the early 1970s, and it has been the standard for the Department of Defense and many other government agencies and educational institutions since the 1980s. TCP/IP is associated with Ethernet and UNIX, but it will run on Token Ring, ARCnet, FDDI, and other topologies, and is supported on DOS, OS/2, Windows, Macintosh, and other operating systems. The now world-wide Internet started by the Defense Advanced Research Projects Agency (DARPA) is based on TCP/IP.

Since the focus of this book is NetWare, and connecting NetWare into existing systems, TCP/IP itself will not be covered in great detail. If you are setting up a TCP/IP network from scratch, there are a number of good books devoted to the subject.

A TCP/IP address is a 32-bit number specifying the network and machine sending or receiving a message. In UNIX systems, a file usually called HOSTS allows users to specify another UNIX workstation or server by name, rather than by a number like 192.42.133.244. What you should know about TCP/IP is that each workstation and server must have an address, and each address must be unique.

If your network is attached to the Internet, you will have a network address and a range of workstation addresses assigned to you by InterNIC. If you are not on the Internet, and never will be, you can assign any valid address you wish. But even if you are assigning your own addresses, you should keep in mind that as your company grows, you will need to provide for growth in your TCP/IP network as well.

The other standard associated with UNIX is NFS, the Network File System standard developed by Sun Microsystems and used by most UNIX vendors. NetWare NFS supports the NFS file standard, allowing UNIX users to access NetWare drives as if they were on their own system. It also includes name space support, which means that the longer filenames supported by NFS can be used on a NetWare drive.

If your NetWare servers aren't running NetWare NFS, you can provide NetWare users with access to UNIX services by running NetWare for UNIX on a UNIX server. This software is available for many different UNIX platforms and allows NetWare users to access files on a UNIX server and print to UNIX printers.

To allow PC users to access UNIX services, Novell markets LAN WorkGroup for 4.2, LAN WorkPlace 5 for MS Windows and DOS, and LAN WorkPlace for Macintosh. These packages allow users on these workstations to access TCP/IP network services. LAN WorkGroup 4.2 allows this software to be loaded from the server and provides access to UNIX functions such as FTP.

For users on UNIX workstations, there is the NUC (NetWare UNIX Client). As described earlier in the chapter, this software is supplied with the NeXTStep operating system and is, or will soon be, available for a number of other systems. It allows a UNIX client to log in to a NetWare server and access NetWare services as if it were a PC client running IPX.

NFS for NetWare Access

NetWare NFS allows UNIX workstations to access NetWare volumes and print services using the TCP/IP protocol. Different protocols can even share the same NIC, so that one NIC can support IPX/SPX, TCP/IP, EtherTalk, and other protocols. IPX packets can also be sent through a TCP/IP-only segment via a process known as *tunneling*, which encapsulates the IPX packets within a TCP/IP packet.

Configuring NFS

TCP/IP transport services are available for NetWare 3.11 and later. They require at least 4 MB of RAM. You should also have the Maximum Physical Receive Packet Size set to 1514 bytes on Ethernet, and whatever size is in use on ARCnet or Token Ring networks (this may be up to 4 KB). The Maximum

Packet Receive Buffer Size should be set to at least 200. Use MONITOR to see how many packet receive buffers are in use and if you need to increase the buffer size parameter.

The NFS name space must be loaded to support UNIX files on your NetWare server. This will use additional RAM. The amount may be calculated by multiplying the size of the disk to which you are adding name space by .032, and dividing the result by the block size. The recommended minimum block size for disks with NFS name space support is 8 KB. For a 660 MB hard disk with NFS name space loaded, this would be (660 x .032) / 8 = 2.64 MB of RAM, in addition to the 5 MB minimum and any other requirements.

The configuration files for NetWare NFS are located in the SYS:ETC directory, and correspond to the files with the same names located in the /etc directory on a UNIX system. Each is a text file containing the UNIX parameter and its associated NetWare parameter:

- HOSTS. This file contains the names and TCP/IP addresses for the workstations, servers, printers, and other TCP/IP network devices that the server can identify.

- NETWORKS. This file associates names with the TCP/IP addresses for networks the server can identify and forward messages to.

- EXPORTS. This file controls what directories or volumes are made available to UNIX workstations.

- USERS. This file maps UNIX user ID numbers to NetWare usernames.

- GROUPS. This file maps UNIX group ID numbers to NetWare groups.

UNIX Services

NetWare NFS supports the following UNIX services:

- Network File System (NFS) version 2, the file system developed by Sun Microsystems. This allows UNIX workstations to use NetWare drives as if they were standard UNIX volumes and supports the NFS name space.

- External Data Representation (XDR). This implements a standard UNIX data-transfer syntax.

- Mount Protocol. This protocol allows UNIX workstations to mount the NetWare volumes as they would UNIX volumes.

- Line Printer Daemon (LPD). This enables UNIX workstations to access NetWare printing services as if they were native. UNIX workstations can print to NetWare queues, and NetWare workstations can print to UNIX queues.

- File Transfer Protocol (FTP). This protocol supports the standard UNIX file-exchange protocol, which allows UNIX workstations to get files from a server without needing to mount the volume (the equivalent of attaching to a server). This allows even UNIX workstations that don't support NFS to access files on the NetWare server.

- Telnet. This allows UNIX users to log in on the NetWare server, using XCONSOLE.NLM, and perform remote management of the server.

- LOCKD (Lock Daemon). This UNIX record-locking utility prevents two or more users from trying to change the same file at the same time.

NetWare and UNIX Permissions

Because of the difference between the NetWare permission structure and the UNIX permission structure, permissions tend to get out of sync with what was originally intended. Additionally, the mapping between UNIX and NetWare rights cannot be matched perfectly because the rights don't correspond perfectly.

NetWare 3.x and 4.x have both trustee rights, which can be granted to a user or a group, and file attributes, which are the same for any user or group. In contrast, UNIX grants three access rights to three entities: the file or directory's owner, its group, and everyone else (the world). A common problem occurs when UNIX users have mounted a NetWare volume and can access it, but are not defined as users on the NetWare server.

A typical default file-creation mask for UNIX users is to give the owner of a file all three rights, and to give the group and the world the rights to read the file and execute it, but not to write to it. When a user with this setup writes a file to a NetWare server on which the user doesn't have an account, the server identifies that person as user -2 (nobody) and group -2 (nogroup). For example, suppose that John, a UNIX user, logs on to a NetWare server where he doesn't have an account, and then he tries to change his own file. But he doesn't have access rights, because a user identified as user -2 or group -2 isn't given rights to files created by unidentified users or groups, for security reasons. This means that John is effectively locked out of his own file or directory.

The way to avoid this problem is to make sure that every UNIX user who will be accessing a NetWare server has a login on that server. Also, if your users will be accessing files from the UNIX side and will need to modify the permissions of files, be sure that the option Modify DOS Attributes in the Export entry is set to Yes. Otherwise, you will be able to change the permissions on the files only from DOS.

Another problem with versions of NetWare NFS prior to version 1.2 is that every time a directory or file is created or the permissions on an existing directory are modified from the UNIX side, another trustee entry is created. This can result in hundreds or thousands of trustee entries, especially in the EVERYONE group. In version 1.2, you can turn this off, but you should then create the file TRUSTEES as described in the NetWare NFS Administration manual.

Troubleshooting TCP/IP Connections

Troubleshooting TCP/IP connections from a NetWare server can be difficult. There is no equivalent to the ping command found in UNIX, which allows you to query another UNIX workstation to see if it is up and its network interface is working. TCPCON will allow you to track packets that are reaching the server and see what happens to them. Add-on utilities to NetWare such as LAN-alyzer for Windows will allow you to do this, and you can also ping the server from a workstation running LAN WorkPlace or a UNIX workstation.

You may also be routing TCP/IP through your NetWare server. If so, there will be two NICs in the server, each with a different TCP/IP address, such as 192.42.172.4 and 192.42.173.60. To check connectivity between a workstation on your network and one on another network, try this:

- Ping the board that connects your network to your NetWare server.

- If the ping shows that the server is responding, then ping the other board.

- If the other board doesn't respond, make sure that the LOAD TCP/IP command in AUTOEXEC.NCF ends with FORWARD=YES. The first board should also be identified as the router in the NET.CFG file for LAN WorkPlace, or in the /etc/hostconfig file for a UNIX workstation. Any UNIX workstation that needs to communicate with other workstations on the other side of a TCP/IP router must have the router identified in its host configuration file or NET.CFG file.

- If the second board responds, ping a workstation on the other TCP/IP network.

- If that workstation responds, then the TCP/IP forwarding is working correctly.

NetWare on UNIX Systems

NetWare for UNIX (formerly Portable NetWare) allows UNIX servers to run NetWare 3.0 or higher as a process. This provides the users on that network with full access to NetWare services, and allows interconnectivity with other NetWare servers and networks.

A major difference from standard NetWare is that NetWare for UNIX is running as a process (an application) on top of the standard UNIX operating system. This adds an extra level where things can go wrong. The UNIX operating system may have other processes running on it that could cause disrupt services or cause NetWare to crash.

Advanced Topics

Troubleshooting
Network
Applications

ETWORK APPLICATIONS PRODUCE some additional fault points for troubleshooting. First, they are accessible to users, who have occasionally been known to misunderstand the proper usage of applications or network services. Second, they interface with Net-Ware, to one degree or another. Finally, they are themselves a fault point. Of the three, the second fault point is the most difficult to diagnose. Users can (usually) be educated, and buggy software can be upgraded or replaced. Discovering how the software is attempting to access NetWare services, and what's going wrong, can be complex. However, the principles of trouble-shooting introduced in Chapter 1 still apply. You can break any problem into its constituent parts, and then isolate the fault.

This chapter addresses three types of network applications:

- Applications that need access to NetWare services, which may either be "NetWare aware"—providing direct access to NetWare services such as print queues—or simple DOS applications that don't have any provision for the existence of a network

- Applications that run from the server

- Applications such as e-mail and fax servers that provide additional net-work services

Applications That Access NetWare Services

HE ESSENTIAL NETWORK SERVICES that applications need to access are file services, print services, networked modems, and sometimes fax services.

Almost all applications save files, but the NetWare drivers make this process essentially identical to accessing the local drive on the workstation. Some programs allow users to select a server's drives by volume name, rather than needing to remember that, for example, drive G: is mapped to VOL1.

Many programs allow users to access print services directly, without going through a CAPTURE command. Some applications even let users select a print queue from a list, rather than needing to set the printer configuration before starting the program.

Networks are beginning to provide users with fax and/or data modem services. For network applications to access these services, they may need to use drivers provided by the modem manufacturer. In some cases, the manufacturer may allow you to set up a print queue that will print to the fax modem instead of to a regular printer, and then the application can simply print to the queue.

The following sections describe how to understand and solve problems with file and print services. Modem services are covered in more detail later in the chapter, in the "Using Networked Modems" section.

File Services

The most basic network service is storing and managing files, a fact that is reflected in the name *file server*. In the most basic case, a user can send a file to the server instead of his or her workstation's hard disk by simply changing the drive entry in the application's Save dialog box from C: to H:. However, there are several considerations even in this most simple case.

Path Names

First is the question of path. Depending on the application, the user may need to remember that the correct directory is G: or J:, depending on what you have set up. In other applications, the user will need to know the server name, volume name, and path. This is a matter of user education.

If your users consistently have problems with path names, you should consider setting up a menu, using macros or icons in Windows to make the process easier for them. You could also set up a "cheat sheet" with path names, program names, and so forth, and distribute it to your users.

File Locks

Second, the primary use for a network is file sharing, not simply storing files on some other computer's disk. The problem is that if a file is shared, two people may try to access it at the same time; and even if this doesn't actually cause a crash, it will generally mean that one of the two will lose his or her work. The way to fix this problem is to lock the file. There are several ways to lock files:

- Through the use of the NetWare file services. NetWare services allow an application to lock a file by designating the file as either locked-exclusive or locked-shareable. Locked-exclusive files cannot be accessed by anyone else while they are in use. Locked-shareable files can be read, but not changed.

- Through the application. Some network applications can keep track of what files are in use by authorized users, and return an error message if a second user attempts to access the file.

- With a lock file, which lets the application know that the file is in use. This method uses a temporary lock file, which is deleted when the file is closed. This file typically has the same name as the file being locked, but with a .LCK or similar extension. If a user attempts to access a file for which there is an equivalent lock file in the same directory (that is, a file currently in use), the application will either deny access or warn the user that the file is in use, and that changes will not be saved. This method of locking is typical of UNIX applications, and can also be seen in network-oriented applications that run on other networks besides NetWare.

Of course, in all of these types of locking, you can use the Save As command and save the file to another location or filename.

The problems that arise from file locking are generally of two sorts: user misunderstanding or application crashes. If users don't understand the message received, they may think that the reason they can't access a file is a system problem, rather than that another user has the file open. Network novices (who aren't necessarily computer novices) need to be educated about the implications of working with files to which others have access. And you may still need to translate particularly cryptic error messages for them.

The second problem is with files that are in use when an application crashes. If the application doesn't exit cleanly, the files may remain locked, or the lock file may not be deleted. In this case, you will need to determine that no other user has the file in use (check Connection Information in MONITOR to see which files each user has open), and then reset the file's status with ATTRIB or FILER, or remove the lock file.

Long Filenames

As Windows 95 becomes more widespread, you may need to deal with the issue of long filenames. OS/2 also supports long filenames, and the same name space is loaded on the server for both OS/2 and Windows 95.

The problem arises when users who are not yet using Windows 95 or OS/2 (or applications that support long filenames) access files created with new applications that do allow long filenames. The users with the older systems will be able to see the files (with the names truncated to the old eight.three formula) and access them, but when they save them, the filenames will be changed to the short name. The users with the newer systems will have trouble finding those files, because their names will be different. For example, a file named SYBEX_NT5.DOC will be truncated to SYBEX_~1.DOC.

Print Services

In general, any application that can print to the local PC's printer port can be made to print to a NetWare queue. Here are some tips for getting print services to work properly:

- The most common sticking point is with applications, such as Windows 3.1 and earlier, that attempt to bypass the DOS LPT port device and send data directly to the physical printer port. If this occurs, the NetWare shell cannot intercept the data and send it to the queue. The problem can often be avoided by instructing the application to print to a file, and when prompted for a filename, entering LPT1. This doesn't actually print to a file, but to the DOS device LPT1, which is then intercepted by the NetWare shell and sent to the queue. (Windows for Workgroups 3.11 and Windows 95 support NetWare queues directly and bypass this problem.)

- The print utilities provided with NetWare have never been famous for stability. If you are using a version of NetWare earlier than 3.12, you should update the printing utilities. Even the utilities provided with the latest versions may not be perfect. You can find updates to the utilities and to PSERVER (.NLM, .VAP, and .EXE) on NetWire or the Novell Web Server.

- You may have several different printers on your network, such as a PostScript printer, a PCL (HP LaserJet compatible), and a dot-matrix (for multi-part forms). A user who needs to print from an application first to one of these printers and then to another must typically enter the CAPTURE statement for the first printer, open the application, print the first document, exit the application, enter the new CAPTURE statement for the next printer, reopen the application, and print the second document. Under Windows 3.11 or later, the user can have both printers (print queues) installed and switch between them using the Printers control panel.

- The NetWare print utilities normally intercept any Tab characters (ASCII 09) and convert them to spaces (the default is eight). This is fine when printing a text file to a text printer. However, if you are printing graphics to an HP LaserJet (or compatible) or PostScript printer, this is not what should happen. In order to prevent the tabs from being replaced, you must use the /NT switch in the CAPTURE statement, or set File Contents to Byte Stream when configuring the print job in PRINTCON.

- When printing PostScript, you should also have the banner page turned off with the /NB switch for CAPTURE, or in the print job configuration. Leaving this on can confuse the printer by sending ASCII text before the PostScript initialization commands.

Accessing NetWare Print Queues Directly

If the application can directly access NetWare queues, then the user can simply tell the application to send the first job to one queue and the second job to the other queue. The application may even give users a list of available queues, so they don't need to remember queue names. The problem with this approach is that, from a programmer's point of view, it further complicates an already complicated subject. Programs that handle this process without errors deserve your respect.

There are several common problems you may encounter with programs that are attempting to access NetWare print services directly. The first is that programs can detect the print queues, but not print to them. If this happens, try printing to LPT1 and using NetWare's redirection capability instead. If that works, make sure that the program is compatible with the version of NetWare you are using—it may be trying to use an outdated method of accessing the NetWare queue. If printing to LPT1 doesn't work either, or you get garbled text, it may be that the application is not configured correctly for the printer you are using. Many users don't understand that you can't print a text file to a Post-Script printer or a PCL graphics file to a dot-matrix printer.

You should also make sure that the correct queue name is entered. If the application allows the user to specify the queue name, but doesn't allow selection from a list, the user may have misspelled the queue name. If the queue name is longer than eight characters, some older programs may truncate the name, which will cause printing to fail.

Printing Fonts

Fonts are another potential problem area, particularly if you are trying to use fonts beyond what the printer provides. Most programs can access the standard fonts fairly easily. However, if you want to add another font, every program that you want to use it with will probably have different requirements for loading it, and different ways for getting the printer to use it. One of the real advantages of Windows is that it provides a unified way for loading and using fonts, although adding fonts to Windows isn't simple either.

If your users need additional fonts, be sure to check the application's manual for special font-loading instructions. You can also refer to several good books on what fonts are available and how to get them to work with your system. Font manufacturers (such as Adobe and Linotype) offer free booklets showing all the fonts they have available.

Printing from Windows Applications

Printing from a Windows application is not like printing from a DOS application. With Windows, the application does not handle the printing itself; it passes the job on to Windows. This means that you only need to configure Windows, instead of every application, for your printer, print queue, and fonts. While the installation and configuration of a printer in Windows can be complex, it is generally a matter of following the directions carefully. The same is true of adding fonts to Windows.

If the users are running on Windows for Workgroups 3.11 (or later) or Windows 95, any application they run under Windows should be able to print to the NetWare queue through Windows. The issues discussed here involve printing with older versions of Windows and DOS. See the next section for more information about Windows for Workgroups 3.11 and Windows 95.

The most common problems in printing from Windows are related to incorrect configuration settings, incorrect paths to directories, and incorrect permissions. These are the items to check first if a printer configuration doesn't work. If you are using the NWTOOLS program (and you should be), you will be able to set configuration options such as No Tabs, No Banner, and Timeout from within Windows, instead of needing to use CAPTURE before starting Windows. However, if all else fails, set Windows to print to LPT1 and set CAPTURE before starting Windows, rather than printing directly to a queue. See the "Accessing NetWare Services from Windows 3.1" section for more information about working with that version.

Accessing NetWare Services from Windows for Workgroups 3.11 or Windows 95

Windows for Workgroups and Windows 95 both directly support NetWare services, including NDS (with the right drivers). This doesn't mean that accessing NetWare will be simple, but with the correct version of the driver, it can be much easier than with older versions. Normally, when Windows is installed, it will detect installed NetWare drivers, or an Ethernet card in a new system, and prompt you to install NetWare support. Once this is done, file and print services can be accessed transparently through Windows.

After the drivers are installed, file servers and print queues should automatically show up in the list of available file servers and printers. From File Manager, you simply attach a network drive. You must still install the printer driver for the correct type of printer (such as HP LaserJet IV), but once that is done, users can select the NetWare queue as if it were a local printer.

The most problematic issue is getting Windows to work with the queue and printer. You can usually fix this by getting the latest driver for that printer and version of Windows, and by making sure that the Print Manager is configured properly for the printer. Install the driver on everyone's system, and printing through Windows should work smoothly.

Accessing NetWare Services from Windows 3.1

Windows 3.1 has its own section here because it is almost a separate operating system. Unlike true operating systems, it loads on top of DOS, but it does offer a unified approach to menus, fonts, file services, and other system services such as fax modems. For that reason, it's often called an "operating environment." If you are using Windows with NetWare, get Windows 3.1 or later. Chapter 12 offers some tips for getting previous versions to work with NetWare, but given the low cost and the added functionality of upgrading to Windows 3.1, it is very difficult to think of any valid reason to stay with older versions.

Getting Windows 3.1 to run on a PC under NetWare can be troublesome. Be sure to use the latest IPX and NETX (or NETx), ODI drivers, or VLMs. Chapter 3 provides some suggestions on appropriate settings.

After Windows is running on the workstation and connecting with NetWare, it offers convenient access to NetWare print services through the Printers Control Panel. You should also get the NetWare Tools for Windows (NWTOOLS.EXE) program, which allows you to use the MAP, ATTACH, CAPTURE, USERLIST, VOLINFO, SETPASS, SEND, MESSAGES, and SESSION utilities from within Windows, instead of needing to exit Windows to reconfigure your NetWare environment from DOS. (However, as noted earlier, if you are having problems accessing a queue from Windows, you may need to exit and set the default queue with CAPTURE or PRINTCON, then restart Windows.)

Another problem you may run into is the result of a difference between the ways DOS and NetWare display files and directories. If you type DIR on a DOS drive, the first two items will be a period and double period, representing the current directory and the parent directory. Windows allows you to double-click on the double period to move back up the directory tree in the File Manager or in file menus. On a NetWare drive, you won't get the period and double period in Windows dialog boxes or the File Manager, unless the entry SHOW DOTS = ON is in the SHELL.CFG or NET.CFG file. This doesn't hurt, so I recommend you use it in your default configuration files.

When installing Windows 3.1 on a workstation connected to an ARCnet network, be sure to run INSTALL with the /I switch. This prevents the automatic hardware detection feature of the Windows installation routine from running, and so prevents the ARCnet network driver from being accidentally unloaded.

Applications Running from the Server

GETTING AN APPLICATION TO RUN from the server may be as simple as copying the APP.EXE file to a network drive and running it, or as complex as performing separate installations for each server and workstation, plus setting up configuration files for each user. Applications written to run on DOS can be run from the server, as long as you understand the implications.

Some programs that run from the server require a configuration file for each user or workstation that will be accessing the software. You may get one user running, and need to do the whole thing over again for the next user. This is another good reason to keep records and default configuration files.

Some applications maintain configuration information within the program code. On a workstation, this isn't a problem. However, if two users try to simultaneously use a program on the server that operates this way, they can both attempt to change the same data at the same time, resulting in a crash for one or both of them. Fortunately, most major applications are available in network versions, which allow multiple users to run the application at the same time. Here are some tips for getting an application to run from the server:

- Many applications have configuration files that contain information on user preferences and the setup of the workstation. Programs designed to run on a network typically have an installation program that installs the program files, and a user installation program that creates the configuration files. If the application isn't started from the directory that contains the configuration files, it may use a default configuration and save a new configuration file in the directory that the application was started from. This can cause crashes because the user doesn't have permission to write a file in that directory, or result in the proliferation of configuration files in many different directories.

- Be sure that the application is marked as shareable. This should be the default with a network-aware installation, but in some cases it may not be set correctly. You may also need to make sure that any user who will be using the application has adequate rights to configuration files, and possibly to copy-protection files as well. Check with the application documentation for information about network installation.

- If you use NCOPY to copy the directory structure for the user's files, use the /E switch in addition to the /S switch, to copy empty directories as well as directories containing configuration files. Some applications look for files in a specific default directory, which may not initially have any files in it.

- If you can't get an application to run from the network, try setting it up as a local application. Most applications offer you the option of either type of installation. If it works from the workstation, this should give you clues about why it won't work from the server. As always, ask yourself, "What's different?" Also try to run the application from another workstation or as another user. This can isolate problems with rights or with configuration files.

- Be cautious about checking the installation of applications as Supervisor. This user has access rights to everything and trustee rights everywhere, so the application may work for you and not for anyone else. Of course, this is a clue in itself—it may mean that the users need additional permissions that they don't have. For example, the Supervisor has permission to write to the root directory of the volume and the user doesn't. You normally won't want to give users permissions to the root directory of a volume (see the next item).

- Some applications expect to be located in a directory directly off the root of a drive—for instance C:\APPDIR. If your standard setup on the network is to have an APPS directory with applications under that, some applications may not run correctly. You can fix this by using the fake root, which makes the application think that the directory is a root directory. A directory set up as a fake root won't allow the user to change directories past that level toward the real root. See the NetWare documentation on the MAP command for more details.

Running LAN WorkGroup

Because LAN WorkGroup runs from the server, it can have the same problems that might affect networked applications in general. Specifically, you need to make sure that the configuration files for each user and workstation are set up correctly, and that the proper search drives are set up for each user with the MAP command. A simple way to do this is to set up a group (called WGUSERS, perhaps) and put a statement in the system login script such as:

```
IF MEMBER OF GROUP WGUSERS  MAP S16:=SYS:/APPLICATIONS/LANWG
```

This statement will set up the appropriate mapping for anyone placed in the group. When you associate the search drive mapping with a group in the login script, instead of putting the mapping in individual users' AUTOEXEC.BAT scripts, you can add or remove search drives for users without going to each of their workstations.

Running Windows 3.x from the Server

Running Windows 3.*x* from the server reduces the space necessary on local workstation drives by 10 MB or more, and makes updates to Windows much easier, especially in large departments. You can also exercise control over the Windows environment—preventing users from changing the Windows configuration, including program groups, the screen saver and colors, and so forth—by denying permission to the appropriate configuration files. You can also prevent users from adding unauthorized (and possibly buggy or virus-infected) programs or utilities to Windows.

This information applies to Windows 3.x—I strongly recommend that you not even try to run Windows 95 from the network server. In fact, doing so is not documented or recommended by Microsoft.

On the other hand, running Windows from the server increases network traffic and can be difficult to set up and manage. And most users will want some control over their Windows setup. If you have different types of workstations, with differing monitor types, different types of pointing devices, or different versions of the NetWare LAN drivers, you will need to have different configuration files on the server for each type of workstation.

You will need about 17 MB free on a server drive to install Windows, and it will take up about 11 MB after it's installed. Windows 3.1 and later is considerably easier to install on the server than previous versions. Just run SETUP with the /A option. Installing the workstation files is also easier—log in on the user's workstation and run SETUP /N. If you create one User Definition File (UDF) directory on the server, and then copy it to everyone else's directory, be sure to change the trustee rights and ownership of the directory and files afterwards. You will also need to make the appropriate changes to CONFIG.SYS and AUTOEXEC.BAT. You can also create the UDF directory on the user's local drive and configure Windows to look for it there, but this makes updates to Windows more complex.

If you are going to be running the SETUP program from a number of workstations that all use the same configuration, you can use the SETUP /H option with an Automatic Installation File (AIF) to automate the installation. Running

SETUP this way doesn't require you to answer the questions for configuration. It allows you to set everything up in the AIF in advance. You will need a different AIF for each different workstation configuration. See the Windows documentation for more details on this option.

The UDF directory contains the files that control how Windows is configured for each user. The files include WIN.COM and the .INI and .GRP files. WIN.COM is not the Windows executable file; it simply starts Windows. The .INI files control various aspects of Windows, and the .GRP files control what applications are shown in each window on the desktop. If you set these files to Read-Only for the users, they won't be able to change their Windows configuration.

The UDF directory must be in the user's directory search path, and must be found before the Windows directory. This will happen automatically if Windows is started from the UDF directory. Otherwise, make sure that the UDF directory is before the Windows directory in the DOS path.

The WIN.COM file in the user's UDF directory assumes a certain video configuration, mouse driver, and version of NetWare. If the user logs in from another workstation and any of these items are different, Windows may hang, drop back to DOS, or give error messages about configuration files not being found. The solution is to create a version of WIN.COM for each display, mouse, and so on that the user might need to use, and rename them along the lines of WINVGA.COM, WINEGA.COM, WINHERC.COM, as seems appropriate. Since this program just starts Windows with the specified configuration, having several such files in the UDF directory won't hurt anything.

You can also have several default UDF directories: one for each type of workstation on your network. This would require that the users replace their UDF directory with a different default directory to change configurations. You could also put the UDF files in a default location, such as C:\UDF, on every workstation. If a user changed the configuration on his or her workstation and then moved to another workstation, that other workstation would still have whatever configuration had already been installed on it, not the user's revised configuration.

Electronic-Mail Applications

THE STANDARD FOR E-MAIL on NetWare is MHS, for Message Handling Service. MHS is a store-and-forward system that holds a message until it can be forwarded to the recipient. In NetWare 3.*x*, and NetWare 4.*x* with bindery emulation turned on, each user has a mail directory, which is a numbered directory in SYS:MAIL. You can get each user's number with SYSCON (User Information/Login Name/Other Information). The Supervisor account always has the directory number 1. In NetWare 4.*x* with bindery emulation disabled, the mail directories will be wherever you specified when you installed MHS. You can use NWADMIN to associate the directory with each user.

The most common problems with e-mail fall into two areas:

- Not attaching correctly to the mail server. The mail server may not be the same server the user normally uses. If it isn't, the user's login script should attach the user to the mail server and set up a mapping to the appropriate directory. (See your e-mail application's documentation for details.)

- Permission problems. If users don't have the correct permissions in their e-mail directory, they won't be able to access their mail.

With the proliferation of alternative mail packages, there are other types of mail that you may run into. One common type is based on the SMTP (Simple Mail Transfer Protocol). It is the standard on the Internet and with most UNIX systems. Most SMTP mail packages also require that TCP/IP be installed. Setting up SMTP, TCP/IP, and the other parts of these systems, such as Domain Name Service (DNS), is beyond the scope of this book. Refer to books on these specific topics.

The key to troubleshooting SMTP is to break it into its parts and isolate faults. Is TCP/IP functioning, enabling the program on the user's workstation to communicate with the mail server? Is the mail message getting to the mail server? Is that server forwarding the message appropriately?

Another standard that is proliferating with Windows is Microsoft Mail. MS Mail setup is another topic that is beyond the scope of this book, but the same principles stated throughout this book work here as well: understand the flow of a mail message from the user to intended recipient, break the process into parts, and check the parts until you find the fault.

Using Networked Modems

AS NETWORKING BECOMES an integral part of computing, the need to access other systems becomes greater. The simplest way to accomplish occasional access is with a modem. Rather than have a modem on every workstation, you can set up a modem on the network that anyone on the network can access, and that can also be used to access the LAN from another location. A fax machine is essentially a specialized modem with a scanner and a printer attached. It is relatively simple to convert a data modem to send the proper signals to a fax modem as well.

Using networked modems requires additional software beyond the standard NetWare shell. This may be software similar to CAPTURE that sends a print job to the fax modem instead of a printer, or software that allows a modem connected by Ethernet to simulate a modem connected to the serial port of the PC. This software is specific to the manufacturer of the modem and is not part of NetWare, with the exception of LAN WorkPlace, which can be used to access the NetWare Access Server. This software usually includes Windows drivers.

The typical problems with modem networking software are incompatibility between the printer driver of the application and the fax modem software, and interrupt conflicts or COM port access problems with data modem software. Make sure that the printer driver used by the application is supported by the fax modem software. With data modem software, the terminal application must be using the DOS port calls, rather than trying to send data directly to the physical port, or the software won't be able to intercept the data and forward it to the network modem.

Networked Data Modems

Novell has solutions such as the NetWare Access Server, which supports up to 16 simultaneous modem connections. There are many products available from other vendors, such as the Shiva NetModem/E, which provides one modem connection accessible from both PCs and Macintoshes. In addition to the hardware and software running on the networked device, you will need to install software on each workstation that needs to access the modem. There is usually one program that allows users on the LAN to dial out, and a second program that allows users elsewhere to dial in and access the LAN.

The additional fault points for a networked modem are:

- The software that intercepts the data that would otherwise be sent to the serial port and reroutes it to the network modem.

- The connection to the network modem.

If the terminal application you are using supports the networked modem, the first fault point is eliminated. If the terminal application is set up to use a COM port, you should make sure that it uses the DOS COM port driver, rather than sending data directly to the physical port, which makes it impossible to intercept the data and route it to the network modem.

Networked Fax Modems

The additional fault points for a network fax modem are:

- The software that simulates a print queue or replaces CAPTURE and sends the data to the fax modem.

- The connection to the fax modem.

- The fax modem itself, especially in the degree to which it is compatible with a standard fax machine.

You may find that a fax modem produces cleaner outgoing faxes than a standard fax machine, because it reduces the number of times the page must be reproduced—the page doesn't need to be printed and then scanned by the fax machine. On the other hand, fax modems may have trouble with incoming faxes, especially if line quality is not good.

Since NetWare doesn't provide direct support for fax modems yet, you must rely on the manufacturer's documentation for troubleshooting information. When possible, test all other parts of the process. For instance, say that the process for faxing is as follows: the application prints PostScript, but to a queue established by the fax modem software, which then sends the output to the fax modem. Make sure that the application can produce PostScript output that prints on a regular PostScript printer. Also make sure that the network fax modem shows up as a node on the network (that it is accessible as a network device). This leaves only the fax modem software and its configuration as potential fault points.

Upgrades to NetWare, Hardware, and Software

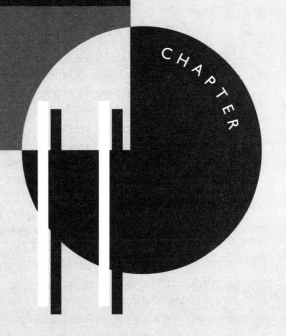

PGRADING COMPUTER SYSTEMS is a process every administrator must go through. The computer industry is advancing at such a rate that two-year-old systems are often obsolete. Upgrades to hardware or application software are generally a matter of removing the old version and installing the new one. NetWare differs in that the data on the server and all the configuration information about your users must be preserved during the upgrade. This chapter discusses practices that can make upgrades easier and decrease the potential for disaster.

Upgrading a system—whether the NetWare operating system, a PC workstation, or application software—can be a traumatic experience. However, this is often because the administrator tries to combine several upgrades at once, rather than taking them one at a time. For instance, when you upgrade a server from NetWare 2.*x* to 3.11, it is also the ideal time to upgrade the server hardware. However, if you aren't cautious, this can make it very difficult to track down problems. If you change several things at once, figuring out which one is causing the problem is much harder. Always make sure that you can retrace your steps—upgrade the hardware first and make sure it's working, then install the new version of NetWare.

Upgrading a system may require that you upgrade related parts. If you change a workstation's NIC to a new, faster NIC, you will also need to upgrade the network driver. Save the old configurations and software, just in case. That way, you always will be able to go back to a working configuration. If possible, this practice should even be followed with servers. It's common to upgrade your system with a new server. First set up the new server, install the new version of NetWare on it, and debug any problems. Then you can transfer the data drives from the old server to the new server, or restore the data from the old server's drive to the new server's drive.

Upgrading NetWare

UPGRADING NETWARE within a version (4.0 to 4.1, for instance) is a relatively trivial operation. If you have good backups, there should be few challenges. Upgrading between versions can be another story. You may find that the new version requires a different network organization or more powerful hardware, or that it has a different permission structure.

Be very sure that you understand the differences between versions before you upgrade. Resources for getting more of this information include the NetWare forums on Compu-Serve, the local chapter of the CNEPA, NetWare Application Notes, and your local NetWare user group.

One thing that you can do to make your upgrades much easier, and make your server more stable as well, is to strictly limit your server's boot drive, the SYS volume, to NetWare directories and applications. Put your user directories and all data directories on other drives. This allows you to upgrade to a new server by changing only the SYS volume. You can set up the new server in advance, then add it to the network and test it, and finally, move the data drives from the old server to the new one. Of course, you should still have backups of the data drives before you begin, just in case. This approach also adds fault tolerance. If the server fails, you can take any workstation, install NetWare on the internal drive, add the external drives, and have a server back online quickly.

Upgrading without Disrupting Work Flow

One of the facts of life for most administrators is working before or after normal hours to minimize network downtime for users. To reduce the time you need to spend outside normal hours, plan the upgrade ahead of time. If you do update the server hardware at the same time as the software, you have the luxury of installing the new version of NetWare any time you wish. The only part you need to do after hours is swapping drives from the old server to the new one.

If you are using the same hardware, write down all the configuration steps you will need to do. Don't just use a check list—write each of the steps down. This procedure is more likely to help you spot problem areas in advance, and it lets you refer to a written configuration sheet while you are actually upgrading the server.

Allow twice the time you think you will need for the upgrade, and then about the same time for testing. Make sure that you can test logins from a couple of different users, particularly users who don't have Supervisor privileges, to make sure that trustee rights have been restored properly.

Planning the Upgrade

When you plan the upgrade, you need to keep three basic questions in mind:

- What do you have now?

- What do you want to end up with?

- How are you going to get there?

Knowing What You Have

To know what you have now, you should have printouts of the following:

- A complete directory map of all existing directories on all volumes, including ownership information

- A copy of all the configuration information about the server, including user information, trustee rights, login scripts, and so forth, as well as hardware settings

- The AUTOEXEC.BAT, CONFIG.SYS, AUTOEXEC.NCF, and STARTUP.NCF files (or their equivalents in older systems)

Knowing What You Want

Next, determine what you want to end up with. Consider these types of questions:

- If permission structures are different, how will that affect the upgrade?

- If you are going to install NetWare 4.*x*, what do you need to change to fit in with the company tree structure?

- Will user login scripts on different servers conflict with each other?

- Are printer or print queue names unique throughout the company?

Decide how the server will be configured. Write out what the new AUTOEXEC.NCF and STARTUP.NCF files should look like.

Deciding How to Get There

Finally, plan how you will make the changes. In some cases, such as the NetWare 3.*x* to 4.*x* upgrade, you should spend a good deal of time consolidating the existing user login scripts, deleting unnecessary files, and planning how your usernames, print queues, groups, and other network resources will fit into the new overall network plan.

Preparing for the Upgrade

The most common upgrades are from NetWare 2.*x* to 3.1*x* and from 3.*x* to 4.*x*. Each of these has special considerations, some of which are covered in the examples later in this chapter. The following sections describe some of the steps you may need to take before you begin an upgrade.

A complete discussion of all considerations is impractical—the NetWare Application Notes April 1993 issue covers some of the considerations of the 3.x to 4.x upgrade in 240 pages. Depending on the complexity of your network and server configurations, you should consider taking the appropriate System Manager or upgrade course at your local Novell Authorized Education Center.

Changing the File Structure

As long as you are going to do the upgrade anyway, it is an ideal time to consider your file systems. Is there anything you would like to do differently? Do you wish your Users directory wasn't on the SYS volume? Now is the ideal time to change it. However, making changes in your file structure will entail some additional steps in the upgrade. You can either use UPGRADE and then move the file structure around, or use the restore method for the upgrade (back up the files, upgrade the server to the new version, and then restore the files into their new directories). Upgrade methods are discussed later in the chapter.

You can make your life simpler by using the SYS volume only for NetWare files and applications. It doesn't hurt to have lots of free space left on SYS. With the prices of hard drives dropping constantly, it's an inexpensive precaution to ensure that you'll always have lots of room for print queues, mail directories, and the NetWare files themselves. The NetWare 3.*x* to 4.*x* upgrade requires as much as 30 additional MB on the SYS drive, and printing PostScript files can create very large temporary queue files (10 to 50 MB is not uncommon when printing books or color PostScript files).

Limiting the files on SYS in this way also reduces the backups necessary on this volume; the only files that will change are the mail files. Applications and the NetWare directories will normally change only when you update the system or add users or new software.

Creating Documentation

If you don't have good documentation of your network now, create it before you upgrade. Not only does it give you a better feel for what you have and what you should change before or during the upgrade, it gives you a hedge against disaster. If the server freezes while UPGRADE.EXE is running, and you can't restore the binderies, you should have enough documentation to re-create every user's environment and trustee rights.

Look at your server and gather all the information you would need to re-create the server if you needed to start from scratch with just the basic NetWare installation and your data files. This information includes documentation of all the NetWare configuration items—the startup files, system login script, print configuration, and any additional configurations (such as NetWare NFS or NetWare for Macintosh). It also includes documentation of every user—their login script, trustee rights, group memberships, and so forth.

Accumulating this information using only NetWare tools can be cumbersome in the extreme. There are a number of utilities that can create reports with all the necessary information, and they range in price from nothing to several hundred dollars. For example, you can download these three utilities from the CompuServe NetWare forum:

- PRINTUSR produces a report on the user's group memberships, security equivalencies, trustee assignments, login script, and disk utilization.

- PRINTGRP provides similar information in a report about groups.

- DUPBIND reports any duplicate names in the bindery—a user and a group with the same name, for instance.

These utilities are provided by Novell, but not supported. See Appendix A for resources to find the utility that's right for you, and Appendix B for details on some of the tools available.

Performing Backups

Always back up the server before starting an upgrade. If you are going to use UPGRADE.EXE to upgrade the server, you should have two backups: the one you did for safety, and the one you'll be working from.

It may take a few hours to back up the server again, but it would take much longer to reconstruct it from scratch if something happens to the only tape you have. Verify the tapes by performing test restores of at least some files (many backup programs won't tell you if the backup can actually be restored). See Chapter 6 for more information about backing up the server.

If you are upgrading the server hardware at the same time, install the new version of NetWare on the new server. You can then restore the data from the backups of the old server to the new server. If you have only one drive in the old server, back it up and then restore the data to the new server's drive, being careful not to restore the binderies (because they are specific to the old drive's partition information). Of course, you won't restore the SYSTEM or PUBLIC directories. You will then need to re-create the trustee rights and ownerships for the restored directories. This is more work than simply using UPGRADE, but it ensures that everything ends up with the correct rights, particularly when upgrading from NetWare 2.*x* to 3.*x* or 4.*x*.

Finally, once you have your new server installed, configured, and running smoothly, back it up. This new backup will give you a reference point to which you can return if trouble occurs.

Meeting Hardware Requirements

The hardware requirements of the new version of NetWare may be different. NetWare 3.*x* requires a minimum of a 386 processor and shouldn't be run with less than 4 MB RAM. NetWare 4.*x* shouldn't be run with less than a fast 486 and 16 MB RAM.

NetWare is less sensitive to processor speed than other network operating systems, but using the fastest workstation possible will not hurt. Depending on the size of your network and the amount of additional network traffic that the NDS database updates will produce, you will probably also want to upgrade the network adapter to a faster model.

Upgrading Support Files

In addition to NetWare itself, you will need to consider the workstations. If you are upgrading to NetWare 4.*x*, you will need to upgrade the workstation Net-Ware files to the VLM drivers. This should be done before the server is upgraded. The advantages of this approach are that it won't interfere with users' access to the 3.11 server, and it lets you handle the relatively time-consuming operation over a period of time.

If you're upgrading to NetWare 3.11 from 2.*x*, you should upgrade your workstation drivers, unless you are already using the latest IPX and NETX or ODI drivers. If you are performing an incremental upgrade, from 2.15 to 2.2, for instance, you probably won't need to update anything on the workstations.

The methods available for upgrading NetWare depend on whether the change is from 2.*x* to 3.*x* or from 3.*x* to 4.*x*. The upgrade from NetWare 2.*x* to 4.*x* actually encompasses both: you must upgrade from 2.*x* to 3.*x* (but you don't need to buy 3.*x*) and then from 3.*x* to 4.*x*.

Upgrading from NetWare 2.x to 3.x

There are two basic methods of upgrading NetWare from 2.*x* to 3.*x*:

- Use the UPGRADE utility to move data from an existing 2.*x* server to a new 3.*x* server (the transfer method).

- Use UPGRADE to back up the server, remove the existing version of NetWare, install the new version of NetWare, then restore the data with UPGRADE (the backup device method).

Each method has advantages and disadvantages.

The Transfer Method

The transfer method—moving data from a 2.x server to a new 3.x server—is simpler, but it does have disadvantages. It can produce errors in the translation of user rights and other bindery elements, and it requires that you have a new server for NetWare 3.*x*. If the server should crash during the upgrade, you will need to restore the old server from tape to its original state, reinstall NetWare on the new server, and begin from scratch. It is a more secure method, however, because you will normally have the old server to fall back on if necessary, and it is often necessary to upgrade the server anyway to support the new version of NetWare.

The Backup Device Method

The other upgrade method is to back up your old server to a Novell Device-Independent Backup Interface (DIBI)-compatible device, reformat the drive, install 3.12, and then restore the files from the backup. The backup device method can be more cumbersome, because you must re-create the users, groups, and trustee rights after the data is restored, but it has the advantage of letting you start from a clean slate. If you are planning changes in the directory structure at the same time, the disadvantage becomes much less significant. If you are planning to use this method, you can make things easier for yourself by making sure that you understand the MAKEUSER utility thoroughly before you start.

The biggest problem you might face with the backup device method is that your data is deleted from the hard drives, forever; if the restore doesn't work, your data is gone. You can reduce the risk by upgrading one hard drive at a time. If the first restore works, you can feel more comfortable about the rest; if it fails, you have lost only some of your data.

If you decide to use the backup device method, it is critical to test your backups by restoring at least some files from them. If several files from different directories can be restored, the tape as a whole is likely to be good, although there is always the chance of a bad block on the tape causing the corruption of a file. This is the reason you should have two backups.

Upgrading from NetWare 3.*x* to 4.*x*

There are three methods of upgrading a server from NetWare 3.*x* to 4.*x*:

- Migrating to an existing NetWare 4.*x* server

- Migrating to a workstation and back to the same server after an upgrade

- Upgrading the server with the files in place

Migrating to an Existing 4.x Server

The first method moves the users, groups, files, print queues, and so on from the existing server to a NetWare 4.x server. This method allows you to set up the new server in advance, and only the transfer itself needs to be done while no one else is on the network. There is no risk of data loss, because the data still exists on the old server. Moreover, you can choose what data goes where in the new directory structure, even consolidating several old servers into one new server, or the reverse. The basic disadvantage is that you must have all new hardware for the new server.

Migrating to a Workstation

The second method is to move all the data to a workstation, using the migration utility. The workstation must have enough disk space to hold all of the server's files. Then you install NetWare 4.x on the server, and migrate the files back to the server. This method has many of the advantages of the first (migrating to a new server), and requires only a workstation with enough hard disk space, rather than a complete new server. You could even accomplish this without any additional hardware by using this method:

1. Unmirror your server's drives.

2. Install the mirror drives on the workstation.

3. Migrate the files.

4. Upgrade the server.

5. Migrate the files back to the server.

6. Remirror the drives.

The risk with this method is slightly higher, because the data is not maintained on a server while the old server is upgraded. If the workstation hard disks fail, you will need to restore the data from tape.

Upgrading the Server In-Place

The third method, the in-place upgrade, requires that the server be running NetWare 3.x or higher. If the server is a 2.x server, you must first upgrade to

3.*x*, then to 4.*x*. This doesn't incur additional cost; the upgrade facility will perform both upgrades. The advantage to this method is that it is the cheapest, because it doesn't require any additional hardware. However, it is the least secure. If the process fails, you will need to restore from tape and begin again. It also requires the most time, especially with a 2.*x* server, which requires two steps and has the least flexibility.

Since there is a good chance you will be upgrading the server hardware at the same time, I strongly recommend using the server-to-server migration if you can get the equipment. It provides complete security of data (you should still make backups first, of course—just for luck), gives you the most flexibility in restructuring the network, and requires the least time outside business hours. You could even make the change while users are working on the network, although I would strongly recommend against it.

Example: NetWare 2.15 to 3.12

There are many considerations involved in planning the upgrade from NetWare 2.*x* to 3.*x*. The NetWare 3.*x* Installation manual covers the process in detail. Here we will cover the typical problem areas and the most important considerations.

Planning and Preparation

When you're upgrading from NetWare 2.15 to 3.12, you need to be aware of a number of differences in the structure of the network operating system. Changes include the partition information on NetWare volumes, the format of the binderies, the number of bindery files, the way rights are assigned and inherited, the format and assignment of user numbers, and the method of password encryption.

PARTITIONS AND RIGHTS The most important changes are those in partitions and rights. The partition changes mean that drives must be repartitioned, which destroys all data on the drive. There is no way of upgrading a NetWare 2.15 volume to a NetWare 3.12 volume without erasing the volume and restoring the information from tape or setting up a new server and moving the data from the old server.

The new rights structure means that there is no exact way to translate rights between the two systems—there will be effective changes in the access users have to files. These changes may be minimal or extensive, depending on what rights users had before.

HARDWARE REQUIREMENTS NetWare 3.12 will require more memory than 2.15, and at least a 386 processor. If you have older NICs, backup tape drives, or other devices in the server, you may need to get updated drivers or change to newer hardware. Of course, if the old server was a 286 PC, you'll need to upgrade to at least a 386 (if you can find one) and at least 4 MB of RAM (I recommend a minimum of 8).

Given the relative differences in price, it makes good sense to get the highest-performance server you can. The difference in price between a 486DX2/66 with 8 MB RAM and an ISA bus and a Pentium 166 with 16 MB RAM and a PCI bus will vary from a couple hundred to a couple thousand dollars, depending on the brand, and the performance difference could be several hundred percent.

Practically, you will probably have trouble finding 486 PCs at all within the year. This means that spare parts and so forth will become hard to get, too. I strongly recommend that you not consider anything less than a Pentium PC for a server, unless your budget just won't handle it.

APPLICATIONS Another consideration is applications. If you use the transfer method, you may need to reinstall some applications. If the application manual recommends that you always install from the original floppies, it's a good indication that you may need to reinstall that application after the upgrade. If the application is copy-protected, you may need to uninstall it and then reinstall it after the upgrade. Some applications that access the NetWare binderies may need to be upgraded to versions that support 3.12.

NETWORK DRIVERS AND MAC NAME SPACES You should update the workstation network drivers to the version that comes with NetWare 3.12. You can do this before the server upgrade. If you are running the Mac VAPs, you'll need to have the Mac name space loaded on the new server before the upgrade.

OTHER PREPARATIONS Run BINDFIX to ensure that the NetWare 2.15 bindery is error-free. Back up NET$OS.EXE and the binderies too. If necessary, you can boot the server from a floppy and restore to it. Print copies of the printer configurations and any other configurations you will need to transfer to the new server.

Performing the Upgrade

As explained earlier, one way to upgrade is to install NetWare 3.12 on an entirely new server, and then connect the old and new servers and run

UPGRADE.EXE from a workstation (the transfer method). The other way is to back up your old server to a Novell DIBI-compatible device, reformat the drive, install 3.12, and then restore the files from the backup. The transfer method is faster, and less chancy, because you'll always have at least one operational server. It does, of course, require a new server, but given the speed with which PCs are growing in capability, this is probably a good idea anyway.

You can perform most of this upgrade piecemeal, before the actual transfer. If you upgrade the workstations at the users' convenience, and get the new server online during normal hours, the only part that you'll need to do after hours is migrating the files from the old server to the new server, and checking user rights on the new server. It's easiest to do this over a weekend. Plan on at least one day for the migration, and one day for checking. If you finish early, fine. If not, you'll have more leeway before the users are banging on your door. Once the upgrade is finished, make a backup of the new server.

Troubleshooting the New Installation

If you have problems after the installation, you will need to determine what has changed and how that change is causing the problem. This may seem simplistic, but the biggest upgrade problems can result from the administrator failing to understand the implications of some change in the features of NetWare or in the default configuration of some part of the system software. Also, the administrator may have left some part of the upgrade undone, such as failing to update login scripts to a new path or syntax.

Ensure before and after the upgrade that your users are aware of the changes you'll be making. At the least, you should provide them with a directory map of the server, showing changes, and a summary of the differences in trustee rights and the new inherited rights. Creating this document may also help you solidify your understanding of the differences. Make sure that the syntax of every login script is correct for any new drive mappings.

There are several areas that could create problems if you aren't aware of them:

- Naming conventions. If you used the 14-character filename capability of NetWare 2.15, the filenames will be truncated to the DOS standard of eight characters and a three-character extension. This may not be a problem unless you have paths set to directories whose names become truncated.

- System and Hidden directories. Any directories that are marked as System or Hidden will not be migrated during the upgrade process. If you have any such directories other than the SYSTEM and PUBLIC directories, or have additional files or applications in the PUBLIC directory that users need, you must transfer them separately, or make sure the directories are unmarked before the upgrade.

▪ Directory depth. NetWare 3.12 has a default maximum directory tree depth of 25 levels. If you have directory structures deeper than this on your 2.15 server, you will need to reduce the directory depth before performing the upgrade, or set the maximum directory depth to more than 25 levels in STARTUP.NCF on the 3.12 server before beginning the upgrade.

Excessive directory depths can cause problems with the backup software, and may also cause PATH statement line lengths in configuration files to exceed the maximum permissible length (256 characters). Some applications may also have problems with excessively long paths. I recommend reducing the directory depth.

Example: NetWare 3.11 to 4.1

Upgrading a network from NetWare 3.11 to NetWare 4.1 is a much more complex proposition than previous upgrades. Because of the WAN-oriented, global nature of NetWare 4.1, your entire corporate internet must be considered when upgrading. You and the other administrators must coordinate nomenclature for users, printers, volumes, groups, and other network resources to ensure that no two objects on your corporate tree use the same name.

You will also need to ensure that users with login scripts on more than one server consolidate the login scripts to avoid conflicts in mappings. Ideally, you should have an overall coordinator responsible for the corporate upgrade. This person should plan the corporate tree structure, install, and administer the master server for the root level, and coordinate all the information necessary to bring the other servers in your company into the NDS structure.

Planning and Preparation

The server will need to have at least 60 MB free on SYS and a minimum of 16 MB RAM (technically, it's 8 MB, but this isn't a place to save $200). Your server should be the fastest PC you can obtain. Desirable options include fast hard drives, an EISA or PCI bus, and 32-bit NICs. See Chapter 2 for more information about NetWare servers.

As explained earlier, you can upgrade by migrating to an existing NetWare 4.1 server, by migrating to a workstation and back to the same server after an upgrade, or with an in-place upgrade. If possible, I recommend the server-to-server migration upgrade. This gives you the maximum in safety and control and allows you to do most of the upgrade at your leisure, without affecting network services. It also gives you good justification to request a new fast server.

Once the new server is ready, run BINDFIX until the binderies are clean. Then use the PRINTUSR, PRINTGRP, and DUPBIND utilities and the NetWare utilities, or the aftermarket utility of your choice, to document all your users, groups, printers, print queues, print servers, binderies, applications, and directory structure.

Consider how your server, the users, and your network resources will fit into the overall corporate structure. Here are some items to look for:

- Are user login scripts consolidated? If the users log in to more than one server, make sure that there are no conflicting commands in the different scripts.

- Are usernames consistent? Make sure that the usernames for the same users are the same on all servers.

- Do you need to upgrade printer definitions and jobs? Run PUPGRADE or MIGPRINT.

- Are all NetWare 2.x and 3.x servers using the Ethernet 802.2 frame type? (Ethernet 802.3 is the default for 2.x and 3.x.) If not, upgrade the whole network, including workstations, to 802.2 before migrating to NetWare 4.1.

- Does your server keep accurate time? Time synchronization across the network is an important part of NetWare 4.1. See the Installation manual for details.

- Have you reviewed the upgrade plan with users, department managers, and your management? This is important, especially with regard to training the users on the requirements of the new system and the new network structure.

- Do you have tested backups of the old server?

- Have you cleaned out obsolete accounts, printer definitions, junk files, and other files you no longer need? The simpler the bindery and file structure of your server is beforehand, the easier the upgrade will be.

- Have you run BINDFIX? Did you run it until there were no errors?

- Is there a new backup that reflects the cleaned-up status of the server?

- Do you have a record of the old server configuration, including BIOS settings, STARTUP.NCF, and AUTOEXEC.NCF?

- Are all clients updated to the VLMs? Are any other necessary updates on the workstations made?

- If you currently have dedicated print servers running PSERVER.EXE, have you planned what to do with them?

- Have all users saved their e-mail to their local drives? It is possible to encounter e-mail problems even when everything else runs smoothly.

These are only some of the issues you will face. The most important thing you can do to prepare for the NetWare 3.*x* to 4.*x* upgrade is to fully understand the new features you will be implementing. Whether you get the information from a class, a book, or just the manuals, you should understand what you have, what you want to achieve with the new network structure, and the steps you will take to implement the new system.

The NetWare Application Notes for April and May 1993 cover many of the issues you should consider before the upgrade. They discuss the 3.12 to 4.0 upgrade, and some issues have changed with 4.1, but they are still well worth reviewing. You might also want to read version-specific guides, such as The Complete Guide to NetWare 4.1, *published by SYBEX.*

After you understand the implications of the upgrade, make sure that the users and managers in your department also understand. Clarifying the upgrade for them will not only reduce the number of problems due to user errors, but it may also raise issues that you haven't considered yet.

Performing the Upgrade

Once you have planned the new network structure and how your new server will fit into it, you can begin the actual process of the upgrade. Assuming this is not the first NetWare 4.*x* server in the company tree (it shouldn't be—the master server should be a new, fast server with no other function than maintaining the master database), you should know where in the tree you will be (which organizational unit and organization).

The upgrade itself should be relatively simple, if you have prepared properly. The migration utility will move the designated files, users, and other bindery objects into the new structure of your NDS tree. If you have already updated the user's workstations to the new VLM network drivers, you will need to switch only some configuration items, such as the login command syntax used in AUTOEXEC.BAT to reflect the new syntax for organizational unit and organization names, rather than server names.

Be sure to allow time to log in as different users and test access to applications and data files, printers, and other network resources. You may spot problems that won't show up for the Supervisor object, with its more extensive permissions.

Troubleshooting the New Installation

Some troubleshooting may be necessary even before you upgrade the server. For instance, you might find that some applications don't work well with the VLMs. You will need to identify each of these applications and either develop methods for fixing the problem or upgrade the applications.

After the server is upgraded, your most common complaint initially will probably be from users who don't understand how NDS has changed the way that they access resources on other servers. If a user can't access network services at all, it may be because the upgrade process has changed their username to prevent conflicts with an existing username in the tree. Similar problems can occur within login scripts. If a user had login scripts on more than one server before the upgrade, that user's usual directory mappings may have been changed, depending on which server was upgraded to NetWare 4.*x* first. If the workstation can't see any servers, make sure that the Ethernet frame types on the server and workstation match; the default for the VLMs is 802.2.

If you have problems with mail directories after an upgrade, try downloading a utility called RENMDIR.NLM from NetWire. When users are migrated from NetWare 3.*x* to NetWare 4.*x*, they get a new (random) user ID number that will not correspond to the old one. This means that their old mail directory number will not match their user ID number. RENMDIR will let you reassign the directories to their correct users.

Upgrading Hardware

F YOU ARE UPGRADING HARDWARE, give yourself a way to return easily to what you had before. Save the old version of the operating system and the configuration files on a floppy before you replace them. Save the old cards, in case you discover conflicts that you can't resolve immediately. You don't need to stockpile the old equipment indefinitely; just keep it long enough for any problems that may arise to show up—say, a couple of weeks.

Hardware Upgrade Considerations

As with any other upgrade, make sure that you understand the implications of the upgrade beforehand. For example, if you upgrade a workstation from a monochrome display to Super VGA, consider these points:

- You may need to change a jumper on the motherboard.

- Most applications will need new display drivers, and they may need to be reinstalled.

- The new display adapter may use additional memory that could cause problems with Windows or other applications.

- You may find that display updates are noticeably slower with the new display, because of higher processor overhead to display color instead of monochrome.

Troubleshooting Hardware Upgrades

You handle troubleshooting an upgrade to hardware in the same manner as troubleshooting a new system. First, make sure that all new configuration settings match the hardware configuration. If the problem persists, return to the most basic configuration possible, and once that works, add the rest of the system back in a piece at a time until you discover the problem. Often, this approach will lead you to the problem by forcing you to methodically compare configuration files with the actual hardware as you verify settings.

As an example, suppose that you are upgrading one of the workstations on your network to the VLM networking software in preparation for installing NetWare 4.*x*. You decide to upgrade the old NE1000 NIC to the faster 16-bit NE2000 at the same time. The ideal process for ease of troubleshooting would be to install the new hardware first and get it running with the old shell, then upgrade the shell; but you decide to save time and do both at once.

You save the old IPX.COM, NETX.COM, AUTOEXEC.BAT, and CONFIG.SYS files on a floppy, then install the new card and reboot the PC. The existing IPX and NETX produce error messages, because they aren't configured for the new adapter, but you were expecting that. You then run the workstation installation program, which installs new ODI and VLM requester files, creates a new NET.CFG file, creates a batch file to start the network services, modifies CONFIG.SYS and AUTOEXEC.BAT, installs the appropriate Windows network drivers, and modifies the Windows .INI files.

Once the installation program is finished, you reboot the PC and execute the STARTNET.BAT file to attach to the network. The message that appears on the screen is "No Servers Available." Going over the configuration in NET.CFG, you notice that the frame type is Ethernet 802.2, and you're still running 802.3 on your NetWare 3.11 server. You change the frame type and restart. The login process begins to run, and then the whole workstation hangs.

After several reboots, the workstation freezing each time, but at different points in the boot sequence, you pull out the configuration worksheet for the PC. You note that the original NIC was set to an alternate configuration, to avoid an interrupt conflict with the serial ports. When you installed the new NIC, you used the default configuration. You pull the card out, set it to the same interrupt as the old card, and change the configuration parameters in NET.CFG. The system works.

Upgrading Software

W ITH SOFTWARE UPGRADES, you should also maintain a path to return to your old configuration. This can be simple on a network—copy the old software (or the entire workstation disk, if necessary) to a network drive. Make sure you have a floppy disk that you can boot from, attach to the network, and copy the old system back to the workstation, if necessary.

Be aware that updating software can affect other software on the workstation. For example, if you update the operating system, you may need to update utilities, TSR programs, Inits, and applications. Upgrading system software or an application to a new version that uses more memory may affect the operation of other applications on the system. The new version may also produce conflicts with existing hardware. Read the hardware requirements for the new version carefully, noting any changes from the old version and checking them against the hardware installed in the workstation.

Upgrading Networking Software and Operating Systems

If you are updating the networking or system software on your network, you can take two approaches:

- If you update all the workstations on the network at once, you may find that some unanticipated incompatibility will affect your entire department. This procedure will also require a fairly large block of time, probably on a weekend or after hours, when you can go from workstation to workstation, making the necessary changes.

- Updating one workstation at a time, on the other hand, while it doesn't require the same large block of time all at once, may produce conflicts between operating system versions.

For instance, updating some Macintoshes on your network to System 7, while others are still using System 6.0x (or even if the Macintoshes are using different incremental versions of System), will cause conflicts between the different LaserWriter drivers. You can fix this by updating the LaserWriter drivers on all systems, using the driver from the new system version with the older systems.

Updating PC operating systems will often require new versions of the NetWare shell as well. For instance, upgrading from MS-DOS 4.0 to a later version will require that you upgrade from NET4.COM to NETX.COM (unless you are already running it) or something newer, such as the ODI drivers or the VLMs. You may also find that the DOS version reported to NetWare will cause problems, if you have upgraded to MS-DOS 5.0 to 6.0. You can fix this by using the DOS command SETVER.EXE in the NETX.COM file and then including SETVER in your CONFIG.SYS file. When you run SETVER.EXE you will want to set NETX.COM to 5.0:

```
SETVER NETX.COM 5.0
```

then, in CONFIG.SYS, add the line:

```
DEVICE=C:\DOS\SETVER.EXE
```

This makes NetWare think that you are using the version of NETX.COM appropriate to the version of DOS.

Upgrading to Windows 95

Upgrading to Windows 95 has some very serious implications in the context of a network—so serious that adoption in the corporate world has been much slower than anticipated. Among the issues are:

- Interface with NetWare

- Long filenames

- 32-bit applications

- Hardware requirements

- Drivers for older components

- Peer-to-peer security of Windows 95

If you are contemplating taking the plunge, review the topics discussed here carefully, then consider setting up a few PCs to see how they interface with the rest of your network. Be sure you understand the total cost of upgrading, including costs for new workstations, new cards, new versions of applications, support time, installation time, and so on. When they're all combined, they make the cost of the Windows 95 software itself seem trivial.

The Interface with NetWare

One of the issues that has slowed adoption has been the length of time it has taken both Microsoft and Novell to release NetWare clients for Windows 95. And even when clients were released, they did not initially support NDS. There are now adequate clients available from both companies, but you should make sure you have the latest, rather than using the drivers installed by default during the Windows 95 installation.

Long Filenames

Windows 95 has jumped on the long-filename bandwagon with the Macintosh and OS/2. It now supports filenames of up to 255 characters, rather than the old limit of 8. However, from the network administrator's point of view, this can cause several problems. First, you must load the OS/2 name space on any drives on which users will be storing files with long names. Second, any application that was not written for Windows 95 will not support the long names and will change the names to the old eight.three type when a file is saved. This can cause problems when some users are running Windows 3.*x* and some are running Windows 95.

32-Bit Applications

To make full use of the capabilities of Windows 95, you will need to upgrade applications to versions written for Windows 95. Full use of the capabilities of Windows 95 includes long filenames and other features that old versions of software don't support. Older programs may run fine, but they won't use the additional features. If you have critical applications that don't yet have Windows 95 versions, test them thoroughly on a Windows 95 PC before committing to an upgrade—they may or may not work well.

Hardware Requirements

Microsoft says that you can run Windows 95 on a 486DX/33 with 8 MB of RAM. It is (just barely) possible, but if you want to run applications other than Notepad, you will need more power. I recommend at least a 486DX4/100 and 16 MB RAM. However, 486 systems are getting hard to find, and the prices of Pentium systems have dropped to less than 486 prices were a year ago. If you have 486 systems, you may be able to upgrade them with faster 486 processors or the Pentium overdrive processors, and more memory. If you have older PCs, you should upgrade to whatever your budget supports.

Drivers for Older Components

If you have PCs installed with older cards in them, you may experience problems with Windows 95's Plug and Play installation. During the installation process, Windows recommends that you allow it to detect any cards in the system and set them up. Windows does a good job of detecting older cards. However, it may not determine an older card's configuration correctly, but assume the default configuration for the card. If this is not what the card is set to, the system may freeze. Make sure you record the settings of all the cards in the system before you begin. You can manually change the interrupt and DMA (direct memory access) settings during the Windows 95 installation.

Peer-to-Peer Security

Windows 95 (and Windows for Workgroups) supports peer-to-peer networking. This does not directly affect a NetWare network, but it can allow users to inadvertently grant any user on the network access to their hard drive. This can cause some real security problems if you aren't aware of it and if you don't monitor the network to look for systems that are exposed.

Tips and Techniques

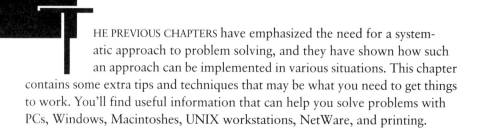

THE PREVIOUS CHAPTERS have emphasized the need for a systematic approach to problem solving, and they have shown how such an approach can be implemented in various situations. This chapter contains some extra tips and techniques that may be what you need to get things to work. You'll find useful information that can help you solve problems with PCs, Windows, Macintoshes, UNIX workstations, NetWare, and printing.

Tips for Troubleshooting PCs (DOS Computers)

THE BIGGEST PROBLEM WITH PCS is their variety and variability—the processor, the type of memory, the bus, the display. Virtually every part of a PC can differ completely from other PCs, and the same is true of the configuration files and software. The tips that may help you with PCs fall into the categories of boot errors, the AUTOEXEC.BAT and CONFIG.SYS files, and IRQs. For details about these and other aspects of troubleshooting PCs, see Chapter 3.

Boot Errors

When error messages appear during the boot process, these tips may help:

- If you have a problem reading the messages that appear as your PC boots, try pressing the Ctrl-NumLock or the Pause key on a 101- or 102-key keyboard. This should pause the boot process until you press another key.

- If your PC's manual doesn't tell you what the POST messages mean, try to find an old IBM XT or AT hardware reference manual. It might be useful for determining whether an error code is hardware related and what part of the system it relates to.

AUTOEXEC.BAT and CONFIG.SYS Errors

When you think your problems may be caused by errors in the AUTOEXEC.BAT or CONFIG.SYS files, the following tips and techniques may apply:

- The single most common cause of problems in system configuration through the AUTOEXEC.BAT and CONFIG.SYS files is spelling and typographical errors. Double-check every line you add to these files.

- Add a PAUSE command in the AUTOEXEC.BAT file before a command if you are trying to trace a problem and aren't sure whether the problem is occurring before or after that command.

- Errors in CONFIG.SYS usually produce an error message that identifies the problem line in the file. If not, the message should at least identify the driver causing the problem. If you see an error message that reads something like "Bad or Missing C:\BOOT\ANSI.SYS," check the spelling and make sure that the path in the file matches the actual path to the directory. Don't rely on the PATH command in AUTOEXEC.BAT; put the whole path to the driver or command in the entry in CONFIG.SYS. If you can't resolve an error, you can temporarily add REM at the beginning of the line to prevent the driver from loading and see if the rest of the lines execute properly.

- With MS-DOS 5.0 or later, you can boot without using CONFIG.SYS or AUTOEXEC.BAT by holding down the F5 key when the message "Starting MS-DOS" appears. If the PC boots without errors, then you can reboot again, holding down F8 at the same time. DOS will step through the commands in CONFIG.SYS one at a time, asking you to confirm that you want to load the driver named there. (You can get the same result with AUTO-EXEC.BAT by using the PAUSE command, as suggested earlier.)

IRQ Conflicts

PCs use IRQs (interrupt channels) to access physical devices. Unfortunately, the number of IRQs can be less than the number of devices that you want to attach to your PC. Trying to use an IRQ for two things can lead to problems. Table 12.1 shows how IRQs are mapped to memory segments and devices. The memory segment is the reserved area of memory used by DOS to hold information about the device. Two devices attempting to use the same memory segment can scramble the data so that neither device can function.

The default IRQ is the IRQ that a PC card is set to at the factory. The installation program for the software that comes with the card will usually assume that you want to use the default settings unless you change them during the installation. Unfortunately, many cards are set to the same default; if you have two cards with the same default, one must be changed to avoid conflicts. For example, a system with an ARCnet adapter and a mouse would be a potential source of interrupt conflict, because the default IRQ for both the mouse and the ARCnet card is 2. Ethernet cards default to IRQ 3 as a rule. Token Ring adapters may use either IRQ 3 or 4 as a default.

T A B L E 12.1 How IRQs are Mapped to Memory Segments and Devices	**IRQ**	**MEMORY SEGMENT**	**DEVICE**
	2	N/A	Actually served by IRQ 9. Use with caution in an AT; IRQ 9 may be in use.
	3	2F8	COM 2, usually the default for LAN adapters. If you aren't using the COM 2 port, this should be safe.
	3	2E0	COM 4 (also COM 2).
	4	3F8	COM 1.
	4	2E8	COM 3 (also COM 1).
	5	3F0	PC-XT hard drive controller.
	5	278	LPT 2.
	6	3F0	Floppy disk drive controller.
	7	378	LPT 1.

Tips for Troubleshooting Windows

THE FOLLOWING SECTIONS DISCUSS the different varieties of Windows, as follows:

- Windows before 3.1

- Windows 3.1 and later

- Windows 95

- Windows NT

For more information about troubleshooting problems with Windows, see Chapter 3.

Windows Versions before 3.1

The basic tip here is: don't. Upgrade to at least Windows 3.1 or Windows for Workgroups 3.11. Those versions offer more compatibility with Windows programs and with NetWare, and better networking support in general. However, if you have an earlier version, these tips may help:

- The original SMARTDRV.SYS supplied with Windows 3.0 can corrupt disk partitions created with utilities other than FDISK, including Speed-Stor from Storage Dimensions, Disk Manager from OnTrack, InnerSpace from Priam Systems, and VFeatures Deluxe from Golden Bow.

- With Windows 3.0, beware of using CHKDSK /F or any utilities that directly access the FAT (file allocation table) or write directly to disk, rather than using the DOS programming calls from within Windows. If you need to use these utilities, exit Windows first, or you may corrupt files or the FAT.

- Running Windows with NetWare versions before 2.2 (2.15c at the very earliest) or 3.11 is possible, but not recommended. Both the workstation network drivers and some of the utilities on the server must be upgraded. And even with a small budget, the time it will take you to get everything working will probably justify the expense of an upgrade, which will also get you a better version of NetWare.

- Get the latest version of the NetWare DOS/Windows Client Kit from your reseller or from NetWire. It includes the latest network drivers, including the ODI drivers, as well as the NetWare Tools for Windows utilities, which allow you to use the MAP, ATTACH, CAPTURE, USERLIST, VOLINFO, SETPASS, SEND, MESSAGES, and SESSION utilities from within Windows, instead of needing to exit Windows to reconfigure your NetWare environment from DOS.

- There is a difference between the ways DOS and NetWare display files with the DIR command. If you type DIR on a DOS drive, the first two items will be a period and double period, representing the current directory and the parent directory. Windows allows you to select the double period to move back up the directory tree. On a NetWare drive, you won't get the period and double period unless the entry SHOW DOTS=ON is in the SHELL.CFG or NET.CFG file. This setting doesn't affect performance or cause any other problems, so I recommend you use it in your default configuration files.

If you use SHOW DOTS=ON and you are running a version of NetWare prior to 2.2, you must replace BINDFIX.EXE with the updated version in the DOS/Windows Client Kit. Otherwise, running BINDFIX could result in the SYS volume being erased.

- If you're planning to use a Windows workstation with a remote printer (running RPRINTER), make sure that you have the latest version of RPRINTER or are using NPRINTER. Older versions can cause the workstation to lock up when anyone attempts to print, and have even been known to cause ABENDs on the server.

Windows 3.1 and Later

Windows for Workgroups 3.11 is probably the best version of Windows currently available for use with a NetWare network. It offers some of the 32-bit advantages of Windows 95, but it's fully understood and debugged, which cannot yet be said of Windows 95 (or NT, which is also much more expensive). Workgroups 3.11 also has good networking support, both for NetWare and other functions, such as TCP/IP. Here are some tips and techniques that apply to Windows 3.1 and later and Windows for Workgroups 3.11:

- If you are running Windows on a NetWare network, use Windows 3.1 or later, and NetWare 2.2, 3.11, or 4.0 or later. You can download the Net-Ware Workstation Kit for DOS/Windows from CompuServe to make sure that you have the latest NetWare drivers.

- If you used NWSETUP from the NetWare Workstation Kit for DOS/Windows to install your network drivers, and Windows now hangs, check your Windows directory for a file called WINSTART.BAT and delete it.

- When you install Windows for Workgroups 3.11, it detects existing network drivers and installs native support. Make sure you know what the actual settings of the network adapter are, and make sure that you set the windows driver to the same settings.

- If you can't get Windows 3.1 to run in Enhanced mode, try running it in Standard or Real mode. (Windows for Workgroups doesn't support this.) Determining the last mode in which it will run should give you clues about what is preventing it from running properly. For example, if Windows will run in Real mode, but not in Standard or Enhanced mode, there may not be enough memory available to Windows, the memory handler (HIMEM.SYS) may not be loading, or the TEMP directory environment variable may not be set to a directory that exists. Similarly, if it will run in Real and Standard modes, but not Enhanced, you may need to install the VPICD.386 driver, WINA20.SYS or EMM386.EXE might not be running correctly, or (most obviously), you might not have a 386 or higher processor.

- Two common problems are a video configuration that doesn't match the video card installed in the PC, and memory conflicts resulting from hardware (such as NICs or TSRs) loaded before Windows trying to use the same parts of memory that Windows uses. See the discussion of the EMMEXCLUDE command in Chapter 3 for details.

- If a user opens a DOS window from within Windows, and there's no prompt, no path, and no environment variables set, Windows is probably not configured for NetWare. Check the configuration with the Control Panel, and if necessary, use SETUP.EXE to add NetWare support.

- One problem often seen with Windows is "Out of Memory" errors. This problem may exist even with large amounts of RAM. The issue is with RAM available under the 640 KB limit. The 640 KB limit still applies to Windows; every program you load uses some of the 640 KB, and if you have a network shell and other software loaded before you start Windows, you may have only 400 KB or less to start with.

Windows 95

Windows 95 has gained very slow acceptance in corporate American due to major problems with existing networks, especially NetWare. You should consider this before planning to switch. See the section on Windows 95 in Chapter 11 for some of the major considerations. If you're having problems with Windows 95, here are some tips and techniques to try:

- There are two ways to give yourself an out when installing Windows 95: either install it in a separate directory from the earlier version and be prepared to reinstall applications and other items or use System Commander, from V Communications, Inc., which will let you choose whether to boot from the old version of Windows or the new one, and will let you uninstall without problems.

- When installing Windows 95 over an existing version of DOS, be sure to disable TSRs and memory managers such as QEMM before you start.

- If you have the extra space (up to 6 MB), save your existing startup files when installing Windows 95.

- Before installing Windows 95, you should delete the existing permanent swap file if you have Windows 3.*x* installed, and let Windows 95 create a new one. After deleting the swap file, you may also wish to defragment the drive.

- Once you have a PC set up with all its drivers, applications installed, and so on, use the Registry Editor (REGEDIT.EXE) to export the registry to a text file (EXAMPLE.REG). Then, when the registry becomes corrupted, and the backup also is corrupted, you can boot in the command prompt mode and type the following command:

```
REGEDIT /C EXAMPLE.REG
```

This will restore the registry to what it was when you made the backup. You should be aware that anything installed since you made the backup may have problems. It's a good idea to back up the registry regularly.

- Don't ever power off a PC running Windows 95 without shutting it down first, because it's almost certain to corrupt the registry. It's quite difficult to lock Windows 95 up to the point that Ctrl-Alt-Del won't exit the troublesome program.

- Get the Windows 95 Resource Kit. It has additional troubleshooting tools, as well as later versions of drivers for some cards.

- Check the Web site or bulletin board of the manufacturers of your cards. A properly optimized driver for Windows 95 can provide a performance increase of 20 percent or more over the standard driver installed by Windows.

- You can use the F8 key to access the startup options of Windows 95. Press F8 as Windows begins to boot, and you'll get a number of options, which may give you a better chance of accessing the system if you're having trouble.

- You can't use DriveSpace if the hard drive is over 512 MB. However, if you have the CD-ROM version of MS Plus!, you can use DriveSpace3, which will work with drives up to 2 GB and delivers higher compression ratios with fast systems.

- Make sure you install the patch that removes read-only access to a hard drive for all users when the file C$ exists on the hard disk and you're using remote administration, and the patch that eliminates the problem that results from OLE links finding files that have been deleted. The patches are available on the Web, in the Windows 95 Resource Kit, or from Microsoft.

- If you're using Stacker with Windows 3.1 and you're about to upgrade to Windows 95, be sure that you have version 4.1 of Stacker. If you install Windows 95 over version 4.0 of Stacker, you can loose all the data on the hard drive.

Windows NT

Microsoft is saying that Windows NT is intended for corporate users, and that Windows 95 is oriented towards consumers. Once NT is available with the cool 95 interface, it may well end up as the platform of choice for both corporate and end users. The current version doesn't do as well as Windows 95 at detecting hardware, but otherwise is much easier for the administrator. Here are some tips for troubleshooting NT systems:

- Many problems with NT can be traced to system requirements. NT workstations should have a minimum of a mid-level Pentium and at the very least, 16 MB RAM; 32 MB is much better. For an NT server, the fastest CPU you can get and 64 MB of RAM are good starting places.

- If you're trying to install NT on a big (over 1 GB) IDE hard drive, and getting an "inaccessible hard drive" message, it's because NT has a problem with IDE drives over 1024 cylinders. You'll need to enable LBA (Logical Block Addressing) in the system or controller BIOS, then reformat the disk with FDISK.

- If you're running an NT server, beware of the new screen savers in version 3.5. Some of them (such as 3DPipes) can cause processor utilization to hit 90 percent!

- Use Windows NT File and Print Services if you want to add an NT server to your network. It will let all your NetWare clients access files and printers on the NT server without needing to load Windows for Workgroups or 95.

Tips for Troubleshooting Macintoshes

YOUR NETWORK may include Macs. When you have problems with them, the following tips and techniques may help. For more details about running Macs in a NetWare network, see Chapter 3.

- If a Macintosh is not booting and you suspect the problem may be caused by Init conflicts, restart the Mac while holding down a Shift key. This prevents all Inits from loading with System 7, and deactivates most under System 6. If the Mac boots without the Inits, remove them all from the System folder or from the Extensions folder in the System folder with System 7. Then add them back in, one at a time, rebooting after each one, until you identify the problem. A simpler solution is to use a utility such as InitPicker, which allows you to designate the order in which Inits load or deactivate them without removing them from the System folder.

- You can identify the order in which Inits load by watching the icons that appear along the bottom of the screen as the Mac boots. If you aren't sure which icon is associated with which Init, open the System or Extensions folder and select Icon View.

- If you can't see any volumes once you log in to a NetWare server, the Macintosh name space may not be loaded. Check on the server by typing VOLUMES at the console. If the volumes don't have the name space listed, you will need to load MAC.NAM and add the Macintosh name space to the volumes.

- If the volume names are dimmed in the login window of the Chooser, the desktop files may be corrupted. To rebuild the desktop files, go back to the server, unload AFP, and then reload it using the CDT option:

```
LOAD AFP CDT
```

Then log in to the server from a Macintosh as Supervisor, highlight each volume that needs to be rebuilt, hold down the Command (flower or apple) and Option keys, and click on OK. Confirm that you wish to rebuild the desktop when prompted.

- During backups, Macs running System 7 may lose their connection to the server, while Macs running System 6 are fine. This is because the binderies are closed for a while during backups and System 6 simply queries the server until the binderies are opened again, while System 7 quits after a few retries. AFIX2.ZIP in NOVLIB1 on CompuServe works with versions 3.0 and 3.01 of NetWare for Macintosh and allows the server to respond to the Macs even while the binderies are closed.

- If you have Macintoshes using System 7 connecting to a NetWare server that has volumes that support the UNIX name space, you may find that the Macs freeze when attempting to access certain volumes or folders. Check to see if the option to calculate folder size automatically is set to On in the Views Control Panel. If it is, the Mac may be attempting to calculate the sizes of folders that were created with UNIX or that contain files created with UNIX. Attempting to get these sizes can cause the Mac to freeze. Set the automatic folder size calculation to Off.

- Insufficient memory can be solved in only one of two ways: unload any unneeded applications, if any exist, or add RAM to the Mac. Fortunately, adding memory to most Macs is a simple matter of installing more or higher-capacity SIMMs (single in-line memory modules). Macs with more than 8 MB of RAM must be running 32-bit addressing to take advantage of the extra memory. If you use this feature, be aware that older applications that are not 32-bit compatible may not run until you switch 32-bit addressing off again and reboot the Mac. If you install more memory, and the About the Macintosh—Finder shows that the system is using more than about 1.5 to 2 MB (probably the amount of memory over 8 MB installed), it means that 32-bit addressing is not switched on. Remember that you must reboot after switching it on.

- If you see an "Insufficient Memory" message while using an application, and there seems to be sufficient memory in the Mac, use the Get Info command in the Finder while the application's icon is selected to see what the Suggested Memory Size is and how much is allocated in Application Memory Size. You may need to increase the Application Memory Size beyond what is suggested, particularly if you are working with large files.

- When configuring your server, remember that the zone name may contain spaces. If you can't get access to a particular zone, try inserting a leading or trailing space in the configuration entry—you may have accidentally put a space at the beginning or end of a zone name when it was initially assigned. This also applies to printer names. A simple way to test for spaces is to use the ATCON NLM to do a lookup test in the suspect zone or on the suspect printer. If the lookup fails with the name spelled as it looks, try adding spaces before or after until the lookup succeeds.

- If you set up NetWare print queues that print to a Macintosh printer, you will see both the NetWare queue and the printer itself in the Macintosh Chooser. You may wish to hide the printer itself, to keep users from printing directly to the printer, which can insert their print jobs ahead of those in the queue. See the NetWare for Macintosh Installation and Maintenance manual for details.

- On a NetWare 3.x server running NetWare for Macintosh, if you get an error message "ATPS can't login ####," you need to delete ATPS with PCONSOLE. Go to Print Server Information, select ATPS, and press the Del key. Confirm the action and exit. When you load ATPS, the server will be re-created.

- With the Macintosh VAPs on 2.*x* servers or bridges (routers), the Apple-Talk address is assigned based on the last two digits of the Ethernet address of the NIC. If those digits are FE, the AppleTalk ID assigned is 254, which is an invalid AppleTalk ID. The only solution is to swap the Ethernet card. PCs don't care about this, so you can swap the card for one from another system.

Tips for Troubleshooting UNIX Workstations

WHEN YOU'RE EXPERIENCING PROBLEMS with the UNIX clients in your network, you can try the following tips and techniques. For more information about UNIX workstations in a NetWare network, see Chapter 3.

- If UNIX workstations can mount a NetWare server's drive but cannot access the files, it may be that the entire volume is not exported (set in the NFSADMIN NLM), but the problem is more likely to be with permissions. A user who doesn't have the Execute permission on a directory won't be able to see the files in that directory. Don't rely on the trustee rights set from a NetWare workstation; the translation of permissions between UNIX and NetWare may not be what you expect, since there is not a one-to-one correspondence between the two permission schemes. Appendix B of the NFS Supervisor's Guide gives information about what the UNIX permissions will be, given specific NetWare trustee assignments.

- If UNIX users will be saving files to your NetWare server, make sure that the Modify DOS Attributes From UNIX option is set to Yes in the Exports information in the NFSADMIN utility. Otherwise, users may be unable to modify their own files or place files in directories they create.

- If you export NetWare volumes with NetWare NFS, users on other systems can access the files without ever having a login account on your system, assuming that the directory trustee rights give the group EVERYONE or the user NOBODY access. However, the user will have a UNIX user ID of -3 and the NetWare name of NOBODY. NOBODY cannot access files created previously by that user (it might not have been the same NOBODY), unless the group (EVERYONE) is also allowed access to the files. Since the typical UNIX file-creation mask turns the Write permission off for the group and the world, users will not be able to open and then save the files they just put on the server. Similarly, they won't be able to delete the files, and may not even be able to put files into a directory they have just created! The solution is to give a NetWare account to each person who needs to access the server through UNIX, or set the file-creation mask on the user's system to give the group write permission.

■ If you are using a version of NetWare NFS prior to 1.2, and have many users accessing volumes on the server through UNIX, get version 1.2b or later. With the older versions, every time that a user accesses a directory, a trustee entry is created for that directory. This can result in thousands of trustee entries, especially for GUEST or EVERYONE. This is not just inconvenient—if the number of entries gets too large, you may not be able to access the binderies with NetWare utilities such as SYSCON, the binderies might become corrupt, or the server could ABEND. With version 1.2 or later, you can turn Create Trustee Rights to OFF. You will need to create a file in each directory hierarchy that lists what the trustee rights should be. See the NetWare NFS 1.2 documentation for details.

Tips for Troubleshooting NetWare

THE FOLLOWING SECTIONS PROVIDE tips and techniques that apply generally to several or all versions of NetWare, followed by version-specific information for NetWare 2.x, 3.x, and 4.x.

BINDFIX

Here are some tips regarding BINDFIX, the NetWare utility for repairing problems that occur with the binderies. For more information about BINDFIX, see Chapter 2.

■ Run BINDFIX until no errors are reported. It will fix some problems each time, but the next time through it may find more problems.

- Don't run BINDFIX from a Windows workstation if NET.CFG contains the statement SHOW DOTS=ON and you are running a version of Net-Ware prior to 2.2. Running BINDFIX could result in the SYS volume being erased. Replace BINDFIX.EXE with the updated version in the DOS/Windows Client Kit.

- When updating to a new version of NetWare, run BINDFIX until no errors are reported. This ensures that the binderies are clean before the upgrade.

PRINTCON

Using print jobs is a much easier way to set the parameters for complex printing, because it allows users to make choices from menus rather than requiring them to enter the exact spelling and syntax for each setting, as with CAPTURE. PRINTCON allows you to designate a default print job and to set up queues associated with each job.

PRINTCON creates a print job definition file named PRINTCON.DAT for the user in their SYS:MAIL directory. You can define a default print job for one user and then copy that file to everyone's mail directory to set everyone's default print job. If you want a user to be able to change the default, make sure to give that person rights to the file (only SUPERVISOR will initially own and have rights to the file). See Chapter 5 for more information about PRINTCON and troubleshooting network printing.

After ABENDs or Power Failures

An ABEND message means that the server software has crashed. This could be caused by an NLM that is incorrectly configured, corrupted, or simply badly written; an incorrectly entered SET command; a printer that is set up incorrectly; or a hardware problem.

You should run VREPAIR any time the server is not properly shut down. Unless the volumes are properly dismounted before the server is taken down, it's possible for the binderies and FATs to become corrupted. This damage may not show up when the server is brought back online, and if left untended, can cause permanent data loss. If the FATs are corrupted, even the backups may not be recoverable. See Chapter 2 for more information about ABEND messages and VREPAIR.

Login Scripts

In NetWare 2.*x* and 3.*x*, each user's login script is stored in a numbered directory in SYS:MAIL, based on a unique user ID number that is assigned by NetWare when a new user is created. You can get each user's number with SYSCON (User Information/Login Name/Other Information).

The login script is a text file called LOGIN. If you need to make changes to many scripts, it can be faster to use a text editor on these files directly, instead of using SYSCON. See Chapter 2 for more information about login scripts.

NetWare 2.*x*

Here are some tips and techniques specific to NetWare 2.*x*. For more version-specific information, see Chapter 2.

- Users upgrading from NetWare version 2.15A to version 2.15B or 2.15C may have severe performance problems if they have two internal MFM (modified frequency modulation) drives on the same controller. Use the ATDISK.DSK driver instead of the ISADISK.DSK driver. Make sure its date is 11/11/88 or later, and the ATDISK.OBJ is dated 10/12/88 or later.

- NetWare 2.2 will use a maximum of 12 MB of RAM on a dedicated server. If you have more installed, it will be recognized but not used. If you are running out of memory, upgrade to NetWare 3.*x* or 4.*x*.

- If you run VREPAIR and the screen blanks and nothing further happens, you should try booting the server with a DOS 3.*x* diskette before running VREPAIR. If you have upgraded the DOS version that the server boots with to a later version, you will need to download a patch from NetWire (see Appendix A for more details) or reboot the server with DOS 3.*x*.

NetWare 3.*x*

The following are some tips and techniques specific to NetWare 3.*x*. For more version-specific information, see Chapter 2.

- To load NetWare without using STARTUP.NCF or AUTOEXEC.NCF, use the following command-line options: SERVER -NS (to skip STARTUP.NCF), SERVER -NA (to skip AUTOEXEC.NCF), or SERVER -NSA (to skip both).

These commands allow you to manually load hard disk drivers, LAN drivers, and so forth, bypassing the usual settings. This can be extremely useful for troubleshooting problems that you can't trace during the normal boot sequence, or for occasions when you've changed the hardware configuration in advance of software, and the new configuration won't boot.

- Load MONITOR with the -p option to get more statistics on your server utilization. It will show you what processes are running and how much of the available processor capacity they are using.

- A typical server setup may have two or more external drives in enclosures. If one of these drives fails, you will receive a message saying that Drive 1 on Adapter 1 has failed. This doesn't tell you anything about the physical location of the drive, however. In some cases, you can use the Disk Information menu item in MONITOR to set the Drive Light Status for each drive to "Flashing" until you have identified all the physical drives by their drive number and volume segment. Of course, if you label the drives before you start, this won't be a problem; the drive numbers generally correspond to the SCSI ID number—the drive with the lowest SCSI ID has the lowest drive number, and so on.

NetWare 4.x

The following are some tips and techniques specific to NetWare 4.*x*. For more version-specific information, see Chapter 2 and Chapter 8, which covers NDS.

- Upgrade workstations to the VLMs from IPX or the ODI shell before you upgrade the server. This will let you debug any problems with applications or TSRs on the workstations before you need to use them to attach to the server. VLMs also use extended memory, conserving precious base memory usage.

- If you're having trouble logging in to a server, try including the entire context in the login command:

```
LOGIN
.CN=login_name.OU=organizational_unit.O=organization
```

If this works, it means the context you've specified in the NET.CFG file may be incorrect, or misspelled.

- If you are running the VLMs and attaching to both NetWare 4.*x* and 3.*x* servers, and the 3.*x* connections are unexpectedly dropping out, look at your NET.CFG file. If CONNECTIONS=## is set to more than 8, connections may be dropped when you run NetWare utilities (such as ATTACH, WHOAMI, or SLIST) on a 3.*x* server.

- Don't delete the Admin object unless you have given Supervisor rights to another object; doing so will leave you with an NDS tree that can't be administered. You will need to either restore the partition from a backup or reinitialize the directory and start from scratch. You won't lose data, but all the structural information will be lost.

- If you can't create, delete, or modify objects, first make sure that you have sufficient rights. Then, if you do, run DSREPAIR. It's a good idea to run this utility every few months to make sure that everything in the database is optimized and that all entries match actual objects.

- Make sure that everything on your LAN is using either Ethernet 802.2 or 802.3—they don't mix well. The default for the NetWare 4.*x* and the VLMs is 802.2, while older systems use 802.3.

- Don't try to define objects such as printers for a domain before you upgrade the server to 4.*x*. This can cause problems with the upgrade that will result in the print queues, print jobs, and other items on the old server being lost during the upgrade.

- Don't use SBACKUP to back up and restore a partition (the NDS information, not the volume) with the initial release of NetWare 4.0. Using SBACKUP can result in the corruption of the partition, which will require that you redefine users, groups, and so on. If you have recorded this information, it shouldn't be too much of a problem to reconstruct, but doing so will cause lots of work, disrupt the network, and waste time. Cheyenne Software's ArcServe 5.0 is a better choice for backups.

Tips for Troubleshooting Printing

THIS SECTION GIVES some tips and techniques that you may find helpful in solving network printing problems. See Chapter 5 for more details.

- If you have a printer attached to the parallel port of a workstation running NPRINTER, RPRINTER, or PSERVER.EXE, and print jobs are not printing, try setting the printer configuration in PCONSOLE to Don't Use Interrupts.

- In NetWare 2.*x* and 3.*x*, print queues are numbered directories in SYS:SYSTEM. You can identify the directory associated with any queue by looking up the print server's ID number in PCONSOLE. Go to the Print Server Information menu, select the print server you are looking for, and then select Print Server ID. Each directory contains hidden files named FILESERV, PRINT, QUEUE, and NOTIFY. You can change the file attributes or use FILER to view them. FILESERV lists the file servers serviced, PRINT has configuration information for the printer, QUEUE contains information on the print queue, and NOTIFY lists the users to be notified of problems. There may be several versions of each file (except FILESERV): one for each printer attached to the print server. The extension will be the same for each defined printer, beginning with 000.

- If you are having problems with printing, and you have deleted print server definitions, check to see if there are queue directories that don't correspond to any existing print server. If there are, delete the directories.

- If you are having problems with a printer on a workstation running RPRINTER, try adding the following items to SHELL.CFG or NET.CFG:

```
IPX RETRY COUNT = 35
SPX ABORT TIMEOUT = 700
```

- If you are running PSERVER.EXE, make sure that you use the latest available network drivers. Older drivers can cause PSERVER to hang the workstation on occasion. Also, make sure that NET.CFG includes the entry:

```
SPX CONNECTIONS = 60
```

The Next Step

F YOU HAVEN'T FOUND THE TIP you were looking for here, don't despair. Appendix A is full of resources you can use to find out more. For instance, through the Internet, you can access some of Novell's best engineers as well as thousands of NetWare administrators around the world and ask them for help with your problem. You can also check Appendix B to find tools that will help you solve the problem yourself.

Appendixes

PART V

Resources for Troubleshooters

WHEN YOU PURCHASE NETWARE, you are entitled to tech support, either from Novell or from the dealer. However, when your initial support agreement lapses, you will need to pay for support. Novell offers tech support over the phone at an hourly rate. There are other options. You may wish to purchase an extended support plan from your Novell authorized reseller or from another firm. You can also get information from online resources (such as CompuServe or NetWire), technical support databases, technical support consultants or companies, or your local chapter of the CNEPA (Certified NetWare Engineer Professional Association) or NetWare Users International (NUI). This appendix describes these and other resources that are useful to troubleshooters. The following topics are covered:

- The NetWare manuals and README files

- Other Novell publications

- Magazines

- Books and catalogs

- Online resources

- The Internet

- Technical support databases

- The CNEPA and NUI

- Aftermarket support services and consultants

- Training

Each possible avenue for tech support and other network-related information has advantages and disadvantages. Cost, speed of response, expertise, convenience of access, and hours of availability are the most important considerations to keep in mind as you evaluate each option.

The NetWare Manuals and README Files

I T IS OFTEN LAUGHINGLY SAID that real administrators don't read manuals. In fact, the opposite is true. It is impossible to get a complete grasp of the Net-Ware software without reading the manuals. Be sure that you also read the README files on the distribution disks, because the information there can be critical to getting your system to work.

A manual set of 1500 pages can be daunting to approach. I don't suggest that you read through the entire set before installing NetWare. The most efficient way to approach the manuals is to first decide what you need to accomplish with your network and your server, then research those particular topics in the manuals. Having an idea of what you need to know will tend to make those topics stand out in your mind and will also allow you to bypass irrelevant information.

Bear in mind that with the standard manual sets, the information you want may be in several places; some in *Installation*, some in *Concepts,* and some in *System Administration*. If you have a chance to install the ElectroText (Dyna-Text in NetWare 4.*x*) online documentation, do so. You may wish to consider installing it on your workstation, if you have enough disk space, so that you will have access to the documentation even if the network is down. The online manuals will let you jump between the different manuals by clicking on a cross-reference, rather than needing to dig out the other manual and page through it.

Other Novell Publications

N OVELL PUBLISHES *NetWare Application Notes*, *Novell Research Reports*, and *Novell Technical Bulletins*. These publications can be ordered from Novell, and some can be downloaded from NetWire. Some are also available in the Network Support Encyclopedia (NSE).

NetWare Application Notes

NetWare Applications Notes is a monthly publication that covers several topics a month relating to troubleshooting or optimizing NetWare. It also includes information about new products, bug fixes, and a tips and techniques section.

I heartily recommend the April and May 1993 issues to anyone contemplating the move to NetWare 4.0. They cover new features, NDS, migration to 4.0, installation of 4.0 planning issues, and so forth.

NetWare Application Notes are available in subscription, on the NSE disk, and online on NetWire. For subscription information, call or write:

Novell Research Order Desk
1601 Park Avenue West
Denver, CO 80216-5199
(800) 377-4136

The current cost is $95 per year, which also includes *Novell Research Reports*. This is probably the best deal around.

Novell Research Reports

Recent *Novell Research Reports* cover topics such as *Integrating NetWare and Windows 3.1*, *Inside NetWare for UNIX*, and *NetWare Security: Configuring and Auditing a Trusted Environment*. These are specialized reports that cover topical issues in depth. They can be ordered through your reseller or from the Novell Research Order Desk address above.

Novell Technical Bulletins

Novell publishes technical bulletins on the NSE disk and on NetWire (in the NOVLIB forum, Technical Bulletins section, on CompuServe). Recent topics include *TCP/IP across Access Server, Printing and NetWare for Macintosh*, and *Using DR DOS LANPack*.

Magazines

I N ADDITION TO a dozen or so magazines dedicated to networking, most magazines that cover the workstation of your choice cover networking products from time to time. All of these magazines can provide you with helpful information, with the specialization that is appropriate for your network. If you have a largely Macintosh network, for instance, you should scan *MacUser*, *MacWeek*, and *MacWorld* for network-related articles.

In general, the weekly magazines will provide information in a more timely manner, so you should pay special attention to reported bugs and their fixes. The monthly magazines usually provide more in-depth coverage of issues, and they are appropriate for researching additions to the network that you are considering.

The magazines mentioned here are only some of the many available. This list is not meant to be all-inclusive, nor to recommend one over another. Many of these magazines also have Web sites that have additional information; the text of articles, programs, and shareware; and links to the Web pages of their advertisers.

Weekly Magazines

Weekly or biweekly magazines include *LAN Times*, *Internetwork*, *Network World*, and *LAN Computing*; the workstation-specific *MacWeek* and *PC Week*; and *InfoWorld*. All of these contain useful information about recently released or soon-to-be-released products.

Monthly Magazines

There are many monthly magazines dedicated to networking topics, as well as more general computing-oriented magazines that publish articles related to networking. *Network News* is produced by the CNEPA, and is dedicated to NetWare-specific topics. It is a benefit of CNEPA membership; one of many.

Corporate Computing covers networking topics from a manager's point of view, with details of cost justification and considerations that may affect other areas of your network, rather than lots of technical specifications. It generally offers a couple of case studies showing how businesses upgraded their networks to meet changing requirements.

Network Computing, *LAN Technology*, *LAN Computing*, and *LAN Magazine* are technically oriented magazines that cover client-server applications from many companies, including, of course, Novell. They generally have one or two comparison tests featuring products from a number of manufacturers. They review new products (such as protocol analyzers and fax modems), feature commentary on industry trends, and predict trends that you will eventually need to deal with. Get a couple of issues of each at the newsstand before subscribing.

You'll see that they all take a different approach to the issues, which you may or may not find relevant to your network.

Networking Management and *Beyond Computing* are two Information Services-related magazines that take a more corporate approach. They tend to cover WAN issues and systems management more than LANs.

For general topics such as hardware and software evaluations, there are many PC-related monthly magazines. I personally subscribe to *PC Magazine*, *PC World*, *PC Computing*, *Windows Sources*, *Windows NT Magazine*, and *BYTE*.

Newsletters

In addition to the magazines, you can find newsletters, which may cover topics as specialized as packet analysis or workgroup publishing. These newsletters may have 10 subscribers or 10,000.

Newsletters tend to be more specific and more opinionated than the larger-circulation magazines. There is even a newsletter for troubleshooters. It's called *Fix Any PC...Fast*, and it's available from AllMicro, Inc. (800) 653-4933. It does concentrate on products that AllMicro carries, but contains lots of useful information.

Computer Select and Other CD-ROM Products

If you don't have the budget to subscribe to a dozen or more magazines, or to flip through them, consider Computer Select. This is a fabulous research tool, containing articles from more than 170 different periodicals in the computer industry on CD-ROM. You can search for a topic, and have every article written in the last year at your fingertips. For more information, call Computer Library at (212) 503-4400 or (800) 827-7889. You will need a PC-compatible system with a CD-ROM drive, 640 KB RAM, and at least 500 KB of hard disk space or a Macintosh with System 6.0.7 or later, 1 MB of RAM, and a CD-ROM drive.

A number of other companies are coming out with reference products on CD-ROM. For example, *LAN Times*, *BYTE*, and *PC Magazine* have or will have products available. Although these are much more limited than Computer Select in scope, they are also much less expensive and may contain other items of interest, such as PC Magazine's test suites for rating the speed of PCs.

Books and Catalogs

FOR MORE DEPTH THAN MAGAZINE ARTICLES, and a different perspective than manuals, you can turn to books. There are perhaps a dozen publishers with lines of computer-related books. Some are consistently good, others are best in certain areas or are oriented to a certain kind of user. For NetWare and networking topics, the two publishers I recommend are Network Press, from SYBEX, and Novell Press. If your local bookstore won't let you read through books to see if they're useful to you, at least peruse the table of contents.

Catalogs shouldn't be overlooked as an information source. Once you get on the mailing lists, you will probably be inundated with catalogs. These may seen to be just a nuisance, but they often contain useful information. Some vendors go to a great deal of trouble to compare product features, and this is the information you need to select the correct product for your application.

Online Resources

NETWIRE HAS SO MANY FEATURES and so much information available that books have been written on it (see below). Other online resources include manufacturers' bulletin boards, forums on the Internet, and other bulletin boards such as BIX. All you need is a modem and a communications program.

NetWire

Using Novell's NetWire, by Laura Chappell and Brent Larson (from Know, Inc., 1992, P.O. Box 50507, Provo UT 84605-0507), deals solely with the NetWire services available on CompuServe. NetWire is accessible from anywhere in the country through CompuServe. You can even try it out for free: call (800) 848-8199 and ask for representative #58. You'll get $15 of usage credit. If you're already a member of CompuServe, type GO NOVELL at the prompt.

Not only can you converse online with many different experts on NetWire, including some of the engineers who created NetWare, you can download the latest versions of NetWare drivers, software, and patches that will fix specific problems.

Other forums on NetWire are devoted to discussions of different NetWare topics and general information; there are also some special and private forums. Novell (GO NOVELL) is a general information area. NOVA, NOVB, NOVC, NETW2X, NETW3X, and DRFORUM are conference forums that feature discussions of various topics. Two forums, NOVDEV and NOVG, are restricted-access forums for developers.

The titles of forums are subject to change, depending on demand for certain topics. You can get a listing of the current forums available when you log in to one of these areas.

Bulletin Boards

Many companies maintain bulletin boards that allow you to ask questions on problems you may be having, or to download patches or new versions of software. Some of these bulletin boards are listed below. Every effort was made to make sure that the information is current. However, these numbers are subject to change.

3Com	(408) 980-8204
Adaptec	(408) 945-7727
AST Technical Support	(714) 727-4723
AT&T NCR (Ethernet and Token Ring drivers)	(612) 638-2854
AT&T Support (PCs)	(201) 769-6397
ATI Support (modems and video cards)	(416) 756-4591
BMUG (Mac support)	(510) 849-2684
Capitol PC User's Group (5500 members)	(703) 750-7809
Cheyenne (ARCSERVE)	(516) 484-3445
CompuCom Customer Support	(408) 738-4990
CrossTalk Technical Support	(404) 740-8428
eSoft Product Support	(303) 699-8222

IBM National Support Center	(404) 835-5300
Intel	(503) 645-6275
LANtastic (support)	(602) 293-8065
Maxtor Technical Support	(303) 678-2020
McAfee Associates (virus information)	(408) 988-4004
Micro Design International (SCSI Express)	(510) 793-3491
Microsoft Product Support	(206) 646-9145
Microsystems Software Inc. (support)	(508) 875-8009
Network World Bulletin Board (LAN and WAN)	(508) 620-1178
NIST Computer Security (virus issues)	(301) 948-5717
Online with Hayes	(404) 446-6336
Oracomm Support	(619) 346-1608
PKWare (PKARC and PKZIP utilities)	(414) 354-8670
PowerNet (REMOTE ACCESS software)	(407) 834-3326
Practical Peripherals (support)	(818) 706-2467
ProComm Support	(314) 474-8477
Qualitas, Inc. (support)	(301) 907-8030
Remote Access HQ 3:690/625	(619) 389-8048
Seagate Technical Support	(408) 438-8771
Searchlight (support)	(516) 689-2566
SemWare Support (QEdit, shareware)	(404) 641-8968
SMC (network interface cards)	(714) 707-2481
Society for Technical Communications	(703) 522-3299
Star-Link Network (75,000 programs)	(718) 972-6099
The Business (Microsoft Windows)	(213) 477-0408
The Micro Foundry (software support)	(415) 598-0398
The Well (popular, hourly charges)	(415) 332-7190
U.S. Robotics	(708) 982-5092

Ventura Professional Forum	(408) 227-4818
Western Digital Technical Support	(714) 753-1068
WordPerfect Customer Support	(801) 225-4444
Xtree	(805) 546-9150
XyQuest Technical Support (XyWrite)	(508) 667-5669
Zenith Technical Support	(800) 888-3058

BIX

BIX (Byte Information eXchange) is an online database of computer knowledge from *BYTE* magazine, designed to help users fix problems and obtain information about specific hardware and software products. For details on joining BIX, call (800) 227-2983 or (603) 924-7681.

World Wire

World Wire is an excellent bulletin board that provides access to a "CNE Lab" through your modem. It includes 3800 NetWare-related files as well as access to a simulated LAN that lets you practice setting up servers and other NetWare products. The direct number for World Wire is (510) 254-1193. If you are participating in the Cyber State University program (mentioned at the end of this appendix), there are toll-free access numbers available.

The Internet

THE INTERNET IS A VAST RESOURCE for finding information about just about any topic in existence. Several resources that should be of particular interest to you are newsgroups (such as comp.os.novell), FTP sites (such as ftp.novell.com), and World Wide Web sites (such as www.novell.com). These resources are taking the place of bulletin boards in many companies because they are more accessible and easier to use, and often provide higher performance as well.

The hard part about the Internet is establishing your connection in the first place. You can join a general service, such as CompuServe or AOL, that provides Internet access as part of its services, or you can join an Internet-specific service, such as Netcom. In either case, once you have set up your software, accessing the Internet is easy, and is becoming easier all the time. There are index programs that can help you find files relating to a certain topic and Web sites that can help you find other Web sites with the information you're looking for.

Internet Newsgroups

If you have access to the Internet, you can join the discussions in the newsgroup comp.os.novell.misc, as well as many other computer-related forums. Most Internet browsers will show you all the available topics in a given area. Topics in the Comp forum include a huge variety of computer manufacturers, and the comp.os section includes most of the popular operating systems in existence, as well as some obscure ones. A large number of Novell employees, including many of the engineers who wrote various parts of NetWare, participate in these forums.

If you want to get all of the messages in comp.os.novell.misc, you can subscribe to the list server by sending mail to novadm@suvm.acs.syr.edu, or novadm@suvm on BITNET, with the following text in the body of the message (the subject doesn't matter): subscribe NOVELL *Your Full Name*.

This will forward all the messages posted on comp.os.novell.misc to your e-mail account. Warning: This could be more than 100 messages per day. Additionally, the FAQ (Frequently Asked Questions) is available via anonymous FTP from 129.65.43.132. It is an extremely useful document full of the answers to the most often-asked questions in the comp.os.novell.misc forum. Kevin Wang (kwang@gauss.elee.calpoly.edu) does a tremendous job of maintaining this document.

I frequently read comp.os.novell.misc, and can be reached by UNIX mail at lharba@aol.com. I welcome comments on this book or suggestions for the next revision.

The following are some other noteworthy newsgroups:

comp.os.ms-windows. apps.winsock.misc

comp.os.ms-windows. apps.winsock.news

comp.os.ms-windows.advocacy

comp.os.ms-windows.announce

comp.os.ms-windows.apps.winsock.mail

comp.os.ms-windows.misc

comp.os.ms-windows.networking

comp.os.ms-windows.networking.misc

comp.os.ms-windows.networking.tcpip

comp.os.ms-windows.networking.windows

comp.os.ms-windows.nt. setup.hardware

comp.os.ms-windows.nt.admin.misc

comp.os.ms-windows.nt.admin.networking

comp.os.ms-windows.nt.announce

comp.os.ms-windows.nt.misc

comp.os.ms-windows.nt.pre-release

comp.os.ms-windows.nt.setup.misc

comp.os.ms-windows.nt.software.backoffice

comp.os.ms-windows.nt.software.compatibility

comp.os.ms-windows.nt.software.services

comp.os.netware.announce

comp.os.netware.connectivity

comp.os.netware.misc (the main NetWare newsgroup)

comp.os.netware.security

comp.os.os2.networking.misc

comp.os.os2.networking.tcpip

FTP Sites

Many companies maintain FTP sites where the latest patches, software revisions, help files, and so forth can be downloaded. After you have loaded your Internet browser software, you enter the name of the site you want to get files from, such as ftp.novell.com. The browser will then show you the files available, and you can select and download them.

If you aren't sure of the name of a company's Internet FTP site, try the company name first, in the format *ftp.company.com*, or just *company.com*. If you have a Web browser, most companies that have FTP sites also have a Web page.

World Wide Web Sites

The World Wide Web has proliferated very rapidly because it makes accessing the Internet much easier. The home page of a Web site can contain pointers to other Web sites, to files that can be downloaded, or to other types of information. Many of Novell's product manuals are available from the Web site, and you can download any patches you might want as well.

Another famous Web site, yahoo, contains links to many other companies, including computer hardware and software companies. If you're not sure of an address, try looking for it at yahoo. Some Web sites that might be useful to you are listed below.

Microsoft	http://www.microsoft.com
Netcom Communications	http://www.netcom.com
Novell	http://www.novell.com
Rocky Mountain NT User Group	budman.cmdl.noaa.gov/rmwntug/ rmwntugg.html
Third-party NetWare service and support	http://www.aimnet.com/~yungi/ lansol.html
Windows 95 shareware	http://www.windows95.com
Windows 95 Internet stuff	http://cws-apps.texas.net
Yahoo	http://www.yahoo.com
Ziff-Davis Publishing	http://www.zdnet.com

This list isn't meant to be all inclusive; there are more than a million Web pages. If you're looking for a particular company or product, try yahoo first. Other sites may be listed in the documentation of the products you're having problems with.

Technical Support Databases

YOU CAN PURCHASE DATABASES that provide technical support information from Novell or many other manufacturers. Two popular databases are the NSE and the one produced by Ziff Desktop Information.

The Network Support Encyclopedia (NSE)

You can subscribe to two versions of the NSE: the Standard Volume and the Professional Volume. Both contain *Novell Technotes*, hardware and software test bulletins, product documentation, the *NetWare Buyer's Guide*, and a listing of all files available on NetWare. The Professional Volume also includes NetWare patches and fixed versions of software, new network drivers and enhanced products, as well as the *Novell Application Notes*.

If you access the NSE frequently on CompuServe, you may find it more economical to purchase a subscription to the CD-ROM distribution. It's also much more convenient.

Support On Site for Networks

Ziff Desktop Information produces a bimonthly CD-ROM that contains the manual sets and support documentation from many software and hardware vendors. If the sources included are ones that you use, it can be a real boon, especially in a heterogeneous networking environment, where you would otherwise need dozens of manuals from many different vendors.

Unfortunately, some major companies haven't yet contributed to the database. Novell has, to the tune of over 13,000 documents, but Apple, for example, has not. At $1,495 per year, this database can be an expensive investment. And it may not cover the products you use, so you may want to try it before you buy.

The Certified NetWare Engineer Professional Association (CNEPA) and NetWare Users International (NUI)

THE CNEPA IS OPEN TO CNEs and anyone who is trying to become a CNE (anyone who has taken one of the tests that lead to the CNE certification). Membership in the CNE has many benefits, including labs that can show you how to configure and troubleshoot Novell products, discounts on software, admission to networking-related events such as NETUCON, and a subscription to *Network News*. The local chapter of the CNEPA is a great place to learn more about networking, and to make contacts with other CNEs who may be able to help you (for a fee, or not) in times of need.

NUI is the world-wide organization of NetWare user groups. In addition to meetings that can help you learn more about NetWare and make contacts with other users, NUI provides a united front that can influence Novell to make changes in NetWare that users want. Membership also includes a subscription to *NetWare Connection*, a bimonthly newsletter that focuses on user (administrator) issues.

900 Numbers and Consultants

CHECK YOUR LOCAL YELLOW PAGES and the network-related magazines for technical support specialists and consultants in your area. These companies can often provide service at a lower price or in a more timely manner than resellers or Novell's tech support department, because they are smaller and have far fewer customers.

Be aware, though, that there is a wide variation in expertise and levels of service provided by technical support specialists and consultants. Ask about companies or consultants at your local CNEPA or NUI meeting before spending money on their services.

Training

N OVELL AUTHORIZED EDUCATION CENTERS (NAECs) can provide you with a complete program that will train you in administering every aspect of NetWare. There are three levels of certification available:

- Certified NetWare Administrator (CNA) certification means that you have taken the System Manager and Advanced System Manager courses for one version of NetWare, or at least passed the tests for those courses.

- A Certified NetWare Engineer (CNE) has demonstrated good general knowledge of NetWare.

- An Enterprise Certified NetWare Engineer (ECNE) has taken additional coursework in WAN-related subjects.

Other sources may provide courses that can provide you with enough knowledge to pass the same tests, or may offer specialized training in some aspects of NetWare networking. Companies such as Data-Tech Institute offer courses in many other computer-related subjects, including maintaining, setting up, and troubleshooting PCs, Macintoshes, or UNIX workstations; setting up and maintaining Windows by itself or on NetWare; and disaster recovery for LANs.

Another source for training on NetWare may be your local community college, adult education center, or university extension program. As NetWare becomes steadily more entrenched as the preeminent LAN operating system, more colleges are offering courses on it. In some cases, the universities may work with Novell to ensure that students who pass the courses are also eligible to obtain CNE certification.

There are many books that may help prepare you for CNE certification. I have found the study guides from Wave Technologies to be useful. You might also want to take a look at Network Press's recent books *The CNA Study Guide for NetWare 4, The CNE-4 Study Guide,* and *The CNE Update to NetWare 4.1.* Also, LearningWare's *The Clark Tests on CD-ROM* is a good interactive CD-ROM that features drills on all the CNE topics and simulations of the tests you will take.

If you want a full-featured CNE program but can't afford the several thousand dollars that many NAECs charge, or you don't have the time to take the courses, you might want to check out Cyber State University, (510) 253-8735. It is a home-study course that includes the LearningWare CD-ROM, an interactive online study program, and access to World Wire (an online NetWare lab).

Tools for Troubleshooters

THROUGHOUT THIS BOOK, I have mentioned types of software that can make your life as an administrator easier. Some of the tools that I've worked with are listed in this appendix. There are also several other sources of information about tools that I can recommend. The standard disclaimers apply; the views expressed are my opinions.

The tools are organized by type, as follows:

- Tool information sources

- Information tools

- Virus-detection software

- Workstation utilities

- Diagnostic tools

- NetWare utilities

- Protocol analyzers

- Inventory tools

- Backup tools

- Fault-tolerance systems

- Disaster-recovery tools

- Shareware, freeware, and demos

Other Sources of Information about Tools

LAN Magazine—LAN Buyer's Guide

The *LAN Magazine, LAN Buyer's Guide Issue*, October 15, 1995, lists hundreds of products in the following categories:

- Cable-testing equipment
- Help desk
- Inventory and asset management
- Network management applications
- Network management platforms
- Probes and monitors
- Protocol analyzers
- Security
- Server management
- Server room/wiring closet accessories
- Storage management software
- Tape drives
- Training
- Troubleshooting tools

Charles River Media—Troubleshooting-oriented CD

Charles River Media produces a CD that's oriented toward troubleshooting NetWare. It, too, has patches and updates, as well as a good search engine for finding the answers or drivers you're looking for. It also includes CNE/CNA questions, Novell technical product information, and a good list of vendors. All for only $29.99! Contact Charles River Media at (800) 382-8505.

EMS Professional Shareware Libraries—NetWare CD-ROM

EMS Professional Shareware Libraries offers a NetWare CD-ROM (and many others on other subjects) that has thousands of files, including patches, version updates, shareware and freeware utilities, and text files describing how to fix various problems. The catalog of files on the CD-ROM is more than 120 pages. You can get the catalog, which includes both the shareware and freeware on the disk, as well as information on commercial products, for $25; the complete CD is $59.95. Contact EMS at (301) 924-3594.

On Technologies—Editor's Choice Catalog

On Technologies has a catalog called *Editor's Choice*. It's a hundred pages of information on commercial products for NetWare. The product descriptions are advertising, rather than impartial, but it's still a very useful collection of information. Contact On Technology at (800) 381-5686 or on the Web at http://www.on.com/edchoice.html. The Web site has the latest catalog information and items that may not be in the catalog.

Information Tools

Novell—Network Support Encyclopedia Pro

This is a relatively expensive but very useful subscription. Rather than printed material, it's a subscription to a CD-ROM that contains software patches, utilities, and the text of recent articles from various groups within Novell. Contact Novell at (800) 638-9273 or on the Web at http://www.novell.com.

Microsoft—Windows 95 Resource Kit

This is a big fat book with a CD-ROM. Between them, they contain everything you ever wanted to know about Windows 95. It's extremely useful for administrators contemplating a company-wide rollout; issues such as network installations and running Windows 95 from a server are addressed. Just remember to take their marketing-oriented verbiage with a grain of salt. The Kit is available in bookstores everywhere.

Micro House—Technical Library, DrivePro

The Micro House Technical Library is an exhaustive database of PC motherboards and adapters. If you've ever needed to change jumpers on a board and couldn't find its manual, this is the product for you. I have yet to find a board that isn't listed.

DrivePro is a hard disk drive utility that will format drives (including reformatting IDE drives), discover the configuration parameters for older systems that can't automatically discover a drive's parameters, reconfigure the master boot record, set up large drives for use with IDE (not EIDE) systems using a boot sector loader, and perform numerous other hard drive-related tasks. Contact Micro House at (800) 926-8299 or on the Web at http://www.microhouse.com.

Micro House/Ziff-Davis Interactive—Support On Site

Support On Site is a series of CD-ROM subscriptions. There's Support On Site for Networks, Support On Site for Application, and Support On Site for Hardware. If you've ever discovered that manuals were missing while trying to troubleshoot or set up a system, you'll appreciate these references. The only caveat is that your product may or may not be on the CD. Given the number of products available, it's impossible to get everything on a CD. Contact Micro House at (800) 926-8299 or on the Web at http://www.microhouse.com.

Virus Detection Software

Security Integration—VirusNet

VirusNet includes a PC-based virus scanner and distribution software that allows you to install it on a PC when the user logs in. It also includes recovery software. Contact Security Integration at (800) 888-5031.

EliaShim Microcomputers—ViruSafe LAN 6.6

ViruSafe LAN is an anti-virus set that includes both an NLM for the server and TSRs for your PCs. It scans Mac, UNIX, and OS/2 files on the server. It also includes software than can repair the damage done by many viruses. Contact EliaShim Microcomputers at (800) 477-5177.

Command Software Systems—Net-Prot 2.1

Net-Prot includes an NLM that runs on the server, plus the rightly famous F-Prot PC anti-virus software. It is very fast and includes 24-hour tech support. This system is highly recommended. Contact Command Software Systems at (800) 423-9147.

McAffee Associates—NetShield and Other Products

NetShield works well with NetWare. It's fast, it maintains a log of scans, and it can scan all incoming files and move infected files to a protected directory. You can specify users who should get notifications of viruses found and designate directories or files to scan regularly. Also, McAffee's virus software is updated regularly, and you can easily get updates from the Internet or CompuServe. Unlike McAffee's SCAN software, which is shareware, NetShield is sold as a 2-year subscription.

McAffee also makes a number of other products, including LAN Inventory, for NetWare 3.*x* and 4.*x*, which automatically or manually inventories hardware and software components for most NetWare clients. It creates a database of components and provides reporting functions. SiteMeter performs application metering and configures applications and user profiles. SiteXpress is a software distribution program. Contact McAffee at (408) 988-3832, BBS: (408) 988-4004, or Internet: support@mcafee.com.

Intel Corporation—LAN Desk Virus Protect

LAN Desk Virus Protect is an NLM that scans for viruses on file servers and workstations on LANs. It reads DOS or Macintosh files in real time before they are written to or read from the file server. When LANProtect detects a virus, the user is given the option of renaming the file to prevent execution, deleting and purging the file, moving it to a protected area for inspection, or leaving the file alone. LPSCAN is the corresponding utility that scans workstations logged into the server. Virus Protect is NetWare 4.1-compatible. Contact Intel at (800) 538-3373 or BBS: (503) 645-6275.

Cheyenne Software—InocuLan 2.0

InocuLan 2.0, an anti-virus NLM, has a wide variety of tools to deal with viruses. Some of InocuLan 2.0's useful tools include its Delete File option, as well as its Purge option, which enables users to delete an infected file so that it is not able to be recovered. In addition, the application includes some time-saving options for managers and has some useful administrative tools, such as the ability to administer the NLM remotely from a workstation and view the activity log. Cheyenne Software can be reached at (516) 465-4000.

Symantec—Untouchable Network

Untouchable Network is an NLM that can scan for both known and unknown viruses (by looking for executable files that have changed in size or contents). It can also scan both compressed and archived files. Symantec can be reached at (800) 441-7234.

Symantec—SAM and SUM II

SAM (Symantec Anti-virus for Macintosh) is the most popular Macintosh anti-virus program. It can be configured for various levels of protection, depending on your estimation of the danger of infection on your network. It also allows you to password-protect the configuration options, so users can bypass the system. SUM II (Symantec Utilities for Macintosh) is a set of Macintosh utilities that provides hard disk optimization, analysis, and repair and security capabilities. Contact Symantec at (800) 441-7234.

Workstation Utilities

Symantec—Norton Utilities

Norton Utilities is a disk-management utility package for the PC and Macintosh. For example, it includes programs to search and edit files, undelete files, and restore damaged files. Contact Symantec at (800) 441-7234.

PKWare—PKZIP

PKWare makes the popular PC shareware compression programs (PK stands for Phil Katz). PKZIP compresses files into a ZIP file, and PKUNZIP decompresses them. PKSFX compresses files into a self-extracting EXE file that decompresses when loaded and doesn't require the PKUNZIP program. ZIP2EXE creates the self-extracting file from an existing ZIP file. These utilities are necessary to uncompress many of the patches and utilities you may wish to download from NetWire or other online services. Contact PKWare at (414) 354-8699.

Quarterdeck—QEMM, MagnaRAM 2

QEMM (Quarterdeck Expanded Memory Manager) is a popular expanded memory manager. It has a well-engineered configuration/installation program that does a good job of detecting TSRs and other programs you may want to load, and accommodating them in upper memory.

MagnaRAM 2 is a Windows utility that compresses files in memory to increase the effective amount of RAM available to Windows. It works with NetWare 3.*x* and Windows 95. Contact Quarterdeck Office Systems at (310) 309-9851 or on the Web at http://www.qdeck.com.

Quarterdeck—WINProbe, CleanSweep

WINProbe is a troubleshooting tool for Windows. It looks for problems with both the software and with hardware. The version I have used is 4.01, which is supposed to be compatible with Windows 95. However, the manual doesn't address Windows 95. When I installed the software, it caused serious registry problems on two different systems. It works very well with 3.*x* versions of Windows.

CleanSweep is a program for Windows that can advise you on files to remove that may no longer be necessary and can also help uninstall software. It can track files added when a program is installed and remove all of them if you want to uninstall the software. This is particularly useful with Windows programs because they often add files to the Windows directory in addition to the ones installed in the program directory. Contact Quarterdeck at (310) 309-9851 or on the Web at http://www.qdeck.com.

V Communications—System Commander

System Commander is an extremely useful utility that allows multiple operating systems on a single hard drive. These can be single-user operating systems such as DOS or Windows (3.*x*, 95, or NT) or multi-user operating systems like NetWare or UNIX. You could have a Windows 95 workstation that could be rebooted to become an NT or a NetWare server! It's also very useful to give you a way of backing out of a Windows 95 install. I've never been able to break this software. I use it to run several versions of NetWare on a single server. When the PC boots, I get a menu and can select from the several versions of NetWare. I highly recommended it if you need to support multiple configurations. Contact V Communications at (408) 296-4224.

CyberMedia—First Aid 95

First Aid 95 is a diagnostics toolkit for Windows 95 and 3.1. It has some excellent diagnostic routines and includes support for multimedia cards and network cards. It also includes crash protection, a feature that may allow you to recover files that were being worked on when a GPF (general protection fault) crash occurred. Contact CyberMedia at (800) 721-7824.

Gibson Research—Spin-Rite II

Spin-Rite II is a nondestructive, low-level formatting program for PCs that reformats the hard disk without erasing the data. It rewrites only the sector ID, which may have drifted over time. Contact Gibson Research at (800) 736-0637.

Diagnostic Tools

Micro 2000—Microscope 6.11 and Post-Probe

This is a hardware and software diagnostics toolkit that really produces results. The Post-Probe card will produce useful POST (power-on self test) codes on its own display, even if the PC's display is not working. The codes allow you to pinpoint low-level hardware problems. It also verifies that the voltages available on the motherboard are correct. The Microscope software will perform tests of higher-level functions, including disk formatting, port testing, memory diagnostics, and so forth. Contact Micro 2000 at (800) 864-8008 or on the Web at http://www.micro2000.com.

NetWare Utilities

Brightworks Development—LAN Utilities

Brightworks Development offers a number of NetWare utilities:

- LAN Server Watch monitors your servers and informs you if parameters exceed set levels. It can even correct some conditions automatically.

- NETremote+ allows you to take over another Windows workstation on the LAN.

- LAN Tachometer is an inexpensive tool that maintains a watch on network traffic and server utilization.

For more information, contact Brightworks at (800) 522-9876.

Frye Computer Systems—Network Management

Frye Computer Systems offers a suite of network management programs for NetWare. They are fairly expensive, but very complete. They include a server monitoring program, an automatic workstation software updating and inventory program, and a mapping utility that will generate a logical map of your network. For more information, contact Frye at (617) 451-5400 or (800) 234-3793.

Protocol Analyzers

Novell—LANalyzer for Windows

This product is in its third generation. It's a stable, well-done program that uses any workstation with a LAN adapter capable of promiscuous mode operation to monitor a LAN for all sorts of potential problems. The online help is not just good, it's proactive, helping you even when you don't know you need help. Contact Novell at (800) 638-9273 or on the Web at http://www.novell.com.

Intel—LANDesk Manager

Intel's LANDesk Manager runs under Windows and provides a wide variety of server and LAN monitoring and control. It can show you packet traffic on the LAN, monitor what applications are running on your server, log peak and average statistics for server and LAN, and inventory workstation hardware and software configurations remotely. Contact Intel at (800) 538-3373.

Network General—Expert Sniffer Analyzer

This sniffer is the Cadillac of protocol analyzers. It has been around the longest and is the most mature. It's also expensive and complex to learn. Expert Sniff Analyzer is an expert's tool and will let an expert perform at levels far beyond the basics. If you need this tool, you should already be aware of it. Contact Network General at (800) 764-3337 or on the Web at http://www.ngc.com.

Triticom—LANdecoder/e, EtherVision

LANdecoder is a software product similar to LANalyzer for Windows. It is less capable and about two-thirds the price. It has a limited list of compatible LAN adapters and isn't as helpful as LANalyzer. It does support all the major protocols and some minor ones, such as SMB, DECnet, and VINES IP.

EtherVision is a LAN traffic monitor that can tell you what levels of utilization you are getting on your network, and how many packets are being generated by which workstations or servers. Contact Triticom at (612) 937-0772 or on the Web at http://www.triticom.com.

Network Communications—LAN Network Probe 4.4

LAN Network Probe includes the functions of the old hardware-based LAN-alyzer with more than 175 diagnostic programs to help you find problems on your Ethernet or Token Ring LAN. It's expensive compared with LANalyzer for Windows, but very fast and with lots of functionality. Contact Network Communications at (800) 451-1984.

INTRAK—ServerTrak

ServerTrak allows monitoring of all the servers on your network from one console. It supports both NetWare 3.*x* and 4.*x* servers, and monitors statistics such as CPU utilization, disk space free, disk activity, and network connection traffic. For more information, contact INTRAK at (800) 233-7494.

Inventory Tools

Preferred Systems—AuditWare

AuditWare creates reports of the information in server binderies across your network. It's an invaluable tool for documenting your server configurations. Contact Preferred Systems at (800) 222-7638.

Backup Tools

Cheyenne—ArcServe 5.0

Cheyenne is one of the major suppliers of backup software for NetWare. Priced at $1,895, ArcServe 5.0 supports automated backups and can also back up workstations to the server. Contact Cheyenne Software at (800) 243-9832, or BBS: (516) 484-3445.

Palindrome Corporation— Storage Manager 4.0

Palindrome's backup software is a strong competitor in the NetWare backup marketplace. It handles NDS especially well. Prices range from $995 for a single-server version to $1,595 for a multiserver package. An unlimited number of clients are supported for free. Contact Palindrome at (800) 288-4912 or on the Web at http://www.palindrome.com.

Fault-Tolerance Systems

Net Guard Systems—SERVivor 3.5

SERVivor is a substitute for Novell's SFT III server mirroring product. It provides much of the functionality of SFT level III and some additional features, such as the ability to mirror more than one server. It is also substantially less expensive than SFT III. Contact Net Guard Systems at (800) 670-0003.

Vinca—StandbyServer32

StandbyServer 32, is a server-mirroring product that provides features like SFT III at a much lower price. It does not require two identical servers, and it uses only one copy of NetWare. Contact Vinca at (800) 934-9530.

Disaster-Recovery Tools

Network Custodian Inc.—Network Custodian PRO

Network Custodian PRO is a disaster prevention and recovery package that includes these features:

- A planning module

- A hardware and software inventory database

- A disaster contact names and numbers directory

- A vendor and service contact and warranty database

- Troubleshooting instructions

- Backup procedures

- A hardware-repair procedures database

Contact Network Custodian at (914) 855-5831.

Shareware, Freeware, and Demo Utilities

The utilities listed here can be categorized as one of three types:

- Shareware, which you must pay for if you use it longer than the evaluation period.

- Freeware, which is, of course, free.

- Demo programs, which may work for only a limited period, or which may be lacking some of the features of the commercial version.

Shareware is *not free*. If you use the software for more than the evaluation period, send in the fee. Not only is this the ethical and legal thing to do, it will ensure that you receive updates.

The utilities are grouped by function as follows:

- Audit

- Backup

- Bindery

- Data recovery

- Diagnostic

- Diagramming

- Macintosh

- NetWare Directory Services (NDS)

- Remote workstation management

- Software management

- User management

- Upgrades

- Virus scanners

For each program, the listing shows the filename, price, function (such as Audit or Backup), and the date it was created. If prices are listed, either the product is a demo version and the price is of the commercial version, or the product is shareware and the price is the registration fee.

The CD-ROMs from Charles River Media and EMS Professional Shareware Libraries, listed at the beginning of this chapter, have some or all of the files as well as many thousands of others. They can also be found on NetWire and the Web sites or bulletin boards of the makers.

Audit Programs

Audit programs give you reports on your network, servers, workstations, traffic, or disk usage. Some can signal you if a particular parameter goes over a threshold; others simply give you a report.

Backwoods Software—DiskWatcher 3.1

DW32 .ZIP   Shareware   Audit   6/30/95

A set of three programs that monitor space on network volumes and provide graphs and reports that show how space is being used in each subdirectory in the volume. DW32DB.ZIP must be used with this program. Contact Backwoods Software at (713) 294-5911, or CompuServe: 70661,3443.

Blue Lance—LAN Auditor

LTA41A.ZIP $995   Audit   4/27/95

Provides an extensive audit trail of LAN usage. Tracks after-hours use, software used, and by whom. Provides lists of deleted and renamed files, files copied off the LAN, and what has gone through the modem. For NetWare 3.11 only. Contact Blue Lance at (713) 680-1187.

Blue Ocean Software, Inc.—Track-It for Windows

TIWDEMO.ZIP $395+   Audit   5/21/95

An integrated PC management system with modules for Inventory, Help Desk, Purchasing, and Training. Provides automatic inventorying of hardware and software. Contact Blue Ocean Software at (813) 977-4553, or CompuServe: 70363,3071.

BlueSky Shareware—Outrider

OR.ZIP $20   Audit   6/16/92

A diagnostic utility. Monitors and displays graphically the status of multiple volumes on multiple servers. Contact BlueSky Shareware at BBS: (914) 897-3936.

Carra Bussa—Novell Check

NVCHK.ZIP   Free   Audit   10/03/94

A suite of programs that can compare versions of all programs loaded on a server and compare your server with the "correctly loaded" Novell file server template. Must have Supervisor access to servers. Contact Carra Bussa at CompuServe: 70662,221.

Christophe Dubios—Wdspace

WDPACE.ZIP   Shareware   Audit   3/01/95

Provides a method to show usage statistics for directories on a NetWare volume. Some features include a display of subdirectories with their NetWare usage size from the selected base directory and an interface to send and graph your stats in Excel. Contact Christophe Dubios at CompuServe: 100341,745.

Circuit Masters—Server Sentry v6.0

SSV6.ZIP   Shareware   Audit   5/12/95

An NLM designed to document ABEND system messages and automatically reboot stuck servers. Network managers can be informed of problems via pagers if a user-definable number of ABENDs occur during a specific time period. There is a 21-day evaluation period. Contact Circuit Masters at (800) 764-5444, or CompuServe: 72103,2327.

C&P Software Systems—NetWare System Monitor (NSM)

NSM.ZIP $20 Shareware   Audit   10/08/93

Monitors four primary areas: server utilization, volume space, the print queues, and user disk space. If a limit is exceeded, NSM beeps and records the event. Contact C&P Software Systems at CompuServe: 76636,433.

Cyco Automation—Showevent

SHOWEV.ZIP   Freeware   Audit   9/18/92

Does real-time tracking of changes to NetWare security. A log of all changes will be saved to disk. Contact Cyco Automation at +31-71-222707, or CompuServe: 75170,1156.

Danasoft—Event Monitoring NLM for NW3.X

EVENTM.ZIP $40   Audit   12/11/93

An informational reporting NLM that logs server events. This event monitor can also be useful for tracking other events, such as file trustee assignments or user login/logout activity. Contact Danasoft at (800) 800-9301.

Danen Software Services—Danen Utilities

TOP20NET.ZIP   Shareware   Audit   4/27/95

A collection of 20 Danen network utilities, which includes programs to audit, batch, inventory equipment, monitor volume usage, and more. Contact Danen Software Services at (403) 471-7210, or CompuServe: 70672,1624.

Danen Software Services—NetWare Disk Usage 2.46

DUSAGE.ZIP $25   Audit   3/25/95

Allows for monitoring of disk usage by the user on a server basis and volume basis. If a user runs low on disk space, this fact is clearly marked on a volume analysis report. Contact Danen Software Services at (403) 471-7210, or CompuServe: 70672,1624.

FSTATS NLM v1.10-File Server

FSTATS.ZIP   Shareware   Audit   8/12/94

A NetWare 3.1*x* NLM that monitors and collects various file server information in log files that can be ported to other viewing programs, such as a spreadsheet or database. Contact at CompuServe: 76040,343.

HawkNet Inc.—NetReport (30-Day Trial)

NR6000.ZIP $695   Audit   6/07/95

Assists network managers with capacity planning and troubleshooting through the use of extensive file server monitoring, reporting, and analysis capabilities. Software provides access to real-time and historical data via Windows-based displays. Contact HawkNet at (800) 429-5638, or BBS: (619) 929-9978.

HawkNet Inc.—NetTune Pro Demo 2.2

NT6000.ZIP   Shareware   Audit   6/19/95

Allows optimization of file server performance by providing network managers with the option to rely on Artificial Intelligence (AI) to perform dynamic parameter turning on NetWare systems. Contact HawkNet at (800) 429-5638, or BBS: (619) 929-9978.

IntraLink Corporation—LanScan

LANSCN.ZIP $99   Audit   5/25/93

LanScan is a network monitoring tool that includes node information reports, software inventory, page server, NetWare reports, and support for multi-server LANs. Contact IntraLink at (212) 389-3135, CompuServe: 76256,1537, or BBS: (914) 528-1772.

Jim Tolliver—Meg

MEG.ZIP $20   Audit   12/10/94

A graphical reporting program to show space and memory usage. Can report from workstations and file servers. Requires VGA. Contact Jim Tolliver at (800) 242-4775 (orders only), CompuServe: 74213,613 (GO SWREG #2259), or Internet: JTJTJTJT@aol.com.

LAN Technologies—Data Access Reliability Test

DART42.ZIP $5   Audit   1/21/94

Provides a method of benchmarking all components in a network, from the user PC and LAN adapter to the server PC, operating system, disk cache, LAN adapter, disk controller, and drive. Also tests the overall data integrity of the network hard drive. Contact LAN Technologies at +64-25-942463, or CompuServe: 100033,2241.

Morgan Adair—Inventry

INVENTRY.ZIP   Free   Audit   8/11/93

INVENTRY and VIEWINVN are two programs that build and view a database of workstation hardware and system information. Source code included. Novell AppNote: *A Workstation Inventory Program for NetWare*, January 1992. Contact Morgan Adair at (801) 429-7757, CompuServe: 76424,410, or Internet: madair@novell.com.

Morgan Adair—SS.EXE

SS.ZIP   Free   Audit   8/11/93

SS.NLM and TOTAL.NLM are two programs for gathering server utilization statistics from a NetWare file server. Includes source code for TOTAL. Part of Novell's AppNote series: *NetWare 3.x Operating System Statistics Exposed!*, July 1991. Contact Morgan Adair at (801) 429-7757, CompuServe: 76424,410, or Internet: madair@novell.com.

NetTech Australia—Dspace

DSPACE.ZIP $15   Audit   11/01/94

A Windows-based program that displays a sorted list of the disk space in use by each user on a Novell file server. Details can be obtained on a volume-by-volume basis. Contact NetTech Australia at CompuServe: 100353,2330.

Network Instruments, LLC—Observer 2.0

OBSDEMO.ZIP $295–$495   Audit   1/01/95

Monitors and analyzes network traffic conditions, warns of a network over-load condition, and captures and decodes packets from a single computer on the LAN. Designed to be used by system administrators or anyone else who needs this information. Contact Network Instruments, LLC at (800) 526-7919, or Internet: info@netinst.com.

P.T. Masters—Sysdoc

SYSDOC.ZIP $195   Audit   11/29/93

A 30-day evaluation of a report generator for SYSCON, FCONSOLE, and PCONSOLE. Can provide reports on a regular basis, either weekly or monthly. Other reports include an audit trail, which monitors changes in the server. Contact P.T. Masters at (713) 530-1075.

Ray Lee—Workstation Automatic Inventory

WAIDB.ZIP $49.95   Audit   12/20/93

Does an automatic inventory of all nodes logging into the NetWare LAN. Some of the information includes server name, short hardware type, memory base-extended and expanded, disk drives installed, serial ports, parallel ports, and video type. Contact Ray Lee at (301) 424-2942.

Roy Coates—FilesFor

FILESFOR.ZIP   Shareware   Audit   1/27/95

A program that will generate a list of all files belonging to a given user on a specified volume. Contact Roy Coates at Internet: roy@mechnet.liv.ac.uk.

Roy Coates—Quota

QUOTA.ZIP   Shareware   Audit   2/01/94

Displays the amount of space left on a Novell volume and how much space is left if a quota restriction is being used. Contact Roy Coates at Internet: roy@mechnet.liv.ac.uk.

Software Solutions—LAN Management & Control System (Evaluation Copy)

LMCSD.ZIP $595   Audit   5/26/93

Provides information control by tracking information about LAN users, file server hardware and software, and server usage. It also detects what software is located on each workstation and can assist with login functions. Software Solutions no longer supports the evaluation program (do not contact the vendor for support). For orders only, call (416) 849-0930.

SYSLOAD—SYSLOAD for NetWare

SYSLOAD.ZIP   Shareware   Audit   7/07/95

A complete package for monitoring NetWare 3.*x* and 4.*x* file servers. Provides constant monitoring of more than 100 server activities with full and transparent historical database capabilities. Can also monitor application usage and print queues. Contact SYSLOAD at +33-1-43992828, or CompuServe: 100135,426.

TGB—Report-Generator

REPOR122.ZIP $89+   Audit   2/26/94

Designed to retrieve detailed configuration information from Novell file servers. Generates fully formatted documentation for your installations with the WinWord Add-on. Information is retrieved from SYSCON, PCONSOLE, DSPACE, FCONSOLE, and more. Contact TGB at +49-9072-3015, or CompuServe: 100020,1721.

Tammy Tran Nga—Base12

BASE12.ZIP   Free   Audit   12/11/94

A DOS program that displays information regarding the connected network. Displays information on the workstation and also the network. Contact Tammy Tran Nga at CompuServe: 74671,1741.

Thompson Software Inc.—Volumes 1.1

VOLUME.ZIP $20 Shareware   Audit   5/20/94

Graphic representation of *all* NetWare disk volume information, including non-default server. Includes printing option and help file/tutorial on NetWare storage and operation. Point and shoot interface. Contact Thompson Software at (302) 684-0335, or CompuServe: 72400,3252.

Triticom—ARGUS/n 1.5

ARGUS.ZIP $245+   Audit   3/22/90

LAN monitoring software. It conducts a hardware inventory and saves it to disk, determines which programs are currently running on the network, provides a history of recently run programs, determines the hardware configuration of individual workstations, and so on. Contact Triticom at (612) 937-0772, or BBS: (612) 829-0135.

Backup Utilities

The utilities listed here back up the two parts of NetWare that the regular backup utilities have trouble with: the binderies and the NDS database.

Jeff Chumbley—BindBack

BINDBACK.ZIP   Free   Backup   11/02/89

Archives the bindery files in Novell NetWare 2.1*x* or 3.*x* so that they can be backed up or copied by normal procedures. Contact Jeff Chumbley at Compu-Serve: 76702,537.

Palindrome Corporation—DSARC and DSREST Backup

DSARC.ZIP   Free   Backup   1/13/96

Two utilities that protect NDS installations. They use Novell's Storage Management Services (SMS) to back up (DSARC) and restore (DSREST) the objects in the NDS database. Contact Palindrome at (800) 288-4912.

Bindery Utilities

The bindery utilities listed here either produce reports on the binderies of your servers or directly manipulate the binderies. These functions are useful if you are unable to delete a user, trustee assignment, etc., through the usual NetWare utility.

AccuSys Computer Services—Grouplist

GRPLST26.ZIP $30   Bindery   3/09/93

Gives a detailed report on users assigned to a NetWare group. Contact AccuSys Computer Services at (416) 734-1992.

Bill Guethlein—List Trustees v0.99

LTRUS099.ZIP   Free   Bindery   6/01/92

Lists all trustees on a server drive. An updated version exists. Contact Bill Guethlein at Internet: wguethlein@ccmail.sunysb.edu.

Computer Tyme—Save/Restore Trustee Info

TRUSTZ.ZIP   Shareware   Bindery   5/9/95

Allows system administrators to save directory trustee information into a text file. Can also be used to modify existing trustee information. Created in MarxMenu and source code included. Contact Computer Tyme at (800) 548-5353, or CompuServe: 71333,427.

Dakware—Bindscan

BSCAN3.ZIP $35   Bindery   4/28/93

Uses the Novell API to scan the bindery for user, group, and file server information. Written in Clarion Professional Developer version 2.0. Contact Dakware at BBS: (207) 827-0512.

David Hendrickson—Strustee and Rtrustee

TRST14.ZIP   Shareware   Bindery   3/22/94

Scans all objects in the bindery and records the trustee rights for each directory on all volumes in to a file. The trustee information is recorded in the file and is also displayed on screen. Contact David Hendrickson at CompuServe: 73311,3725.

Fachhochschule Hamburg—Edbin

EDBIN.ZIP   Free   Bindery   2/15/95

A bindery editor that allows for editing of every possible item in the bindery, including type, add, remove, change, and copy properties. Contact Fachhochschule Hamburg at Internet: arpe@etech.fh-hamburg.de.

Kurt Kellner—BS.EXE

BS.ZIP $10   Bindery   10/11/93

A NetWare bindery scanning utility. It displays all items, both static and dynamic, found in a NetWare server's bindery. Contact Kurt Kellner at CompuServe: 72410,3004, or Internet: Kurt_Kellner@mail.amsinc.com.

Novell—B2DS

B2DS.ZIP   Free   Bindery   4/22/93

Creates a UIMPORT file from a pre-volume 4.0 bindery. Source code is included. Contact at CompuServe: 75600,2565, or Internet: BKUNZE@novell.com.

Novell—GMCopy

GMCOPY.ZIP   Free   Bindery   7/16/90

Permits the Supervisor to copy a print job configuration, user login script, or another configuration file from an individual user to a list of users on the default server. Contact Novell at (800) NETWARE, or Internet (Web): http://www.novell.com.

Morgan Adair—Bindery

BINDERY.ZIP   Free   Bindery   8/11/93

Displays the contents of a NetWare file server's bindery database. Visual Basic source code is included. AppNote: *Interfacing Visual Basic for Windows and NetWare*, October 1992. Contact Morgan Adair at (801) 429-7757, CompuServe: 76424,410, or Internet: madair@novell.com.

Roy Coates—UserDump 1.1

USERDUMP.ZIP   Shareware   Bindery   1/26/95

Lists all users in the bindery. Tested under NetWare 3.11 and 3.12. Contact Roy Coates at Internet: roy@mechnet.liv.ac.uk.

Wolfgang Schreiber—SaveUser and MakeUser

SAVEUSR.ZIP   Free   Bindery   5/22/91

Creates a MAKEUSER input file from an existing server environment, to bring user definitions of one file server to another or to save user definitions for documentation or later use. No separate documentation. SAVEUSER has limited built-in help. Contact Wolfgang Schreiber at +49-211-4380026, or CompuServe: 75170,124.

Wolfgang Schreiber—Vspace

VSPACE.ZIP   Free   Bindery   12/30/93

Lists all or selected users, their volume restrictions, and their currently used disk space per volume. Contact Wolfgang Schreiber at +49-211-4380026, or CompuServe: 75170,124.

Data-Recovery Utilities

Rescue v2.10

RSCU21.ZIP   Shareware   Data Recovery   2/21/95

A data-recovery NLM that is loaded on the NetWare server. It provides recovery tasks for drives that have read/write or SCSI failures. It also allows users to control the process of the recovery and does a continuous log of the recovery process. Contact CompuServe Shareware service: Reg ID 2384 from member 75277,1061.

Diagnostic Utilities

These diagnostic utilities will help you find problems with your physical network. They include protocol analyzers, packet capture programs, data load simulation programs, and discovery utilities.

ACS—WSDiag 3.53

DIAGS.ZIP   Shareware   Diagnostic   3/16/95

Full workstation IPX diagnostics using internet Novell data tables. No TSRs or extra modules needed. Produces seven pages of detailed diagnostic information. Supports NetWare 2.x–4.x server connections, including 1000 user NetWare 4.x licenses. Contact ACS at CompuServe: 71753,3522.

Artefact—NetCure

NETCURE.ZIP   Free   Diagnostic   3/16/91

Ethernet monitor and analyzer developed at Ingenieursbureau voor Informatica. Limited documentation in this distribution; full printed documentation for $100, with registration. Contact Artefact at +31-15-617532, BBS: +31-15-620790, or CompuServe: 72571,73.

Auto Exec—NicInfo

NICINFO.ZIP $5 Shareware   Diagnostic   10/16/91

Returns the username, connection number, server, date on, time on, and NIC number. Contact Auto Exec at BBS: (508) 833-0508.

Auto Exec—Nutilize

NUTILIZE.ZIP $5 Shareware   Diagnostic   10/17/91

Graphically shows utilization on the server, including current number of connections, current files open, maximum files open, and maximum utilization during session. Contact Auto Exec at BBS: (508) 833-0508.

DAC Micro Systems—Lanbench

LANBEN.ZIP   Free   Diagnostic   8/15/93

Determines and measures packet speed between a workstation and the file server. Very good for measuring increase or decrease in system performance after a change in the local workstation. Contact DAC Micro Systems at (800) 776-1322, or BBS: (805) 264-1219.

Darwin Collins—NCard

NCARD.ZIP $25 Shareware   Diagnostic   8/26/91

Displays statistics on a given station or network connection. Polls all attached workstations for their diagnostic packets. Can display the three with the most errors and write a report on all station diagnostics ready for spreadsheet/database import. Contact Darwin Collins at (214) 749-3022, or CompuServe: 75600,2274.

Denmac Systems Inc.—TrenData 2.02 (Evaluation Copy)

TD202E.ZIP   Shareware   Diagnostic   5/26/95

Provides a method of doing capacity planning and network growth forecasting on the physical layer of the network. A long-term trending and report-generating device, which gathers information from NetWare LANalyzers as well as other third-party RMON (remote network monitoring). Contact Denmac Systems at (708) 291-7760, CompuServe: 71521,3074, or Internet: Denmac@interacess.com.

Hans-Joachim Roy—IPX Diagnostics for Windows

IDIAGW.ZIP $39   Diagnostic   6/17/95

A Windows-based diagnostic program that scans the entire network for connected nodes. It reports the internal statistics of those nodes provided by IPX/SPX and also the installed network interface card. Contact Hans-Joachim Roy at CompuServe: 100024,110.

Ingenieursbr voor Informatica—Beholder

BEHOLD.ZIP   Free   Diagnostic   6/01/91

SNMP-able Ethernet monitor for standard PC hardware. Contact Ingenieursbr voor Informatica at +31-15-617532, CompuServe: 72571,73, or BBS: +31-15-620790.

Ingenieursbr voor Informatica—Gobbler

GOBBLR.ZIP   Free   Diagnostic   11/14/91

Grabs packets from an Ethernet network and presents contents in human readable form. Handles TCP/IP, IPX, and other types of packets. Filters can be set to destination, source, protocol, contents, device number, and packet length. Contact Ingenieursbr voor Informatica at +31-15-617532, CompuServe: 72571,73, or BBS: +31-15-620790.

Justin Jones—SAPTrack v1.0

SAPTRK.ZIP   Free   Diagnostic   9/05/93

A network analysis utility that provides continuous monitoring of Novell SAP (Service Advertisement Protocol) and RIP (Routing Information Protocol) broadcasts. Contact Justin Jones at (800) 800-0210.

Kurt Kellner—SNET.EXE

SNET.ZIP $10   Diagnostic   10/10/93

Scans a NetWare network for nodes. A node can be a workstation, a bridge, a printer server, or any device that has IPX/SPX loaded. Contact Kurt Kellner at CompuServe: 72410,3004, or Internet: Kurt_Kellner@mail.amsinc.com.

Borland—Lantraffic

LANTRAF.ZIP   Shareware   Diagnostic   2/04/88

A LAN management tool to track traffic passing through each workstation. Provides the LAN supervisor with information about the load that each workstation is placing on the network. Includes a stand-alone program to archive and export data files to dBASE or 1-2-3. Contact Borland at (800) 331-0877.

Network Instruments—Analyst/Probe

APDEMO.ZIP $795   Diagnostic   10/15/95

A Windows-based, multi-segment LAN/WAN software protocol analyzer. Capture and decode TCP/IP, IPX/SPX, or NetBIOS/NetBEUI packets. Provides graphical displays of outputs. Compatible with Windows, Windows 95, and Windows NT. Contact Network Instruments at (800) 526-7919, or Internet: info@netinst.com; ftp.netinst.com.

Novell—Comchek Utility

COMCHK.ZIP   Free   Diagnostic   11/22/93

A diagnostic utility for troubleshooting hardware or network interface card driver problems. This file contains the executable and support files needed to run Comchek. Contact Novell at (800) NETWARE, or Internet (Web): http://www.novell.com.

RealTech Systems Corporation—SAPTrack 2.0

SPTRK.ZIP   Shareware   Diagnostic   4/12/94

A network analysis utility that provides continuous monitoring of Novell SAP (Service Advertisement Protocol) and RIP (Routing Information Protocol) broadcasts, with identification of all advertised services and networks and identification of alarms. Contact RealTech Systems at Internet: info@realtech.com.

Ryu Consulting—Snoop

SNOOP1.ZIP   Free   Diagnostic   5/27/94

Lets you examine Ethernet data on NE2000 compatible network interface cards. Can be used to monitor and analyze the network traffic in real time. Contact Ryu Consulting at (916) 722-1939, or BBS: (916) 722-1984.

Scott Taylor—TestNet v1.4

TESTNET4.ZIP   Shareware   Diagnostic   8/03/90

Measures file I/O on network. Performs sequential or overlaid reads and writes and reports throughput. Can also be used to test stand-alone PCs or compare environments. It is well-documented. Contact Scott Taylor at (301) 921-0437.

Software Systems—Card-Network Scanner

CARD.ZIP   Free   Diagnostic   10/23/93

Retrieves network card information from all workstations in a NetWare LAN system. On an Ethernet system, more than 90 board manufacturers are identified. Can be run on systems up to 1000 workstations. Contact Software Systems at +49-841-760148, or CompuServe: 100066,52.

Standard Microsystems—PC Agent/SNMP

AGT131.ZIP   Free   Diagnostic   7/13/93

A true SNMP (Simple Network Monitoring Protocol) TSR program, which operates with SMS LAN adapters. Provides SNMP support for both large mainframe connections and NetWare-based systems. Contact Standard Microsystems at (800) 762-4968.

Symbios Logic—IOBENCH.NLM

IOBNCH.ZIP   Free   Diagnostic   3/16/95
   Benchmarks disk activity across a NetWare network. Tests variable read/
write ratios, I/O size, queue depth, and seek range and duration. Results can be
exported to spreadsheets or other programs. For NetWare 3.x and 4.x. Contact
Symbios Logic at (316) 636-8340, or CompuServe: 76207,1433.

Virtual Networks—NetWatch

NWNETWAT.ZIP $195   Diagnostic   11/03/90
   Allows viewing statistical and configuration information for any workstation
or server on the network. It can find network problems or keep track of configuration parameters. Contact Virtual Networks at CompuServe: 75360,2001.

Network Diagramming Tools

The programs listed here can help you draw maps of your physical and logical
network topologies.

Network Performance Institute—LCAD Demo Network

LCADDM.ZIP   Shareware   Diagramming   7/28/94
   Lets you diagram a LAN or WAN in Windows. Shows network devices,
wiring paths, wiring lengths, and obstructions. Requires 4 MB of RAM, Win-
dows, and VGA. Help for this package is included in another file called
LCADHL.ZIP. Contact Network Performance Institute at (305) 864-2744,
CompuServe: 70373,1350, or Internet: npi@shadow.net.

I-Soft—LANDoc 1.1 Demo Network

LDOC1.ZIP, LDOC2.ZIP, LDOC3.ZIP Shareware Diagramming   7/19/94
   A Windows-based graphical documenting system for designing and mapping
a network. Each piece of equipment can be detailed and documented. The
system is made up of zip files. Contact I-Soft at CompuServe: 71033,1617.

Macintosh Utilities

Novell/Dayna—Desktop Rebuild

RBUILD.ZIP   Free   Macintosh   6/07/95

Makes it possible to rebuild a NetWare for Macintosh volume's desktop from a Macintosh workstation on the network running a System 6.*x* or 7.*x* operating system. Contact Novell at (800) NETWARE, or Internet (Web): http://www.novell.com.

NDS Tools

These utilities can help you learn more about your NDS tree and fix problems with it.

Laurent Dupuis—Net Tree

NETTRE.ZIP   Free   NDS   7/09/94

Displays all of the NDS tree for all volumes on all attached servers. It's good for supervisors who wish to see the tree across other servers. Contact Laurent Dupuis at CompuServe: 100041,2441.

Mark Mosko—NDSScan 1.00

NDSCAN.ZIP $20   NDS   1/25/94

Reports all information about objects defined in the NDS database, with detailed scans showing all properties and their values. Also reports some non-NDS information about Novell file servers defined in the NDS tree. For NetWare 4.*x* only. Contact Mark Mosko at CompuServe: 76234,3176, or Internet: mmosko@netcom.com.

Novell—Dsrepair.Nlm v2.01

DSREPS.ZIP   Free   NDS   6/21/94

An NDS utility for NetWare 4.01. Contact Novell at (800) NETWARE, or Internet (Web): http://www.novell.com.

Remote Workstation Management Utilities

These applications allow you to take over a user's workstation and see what's going on without needing to physically go to the user's desk. If your campus is spread out, this type of program can be an enormous time-saver.

Intel Corporation—LANDesk Express v2.60 (Evaluation Copy)

LDXPRS.ZIP   Shareware   Remote   9/27/94

A Windows-based, flexible network management tool that allows monitoring any DOS or Windows workstation attached to a NetWare LAN. Contact Intel at (800) 538-3373, or BBS: (503) 645-6275.

KDS Software—LAN Hijack

LANHJ2.ZIP $69 Shareware   Remote   1/05/91

A TSR utility that allows you to control other PCs on the network. Access modems, FAX cards, CD-ROMs, and other hardware in other workstations. It provides WAN support and conferencing. The trial version excludes graphics support and run-time limits. Contact KDS Software at 2125 W. Coronet Ave., Anaheim, CA 92801.

Software Management Tools

These tools allow you to manage software upgrades and configuration from a single location, instead of needing to upgrade all your users individually. This can obviously be an incredible boon to the administrator supporting lots of users.

David Carter—FRED

FRED.ZIP   Free   Software Management   1/31/95

Allows administrators to update files on the workstations with a level of automation by scripting. Contact David Carter at (612) 871-5554.

Hans-Georg Michna—Remote Software Update 1.4a

RSUX.ZIP   Free   Software Management   3/14/95

Distributes software over a LAN. Can perform complex INI and text file modifications, replicate directories, detect hardware, and more. The update is $50 for 100 users and free for individual non-network use. Contact Hans-Georg Michna at +49-89-605063, or CompuServe: 74776,2361.

Laurent Clerc—SmartCOPY 2.0

SMCOPY.ZIP   Free   Software Management   5/20/94

Supports automatic software distribution over NetWare 3.*x* networks and DOS up to 5.0. Enforces software version checking and automatic download on the workstation via batch files. Contact Laurent Clerc at CompuServe: 100144,203.

Maurice Smulders—Complete 4.x Tree Update

4XUPD.ZIP   Free   Software Management   7/21/95

DOS batch files to update all servers in a NDS tree. Contact Maurice Smulders at CompuServe: 72773,230.

McAffee Associates—NetTools v5.2

NN520D5.ZIP   Shareware Software Management   2/28/95

Allows administrators to manage Windows desktops quickly and easily. Assists with creating centralized and secure environments for workstations running Windows. Provides for restriction of certain applications per workstation. The package consists of seven disks. Contact McAffee Associates at (408) 988-3832, BBS: (408) 988-4004, or Internet: support@mcafee.com.

User Management Tools

Some user management utilities allow you to create standard sets of rights, permissions, home directories, or print configurations for many users at once. Some make your work easier by letting you copy files and retrieve directory and user listings at the file server console. Other utilities can help you figure out who is still using the server when you need to shut it down. They will tell you which users have files open and can send messages to the users asking them to log out.

Dave Barnes—Setuser v1.1

SETUSR.ZIP $25 User Management 3/23/93

Automates the creation and maintenance of home and application directory structures and files on the LAN system. Contact Dave Barnes at (604) 743-4077.

Classic Software—Console Plus

CSCON.ZIP $25 User Management 07/02/94

An NLM for NetWare 3.*x* that adds features for copying files, retrieving a directory listing, and listing all the users on the system at the file server console. Contact Classic Software at CompuServe: 72460,33.

Holmstead Partners—Mass User Management (MUM) 1.3

MUM13B.ZIP $390 User Management 7/06/94

Allows supervisors to add, delete, update, and monitor user accounts. Essential for servers with large number of users. User restrictions can be manipulated for entire groups, for selected accounts, etc. Contact Holmstead Partners at (801) 375-8890, or Internet: Partners@world.std.com.

Jens Jacobi—Whathave 2.0

WHATHAVE.ZIP Shareware User Management 6/07/95

Displays a list of open files by user, username, and connection identification. This utility has been tested with NetWare 3.*x* and 4.*x*. Contact Jens Jacobi at CompuServe: 100335,1606.

John C. Leon—JCLUTL

JCLUTL.ZIP Shareware User Management 3/5/94

Gives network administrators quick, direct access to important information not easily available from the tools shipped with NetWare. There are three utilities: Multconn, Nopword, and Nwdisabl. Contact John C. Leon at (713) 359-3461, or CompuServe: 72426,2077.

William Madonna, Jr.—WmWhoHas

WMWHOHAS.ZIP $20   User Management   7/10/95

Displays a list of all users who currently have a file open on the server. Screen updates can be set to a time interval. Also allows you to send messages to tell those users to close open files. Contact William Madonna, Jr., at (208) 664-3413, or CompuServe: 71072,573.

Netmagic Systems Inc.—NetMagic

NETDEM.ZIP   Shareware   User Management   6/29/94

A replacement for SYSCON, PCONSOLE, and FCONSOLE. Allows global editing of hundreds of users at one time. Also provides support for managing print queues and groups from Windows 3.*x*. Contact Netmagic Systems at (914) 739-4579, Ext. 14.

Ric Ridderhof—Nwuserlist v1.3b

NWULIS.ZIP   Shareware   User Management   6/13/94

Displays currently logged in users in a NetWare 2.*x* or 3.*x* environment. Supports multiple servers. Contact Ric Ridderhof at CompuServe: 100265,1405.

Stephen Smith—NetWare Clear Connection

CLRCON.ZIP   Free   User Management   2/04/95

Allows for mass clearing of NetWare connections. Gives the capabilities of clearing one or more connections with a single keystroke. Also allows for a delay before clearing the connection and can send a message to users being cleared. Contact Stephen Smith at CompuServe: 72623,3644.

Upgrade Utilities

These programs are intended to ease the migration from one version of NetWare to another. They help you figure out what you currently have on your existing server and can move configurations to your new server.

Novell—Migrate

MIGRAT.ZIP   Free   Upgrade   6/18/93

Assists in upgrading an existing NetWare 2.*x* file system to a 3.*x* file system. Assists in keeping existing file structures between 2.*x* to 3.*x*. It now has support for going to NetWare 4.*x*. Contact Novell at (800) NETWARE, or Internet (Web): http://www.novell.com.

Novell—Printuser, Printgrp, Dupbind

AN304X.ZIP   Free   Upgrade   3/29/93

Three utilities that assist in the migration of the bindery information from Novell 2.*x*/3.*x* to 4.*x*. Contact Morgan Adair at (801) 429-7757, CompuServe: 76424,410, or Internet: madair@novell.com.

Novell—Uimport.Exe for NetWare 4.01

UIM413.ZIP   Free   Upgrade   6/07/94

Latest version of UIMPORT, which is targeted for NetWare 4.02. This version may solve problems creating home directories on certain file servers. Contact Novell at (800) NETWARE, or Internet (Web): http://www.novell.com.

Virus Scanners

These programs check for viruses on the workstation, on the server, or on both. NLM-based checkers may provide higher levels of performance, but they are also usually more expensive. The most important thing to remember is that any virus-checking software you have is probably good for two months at the outside. Update your software regularly; most of the companies below offer a subscription or free updates through a bulletin board or Web site.

ANTaLION Software—FxREPEAT 4.00

FREP40.ZIP   Free/Evaluation   Virus   1/17/95

Automates virus scanning of workstations with Frisk Software's F-PROT program. This is not a TSR. You can get it as freeware for individual use or an evaluation copy for commercial/business use. Contact ANTaLION Software at CompuServe: 74720,224.

ANTaLION Software—Repeat Program Group v3.x

FXREP310.ZIP $50 Virus 8/01/93

A virus-scanning shell for Frisk Software's F-PROT program. Periodic scanning (hours/days) is determined by a command-line parameter. When a virus is found, an alarm is sounded, a message is displayed, and the keyboard is locked. This is not a TSR. Contact ANTaLION Software at CompuServe: 74720,224.

ANTaLION Software—TxRepeat v1.62

TREP16.ZIP Free/Evaluation Virus 1/19/95

Automates virus scanning of workstations. This is not a TSR. Scanning is done only when a user-defined date or time interval is exceeded. It's freeware updated for use with Thunderbyte's TbSCAN version 6.24. Contact ANTaLION Software at CompuServe: 74720,224.

Cheyenne Software, Inc.—InocuLAN (30-Day NLM)

IL0025.ZIP Shareware Virus 7/19/94

For use with NetWare 3.1x and above. Prevents known viruses and halts the execution of unknown viruses. You can get a 30-day evaluation NLM version. Contact Cheyenne Software at (800) 243-9832, or BBS: (516) 484-3445.

Datawatch Corporation—VIRx

VIRX.ZIP $69 Virus 4/30/95

Detection-only version of vendor's VPCScan. Scans executable (including PKLite- and LZEXE-compressed) files for certain viruses. Improved handling of NetWare volumes. Contact Datawatch at (919) 549-0711, or BBS: (919) 419-1602.

Frisk Software International—F-PROT v2.12

FPROT2.ZIP   Free/Shareware   Virus   4/27/94

Comprehensive computer-prophylactic package, including an additional program specifically for protecting a NetWare environment. Recognizes well over 2000 virus variants and is able to disinfect most of them. Heuristic scan for new viruses. Contact Frisk Software International at Internet: frisk@complex.is.

H+ BEDV GmbH—AVScan 2.30

AVSCAN.ZIP   Shareware   Virus   7/09/95

Searches for about 3600 signatures for viruses plus other special identification features (to handle polymorphic viruses). Contact H+ BEDV GmbH at +49-7542-83040, or CompuServe: 71310,3143.

Intel Corporation—KAOS4 Virus Protection

NOKAOS.ZIP   Shareware   Virus   8/1/94

A subset of the LanDesk Virus Protect 2.1 software that detects the KAOS4 virus, along with others. Uses virus pattern version .061. Contact Intel at (800) 538-3373, or BBS: (503) 645-6275.

McAffeeAssociates—Clean v1.17

CLEAN117.ZIP   Shareware   Virus   7/15/94

Removes any viruses found by NetScan, also made by McAffee Associates. Contact McAffee Associates at (408) 988-3832, BBS: (408) 988-4004, or Internet: support@mcafee.com.

McAffee Associates—Netscan

NETSC102.ZIP   Shareware   Virus   2/27/93

A network version of the well-known McAffee virus-scanning program. Scans network drives and identifies preexisting viruses on file servers. Site-licensing fees vary according to the installed base. Updated frequently. Call BBS for latest version. Contact McAffee Associates at (408) 988-3832, BBS: (408) 988-4004, or Internet: support@mcafee.com.

McAffee Associates—Netshield

NSH211E.ZIP   Shareware   Virus   4/19/95

An NLM for NetWare version 3.11 systems. Netshield checks file servers for all know computer viruses using the Viruscan technology. As an NLM, Netshield checks files as they are accessed on the server. Requires 560 KB free memory. Contact McAffee Associates at (408) 988-3832, BBS: (408) 988-4004, or Internet: support@mcafee.com.

McAffee Associates—Scan v2.00

SCN210E.ZIP   Shareware   Virus   7/19/94

A virus detector for stand-alone PCs and network workstations. Good for office and multi-PC environments since site licenses are available. Contact McAffee Associates at (408) 988-3832, BBS: (408) 988-4004, or Internet: support@mcafee.com.

McAffee Associates—Virusscan v2.1.7

SCN217E.ZIP   Shareware   Virus   3/08/95

Another in the line of McAffee virus-scanning programs, this one is designed for the stand-alone PC or network workstation. Detects most of the known viruses in the world. Contact McAffee Associates at (408) 988-3832, BBS: (408) 988-4004, or Internet: support@mcafee.com.

McAffee Associates—Virus Shield v2.1.7

VSH217E.ZIP   Shareware   Virus   3/08/95

A TSR program that will do real-time detection of viruses during file accesses on local and server drives. Contact McAffee Associates at (408) 988-3832, BBS: (408) 988-4004, or Internet: support@mcafee.com.

Morgan Adair—Pinch

PINCH.ZIP   Free   Virus   8/11/93

An NLM that builds a database of file information for NetWare file servers. PINCH (Program INtegrity CHecker) can be used to detect virus infections or data corruption. Source code included. Novell AppNote *Detecting Viruses in NetWare*. Contact Morgan Adair at (801) 429-7757, CompuServe: 76424,410, or Internet: madair@novell.com.

SafetyNet Inc.—VirusNet LAN 2.17d

VNLAN.ZIP　　　$695　　　Virus　　　5/04/95

　　Detects and removes existing viruses before they cause damage. Consists of a scanner, a 3 KB TSR virus monitor, and an informative virus reference database. Does continuous checking to prevent infected programs from running or being copied. Contact SafetyNet at (800) 851-0188, or BBS: (201) 467-1581.

Stiller Research—Integrity Master 2.42c

IMAST.ZIP　　　$39.50　　　Virus　　　3/23/95

　　Easy to use anti-virus and PC integrity program that also provides security, CMOS protection, and disk diagnostics. Does not require periodic updates, yet identifies known viruses by name as well as unknown viruses. Contact Stiller Research, Dept. I211 at (800) 622-2793, or CompuServe: 72571,3352.

Thompson Network Software—DocNLM

DOCNLM.ZIP　　　$300　　　Virus　　　8/01/94

　　An NLM virus scanner that will check files on a time-schedule basis. Any infected files will be moved to another file and isolated from the network. Contact Thompson Network Software at (404) 971-8900, or BBS: (404) 971-8886.

Trend Micro Devices Inc.—Pcscan

PCSCAN.ZIP　　　Shareware　　　Virus　　　9/07/94

　　A new-generation virus scanner that provides protection, both at the local workstation and network drives, against stealth and mutation engine viruses using a new technology called Multi-Clean and DeepScan. Contact Trend Micro Devices at (800) 228-5651, or BBS: (310) 320-2523.

Network Record Keeping Forms

APPENDIX

C

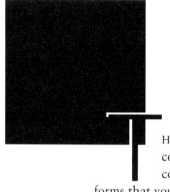

HIS APPENDIX CONTAINS forms that you can use to record the configuration of your network and its components. They can be copied and used as they are, or they can serve as the basis for forms that you design yourself. The worksheets are:

- Server configuration worksheet (two sides)

- Workstation configuration worksheet

- Network configuration worksheet

- User configuration information worksheet

- Printer configuration worksheet

- Print queue and print server configuration worksheet

As examples, filled-in versions of the server configuration and workstation configuration worksheets are included.

These forms are available as Macintosh and PC Adobe Illustrator files on the CD-ROM included with this book. You can open them and make any changes you like.

FIGURE C.I
Server configuration
worksheet

Server Configuration Worksheet
Side One

Name: _____ Location: _____ Date: _____

Internal IPX Number: _____ Department: _____

Brand/Model: _____

Support Phone Number: _____ Serial Number: _____

Memory Installed: _____ Possible: _____ Type: _____

Board : _____
Brand: _____
Support #: _____
Model #: _____
I/O Port: _____
Memory Address: _____
Interrupt: _____
DMA: _____
Slot Number: _____
Driver: _____
BIOS Version: _____
Network Number: _____

Board : _____
Brand: _____
Support #: _____
Model #: _____
I/O Port: _____
Memory Address: _____
Interrupt: _____
DMA: _____
Slot Number: _____
Driver: _____
BIOS Version: _____
Network Number: _____

Board : _____
Brand: _____
Support #: _____
Model #: _____
I/O Port: _____
Memory Address: _____
Interrupt: _____
DMA: _____
Slot Number: _____
Driver: _____
BIOS Version: _____
Network Number: _____

Board : _____
Brand: _____
Support #: _____
Model #: _____
I/O Port: _____
Memory Address: _____
Interrupt: _____
DMA: _____
Slot Number: _____
Driver: _____
BIOS Version: _____
Network Number: _____

Disks - see other side

FIGURE C.1
Server configuration
worksheet (continued)

Server Configuration Worksheet
Side Two — Disks

Controller: _____   Int: ____ DMA: _____ Slot #: ____

Support #: _____   Driver: _____

Port: ____ Mem. Address: ____   BIOS Version: _____

Disk	Size	Heads	Cylinders	Device Code (5-digit)	Logical Device	Physical Partition	Mirrored With

Controller: _____   Int: ____ DMA: _____ Slot #: ____

Support #: _____   Driver: _____

Port: ____ Mem. Address: ____   BIOS Version: _____

Disk	Size	Heads	Cylinders	Device Code (5-digit)	Logical Device	Physical Partition	Mirrored With

Server Configuration Worksheet
Side One

Name: _Asmodeus_   Location: _Office 1141_   Date: _3/30/96_

Internal IPX Number: _C11412385_   Department: _Marketing_

Brand/Model: _ACMA 150 Mhz Pentium PC1 Tower Award BIOS 6.11_

Support Phone Number: _408 555-1491_   Serial Number: _A11093B31_

Memory Installed: _64 Mb_ Possible: _256 Mb_ Type: _16x32 SIMM_

Board : _____LAN Adapter_____	**Board** : _____LAN Adapter_____
Brand: _____3Com_____	Brand: _____3Com_____
Support #: _408 764-6399_	Support #: _408 764-6399_
Model #: _____36590TP_____	Model #: _____3C590TP_____
I/O Port: _____	I/O Port: _____
Memory Address: _____	Memory Address: _____
Interrupt: _____	Interrupt: _____
DMA: _____	DMA: _____
Slot Number: _____3_____	Slot Number: _____2_____
Driver: _____3C590.LAN_____	Driver: _____3C590.LAN_____
BIOS Version: _____1.21_____	BIOS Version: _____1.21_____
Network Number: _1A114100_	Network Number: _2B114100_
Board : _____SVGA_____	**Board** : _____
Brand: _On Motherboard_	Brand: _____
Support #: _____	Support #: _____
Model #: _____	Model #: _____
I/O Port: _____	I/O Port: _____
Memory Address: _B000-B7FF_	Memory Address: _____
Interrupt: _____	Interrupt: _____
DMA: _____	DMA: _____
Slot Number: _____	Slot Number: _____
Driver: _____	Driver: _____
BIOS Version: _____	BIOS Version: _____
Network Number: _____	Network Number: _____

Disks - see other side

FIGURE C.2

Server configuration
worksheet—filled in
(continued)

Server Configuration Worksheet
Side Two — Disks

Controller: Adaptec 1742B (EISA)   Int: — DMA: ____ Slot #: _4_
Support #: 510 555-3201   Driver: AHA1740.DSK
Port: — Mem. Address: —   BIOS Version: 6.02

Disk	Size	Heads	Cylinders	Device Code (5-digit)	Logical Device	Physical Partition	Mirrored With
Maxtor PO-12S	1 Gb	15	4196	21100	1	0	1
Maxtor PO-12S	1 Gb	15	4196	21200	2	1	—

Controller: Motherboard   Int: _E_ DMA: ____ Slot #: ____
Support #: 415 555-8195   Driver: ISADISK
Port: 1f0 Mem. Address: ____   BIOS Version: _____

Disk	Size	Heads	Cylinders	Device Code (5-digit)	Logical Device	Physical Partition	Mirrored With
Quantum IDE 105S	100	8	995	11000	1	0	—

FIGURE C.3
Workstation
configuration worksheet

Workstation Configuration Worksheet

User: _____   Location: _____   Date: _____

Network Node Address: _____   Department: _____

Brand/Model: _____

Support Phone Number: _____   Serial Number: _____

Memory Installed: _____   Possible: _____   Type: _____

Ports Enabled: LPT1☐ LPT2☐ LPT3☐ COM1☐ COM2☐ COM3☐ COM4☐

Floppys: 3.5"- DD ___ HD ___ 5.25"- DD ___ HD ___ Mouse: _____

Hard Disk 1: Brand _____ Controller _____ Type ____ Heads ____
             Cyl ____ PreComp ____ LZ ____Partition _____ Size _____

Hard Disk 2: Brand _____ Controller _____ Type ____ Heads ____
             Cyl ____ PreComp ____ LZ ____Partition _____ Size _____

Boards:

Brand/Model _____ Support # _____

Int ____ DMA _____Port _____ Mem. Addr. _____ Slot ___ BIOS Ver. _____

Brand/Model _____ Support # _____

Int ____ DMA _____Port _____ Mem. Addr. _____ Slot ___ BIOS Ver. _____

Brand/Model _____ Support # _____

Int ____ DMA _____Port _____ Mem. Addr. _____ Slot ___ BIOS Ver. _____

Brand/Model _____ Support # _____

Int ____ DMA _____Port _____ Mem. Addr. _____ Slot ___ BIOS Ver. _____

Operating System Version: _____

Networking Software: _____

TSRs and Other Drivers: _____

Comments: _____

             _____

FIGURE C.4
Workstation
configuration
worksheet—filled in

Workstation Configuration Worksheet

User: _Bosco Ninnyhammer_   Location: _Cube 1510_   Date: _3/10/92_

Network Node Address: _FC3010014C13_   Department: _Engineering_

Brand/Model: _ACMA 486/33 ISA with AMI BIOS v. 4.26_

Support Phone Number: _415 555-7717_   Serial Number: _A551C-30-1147_

Memory Installed: _16 Mb_ Possible: _32 Mb_ Type: _4 Mb x 9 SIMMs_

Ports Enabled: LPT1 ☐ LPT2 ☐ LPT3 ☐ COM1 ☐ COM2 ☐ COM3 ☐ COM4 ☐

Floppys: 3.5"- DD ___ HD _A:_ 5.25"- DD ___ HD _B:_ Mouse: _Logitech Bus_

Hard Disk 1: Brand _Conner_   Controller _IDE_ Type _45_ Heads _8_
     Cyl _960_ PreComp _0_ LZ _960_ Partition _MS DOS 5_ Size _210 Mb_

Hard Disk 2: Brand _____ Controller _____ Type ____ Heads ____
     Cyl ____ PreComp ____ LZ ____ Partition _____ Size _____

Boards:

Brand/Model _Orchid SVGA 1150_ _____ Support # _703 555-4491_

Int ____ DMA ____ Port ____ Mem. Addr. ____ Slot _5_ BIOS Ver. _1.31_

Brand/Model _Eagle NE2000 10BaseT_ _____ Support # _408 555-7171_

Int _3_ DMA ____ Port _300_ Mem. Addr. ____ Slot _3_ BIOS Ver. _4.6_

Brand/Model _____ Support # _____

Int ____ DMA ____ Port ____ Mem. Addr. ____ Slot ___ BIOS Ver. _____

Brand/Model _____ Support # _____

Int ____ DMA ____ Port ____ Mem. Addr. ____ Slot ___ BIOS Ver. _____

Operating System Version: _DR DOS 6.0_

Networking Software: _NETX v 3.26, IPX 3.1, NET.CFG_

TSRs and Other Drivers: _SMARTDRV.SYS_

Comments: _Runs Windows 3.1, NE1000 failed 11/28/91, Bosco eats over the
      keyboard - vacumn regularly._

Network Configuration Worksheet

Server Name _____ Network Type and # _____
(One Worksheet per protocol)

User _____ Node # _____ Protocol Addr: _____

User _____ Node # _____ Protocol Addr: _____

User _____ Node # _____ Protocol Addr: _____

User _____ Node # _____ Protocol Addr: _____

User _____ Node # _____ Protocol Addr: _____

User _____ Node # _____ Protocol Addr: _____

User _____ Node # _____ Protocol Addr: _____

User _____ Node # _____ Protocol Addr: _____

User _____ Node # _____ Protocol Addr: _____

User _____ Node # _____ Protocol Addr: _____

User _____ Node # _____ Protocol Addr: _____

User _____ Node # _____ Protocol Addr: _____

User _____ Node # _____ Protocol Addr: _____

User _____ Node # _____ Protocol Addr: _____

User _____ Node # _____ Protocol Addr: _____

User _____ Node # _____ Protocol Addr: _____

User _____ Node # _____ Protocol Addr: _____

User _____ Node # _____ Protocol Addr: _____

User _____ Node # _____ Protocol Addr: _____

User _____ Node # _____ Protocol Addr: _____

FIGURE C.6
User information
configuration worksheet

User Configuration Worksheet

Date: _____

User Name: _____   Location: _____

Workstation: _____   Phone: _____

Groups: _____

Managed Users & Groups,
Security Equivalences: _____

Time, Station, Volume
Restrictions: _____

Login Script: Trustee Assignments:

_____   _____

_____   _____

_____   _____

_____   _____

_____   _____

_____   _____

_____   _____

_____   _____

_____   _____

_____   _____

_____   _____

_____   _____

_____   _____

FIGURE C.7
Printer configuration
worksheet

Printer Configuration Worksheet

Date: _____

Printer Name: _____   Type: _____

Manufacturer: _____   Phone: _____
                                               (Tech Support)

Location: _____ PSERVER Name: _____

Print queue(s): _____ AppleTalk ☐ Name: _____

Parallel ☐ Interrupt: _____ Ethernet ☐ Addr: _____

Serial ☐ Baud: ___ Data bits: ___ Stop bits: ___ Parity: ___ XON/XOFF: ___

Hard Disk ☐ Size: _____

Mode: _____
                (Text, PostScript, PCL etc)

Forms Defined:	Queues Serviced:	Notify List:
_____	_____	_____
_____	_____	_____
_____	_____	_____
_____	_____	_____
_____	_____	_____
_____	_____	_____

Notes: _____

_____

_____

FIGURE C.8

Print server and queue
configuration worksheet

Print Server and Print Queue Configuration Worksheet
Print Server

Name: _____   File Server(s): _____

ID: _____   _____

Printer 0: _____   Queue(s) Attached: _____

Printer 1: _____   Queue(s) Attached: _____

Printer 2: _____   Queue(s) Attached: _____

Printer 3: _____   Queue(s) Attached: _____

Printer 4: _____   Queue(s) Attached: _____

Printer 5: _____   Queue(s) Attached: _____

Printer 6: _____   Queue(s) Attached: _____

Printer 7: _____   Queue(s) Attached: _____

Operators: _____

Users: _____

Print Queues Attached to this Print Server

Queues: _____ ID: _____   Queues: _____ ID: _____

Operators: _____   Operators: _____

_____   _____

Users: _____   Users: _____

_____   _____

Queues: _____ ID: _____   Queues: _____ ID: _____

Operators: _____   Operators: _____

_____   _____

Users: _____   Users: _____

_____   _____

Glossary of
Terms

GLOSSARY

ABEND (Abnormal End)

The dreaded ABEND message indicates that the server has crashed. The message may or may not indicate why. If there is an error code or meaningful error message, it can help you determine the root cause of the crash.

active hub

See *hub*.

active star

A network topology that provides regeneration of signals in the central hub. Typical of ARCnet. See also *passive star*.

ADB (Apple Desktop Bus)

A Macintosh communications standard for keyboards, mice, trackballs, graphics tablets, and other input devices.

Address Resolution Protocol (ARP)

A process in Internet Protocol (IP) and AppleTalk networks that allows a host to find the physical address of a target host on the same physical network when it knows only the target's logical address. Under ARP, a network board contains a table that maps logical addresses to the hardware addresses of the objects on the network.

AFP

See *AppleTalk Filing Protocol*.

AIX (Advanced Interactive eXecutive)

IBM's version of UNIX for 386-based PS/2s, RTs, and mainframes. It is based on AT&T's UNIX System V with Berkeley extensions.

analog

Signals that carry information that directly represents the physical data, as in a phone connection or a phonograph record. Contrasts with digital, where information is broken down into yes/no pulses, as in a LAN connection or a CD.

ANSI (American National Standards Institute)

American body that sets standards and is a voting member of ISO.

ANSI.SYS

A driver used for screen control (such as cursor movement and screen clearing) and as a keyboard macro processor to assign commands to function keys or reassign keys. Some applications require ANSI.SYS.

APPC (Advanced Program-to-Program Communications)

An IBM marketing term for communications between programs using SNA LU 6.2 protocols.

AppleShare

Networking software from Apple Computer, Inc. that enables a Macintosh computer to function as a file server in an AppleTalk network.

AppleTalk Filing Protocol (AFP)

A network file-system model from Apple Computer, Inc., that allows workstations to share files and programs on an AppleShare file server.

AppleTalk protocols

The underlying forms and rules that determine communication between nodes on an AppleTalk network. These protocols govern the AppleTalk network, from the network board to the application software.

- **Link Access Protocol (LAP):** Works at the Data-Link layer (the bottom layer of the network), receiving packets of information and converting them into the proper signals for your network board. Examples of LAPs include LLAP (LocalTalk LAP), ELAP (Ethernet LAP), and DTLAP (Token Ring LAP).

- **Datagram Delivery Protocol (DDP):** Works at the Network layer and prepares packets of data to send on network cables. These packets, called datagrams, include network address information and data formatting. They are delivered to one of the LAPs (LLAP, ELAP, or TLAP), according to the hardware in the computer.

- **Name Binding Protocol (NBP):** Each network process or device has a name that corresponds to network and node addresses. AppleTalk uses an NBP to conceal those addresses from users.

- **Routing Table Maintenance Protocol (RTMP):** When many small networks are connected, a router connects them together in an internetwork. Information about other networks is stored in routing tables. Routers update routing tables by using an RTMP to communicate with each other.

- **Zone Information Protocol (ZIP):** In a large internetwork, all AppleTalk nodes are divided into groups, called *zones*, for ease of locating an object. The NBP uses a ZIP to assist in finding the correct network and node addresses from a zone list. Zones are referred to by names, which can be up to 32 characters each. The zone names are converted to addresses on the internetwork by the NBP and the ZIP. (In a network without routers, only one zone exists, and the zone name is invisible to users.) Zone names and addresses are maintained in a zone information table within each router. A NetWare server can act as a router for AppleTalk nodes connected to it.

- **Printer Access Protocol (PAP):** When a network node prints to a network printer, the PAP prepares a path to the requested printer using NBP.

Application layer

See *OSI model*.

APPN (Advanced Peer-to-Peer Networking)

SNA extensions that provide intermediate node routing, dynamic network services, and improved administration. APPN makes use of LU 6.2 protocols and is implemented in SNA Node Type 2.1.

ARCnet (Attached Resource Computer NETwork)

The LAN introduced in 1968 by Datapoint Corporation. It was the first LAN. It uses a token-passing access method at 2.5 Mbps with a distributed star topology for up to 255 nodes.

ARP

See *Address Resolution Protocol*.

ARPANET (Advanced Research Projects Agency NETwork)

The research network funded by DARPA (originally ARPA) and built by BBN, Inc., in 1969. It pioneered packet-switching technology and was the original backbone and test bed for the now-gigantic Internet. In 1983, the military communications part of it was split off into MILNET.

AS/400 (Application System/400)

The IBM minicomputer series introduced in 1988 that supersedes and advances the System/36 and System/38. The AS/400 serves in a variety of networking configurations: as a host or intermediate node to other AS/400s and System/3*x* machines, as a remote system to mainframe-controlled networks, and as a network server to PCs. The AS/400 offered the widest range of connectivity in an IBM introduction.

ASCII (American Standard Code for Information Interchange)

A binary code for data that is used in communications, most minicomputers, and all personal computers. ASCII is a 7-bit binary code providing 128 possible character combinations, the first 32 of which are used for printing and transmission control. Since the common storage unit is an 8-bit byte (256 combinations) and ASCII uses only 128, the extra bit is used to hold a parity bit or special symbols. For example, the PC uses the additional values for foreign-language and graphics symbols.

asynchronous protocol

A protocol that separates data into characters, with each character separated with a start and stop bit. Asynchronous communication protocols include ASCII, TTY, Kermit, and Xmodem.

asynchronous transmission

Transmission of data in which each character is a self-contained unit with its own start and stop bits. Intervals between characters may be uneven. It is the common method of transmission between a computer and a modem, although the modem may switch to synchronous transmission to communicate with the other modem. Also called start/stop transmission. See also *synchronous transmission*.

ATM (Asynchronous Transfer Mode)

A high-speed packet-switching technique suitable for MANs and Broadband ISDN transmission. Designed to send parts of a transmission over different routes as they become available. Works very well with mixed video and data transmissions. Allows up to 622 Mbps (current implementations are up to 155 Mbps).

AUTOEXEC.BAT

A DOS batch file (AUTOmatic EXECute BATch) that executes when the computer is started. For OS/2, see *STARTUP.CMD*.

B

backbone

The part of a network that handles the major traffic. It may interconnect multiple locations, and smaller networks may be attached to it. It often uses a higher-speed protocol than the LAN segments.

base address

The location in memory where the beginning of a program is stored. The relative address from the instruction in the program is added to the base address to derive the absolute address.

baseband

A communications technique in which digital signals are placed onto the transmission line without change in modulation. It is usually limited to a couple of miles and does not require the complex modems used in broadband transmissions. Common baseband LAN techniques are token-passing ring (Token Ring) and CSMA/CD (Ethernet). In baseband, the full bandwidth of the channel is used, and simultaneous transmission of multiple sets of data is accomplished by interleaving pulses using TDM (time division multiplexing). See also *broadband*; *TDM*.

baseline

Information representing the normal operation of your network, server, or other device. This can range from a feeling for how often the collision lights on your hub should be blinking to detailed data, such as the number of each type of bad packet generated by each node on the network during any given day in the last six months.

baud rate

The signaling rate of a line. It is the switching speed, or number of transitions (voltage or frequency changes) that are made per second. Only at low speeds are bauds equal to bits per second; for example, 300 baud is equal to 300 Bps. However, one baud can be made to represent more than one bit per second. For example, the V.22bis modem generates 1200 Bps at 600 baud.

BIOS (Basic Input/Output System)

A set of routines, usually in firmware, that enables each computer's central processing unit to communicate with printers, disks, keyboards, consoles, and other attached input and output devices. In the PC, it resides in ROM and contains the microcode to handle requests for I/O from both the operating system and application programs. It searches for other BIOSs on the plug-in boards and sets up pointers (interrupt vectors) in memory to access all BIOS routines during system startup. It loads the operating system and passes control to it.

B/ISDN (Broadband/ISDN)

See *ISDN*.

bisync

A major category of synchronous communication protocols used in mainframe networks. Bisync (for binary synchronous) communications require that both sending and receiving devices be synchronized before transmission of data is started.

BNC

A commonly used connector for coaxial cable. The plug looks like a cylinder with two short pins on the outer edge on opposite sides. After the plug is inserted, the socket is turned, causing the pins to tighten the plug within it.

bridge

A device that retransmits packets from one segment of the network to another segment. A bridge will forward a packet only if it is intended for the other segment. A router, on the other hand, is a device that receives instructions for forwarding packets between topologies and determines the most efficient path.

broadband

A technique for transmitting large amounts of data, voice, and video over long distances. Using high-frequency transmission over coaxial or fiber-optic cable, broadband transmission requires modems for connecting terminals and computers to the network. Using the same FDM (frequency division multiplexing) technique as cable television, several streams of data can be transmitted simultaneously. See also *baseband; FDM.*

brouter

A communications device that performs functions of both a bridge and a router. Like a bridge, the brouter functions at the OSI Data-Link level (layer 2) and remains independent of higher protocols. But like a router, it manages multiple lines and routes messages accordingly.

BTAM (Basic Telecommunications Access Method)

An IBM communications program that is used in bisync, non-SNA mainframe networks. Application programs must interface directly with BTAM.

C

cache

A reserved section of memory used to improve performance. A hardware disk cache is memory on the disk controller board. When the disk is read, a large block of data is copied into the cache. If subsequent requests for data can be satisfied in the cache, a slower disk access is not required. If the cache is used for writing, data is queued up in memory and written to the disk in larger blocks. A memory cache is an extra high-speed memory bank between memory and the CPU. Blocks of instructions and data are copied into the cache, and instruction execution and data updating are performed in the higher-speed memory.

CCITT (Consultative Committee for International Telephony and Telegraphy)

An international organization that sets telecommunications standards, including X.25, V.22, V.32, V.42, X.400, and X.500. It is one of four organs of the International Telecommunications Union, founded in 1865, headquartered in Geneva and composed of over 150 member countries.

CDEV (Control panel DEVice)

Customizable settings in the Macintosh Control Panel that pertain to a particular program or device. CDEVs for the mouse, keyboard, and startup disk, among others, come with the Mac. Others are provided with software packages and utilities.

CD-ROM (Compact Disc Read Only Memory)

A CD format used to hold text, graphics, and hi-fi stereo sound. It's like a music CD but uses a different track format for data. A music CD player cannot play CD-ROMs, but CD-ROM players usually can play music CDs and have headphone and amplifier jacks. CD-ROMs hold about 660 MB of data, which is equivalent to more than 250,000 pages of text or 20,000 medium-resolution images. Audio and data reside on separate tracks and cannot be heard and viewed together. See also *CD-ROM XA*.

CD-ROM extensions

Software required to use a CD-ROM player on a PC running DOS. It usually comes with the player and includes a driver specialized for the player and Microsoft's MSCDEX.EXE RAM resident program.

CD-ROM XA (CD-ROM eXtended Architecture)

A CD-ROM enhancement introduced in 1988 by Philips, Sony, and Microsoft that allows concurrent audio and video. It provides up to 9.5 hours of AM-quality stereo or up to 19 hours of monophonic audio. It also functions as a bridge between CD-ROM and CD-I, since CD-ROM XA discs will play on a CD-I player.

channel

The logical location of hard-disk controller hardware for the flow of data. For instance, a hard-disk controller in a PC is installed in a channel. An HBA (host bus adapter) and its disk subsystems also make up a disk channel. Available channels are usually 0 through 4. Channel 0 is normally used by internal controllers and hard disks.

checksum

A value used to ensure that data is transmitted without error. It is created by adding the binary value of each alphanumeric character in a block of data and sending it with the data. At the receiving end, a new checksum is computed and matched against the transmitted checksum. A non-match indicates an error. Just as a check digit tests the accuracy of a single number, a checksum tests a block of data. Checksums detect single-bit errors and some multiple-bit errors, but are not as effective as the CRC method.

Chooser

The Macintosh desk accessory that allows the user to select a printer, file server, or network device, such as a network modem. Found under the Apple icon.

client

A workstation accessing the network. Under NetWare, client types include DOS, Macintosh, OS/2, UNIX, and Windows. With the respective client software, users can access network drives, printers, and applications.

CMIP (Common Management Information Protocol)

The OSI protocol that defines the format for network monitoring and control information.

CMIS (Common Management Information Services)

The OSI standard functions for network monitoring and control.

CMOS RAM (Complementary Metal-Oxide Semiconductor RAM)

RAM used for storing system configuration data (such as number of drives, types of drives, and amount of memory). CMOS RAM is battery-powered to retain data while the computer is turned off. If the batteries die or are disconnected, the configuration information is lost.

CNA (Certified NetWare Administrator)

The most basic level of certification for NetWare professionals. You must successfully pass a series of tests designed to make sure you have a minimum level on knowledge of NetWare. There are many ways of preparing for the tests, including Authorized NetWare Education Centers. See also *CNE; CNEPA; ECNE.*

CNE (Certified NetWare Engineer)

The original certification for NetWare professionals. Requires more knowledge than a CNA, but less than an ECNE. You must successfully pass a series of tests on NetWare, specializing in NetWare 3.*x* or 4.*x*. There are many ways of preparing for the tests, including Authorized NetWare Education Centers. See also *CNE; CNEPA; ECNE.*

CNEPA (Certified NetWare Engineer Professional Association)

An association of NetWare professionals, limited to people who have received certification or are working toward it. A superb resource for the administrator seeking to learn more about networking and to network with other NetWare professionals. See also *CNA; CNE; ECNE.*

coaxial cable

High-capacity cable used in communications and video, commonly called *coax*. It contains an insulated solid or stranded wire that is surrounded by a solid or braided metallic shield, which is wrapped in an external cover. Fire-safe Teflon coating is optional. There are several types of coaxial cable, each designed with a different width and impedance for a particular purpose (television, baseband, or broadband). Coax provides a much higher bandwidth than twisted-pair wire.

COM ports

Asynchronous serial ports on IBM PC-compatible computers. DOS versions 3.3 and above support up to four COM ports, and OS/2 supports eight.

COMSPEC

A DOS environment variable, set in CONFIG.SYS, that specifies the path to COMMAND.COM and the environment space allotted.

concentrator

A device that joins several communications channels together. The central unit that ties a star topology together. See also *hub*.

CONFIG.SYS

A DOS and OS/2 configuration file that is examined upon startup. It resides in the root directory and is primarily used to load drivers for peripherals that have been added to the system.

connection number

A number assigned to any workstation that attaches to a NetWare server; it may be a different number each time a station attaches. Connection numbers are also assigned to processes, print servers, and applications that use server connections.

connectionless

A protocol in which the source and destination addresses are included within each packet so that a direct connection or established session between nodes is not required. See also *connection-oriented*.

connection-oriented

A protocol that requires a direct connection or established session between two nodes before communication takes place. See also *connectionless*.

container object

NetWare 4.*x* represents all parts of your network with objects. The container object is a logical grouping of network resources. Containers can hold other containers or network resources (leaf objects) such as servers, disk drives, printers, and users. See also *leaf object; Organization; Organizational Unit; NDS tree.*

contention

A condition that arises when two devices attempt to use a single resource at the same time. See also *CSMA/CD.*

Control Panel

Software that changes the computer's environment settings, such as keyboard and mouse sensitivity, sounds, colors, communications, and printer access. It is a desk accessory in the Macintosh and a utility program in Windows.

CRC (cyclic redundancy check)

A numeric value derived from the bits in a message. The transmitting station uses a formula to produce a number that is attached to the message. The receiving station applies the same formula and should derive the same number. If the numbers are not the same, the receiving station signals an error.

CSMA/CD (Carrier Sense Multiple Access/Collision Detection)

A baseband communications access method that uses a collision-detection technique. When a device wants to gain access to the network, it checks to see if the network is free. If it is not, it waits a random amount of time before retrying. If the network is free and two devices attempt access at exactly the same time, they both back off to avoid a collision, and each waits a random amount of time before retrying. Typical of Ethernet.

daemon

A program that waits in the background ready to perform some action when a certain event occurs. Used in OS/2 and UNIX.

DARPA (Defense Advanced Research Projects Agency)

See *ARPANET*.

DAT (digital audio tape)

A magnetic medium suitable for mass storage of digital data. The most common format is a 4mm, helical-scan DAT drive that holds 1.3 GB or more, with extended-length tapes or compression, up to 8 GB.

data fork

The part of a Macintosh file that contains data. For example, in a HyperCard file text, graphics and HyperTalk scripts reside in the data fork, while fonts, sounds, control information, and external functions reside in the resource fork.

datagram

A TCP/IP message unit that contains Internet source and destination addresses and data.

data-link protocol

The protocol that controls the transmission of a unit of data from one node to another (OSI layer 2). It ensures that the bits received are the same as the bits sent.

DCB

See *disk coprocessor board*.

DCE (Data Communications Equipment; Data Circuit-terminating Equipment)

A device that establishes, maintains, and terminates a session on a network. It may also convert signals for transmission. Typically, a modem. See also *DTE*.

DCE (Distributed Computing Environment)

See *OSF*.

desk accessory

On the Macintosh, a program that is always available from the Apple menu no matter what application is running. With System 7, all applications can be turned into desk accessories.

device driver

Software that forms the interface between the operating system and devices such as hard disks or network boards. See also *disk driver*; *LAN driver*.

device numbering

A method of identifying a device, such as a hard disk, to allow the device to work on the network. Devices are identified by three numbers:

- **Physical address:** Set with jumpers on the boards, controllers, and hard disks. The physical address is determined by the driver, based on those jumper settings.

- **Device code:** Determined by the physical address of the board, controller, and hard disk. In the device code #00101, the first two digits (00) are reserved for the disk type. The third digit (1) is the board number; the fourth (0), the controller number; and the fifth (1), the disk number.

- **Logical number:** Determined by the order in which the disk drivers are loaded and by the physical address of the controller and hard disk.

All physical partitions are assigned logical partition numbers. These numbers are assigned to both the mirrored disks and the DOS partition. Mirroring messages use the logical partition number to record which hard disks are being remirrored or unmirrored.

digital

Signals that carry information that is broken down into yes/no pulses, as in a LAN connection or a CD. See also *analog*.

directory table

A table that contains basic information about files, directories, directory trustees, or other entities on the volume. The directory table occupies one or more directory blocks on the volume. Each block is 4 KB. A directory entry is 32 bytes long, so each block can hold 128 directory entries. Volume SYS: starts out with seven blocks for its directory table and allocates more blocks as necessary. The maximum number of directory blocks per volume is 65,536. Since each block can accommodate 32 entries, the maximum directory table entries per volume is 2,097,152.

disk driver

The software that forms the interface between the operating system and the hard disks. The disk driver talks to an adapter that is connected to the disk drives.

disk duplexing

A data-protection technique that consists of duplicating data on two hard disks, each on a separate disk channel and with a separate power supply. This protects data against the failure of a hard disk or the channel between the disk and the server. The hard disk channel includes the disk controller and cable. If any component on one channel fails, the other disk can continue to operate without data loss or interruption. See also *disk mirroring*.

disk mirroring

A data-protection technique that uses two or more hard disks on the same channel that hold the same data. Blocks of data written to the original (primary) disk are also written to the duplicate (secondary) disk. The disks are constantly storing and updating the same files. Should one of the disks fail, the other disk can continue to operate without data loss or interruption. See also *disk duplexing*.

disk partition

A logical unit for dividing hard disks. A PC may have more than one partition; for example, one or more DOS partitions or other partitions such as OS/2 or UnixWare.

DMA (direct memory access)

Specialized circuitry or a dedicated microprocessor that transfers data from one place in memory to another without using the CPU. Although DMA may periodically steal cycles from the CPU, data is transferred much faster than using the CPU for every byte of transfer.

DME (Distributed Management Environment)

See *OSF*.

DNS (Domain Naming System)

An electronic-mail addressing system used in networks such as the Internet and BITNET.

DOS boot record

A record containing information that the BIOS uses to determine which device to boot from. The boot record can be on a floppy diskette, a local hard disk, or a remote boot chip. The BIOS determines from the boot record the disk format and location of system files and directories. The BIOS then loads the system files and COMMAND.COM.

DQDB (Distributed Queue Dual Bus)

A proposed IEEE standard (802.6) for MANs. It uses multiple channels to achieve very high speeds—from hundreds of Mbps to 1 Gbps. It is also designed to provide service over a greater area than is possible with FDDI, which is limited to about 60 miles.

DS (Digital Signal)

Digital signal speed measurements, as follows:

DS-0	64 Kbps
DS-1	1.544 Mbps (T-1)
DS-1C	3.152 Mbps
DS-2	6.312 Mbps (T-2)
DS-3	44.736 Mbps (T-3)
DS-4	274.176 Mbps (T-4)

DSR (Data Set Ready)

The RS-232 signal sent from the modem to the computer or terminal indicating that it is able to accept data. See also *DTR*.

DSU/CSU (data service unit/channel service unit)

A communications device that connects an in-house line to an external digital circuit (T-1, T-3, or DDS). The DSU converts data into the required format; the CSU terminates the line and provides signal regeneration and remote testing.

DTE (Data Terminating Equipment)

A communications device that is the source or destination of signals on a network. It is typically a terminal or computer. See also *DCE*.

DTR (Data Terminal Ready)

The RS-232 signal sent from the computer or terminal to the modem indicating that it is able to accept data. See also *DSR*.

E

ECNE (Enterprise Certified NetWare Engineer)

Currently the most advanced level of certification for NetWare professionals. You must successfully pass a series of tests designed to make sure you have a respectable knowledge of NetWare and wide-area networking. There are many ways of preparing for the tests, including Authorized NetWare Education Centers. See also *CNA; CNE; CNEPA*.

EISA (Extended Industry Standard Architecture)

A PC bus standard that extends the AT bus to 32 bits and allows bus mastering.

Embedded SCSI

A hard disk that has a SCSI and a hard disk controller built into the hard disk unit.

encapsulation

In communications, a technique for inserting the frame header and data from a higher-level protocol into the data frame of a lower-level protocol.

ESDI (Enhanced Small Device Interface)

A hard disk interface that typically transfers data in the 1 to 3 MB per second range.

Ethernet configuration

The setup that allows communication using an Ethernet environment. In an Ethernet environment, stations communicate with each other by sending data in frames along an Ethernet cabling system. Different Ethernet standards use different frame formats. NetWare 4.*x* uses the IEEE 802.2 standard by default. In addition to 802.2, you can use one of the following frame types:

- **Ethernet 802.3:** The default frame type used in NetWare 3.11 and earlier. This frame type is also referred to as the raw frame.

- **Ethernet II:** The frame type used on networks that communicate with DEC minicomputers, and on computers that use TCP/IP or AppleTalk Phase I.

- **Ethernet SNAP:** The IEEE standard 802.2 frame type with an extension (SNAP) added to the header. Use this frame on networks that communicate with workstations that use protocols such as AppleTalk Phase II.

Using Novell's ODI technology, NetWare allows stations with different Ethernet frame types to coexist on the same Ethernet cabling system.

EtherTalk

The AppleTalk implementation that runs over Ethernet. See also *AppleTalk protocols*.

fake root

A subdirectory that functions as a root directory. NetWare allows you to map a drive to a fake root (a directory where rights can be assigned to users). Some applications cannot be run from subdirectories; they read files from and write files to the root directory. However, for security, do not assign users rights at the root or volume directory level. Instead, load the files in a subdirectory and designate it as a fake root directory in the login script. Fake roots do not exist for OS/2 clients. Under OS/2, all mapped drives are roots, and search drives don't exist.

fast Ethernet

There are two main types of fast Ethernet: 100BaseTX and 100VGAnyLan. 100BaseTX uses standard twisted-pair wiring (although it must be Category 5) and the same CSMA/CD protocol as 10BaseT Ethernet. It requires new network adapters and concentrators. 100VG uses all four pairs of wires in twisted-pair cabling, also requires new network adapters and concentrators, and uses a different protocol known as demand-priority access.

FAT (file allocation table)

An index table that points to the disk areas where a file is located. Because one file may be in any number of blocks spread over the disk, the FAT links the file together. In NetWare, the FAT is accessed from the directory entry table (DET). The FAT is cached in server memory, allowing the server to access the data quickly.

fault tolerance

A means of protecting data by providing data duplication on multiple storage devices. See also *System Fault Tolerance (SFT)*.

FCC Class

The FCC certification of radiation limits on digital devices. Class A certification is for business use. Class B for residential use is more stringent in order to avoid interference with television and other home reception.

FDDI (Fiber-optic Data Distribution Interface)

An ANSI standard for fiber-optic LANs. It deals with OSI layers 1 and 2 and transmits at 100 Mbps.

FDM (frequency division multiplexing)

A method used to transmit multiple signals over a single channel. Each signal (data, voice, etc.) is modulated onto a carrier of a different frequency, and all signals travel simultaneously over the channel. See also *baseband, TDM.*

fiber channel

A future ANSI standard under development for a high-speed computer channel that incorporates IPI, SCSI, and HiPPI command sets. Speeds range from 12.5 to 100 MB per second using coaxial and fiber-optic cable.

file allocation table

See *FAT.*

file locking

The means of ensuring that a file is updated correctly before another user, application, or process can access the file. For example, without file locking, if two users attempt to update the same word processing file simultaneously, one user could overwrite the file update of the other user.

Finder

The part of the Macintosh operating system that manages the desktop. It keeps track of icons, controls the Clipboard and Scrapbook, and allows files to be copied. Finder manages one application at a time. MultiFinder manages multiple applications.

FOIRL (Fiber Optic Inter Repeater Link)

The IEEE standard for fiber-optic Ethernet.

Fractional T-1

The division of a T-1 channel into subchannels that provide between 64 and 768 Kbps. See also *T-carrier*.

frame

A packet data format for a given media. Some media support multiple packet formats, such as Ethernet 802.2, Ethernet 802.3, Ethernet II, Ethernet SNAP, Token Ring, or Token Ring SNAP.

Frame Relay

A high-speed packet switching protocol similar to X.25 in that it provides access to a public network (the "cloud" shown in many illustrations), but at speeds from 64 Kbps (fractional T-1) to 45 Mbps (T-3).

FTAM (File Transfer Access and Management)

A communication protocol for the transfer of files between systems of different vendors.

FTP (File Transfer Protocol)

The TCP/IP protocol that is used to log on to the network, list directories, and copy files. It can also translate between ASCII and EBCDIC.

G

gateway

A link between two networks. A gateway allows communication between dissimilar protocols (for example, NetWare and UNIX networks) using industry-standard protocols such as TCP/IP, X.25, or SNA. See also *bridge*; *brouter*; *router*.

GOSIP (Government Open Systems Interconnection Profile)

The government mandate that after 8/15/90 all new network procurements must comply with OSI. Testing is performed at the NIST, which maintains a database of OSI-compliant commercial products. (TCP/IP protocols can also still be used.)

GVPN (Global Virtual Private Network)

A service from cooperating carriers that provides international digital communications for multinational companies.

H

handle

A pointer used by a computer to identify a resource or feature. For example, a directory handle identifies a volume and a directory, such as SYS:PUBLIC. Other types of handles used to access NetWare include file handles, video handles, request handles, device handles, and volume handles.

handshaking

The initial exchange between two data communication systems prior to and during data transmission to ensure proper data transmission. A handshake method (such as XON/XOFF) is part of the complete transmission protocol.

HBA

See *host bus adapter*.

HCSS

See *High-Capacity Storage System*.

HDLC (High-level Data-Link Control)

An ISO communications protocol used in X.25 packet-switching networks. It provides error correction at the Data-Link layer. SDLC, LAP, and LAPB are subsets of HDLC.

header

The first part of a packet that contains controlling data, such as originating and destination stations, message type, and priority level.

hexadecimal

A base-16 alphanumeric numbering system used to specify addresses in computer memory. In hexadecimal notation, the decimal numbers 0 through 15 are represented by the decimal digits 0 through 9 and the alphabetic digits A through F (A = decimal 10, B = decimal 11, etc.).

HFS (Hierarchical File System)

The Macintosh file system that currently supports NetWare volume sizes up to 2 GB.

High Capacity Storage System (HCSS)

In NetWare 4.*x*, the system that supports optical storage. It allows migration of files that have not been used for a while to the slower optical media, and also allows transparent access when the files are requested.

HIMEM.SYS

An XMS driver from Microsoft that allows programs to cooperatively use extended memory in 286 and higher machines. It also manages the HMA (high memory area), the 64 KB block of memory just above 1 MB.

hop count

The number of network boards a message packet passes through on the way to its destination on an internetwork. The destination network can be no more than 16 hops (NetWare servers or routers) from the source.

host

The mainframe computer in a distributed processing environment. It typically refers to a large, time-sharing computer or a central computer that controls a network.

host bus adapter (HBA)

A special-purpose board that relieves the host microprocessor of data storage and retrieval tasks, usually improving the computer's performance time. An HBA and its disk subsystems make up a disk channel.

Hot Fix

A method NetWare uses to ensure that data is stored safely. Data blocks are re-directed from faulty blocks on the server's disk to a small portion of disk space set aside as the Hot Fix redirection area. Once the operating system records the address of the defective block in a section of the Hot Fix area reserved for that purpose, the server will not attempt to store data in defective blocks.

HPFS (High Performance File System)

The file system introduced with OS/2 version 1.2 that handles larger disks (2 TB volumes and 2 GB files) and long filenames (256 bytes).

hub

A device that modifies transmission signals, allowing the network to be lengthened or expanded with additional workstations. There are two kinds of hubs:

- **Active hub:** Amplifies transmission signals in network topologies to allow additional workstations on a network or to extend the cable distance between stations and the server.

- **Passive hub:** In certain network topologies, splits a transmission signal, allowing additional workstations to be added. A passive hub can't amplify the signal, so it must be cabled directly to a station or to an active hub.

I

IDE (Integrated Drive Electronics)

A hard disk and built-in controller. IDE-ready motherboards have a 40-pin socket that connects directly to an IDE drive, eliminating the use of an expansion slot.

IEC (International Electrotechnical Commission)

The organization that sets electrical and electronics standards. IEC, founded in 1906 and headquartered in Geneva, is made up of national committees from more than 40 countries.

IEEE (Institute of Electrical and Electronic Engineers)

The membership organization that includes engineers, scientists, and students in electronics and allied fields. It has more than 300,000 members and is involved with setting standards for computers and communications. The Computer Society of the IEEE has over 100,000 members and holds meetings and technical conferences on computers.

- 802.1: Covers network management and other aspects related to LANs. The IEEE standard for LANs.

- 802.2: Specifies the Data-Link layer for the following access methods.

- 802.3: Specifies CSMA/CD, popularized by Ethernet.

- 802.4: Specifies a token-passing bus.

- 802.5: Specifies a token-passing ring, popularized by IBM's Token Ring.

Init

A Macintosh program that is run when the computer is started (Init for Initiate). Used to load and activate drivers and system routines. Many Inits are memory resident and may conflict with each other, similar to TSRs in the PC environment.

The Internet

The huge network of military, business, and university computers that stretches around the world and reaches millions of people. The Internet is based on the TCP/IP protocol. See also *ARPANET*.

internetwork

Two or more networks connected by a router. Users on an internetwork can access the resources (such as files, printers, and hard disks) of all connected networks, provided they have the appropriate rights.

InterNIC

The authority responsible for assigning TCP/IP address ranges. This organization has the primary responsibility for the organization of the Internet.

IPX (Internetwork Packet eXchange)

The NetWare communication protocol used to route messages from one node to another. Application programs that manage their own client/server or peer-to-peer communications in a Novell network can access IPX, or NetWare's SPX protocol, directly. Unlike SPX, IPX does not guarantee delivery of a message.

IPX external network number

A network number that uniquely identifies a network cable segment. An IPX external network number is a hexadecimal number from one to eight digits in length (1 to FFFFFFFE). The number is assigned when the IPX protocol is bound to a network board in the server.

IPX internal network number

A logical network number that identifies an individual NetWare server. Each server on a network must have a unique IPX internal network number. The internal network number is a hexadecimal number from one to eight digits in length (1 to FFFFFFFE). The number is assigned to the server during installation.

IPX internetwork address

A 12-byte number (represented by 24 hexadecimal characters) divided into three parts. The first part is the 4-byte (8-character) IPX external network number, the second is the 6-byte (12-character) node number, and the third is the 2-byte (4-character) socket number.

IPXODI (Internetwork Packet eXchange Open Data-link Interface)

A module that takes workstation requests that the DOS Requester has determined are for the network, packages them with transmission information (such as their destination), and hands them to the LSL. IPXODI attaches a header to each data packet. The header specifies information that targets network delivery, announcing where the packet came from, where it's going, and what happens after delivery. Because IPXODI transmits data packets as datagrams (self-contained packages that move independently from source to destination), it can only deliver the packets on a best-effort basis. Delivery is assured by SPX.

IRQ (interrupt)

An interrupt used by the operating system to communicate with a physical device. This device can be a hard disk adapter, an NIC, a mouse, or any other type of device connected to a PC. The problem with interrupts arises from the fact that there are a limited number of interrupts, and there may be more devices that there are interrupts to go around (especially with servers). If two devices use the same interrupt, they may cause the PC to freeze, or they may just interfere with each other.

ISA (Industry Standard Architecture)

The original PC bus architecture, specifically the 16-bit AT bus. See also *EISA; Micro Channel; PCI.*

ISDN (Integrated Services Digital Network)

The international telecommunications standard for transmitting voice, video, and data over a digital communications line. It uses out-of-band signaling, which provides a separate channel for control information. ISDN services come in two forms: Basic Rate Interface (BRI) and Primary Rate Interface (PRI). BRI provides 144 Kbps service, which includes two 64 Kbps B channels for voice, data, or video, and one 16 Kbps D channel for control information. (You might think this is really only 128 Kbps, but regular modems must use part of their bandwidth for control information.) PRI provides 1.54 Mbps, allowing 23 64 Kbps B channels and one 64 Kbps D channel. ISDN's 64 Kbps transmission rate provides a big boost for PCs communicating via modem, even compared to high-speed modems communicating at 9600 or 19,200 Bps, but it does not provide a viable alternative for interconnecting LANs transmitting in the 10+ Mbps range. Broadband ISDN (B/ISDN) should begin to be available in the near future. It utilizes broadband transmission and fiber-optic cables to jump transmission speed to 150 Mbps.

ISO (International Standards Organization)

Founded in 1946 and headquartered in Geneva, this organization deals with all fields except electrical and electronics standards, which are governed by the older International Electrotechnical Commission (IEC). With regard to information processing, ISO and IEC created JTC1, the Joint Technical Committee for information technology. It carries out its work through more than 160 technical committees and 2300 subcommittees and working groups and is made up of standards organizations from more than 75 countries, some of them serving as secretariats for these technical bodies. ANSI is the U.S. member body.

L

LAN (local-area network)

A network located within a small area or common environment, such as in a building or a building complex. A LAN has only one network address.

Large Internet Packet (LIP)

A NetWare feature that allows the internetwork packet size limit to be increased from the default 576 bytes. By allowing the NetWare packet size to be increased, LIP enhances the throughput over bridges and routers.

leaf object

NetWare 4.*x* represents all the parts of your network with objects. Leaf objects are network resources such as servers, disk drives, printers, and users. Leaf objects are organized into containers. See also *container object; Organization; Organizational Unit; NDS tree.*

Link Support Layer (LSL)

An implementation of the ODI specification that serves as an intermediary between the NetWare server's LAN drivers and communication protocols, such as IPX, AFP, or TCP/IP. The LSL allows network boards to service one or more protocol stacks.

local-area network

See *LAN*.

LocalTalk

A LAN access method from Apple Computer, Inc., that uses twisted-pair wires and transmits at 230,400 Bps. Third-party products allow it to hook up with bus, passive star, and active star topologies.

login script

A file that contains commands to be executed initially when a user logs in to the network. There are three login scripts in NetWare 4.*x*: the default login script, the container login script, and the user login script. The default login script will execute if no container or user login script exists. The container login script executes next, and should contain commands that are necessary to set up all users. The user's login script executes last, and it contains the commands that configure the user's environment. There is another login script for groups (called the profile login script), which takes the place of the IF MEMBER OF construction in the system login script under previous versions. This is necessary because groups are global in a network and can be accessed by members from any server.

LPT1

The first parallel printer port of a personal computer. Refers to the hardware device. The DOS device is called PRN which is sometimes confused with the first parallel port.

LSL

See *Link Support Layer*.

Macintosh file

A Macintosh file contains two parts, the data fork and the resource fork:

- The *data fork* contains data specified by the user.

- The *resource fork* contains file resources, such as the windows, icons or fonts used with the file.

When a Macintosh client accesses the file stored on the server, it accesses both the data and resource forks. When a non-Macintosh client accesses the file, only the data fork is used.

MAN (metropolitan-area network)

A communications network that covers a geographic area such as a city or suburb. See also *LAN*; *WAN*.

MAU (Multi-Station Access Unit)

The central hub in a Token Ring LAN. Also MSAU.

MFM (Modified Frequency Modulation)

A magnetic disk encoding method used on floppy disks and most hard disks under 40 MB.

MHS (Message Handling Service)

An electronic-mail system from Action Technologies, Inc., licensed by Novell for its NetWare operating systems. It allows for the transfer and routing of messages between users and provides storage and forwarding capabilities. It also provides gateways into PROFS, All-in-1, X.400, and other message systems.

Micro Channel

The IBM bus architecture used in high-end PS/2 models, the RS/6000 series, and certain ES/9370 models. It is a 32-bit bus that provides bus mastering. It transfers data at 20 MB per second and has modes for increasing speeds to 40 and 80 MB per second.

MLID

See *Multiple Layer Interface Driver*.

MPC (Multimedia PC) I (1990)

The specification of minimum requirements for a multimedia PC:

- 10 MHz 286 CPU
- VGA display
- 2 MB RAM
- 30 MB hard disk
- Two-button mouse
- CD-ROM with CD-ROM extensions 2.2
- Audio board with 8-bit linear PCM sampling, music synthesizer, and analog mixing capabilities
- Serial, parallel, MIDI, and joystick ports
- DOS 3.1 or later, Windows 3.0 or later, with multimedia extensions

MPC (Multimedia PC) 2 (1993)

The second-generation specification of minimum requirements for a multimedia PC:

- 486SX/25 CPU

- VGA display (64,000 colors at 640x480)

- 4 MB RAM

- 160 MB hard disk

- Two-button mouse

- 2x CD-ROM

- 16-bit audio board that can record and play back CD-quality stereo sound, digital audio, and .WAV and MIDI files.

- Serial, parallel, MIDI, and joystick ports

- DOS 3.3 or later, Windows 3.1 or later, with multimedia extensions

MPC (Multimedia PC) 3

The third-generation specification of minimum requirements for a multimedia PC:

- Pentium 75 MHz CPU

- VGA display 64,000 colors at 640x480

- 8 MB RAM

- 540 MB hard disk

- Two-button mouse

- 4x CD-ROM compatible with XA and multisession PhotoCD standards

- 16-bit audio board that can record and play back CD-quality stereo sound, digital audio, WAV and MIDI files, and wave table synthesis

- Serial, parallel, MIDI, and joystick ports

MPC 3 systems are not required to support video capture, but their graphics accelerators must be capable of YUV color-space conversion and X and Y scaling. They also must comply with the DirectDraw 2.0 specification. Support for MPEG-1 full-screen video playback is also required.

multiple-byte character

A single character made up of more than one byte. One byte allows 256 different characters. Since the number of ASCII characters equals 256, a computer can handle any ASCII character with one byte. However, other character sets, such as Japanese or Arabic, include more than 256 characters; for this reason, a computer must use two bytes for each character in some character sets.

Multiple Layer Interface Driver (MLID)

A device driver written to the ODI specification that handles the sending and receiving of packets to and from a physical or logical LAN medium.

multiplexing

The method for transmitting multiple signals over a single communications line or computer channel. The two common multiplexing techniques are FDM, which separates signals by modulating the data onto different carrier frequencies, and TDM, which separates signals by interleaving bits one after the other.

multiplexer (MUX)

A device that merges several low-speed transmissions into one high-speed transmission and vice versa. Useful for combining several low-speed channels to create one useful WAN link.

N

name space

A special NLM that allows you to store non-DOS files on a NetWare server. Files appear as they would on the workstation. File types such as Macintosh or

OS/2 must have a name space NLM linked with the operating system before the NetWare server can store such files. Name-space NLMs have an NAM extension. When name space support is added to a volume, another entry is created in the directory table for the directory and file-naming conventions of that name space.

NBP (Name Binding Protocol)

See *AppleTalk protocols.*

NCB (Network Control Block)

The packet structure used by the NetBIOS transport protocol.

NCP

See *NetWare Core Protocol.*

NDIS (Network Driver Interface Specification)

See *ODINSUP.*

NDS tree

The major new feature of NetWare 4.*x* is the NetWare Directory Services (NDS) structure. It allows a large organization's network to be organized logically rather than by server. The NDS tree contains many objects, beginning with Organizations, then Organizational Units, then leaf objects for network resources (such as server disks or printers). See also *container object; leaf object; Organization; Organizational Unit.*

NetBEUI (NetBIOS Extended User Interface)

The implementation of the NetBIOS transport protocol used by LAN Manager, LAN Server, Windows for Workgroups, Windows 95, and Windows NT. It communicates to the network adapter via NDIS.

NETBIOS.EXE

NetWare's NetBIOS emulator program that allows workstations to run applications written for peer-to-peer communication or distributed processing on IBM's PC Network or MS-Net and LAN Manager. The INT2F.COM file is used with NETBIOS.EXE.

NET.CFG

A workstation boot file, similar to CONFIG.SYS, that contains configuration values for the network shell that are read and interpreted when the workstation boots. These configuration values control the operating parameters of the NetWare DOS Requester, IPX, and other workstation software. Also called *SHELL.CFG*.

NetView

IBM's SNA network management software that provides centralized monitoring and control for SNA, non-SNA, and non-IBM devices. NetView/PC interconnects NetView with Token Ring LANs, Rolm CBXs, and non-IBM modems, while maintaining control in the host.

NetWare Core Protocol (NCP)

Procedures that NetWare follows to accept and respond to workstation requests. NCPs exist for every service a station might request from a server. Common requests handled by an NCP include creating or destroying a service connection, manipulating directories and files, opening semaphores, altering the Directory, and printing.

NetWare Express

Novell's private electronic information service that provides access to Novell's Network Support Encyclopedia. NetWare Express uses the GE Information Services network and software and requires a connection through an asynchronous modem.

NetWare Management Agents

A group of NLMs that bring together software, hardware, and data components of a NetWare server and an external network management software package. When NetWare Management Agents are loaded, they create a hierarchical representation of all managed objects and their attributes.

NetWare protocols

NetWare 4.x has six layers of communication between an application and the hardware in the computer. These layers are based on the OSI model. The following are the six communication layers:

- Application

- Service Protocol

- Communication Protocol

- Link Support

- Driver

- Hardware

In the server, communication protocols allow the Service Protocol Layer to communicate with the Link Support Layer (LSL). IPX, part of the operating system, is the default communication protocol. You can use more than one protocol on the same cabling scheme because the LSL, part of ODI, allows the LAN driver for a network board to service more than one protocol.

NetWare Requester for OS/2

Software that connects OS/2 workstations to NetWare networks, allowing OS/2 users to share network resources. The NetWare Requester directs network requests from the workstation to the network and allows application servers (such as SQL Server) and their workstations to communicate on the network without using a NetWare server. DOS and OS/2 users can access data on OS/2 application servers without using a NetWare server.

NetWare Runtime

A single-user version of NetWare. It supports front-end or back-end applications as well as basic NLM services, such as communication services, database servers, electronic mail, and other third-party applications.

NetWire

Novell's online information service, which provides access to Novell product information, Novell services information, and time-sensitive technical information for NetWare users. NetWire is accessed through the CompuServe Information Service. It requires a modem and a communications program.

Network Driver Interface Specification (NDIS)

See *ODINSUP*.

network interface card (NIC)

A board installed in each workstation to allow stations to communicate with each other and with the NetWare server. NetWare documentation uses the term *network board* instead of *network interface card*.

network node

A device connected to a network by a network board and a communication medium. A network node can be a server, workstation, router, printer, or fax machine.

Network Support Encyclopedia (NSE)

Novell's electronic information database containing comprehensive information about network technology. The NSE includes NetWare patches, fixes, drivers, and utilities as well as Novell technical bulletins and manuals. NSE contains *NetWare Application Notes* (with graphics), the *NetWare Buyer's Guide*, Novell press releases, and additional product information. The NSE also includes Novell Labs' hardware and software compatibility test results. The NSE is available as a CD-ROM subscription or through NetWare Express.

NETX

The shell for NetWare 2.*x* and 3.*x* network clients. In NetWare 4.*x*, a VLM (NETX.VLM) under the NetWare DOS Requester that provides backward compatibility with NETX and other older versions of the shell.

NFS (Network File System)

The distributed file system from Sun that allows data to be shared with many users in a network regardless of processor type, operating system, network architecture, or protocol.

NIC

See *network interface card*.

NIST (National Institute of Standards and Technology)

The standards-defining agency of the U.S. government, formerly called the National Bureau of Standards.

NLM (NetWare Loadable Module)

An NLM is a program that adds functionality to NetWare. NLMs can be loaded and unloaded while NetWare is running. Typical NLMs are of the following four types:

- Disk drivers to allow the use of different types of disk drives (*.DSK).

- LAN drivers for running different protocols on various LAN adapters (*.LAN).

- Name space modules to allow operating systems other than DOS to access and store files on the server. These include modules for Macintosh, NFS (UNIX), and OS/2 (*.NAM).

- Management utilities and server applications, such as MONITOR, INSTALL, and UPS. These allow you to configure and manage the server or add functionality (*.NLM).

NMI (non-maskable interrupt)

A high-priority interrupt that cannot be disabled by another interrupt. It is used to report malfunctions such as parity, bus, and math coprocessor errors.

node number

A number that uniquely identifies a network board. Every node must have at least one network board, by which the node is connected to the network. Each network board must have a unique node number to distinguish it from all other network boards on that network. Node numbers are assigned in several ways, depending on the network board type:

- Ethernet boards are factory set. (No two Ethernet boards have the same number.)

- ARCnet and Token Ring board numbers are set with jumpers or switches.

NOS (network operating system)

A system designed to support multiple users. Common examples are NetWare, Windows NT, OS/2 server, and UNIX. It is interesting to note that of these examples, only NetWare is dedicated to being a server. The others can also be used as clients or stand-alone workstations.

NSE

See *Network Support Encyclopedia*.

NuBus

A 32-bit bus architecture originally developed at MIT. Rights to the bus were purchased by Western Digital and TI. Apple licenses it from TI and has changed its electrical and physical specifications for the Macintosh.

NUI (NetWare Users International)

NetWare user groups.

ODI (Open Data-link Interface)

An architecture that allows multiple LAN drivers and protocols to coexist on network systems. The ODI specification describes the set of interface and software modules used to decouple device drivers from protocol stacks and to enable multiple protocol stacks to share the network hardware and media transparently. The following are the major components of the ODI architecture:

- **Multiple Layer Interface Driver (MLID):** A device driver written to the ODI specification that handles the sending and receiving of packets to and from a physical or logical LAN medium. Each driver is unique due to the adapter hardware and media, but ODI eliminates the need to write separate drivers for each protocol stack. ODI allows LAN drivers to function with protocol stacks independent of the media frame type and protocol stack details. MLIDs interface with a network board and handle the appending and stripping of media frame headers. They also help de-multiplex the incoming packets by determining their frame format.

- **Link Support Layer (LSL):** A software module that implements the interface between drivers and protocol stacks. It essentially acts like a switchboard, directing packets between the drivers and protocol stacks. Any ODI LAN driver can communicate with any ODI protocol stack through the LSL. The LSL handles the communication between protocol stacks and MLIDs.

- **Media Support Module (MSM):** A module that standardizes and manages primary details of interfacing ODI MLIDs to the LSL and operating system. The MSM handles generic initialization and run-time issues common to all drivers.

- **Topology-Specific Module (TSM):** A module that manages operations unique to a specific media type, such as Ethernet or Token Ring. Multiple frame support is implemented in the TSM so that all frame types for a given media type are supported.

- **Hardware-Specific Module (HSM):** A module created for a specific network board. The HSM handles all hardware interactions. Its primary functions include adapter initialization, reset, shutdown, and removal. It also handles packet reception and transmission. Additional procedures may also provide support for timeout detection, multicast addressing, and promiscuous mode reception.

ODINSUP (Open Data-link Interface/Network driver interface specification SUPport)

An interface that allows the coexistence of two network driver interfaces: the Network Driver Interface Specification (NDIS) and the ODI specification. ODINSUP allows you to connect to dissimilar networks from your workstation and use them as if they were one network. ODINSUP also allows NDIS protocol stacks to communicate through the ODI's LSL and MLID. This way, NDIS and ODI protocol stacks can coexist in the same system, making use of a single ODI MLID.

Open Data-link Interface

See *ODI.*

optical disk

A form of removable media used to store data. An optical disk can be one- or two-sided. Some optical disks are read-only; others can be written to as well.

Organization

The first level of organization in the NDS tree. Your network may have several Organizations, each with Organizational Units, each with leaf objects, which represent the actual network resources such as printers and server disks. See also *container object; leaf object; Organizational Unit; NDS tree.*

Organizational Unit

NetWare 4.*x* represents all the parts of your network with objects. The Organizational Unit is a logical group under an Organization object. See also *container object; leaf object; Organization; NDS tree.*

OSF (Open Software Foundation)

A nonprofit organization dedicated to delivering an open computing environment based on standards. Formed in 1988, it solicits contributions from industry and invites member participation to set technical direction. The following are the major OSF standards:

- The OSF/1 operating system uses Carnegie-Mellon's Mach kernel. It is a B1-secure, symmetric multiprocessing operating system that can run on multiple processors within the same machine. It is compliant with POSIX, XPG3, and SVID base and kernel extensions.

- Motif is a graphical user interface similar to Presentation Manager for applications running on any system with X Windows version 11. It is compliant with POSIX, ANSI C, and XPG3.

- Distributed Computing Environment (DCE) is a set of integrated programs that provides an environment for creating, using, and maintaining client/server applications on a network. It includes security, directory naming, time synchronization, file sharing, RPCs, and multithreading services.

- Distributed Management Environment (DME) is a set of integrated programs that provides coherent management of systems and networks.

- Architecture Neutral Distributed Format (ANDF) supports developing portable applications by generating an intermediate language executed by an interpreter in the target machine. It allows shrink-wrapped software to be developed for UNIX.

OSI (Open System Interconnection) Model

The ISO standard for communications that defines a framework for implementing protocols in seven layers:

- Application

- Presentation

- Session

- Transport

- Network

- Data-Link

- Physical

Control is passed from one layer to the next, starting at the Application layer in one station, proceeding to the bottom layer, over the channel to the next station and back up the hierarchy. Similar functionality exists in all communications networks, although layers may not correspond exactly. Most vendors have agreed to support OSI in one form or another.

P

packet

A unit of information used in network communication. Messages sent between network devices are formed into packets at the source device. The packets are reassembled, if necessary, into complete messages when they reach their destination.

Packet Burst Protocol

A protocol built on top of IPX that speeds the transfer of multiple-packet NCP (NetWare Core Protocol) file reads and writes. The Packet Burst Protocol speeds the transfer of NCP data between a workstation and a NetWare server by eliminating the need to sequence and acknowledge each packet. Packet Burst Protocol is more efficient than the one-request/one-response protocol in NetWare versions prior to 3.11/4.0. With Packet Burst Protocol, the server or workstation can send a whole set (burst) of packets before it requires an acknowledgment. By allowing multiple packets to be acknowledged, Packet Burst Protocol reduces network traffic.

packet switching

A technique for handling high-volume traffic in a network by breaking apart messages into fixed-length packets that are transmitted to their destination through the most expedient route. All packets in a single message may not travel the same route (dynamic routing). The destination computer reassembles the packets into their proper sequence. This method is used to efficiently handle messages of different lengths and priorities in large networks, such as Telenet, Tymnet, and AT&T's Accunet. X.25 is the international standard for such a network. ATM is a higher-speed version of packet switching. Packet-switching networks also provide value-added services, such as protocol conversion and electronic mail.

PAP (Printer Access Protocol)

See *AppleTalk protocols*.

parallel port

A printer interface that allows data to be transmitted a byte at a time, all eight bits moving in parallel. LPT1 to LPT3 are parallel ports. See also *serial port*.

parity

A method of checking for errors in transmitted data.

passive hub

See *hub*.

passive star

A network topology that joins wires from several nodes without providing any additional processing. See also *active star*.

path

The location of a file or directory in the file system. For example, the path for file REPORT.FIL in subdirectory ACCTG in directory CORP on volume SYS: of server ADMIN is:

ADMIN\SYS:CORP\ACCTG\REPORT.FIL

PCI (Peripheral Component Interconnect)

A 64-bit interface that has replaced previous buses (AT, MCA, EISA, VL-bus) in most new systems. It features bus mastering and operates at speeds of 30 MHz and higher.

PCL (Printer Control Language)

The command language for the HP LaserJet printers. It has become a de facto standard used in many printers and typesetters. PCL Level 5, introduced with the LaserJet III in 1990, also supports Compugraphic's Intellifont scaleable fonts.

PhoneNET

Communications products from Farallon Computing, Inc. that extend Local-Talk distances to 3000 feet and use unshielded twisted phone lines instead of shielded twisted pair. Configurations include daisy chain and passive star as well as active star topologies for both EtherTalk and LocalTalk. Optional Traffic Watch software provides network management and administration.

PING

A program used to check an address on the network to see if there is an operational machine at that address. It was first developed for UNIX systems running the TCP/IP protocol. Similar programs now exist for other environments.

Plug and Play

A specification designed to make PCs almost as easy to configure as Macintoshes. The standard specifies how cards identify themselves to the PC hardware and the operating system.

port

A *hardware port* is a connecting component that allows a microprocessor to communicate with a compatible peripheral. On the PC, there are serial and parallel ports. The Macintosh includes a SCSI port.

A *software port* is a memory address that identifies the physical circuit used to transfer information between a microprocessor and a peripheral. The DOS devices COM1 to COM4 and LPT1 to LPT3 are software ports.

POST (power-on self test)

A series of built-in diagnostics that are performed when the computer is first started. Proprietary codes (POST codes) are generated to indicate test results.

PostScript

A page-description language from Adobe Systems, Inc., used in a wide variety of printers. Software that provides PostScript output is able to print text and graphics on any PostScript printer or imagesetter. PostScript printers have a built-in interpreter that translates PostScript instructions into the printer's machine language, which generates the required dot patterns. Fonts are scaled to size by the interpreter, thus eliminating the need to store a variety of font sizes on the disk.

PROM (programmable read-only memory)

A specialized type of read-only memory used to add functionality to circuit boards. Typical applications include the PROM on an NIC that allows a user to boot a diskless workstation, and the PROM on a SCSI adapter that allows a PC to boot from a SCSI device.

Protected mode

A type of operation that provides the capability of multitasking (running more than one application or process at a time). Protected mode allocates memory to various processes running concurrently so that memory used by one process does not overlap memory used by another process. By contrast, 8086 and 8088 processors can address only 1 MB of memory and can run only one application or process at a time. 80286 and later processors can be set to run in *Real mode*, in which case they emulate an 8086 processor (and are subject to its memory constraints).

protocol analyzer

A device that intercepts LAN traffic and decodes the information, allowing the administrator to see how packets are being routed across the network and to determine whether the packets are being mangled en route.

PU (Physical Unit)

In SNA, software responsible for managing the resources of a node, such as data links. A PU supports a connection to the host (SSCP) for gathering network management statistics.

R

RAID (Redundant Arrays of Independent Disks)

A cluster of disks in which data is copied onto multiple drives. It provides faster throughput, fault tolerance (mirroring), and error correction. Level 3 is used for large block transfers (such as images and satellite feeds). Level 5 is most common. RAID has the following levels:

- **Level 0:** Disk striping or spanning

- **Level 1:** Disk mirroring or duplexing (100 percent duplication)

- **Level 2:** Data striping, bit interleaving, checksum drive(s)

- **Level 3:** Data striping, bit interleaving, parity drive

- **Level 4:** Independent transfer, data striping, block interleaving, parity drive

- **Level 5:** Independent transfer, data striping, block interleaving, no parity drive (distributed parity)

RBOC (Regional Bell Operating Company)

One of seven regional telephone companies created by divestiture. They are Nynex, Bell Atlantic, BellSouth, Southwestern Bell, US West, Pacific Telesis, and Ameritech.

Real mode

See *Protected mode.*

redirection

The method of diverting data from its normal destination to another; for example, to a print queue instead of the printer port or to a server's disk instead of the local disk.

registry

The database used in some versions of Windows instead of or in addition to the configuration files WIN.INI and SYSTEM.INI. Windows 95 uses the registry more or less exclusively, although the configuration files are retained. Windows NT uses both the registry and the configuration files. The registry is a nontext database; it must be edited with a special editor, REGEDIT.

remote connection

A connection between a LAN on one end and a workstation or network on the other, often using telephone lines and modems. A remote connection allows data to be sent and received across greater distances than those allowed by normal cabling.

Remote Procedure Call (RPC)

The protocol that governs how an application makes requests of network resources and retrieves the results.

repeater

A device that amplifies or regenerates the data signal in order to extend the distance of the transmission. Available for both analog and digital signals.

ResEdit (Resource Editor)

A Macintosh system utility used to edit the resource fork.

resource fork

See *Macintosh file.*

RIP

See *Router Information Protocol.*

RLL (Run-Length Limited)

A magnetic disk encoding method that packs 50 percent more bits into the same space than the earlier MFM method. It is used with RLL, IDE, ESDI, SCSI, SMD, and IPI interfaces.

router

A device that examines the destination address of a message and selects the most effective route. It is used in complex networks where there are many pathways between users. A NetWare router can run internally as part of a NetWare server. It connects separate network cabling topologies or separate networks with functions built into NetWare.

Router Information Protocol (RIP)

A protocol that provides a way for routers to exchange routing information on a NetWare internetwork. RIP allows NetWare routers to create and maintain a database (or router table) of current internetwork routing information. Workstations can query the nearest router to find the fastest route to a distant network by broadcasting a RIP request packet. Routers send periodic RIP broadcast packets containing current routing information to keep all routers on the internetwork synchronized. Routers also send RIP update broadcasts whenever they detect a change in the internetwork configuration.

RS-232-C

An EIA standard for a serial interface between computers and peripheral devices (modem, mouse, etc.). It uses a 25-pin DB-25 or 9-pin DB-9 connector. Its normal cable limitation of 50 feet can be extended to several hundred feet with high-quality cable. RS-232 defines the purposes, electrical characteristics, and timing of the signals for each of the 25 lines. However, all 25 are not always used; many applications use less than a dozen.

RTMP (Routing Table Maintenance Protocol)

See *AppleTalk protocols.*

RTS (Request To Send)

An RS-232 signal sent from the transmitting station to the receiving station requesting permission to transmit. See also *CTS.*

S

SAA (System Application Architecture)

Introduced in 1987, a set of IBM standards that provides consistent interfaces among all IBM computers from micro to mainframe. It is made up of user interfaces, programming interfaces, and communication protocols, as follows:

- **Common User Access (CUA):** Interfaces based on the graphics-based Presentation Manager of OS/2 and the character-oriented interfaces of 3270 terminals.

- **Common Programming Interface (CPI):** A common set of application programming interfaces (APIs) that, for example, allow a program developed on the PC to be easily moved to a mainframe. The standard database language is SQL.

- **Common Communications Support (CCS):** A common set of protocols, including LU 6.2 (APPC) and HLLAPI.

SAP

See *Service Advertising Protocol*.

SCSI (Small Computer System Interface)

An industry standard that sets guidelines for connecting peripheral devices and their controllers to a microprocessor. The SCSI interface defines both hardware and software standards for communication between a host computer and a peripheral. SCSI (SCSI-1) provides up to 5 MB per second data transfer and can connect multiple peripherals while taking only one expansion slot in the computer. SCSI-2 provides command queuing and a Fast SCSI synchronous option that provides up to 20 MB data transfer (8-bit). Fast wide SCSI provides up to 40 MB transfer (with a 68-conductor cable). SCSI-3 includes enhanced features and the ability to handle more than eight devices.

SDLC (Synchronous Data-Link Control)

The primary data-link protocol used in IBM's SNA networks. It is a bit-oriented, synchronous protocol that is a subset of the HDLC protocol.

Sequenced Packet Exchange

See *SPX*.

serial communication

The transmission of data between devices over a single line, one bit at a time. See also *parallel port*.

serial port

A port that allows data to be transmitted asynchronously, one bit at a time. Typically, serial ports are used for modems or serial printers. On IBM PC compatible computers, COM1 through COM4 are asynchronous serial ports.

serialization

The process of serializing software to prevent unlawful software duplication. Each NetWare operating system has a unique serial number. If two NetWare operating systems with the same serial number exist on the same internetwork, each NetWare server displays a copyright violation warning at the server console, and at each logged-in workstation. Depending on the version of NetWare, copyright violation error messages may mention serialization.

Service Advertising Protocol (SAP)

The protocol NetWare servers use to advertise their services, allowing routers to create and maintain a database of current internetwork server information. Routers send periodic SAP broadcasts to keep all routers on the internetwork synchronized. Routers also send SAP update broadcasts whenever they detect a change in the internetwork configuration. Workstations can query the network to find a server by broadcasting SAP request packets. When a workstation logs in to a network, it broadcasts a "Get Nearest Server" SAP request and attaches to the first server that replies.

SETUP

The routine that sets up the system configuration of a client or server PC. The setup routine records the system's built-in features: add-on boards, hard drives, disk drives, ports, math coprocessor, and available system memory. It also lets you set the date and time, password, and keyboard speed. The system configuration may be accessed from a program on diskette or from the BIOS.

SFT

See *System Fault Tolerance.*

SIMM (Single In-line Memory Module)

A narrow printed circuit board about 3 inches long that holds eight or nine memory chips. It plugs into a SIMM socket on the circuit board.

SIP (Single In-line Package)

A type of chip module that is similar to a SIMM, but uses pins rather than edge connectors. SIPs are sometimes called SIPPs (Single In-line Pin Packages).

SMB (Server Message Block)

The message format used in the Microsoft/3Com file-sharing protocol for PC Network, MS-Net, and LAN Manager. Used to transfer file requests between workstations and servers as well as within the server for internal operations. For network transfer, SMBs are carried within the NetBIOS network control block (NCB) packet.

SMDS (Switched Multimegabit Data Services)

High-speed data services in the 45 Mbps range proposed by local telephone companies that will allow companies to build private MANs.

SMT (Station ManagemenT)

An FDDI network management protocol that provides direct management. Only one node requires the software.

SMTP (Simple Mail Transfer Protocol)

An electronic-mail protocol used in TCP/IP networks.

SNA (Systems Network Architecture)

IBM's primary networking strategy, introduced in 1974. SNA is made up of a variety of hardware and software products that all interact together. In SNA, nodes are end points or junctions, and data links are the pathways between them. Nodes are defined as Type 5 (hosts), Type 4 (communications controllers), and Type 2 (peripheral; terminals, PCs, and midrange computers). Type 2.0 nodes can communicate only with the host, and Type 2.1 nodes can communicate with other 2.1 nodes (peer-to-peer) without going to the host. Data links include high-speed local channels, the SDLC data-link protocol, and Token Ring.

The heart of a mainframe-based SNA network is the SSCP (System Services Control Point) software that resides in the host. It manages all resources in its domain. Within all nodes of an SNA network, except for Type 2.1, there is PU (Physical Unit) software that manages node resources, such as data links, and controls the transmission of network management information. In Node Type 2.1, Control Point software performs these functions. In order to communicate user data, a session path is created between two end points, or LUs (Logical Units). When a session takes place, an LU-LU session is established between an LU in the host (CICS, TSO, user application, etc.) and an LU in the terminal controller or PC. An LU 6.2 session provides peer-to-peer communication and lets either side initiate the session.

VTAM (Virtual Telecommunications Access Method) resides in the host and contains the SSCP, the PU for the host, and establishes the LU sessions within the host. NCP (Network Control Program) resides in the communications controller (front-end processor) and manages the routing and data-link protocols, such as SDLC and Token Ring.

SNA is implemented in functional layers with each layer passing control to the next layer. This layering is called a protocol stack. SNA had major influence on the international OSI model; however, OSI does not implement every layer in the same way.

SNA	OSI
Transaction	Application
Presentation	Presentation
Data Flow	Session
Transmission	Transport
Path Control	Network

SNA	OSI
Data Link	Data Link
Physical	Physical

SNADS (SNA Distribution Services)

An IBM electronic-mail system for SNA networks. It also provides storage and forwarding capabilities if a user's machine is unavailable to receive a transmission.

SNMP (Simple Network Management Protocol)

A format used for network management data. Data is passed between SNMP agents (processes that monitor activity in hubs, routers, bridges, etc.) and the workstation used to oversee the network. Originating in the UNIX community, it has spread to VMS, DOS, NetWare, and other environments.

socket

The part of an IPX internetwork address, within a network node, that represents the destination of an IPX packet. Some sockets are reserved by NetWare for specific applications. For example, IPX delivers all NCP request packets to socket 451h. Third-party developers can also reserve socket numbers for specific purposes by registering those numbers with Novell.

SONET (Synchronous Optical NETwork)

An international standard for broadband transmission through fiber-optic cables in the 50 megabit to 13 gigabit per second range. It is included in the Broadband ISDN (B/ISDN) specification.

source routing

IBM's method of routing data across source-routing bridges. NetWare source-routing programs allow an IBM Token Ring network bridge to forward NetWare packets (or frames). IBM bridges can be configured as either single-route broadcast or all-routes broadcast. The default is single-route broadcast.

- **Single-route broadcasting:** Only designated single-route bridges pass the packet and only one copy of the packet arrives on each ring in the network. Single-route bridges can transmit single-route, all-routes, and specifically routed packets.

- **All-routes broadcasting:** The packet is sent across every possible route in the network, resulting in as many copies of the frame at the destination as there are bridges in the network. All-routes bridges pass both all-routes broadcasts and specifically routed packets.

sparse file

A file with at least one empty block. NetWare won't write any block that is completely empty. Databases often create sparse files. For example, suppose the disk allocation block size for volume VOL1 is 4 KB. Also suppose that a database opens a new file, seeks out the 1,048,576th byte, writes 5 bytes, and closes the file. It would be inefficient to save the entire file to disk. The file would be comprised of 256 zero-filled disk allocation blocks (the first 1 MB) and one more disk allocation block with 5 bytes of data and 4091 zeros. Instead, NetWare writes only the last block to disk, saving time and disk space. The NetWare NCOPY command does not create sparse files automatically. NCOPY has a /f option that forces the operating system to create sparse files.

SPS (Standby Power System)

A system that switches to battery backup upon detection of a power failure. See also *UPS*.

SPX (Sequenced Packet Exchange)

A NetWare DOS Requester module that enhances the IPX protocol by supervising data sent out across the network. SPX verifies and acknowledges successful packet delivery to any network destination by requesting a verification from the destination that the data was received. The SPX verification must include a value that matches the value calculated from the data before transmission. By comparing these values, SPX ensures not only that the data packet made it to the destination, but that it arrived intact. SPX can track data transmissions consisting of a series of separate packets. If an acknowledgment request brings no response within a specified time, SPX retransmits it. After a reasonable number of retransmissions fail to return a positive acknowledgment, SPX assumes the connection has failed and warns the operator of the failure.

ST412

An enhancement to the ST506 standard. All new ST506 drives/controllers incorporate this; thus ST412, ST506/412, and current ST506 units are the same.

ST506

A hard disk interface commonly used in drives 40 MB and less. It transfers data at 625 KB per second and uses the MFM encoding method. See also *ST412*.

ST506 RLL (ST506 Run-Length Limited)

A hard disk interface (also called RLL interface) that increases capacity and speed by 50 percent over ST506 MFM drives and transfers data at 937 KB per second. With MFM drives certified for increased capacity, the ST506 MFM controller can be replaced with an ST506 RLL controller and the drive can be reformatted.

star network

A communications network in which all terminals are connected to a central computer or central hub. PBXs, as well as IBM's Token Ring and AT&T's Starlan LANs, are prime examples.

STARTUP.CMD

An OS/2 file executed immediately upon startup (STARTUP.CoMmanD). It contains instructions that can initialize operating system settings and call in a specific application program. The DOS counterpart is AUTOEXEC.BAT.

statistical multiplexer (stat mux)

A method that divides bandwidth on a WAN connection between users based on how much each user needs, rather than a strict allocation of the same amount to everyone, whether they need it or not.

stop bit

A signal that indicates the end of a character in communication protocols.

STP (shielded twisted-pair)

Telephone wire wrapped in a metal sheath to eliminate external interference. See also *twisted-pair*.

surge protector

A device that protects a computer from excessive voltage (spikes and surges) in the power line. See also *UPS*.

synchronous protocol

A communication protocol that controls a synchronous transmission, such as bi-sync, SDLC, and HDLC. Synchronous protocols always have error checking. See also *asynchronous protocol*.

synchronous transmission

Transmission of data in which contiguous blocks of data are sent, with both sending and receiving stations synchronized to each other. It was developed for mainframe networks using higher speeds than teletype terminals. Examples of synchronous protocols are IBM's SDLC, Digital's DDCMP, and the international HDLC. Modems that transmit at 1200 Bps and higher often convert the asynchronous signals from a computer's serial port into synchronous transmission over the transmission line. See also *asynchronous transmission*.

System Fault Tolerance (SFT)

A means of protecting data by providing data duplication on multiple storage devices. If one storage device fails, the data is available from another device. There are several levels of hardware and software system fault tolerance; each level of redundancy decreases the possibility of data loss.

System folder

The operating system folder in the Macintosh that contains the System, Finder, and MultiFinder, printer drivers, fonts, desk accessories, Inits, and CDEVs.

T

T-1

A 1.544 megabit T-carrier channel that can handle 24 voice or data channels at 64 Kbps. The standard T-1 frame is 193 bits long, which holds 24 eight-bit voice samples and one synchronization bit. 8000 frames are transmitted per second.

T-3

A 44.736 megabit T-carrier channel that can handle 672 voice or data channels at 64 Kbps. T-3 requires fiber-optic cable.

T-carrier

Digital transmission service from a common carrier. T-carrier service requires multiplexers at both ends that merge the various signals together for transmission and split them at the destination. Multiplexers can analyze the traffic load and vary channel speeds for optimum transmission.

TCP/IP (Transmission Control Protocol/Internet Protocol)

An industry-standard suite of networking protocols, enabling dissimilar nodes in a heterogeneous environment to communicate with one another. TCP/IP is built upon four layers that roughly correspond to the seven-layer OSI model. The TCP/IP layers are:

- Process/application
- Host-to-host
- Internet
- Network access

The File Transfer Protocol (FTP) and Simple Mail Transfer Protocol (SMTP) provide file transfer and e-mail capability. The TELNET protocol provides a terminal-emulation capability that allows a user to interact with any other type of computer in the network. TCP controls the transfer of the data, and IP provides the routing mechanism.

TDM (time division multiplexing)

A technique that interleaves several low-speed signals into one high-speed transmission. For example, if A, B, and C are three digital signals of 1000 Bps each, they can be mixed into one 3000 Bps as follows: AABBCCAABBCCAABBCC. The receiving end divides the single stream back into its original signals. See also *baseband; FDM.*

termination

Placing a terminating resistor at the end of a bus, line, chain, or cable to prevent signals from being reflected or echoed.

token passing

A communications network access method that uses a continuously repeating frame (the token) that is transmitted onto the network by the controlling computer. When a terminal or computer wants to send a message, it waits for an empty token. When it finds one, it fills it with the address of the destination station and some or all of its message. Every computer and terminal on the network constantly monitors the passing tokens to determine if it is a recipient of a message, in which case it "grabs" the message and resets the token status to empty. Token passing uses bus and ring topologies.

Token Ring network

An IBM LAN that uses a special twisted-wire cable and the token-passing access method transmitting at four or 16 Mbps. It uses a star topology in which all computers connect to a central wiring hub, but pass tokens to each of up to 255 stations in a sequential, ring-like sequence. Token Ring conforms to the IEEE 802.5 standard.

TokenTalk

Software for the Macintosh from Apple that accompanies its TokenTalk NB board and adapts the Macintosh to 4 Mbps Token Ring networks.

topology

The structure of a network. There are two types of topology: logical and physical. Logical topology describes the route that packets take en route from the sender to the intended recipient. The physical topology is the actual layout of cabling from each workstation to the next.

Trojan horse

A program routine that invades a computer system by being secretly attached to a valid program that will be downloaded into the computer. It may be used to locate password information, or it may alter an existing program to make it easier to gain access to it. A virus is a Trojan horse that continues to infect programs over and over.

TSR (terminate and stay resident)

A program that remains in memory so that it can be instantly popped up over some other application by pressing a hotkey. The program may be displayed in a small window on top of the existing text or image or it may take up the full screen. When the program is exited, the previous screen contents are restored. On PCs, TSRs have become popular in order to have quick access to a calculator, calendar, or dictionary; however, conflicts may arise when multiple TSRs are loaded. Older ones may not always work with newer ones. Task-switching environments, such as Windows and DESQview, provide the ability to switch back and forth between applications, thus making all programs function as a TSR. In this context, the term refers to loading a program, then terminating its action but not removing it from memory.

twisted-pair

A pair of thin-diameter (22 to 26 gauge) insulated wires commonly used in telephone wiring. The wires are twisted around each other to minimize interference from other twisted pairs in the cable. Twisted pairs have less bandwidth than coaxial or fiber-optic cable.

UDP (User Datagram Protocol)

A TCP/IP protocol that allows an application to send a message to one of several applications running in the destination machine. The application is responsible for reliable delivery.

uninterruptible power supply

See *UPS.*

UPS (uninterruptible power supply)

A backup power unit that supplies uninterrupted power if a commercial power outage occurs. Attaching a UPS to a server enables the server to properly close files and rewrite the system directory to disk in the event of a power failure. There are two types of UPSs:

- **Online UPS:** Actively modifies the power as it moves through the unit. If a power outage occurs, the unit is already active and continues to provide power. An online UPS is usually more expensive than an offline UPS, but provides a nearly constant source of energy during power outages.

- **Offline UPS:** Monitors the power line. When power drops, the UPS is activated. The drawback to this method is the slight lag before the offline UPS becomes active. However, most offline UPS systems are fast enough to offset this lag. Also known as SPS (standby power supply).

UPS monitoring

The process a NetWare server uses to ensure that an attached UPS is functioning properly. A Novell-certified UPS is attached to a server to provide backup power. When a power failure occurs, NetWare notifies users. After a timeout specified in SERVER.CFG, the server logs out remaining users, closes open files, and shuts itself down.

UTP (unshielded twisted-pair)

See *twisted-pair*.

V.22

The CCITT standard (1980) for asynchronous and synchronous 600 and 1200 Bps full-duplex modems for use on dial-up lines. It uses DPSK (differential phase shift keying) modulation.

V.22bis

The CCITT standard (1984) for asynchronous and synchronous 2400 Bps full-duplex modems for use on dial-up lines and two-wire leased lines, with fallback to V.22 1200 Bps operation. It uses QAM (quadrature amplitude modulation).

V.32

The CCITT standard (1984) for asynchronous and synchronous 4800 and 9600 Bps full-duplex modems using TCM (trellis coded modulation) over dial-up or two-wire leased lines. TCM encoding may be optionally added. V.32 uses echo cancellation to achieve full-duplex transmission.

V.32bis

The CCITT standard (1991) for asynchronous and synchronous 4800, 7200, 9600, 12,000, and 14,400 Bps full-duplex modems using TCM (trellis coded modulation) and echo cancellation. It supports rate renegotiation, which allows modems to change speeds as required.

V.35

The CCITT standard (1968) for group band modems that combine the bandwidth of several telephone circuits to achieve high data rates. V.35 has become known as a high-speed RS-232 interface rather than a type of modem. The large, rectangular V.35 connector was never specified in V.35, but has become a de facto standard for a high-speed interface.

V.42

The CCITT standard (1989) for modem error correction that uses LAPM (Link Access Procedure, Modem) as the primary protocol and provides MNP (Microcom Networking Protocol) Classes 2 through 4 as an alternative protocol for compatibility.

V.42bis

The CCITT standard (1989) for modem error correction and data compression. It uses V.42 error correction with a compression technique (British Telecom Lempel Ziv) that increases transmission speed up to four times the Bps rating.

Value-Added Process (VAP)

A process that ties enhanced operating system features to a NetWare 2.*x* operating system without interfering with the network's normal operation. VAPs run on top of the operating system in much the same way a word processing or spreadsheet application runs on top of DOS. NLMs provide this type of enhancement for NetWare 3.*x* and 4.*x*.

VCPI (Virtual Control Program Interface)

A DOS extender specification that allows multiple Real mode programs and multiple DOS-extended programs to run at the same time in 386 and higher machines.

VLM (Virtual Loadable Module)

A program that runs on a NetWare client PC to enable the PC to communicate with the network. VLM.EXE is a TSR that loads first and coordinates loading the rest of the VLMs.

VSAT (very small aperture satellite terminal)

A small earth station for satellite transmission that handles up to 56 Kbps of digital transmission. VSATs that handle the T-1 data rate (up to 1.544 Mbps) are called TSATs.

VTAM (Virtual Telecommunications Access Method)

Also called ACF/VTAM (Advanced Communications Function/VTAM), software that controls communications in an IBM SNA environment. It usually resides in the mainframe under MVS or VM, but may be off-loaded into a front-end processor that is tightly coupled to the mainframe. It supports a wide variety of network protocols, including SDLC and Token Ring. VTAM can be thought of as the network operating system of SNA.

wait state

A period of time when the processor does nothing; it simply waits. A wait state is used to synchronize circuitry or devices operating at different speeds. For example, wait states used in memory access slow down the CPU so that processing doesn't get ahead of memory access.

WAN (wide-area network)

A network that communicates over a long distance, such as across a city or around the world. A LAN becomes a part of a WAN when a link is established (using modems, remote routers, phone lines, satellites, or a microwave connection) to a mainframe system, a public data network, or another LAN.

watchdog

A type of packet used to make sure workstations are still connected to the NetWare server. If the server has not received a packet from a station in a certain time, a watchdog packet is sent to the station. If the station does not respond within a certain time, another watchdog packet is sent. If the station still does not respond to a certain number of watchdog packets, the server assumes that the station is no longer connected and clears the station's connection.

watt

A measurement of electrical power. One watt is one ampere of current flowing at one volt. Watts are typically rated as *amps* x *volts*; however, *amps* x *volts*, or *volt-amp* (V-A) ratings and watts are only equivalent when powering devices that absorb all the energy such as electric heating coils or incandescent light bulbs. With computer power supplies, the actual watt rating is only 60 to 70 percent of the volt-amp rating.

wide-area network

See *WAN.*

X.25

A CCITT standard (1976) for the protocols and message formats that define the interface between a terminal and a packet-switching network.

X.32

A CCITT standard (1984) for connecting to an X.25 network by dial up. It defines how the network identifies the terminal for billing and security purposes and how default parameters are negotiated for the connection.

X.400

A CCITT standard mail and messaging protocol that is OSI compliant.

X.500

A CCITT standard mail and messaging protocol that includes the capability of maintaining directories of users. X.500 is OSI compliant.

Xmodem

A widely used asynchronous file transfer protocol. Early versions used a checksum to detect/correct transmission errors; later versions used the more effective CRC method (Xmodem-CRC). Xmodem programs typically handle both methods. Xmodem transmits 128-byte blocks. Xmodem-1K transmits 1024-byte blocks. Xmodem-1K-G transmits without acknowledgment (for error-free channels or when modems are self correcting), but transmission is canceled upon any error.

XON/XOFF

A handshake protocol that prevents a sending system from transmitting data faster than a receiving system can accept it.

Ymodem

An asynchronous file transfer protocol identical to Xmodem-1K plus batch file transfer (also called Ymodem Batch). Ymodem-G transmits without acknowledgment (for error-free channels or when modems are self correcting), but transmission is canceled upon any error.

Zmodem

An asynchronous file transfer protocol that is more efficient than Xmodem. It sends file name, date, and size first. Zmodem responds well to changing line conditions, thanks to its variable-length blocks. It uses CRC error correction and is effective in delay-induced satellite transmission.

zone

See *AppleTalk protocols.*

Index

Page numbers in *italics* refer to figures; page numbers in **bold** refer to primary discussions of the topic.

Symbols and Numbers

(pound sign), to comment out configuration file line, 40
00006f00.000 file, 50
100 Mbps standard, cable for, 138
10BaseT Ethernet, 125, 131, 132. *See also* twisted-pair Ethernet
   hub in, 122
16550 UART chip, 265
32-bit addressing, on Macintosh, 356
32-bit applications, in Windows 95, 342
486 VL-bus server, 32
586 VL-bus server, 32

A

ABEND (Abnormal End), **43**, **47**, 348, 350, 438
   UNIX workstations after, **359**
AccuSys Computer Services, Grouplist, 405
active hubs, 464
   for ARCnet, **134–135**
active star, 438
Adair, Morgan
   Bindery, 407
   Inventry, 401
   Pinch, 422–423
   SS.EXE, 402
Adaptec VL-bus SCSI controllers, 32
adapter cards
   Apple Coax/Twinax, 297
   loading in new workstation, 105
   for Macintosh, **98**
   moving, 210
   on PC workstations, 75, **81–82**
   default IRQ, 348
   Plug and Play, 33

ADB (Apple Desktop Bus), 438
addresses. *See also* network addresses
   for TCP/IP, 297–298
Address Resolution Protocol (ARP), 438
Admin object, 362
Advanced Interactive eXecutive (AIX), 439
Advanced Peer-to-Peer Networking (APPN), 441
Advanced Program-to-Program Communications (APPC), 439
Advanced Research Projects Agency NETwork (ARPANET), 441
AFP (AppleTalk Filing Protocol), 283, 294, 439
AFP.NLM, loading and unloading, 295
AFP servers, 282–283
AIX (Advanced Interactive eXecutive), 439
aliases, 283
Alloc Short Term Memory statistic, 217
all-routes broadcasting, 496
American National Standards Institute (ANSI), 259, 439
American Standard Code for Information Interchange (ASCII), 442
analog, 439
analog dial-up connections, 257
Analyst/Probe (Network Instruments), 411
ANDF (Architecture Neutral Distributed Format), 482
ANSI (American National Standards Institute), 259, 439
ANSI.SYS, 439
ANTaLION Software
   FxREPEAT, 419–420
   Repeat Program Group, 420
   TxRepeat, 420

anti-static precautions, **209–210**, 244
Anti-virus for Macintosh (Symantec), 389
APPC (Advanced Program-to-Program Communications), 439
APPLDATA.AFP, 395
Apple Coax/Twinax card, 297
Apple Desktop Bus (ADB), 438
AppleShare, 439
AppleTalk, 102, 128, 293
   address, 357
   configuring support, **294–295**
   fault point chain for, 154–155
   gateways for, **296–297**
   or parallel interface, for printer, 181
   protocols, 440
      scenario, **152–155**
   support on PCs, **296**
AppleTalk Filing Protocol (AFP), 283, 294, 439
AppleTalk Phase II, 294
AppleTalk Print Service (ATPS), 294
AppleTalk zone
   printer on, 164
   in WAN environment, 42
application layer (OSI model), 129
Application System/400 (AS/400), 441
applications. *See* software
applications server, 290
APPN (Advanced Peer-to-Peer Networking), 441
Architecture Neutral Distributed Format (ANDF), 482
ARCnet (Attached Resource Computer NETwork), **134–135**, 441
   cabling requirements, 136
   Windows 3.1 on connected workstation, 313
ArcServe 5.0 (Cheyenne Software), 362, 395

ARGUS/n 1.5 (Triticom), **404**
ARP (Address Resolution Protocol), 438
ARPANET (Advanced Research Projects Agency NETwork), 441
Artefact, NetCure, 408
AS/400 (Application System/400), 441
ASC, WSCDiag, 408
ASCII (American Standard Code for Information Interchange), 442
ASCII-only printer, 176
asynchronous protocol, 442
Asynchronous Transfer Mode (ATM), 259, 442
asynchronous transmission, 442
ATCON.NLM, 294
ATDISK.DSK driver, 360
ATM (Asynchronous Transfer Mode), 259, 442
ATPS (AppleTalk Print Service), 294
"ATPS can't login ####" message, 356
ATPS.CFG, printer name in, 178
Attached Resource Computer NETwork (ARCnet). *See* ARCnet
ATTACH.EXE, 279, 292
    using within Windows, 313
attitude
    in disaster recovery, **231**
    when troubleshooting, 9–10
audit programs, **397–404**
AuditWare (Preferred Systems), 394
Auto Exec
    Nicinfo, 409
    Nutilize, 409
AUTOEXEC.BAT, 75, 85, 191, 442
    backups of, 213
    errors on PCs, **347**
    login name in, 224
    saving old versions, 211
    viewing message from, 80
AUTOEXEC.NCF, 360
    LOAD TCP/IP command, 301
    in version 3, 28, 40, 51, 58
AUTOEXEC.SYS, in version 2.*x,* 28, 40, 51

Automatic Installation File (AIF), 316–317
Available Cache Buffers, from MONITOR, 217
AVScan (H+ BEDV GmbH), 421

B

B2DS (Novell), 407
backbone, 123, 138, 443
backup device method, to upgrade NetWare, **329**
backup systems, 198, **199–205**
    developing plan, **204**
    evaluating, **200–204**
    name space support by, 237
    for workstations, **205**
backups, 230
    before NetWare upgrade, 51, **327**
    of binderies, 50, 237, 327
    lost Macintosh connection during, 355
    of NET$OS.EXE, 22
    of NetWare Directory Services database, **203**
    off-site storage of, 204, 233, 246
    restoring from, **236–239**
    testing, 247, 329
    tools for, **395**
    utilities, **404–405**
Backwoods Software, Disk Watcher 3.1, 398
bad blocks, 39
bad packets, 269
Barnes, Dave, Setuser, 417
Base12 (Tran Nga), 404
base address, 443
baseband, 443
baselining, 6, **215–220**, 245, 443
    server monitoring, **216–219**
    utilities for, **219–220**
    for WAN traffic, 268
Basic Rate Interface (BRI), 266, 467
Basic Telecommunications Access Method (BTAM), 445

batch file, commands for multiple logins, 279
battery in computer, 75
    and SETUP information, 83
baud rate, **444**
Beholder (Ingenieursbr voor Informatica), 410
Beyond Computing, 372
bidirectional printing, for UNIX printers, 178
BinBack (Chumbley), 405
BIND command, 42
binderies
    back up and restoring, 50, 237, 327
    managing, 50
    utilities, **405–408**
Bindery (Adair), 407
bindery objects, 283
bindery queues, 283
BINDFIX utility, 47, 50, 233, 235, **358–359**
    before NetWare upgrade, 332, 335
Bindscan (Dakware), 406
BIOS (Basic Input/Output System), 25, 107, **444**
    automatic loading in upper memory, 37
    failure, 75
    on server card, 26
    for Windows workstation, 115
B/ISDN (Broadband/ISDN), 259, 467. *See also* ISDN
bisync, **444**
BIX (Byte Information eXchange), 376
blackouts, 244
BLOCK.NDS file, 50
Blue Lance, LAN Auditor, 398
Blue Ocean Software, Inc., Track-it for Windows, 398
BlueSky Shareware, Outrider, 398
BNC, **444**
books, **373**
boot device, on workstation, 77
boot drive, SCSI drive as, 34
boot errors, in PC systems, 346

booting DOS
    record for, 455
    on server, 31
    to test server, 21
booting workstation, 66
    Macintosh with extensions off, 71
    sequence for PC, 80
Borland, Lantraffic, 411
BRI (Basic Rate Interface), 266, 467
bridges, 140, **254**, 256, 445
    problems with, **263**
Brightworks Development, LAN Utilities, 392
broadband, 445
broadband ISDN (B/ISDN), 259, 467
brouters, **255**, 445
brownouts, 206, 244
BS.EXE (Kellner), 406
BTAM (Basic Telecommunications Access Method), 445
BUFFERS statement, in CONFIG .SYS, 91
bulletin boards, 374–376
bus-mastering card, 34
bus-mastering mode, 38
bus type, on servers, **32–33**
Byte Information eXchange (BIX), 376
Byte Stream, 176

C

C&P Software Systems, NetWare System Monitor (NSM), 399
cabling
    ARCnet requirements, 136
    documentation of, **140–141**
    for Ethernet, 131
    fault point chain for, 120, *121*, 143–144
    increasing maximum, 185
    on new network, 118
    for printer, 168
    repeater to extend, 256
    scenario, **141–144**
    for serial printer, 175

Token Ring network requirements, 134
    tracking problems, **135–140**, 275
    twisted-pair, 122, 138
    types and lengths of, 138
    unshielded or shielded twisted-pair, 133
    for workstations, 77
cache, 445–446
Cache Buffer Early Warning, 219
Cache Buffer Hits statistic, 219
cache buffers
    for NetWare, 216
    number available, 217
capacity, of backup system, **201**
CAPTURE.EXE, 169, 186, 279, 307, 310
    batch file for multiple logins, 279
    default printer, 191
    and print jobs, **171–172**
    using within Windows, 313
Card-Network Scanner (Software Systems), 412
cards. *See* adapter cards
Carra Bussa, Novell Check, 398
Carrier Sense Multiple Access/Collision Detection (CSMA/CD), 451
Carter, David, FRED, 415
cartridge drives, 34
case-sensitivity, in configuration file, 41
catalogs, **373**
CCITT (Consultative Committee for International Telephony and Telegraphy), 259, 446
CCS (Common Communications Support), 491
CDEV (Control panel DEVice), 446
    on Macintosh, 102
CD-ROM (Compact Disk Read Only Memory), 239, 372, 446
    information on, 13
CD-ROM drives, 34
CD-ROM extensions, 446
CD-ROM XA (CD-ROM) eXtended Architecture, 447
certification, levels of, 382

Certified NetWare Administrator (CNA), 382, 448
Certified NetWare Engineer (CNE), 382, 448
Certified NetWare Engineer Professional Association (CNEPA), 13, **381**, 448
channel, 447
Charles River Media, 385
checksum, 447
Cheyenne Software
    ArcServe 5.0, 395
    InocuLAN, 389, 420
Chooser, 447
Chooser document, 101
Chumbley, Jeff, BinBack, 405
Circuit Masters, Server Sentry v.6.0, 399
Classic Software, Console Plus, 417
Clean (McAfee Associates), 421
CleanSweep (Quarterdeck), 391
Clerc, Laurent, SmartCOPY, 416
client, 447
client software, 289
CMIP (Common Management Information Protocol), 448
CMIS (Common Management Information Services), 448
CMOS, 75
CMOS RAM (Complementary Metal-Oxide Semiconductor RAM), 448
CNA (Certified NetWare Administrator), 382, 448
CNE (Certified NetWare Engineer), 382, 448
CNEPA (Certified NetWare Engineer Professional Association), 13, **381**, 448
Coates, Roy
    FilesFor, 403
    Quota, 403
    UserDump, 407
coaxial cable, 449
cold boot loader, 28, 39
Collins, Darwin, NCard, 409

color video adapters, SCSI on Mac for, 99

Comchek Utility (Novell), 411

COMMAND.COM, 21, 85

Command Software Systems, Net-Prot 2.1, 388

commenting out line in configuration file, 40

Common Communications Support (CCS), 491

Common Management Information Protocol (CMIP), 448

Common Management Information Services (CMIS), 448

Common Programming Interface (CPI), 491

Common User Access (CUA), 491

communication buffers, 45
  for data packets, 28

communications settings, for dial-in/dial out communications, 265–266

Compact Disk Read Only Memory (CD-ROM), 446

Complementary Metal-Oxide Semiconductor RAM (CMOS RAM), 448

Complete 4.x Tree Update (Smulders), 416

components
  conflict between, 7
  testing for failure, 108, 109

COM ports, 265, 449

compression of files, 30

COMPSURF, 39

CompuServe, 13
  forums, 154
  NetWare Workstation Kit for DOS/Windows, 351

computer bulletin boards, 13

computer objects, 283

Computer Select, **372**

Computer Tyme, Save/Restore Trustee Info, 406

COMSPEC, 449

concentrators, 122, 139, 142, 256, 449

CONFIG.SYS, 75, 85, 449
  backups of, 213
  BUFFERS statement, 91
  errors on PCs, **347**
  FILES statement, 91
  LASTDRIVE, 89
  viewing messages from, 80

configuration
  tracking details, 7–8
  utilities for WANs, 268

configuration files
  for network applications on server, 314
  in new servers, **40–41**

conflict, between components, 7

connecting to other systems, 286–302
  Macintoshes, 293–297
  methods, 287–289
  with PC operating systems, 289–293
  TCP/IP and Unix connectivity, 297–302

connection number, 449

connection-oriented, 450

connectionless protocol, 129, 450

connections
  between network card and physical wiring, 15
  checking, **209**
  in workstations, 77–78, 81–82
  workstations to network, 74–75

connectors, 138
  quality of, 151

Console Plus (Classic Software), 417

consultants, **381**

Consultative Committee for International Telephony and Telegraphy (CCITT), 259, 446

container login script, 43

container objects, 280–281, 450

contaminants, **209**

contention, 450

contexts, 284

continuity testers, 276

Control Panel, 450
  hardware problems from settings, 100

Control panel DEVice (CDEV), 102, 446

Control Panel document (Macintosh), 101

Corporate Computing, 371

corruption of files, 267

CPI (Common Programming Interface), 491

CPU (central processing unit), percentage utilized, 217

crashes
  and locked file, 308–309
  of server software, 47

CRC (cyclic redundancy check), 450

cross training, 17

CSMA/CD (Carrier Sense Multiple Access/Collision Detection), 451

CUA (Common User Access), 491

CyberMedia, First Aid 95, 391

Cyber State University, 382

cyclic redundancy check (CRC), 450

Cyco Automation, Showevent, 399

D

DAC Micro Systems, Lanbench, 409

daemon, 451

daisy chain, 34, *35*

Dakware, Bindscan, 406

Danasoft, Event Monitoring NLM for NW3.x, 399

Danen Software Services
  Danen Utilities, 400
  NetWare Disk Usage 2.46, 400

Danen Utilities (Danen Software Services), 400

Data Access Reliability Test (LAN Technologies), 401

Data Circuit-terminating Equipment, 452

data communication protocols, **125–129**

Data Communications Equipment (DCE), 452

data fork, 451, 470

datagram, 452

Datagram Delivery Protocol (DDP), 440

Datalink layer, in OSI, 129

data-link protocol, 452

data modem services, network applications to access, 307

data packets
bad, 269
communication buffers to hold, 28

data recovery
after mechanical failure, 235–236
services for, 230
utilities, 408

data service unit/channel service unit (DSU/CSU), 456

Data Set Ready (DSR), 456

Data-Tech Institute, 382

Data Terminal Ready (DTR), 456

Data Terminating Equipment (DTE), 456

Datawatch Corporation, VIRx, 420

DAT (digital audio tape), 451

DCB (disk coprocessor board), 22, 28

DCE (Data Communications Equipment), 452

DCE (Distributed Computing Environment), 482

DDP (Datagram Delivery Protocol), 440

debugging failed process, installing NetWare, 39–43

default login script, 43

Defense Data Network, Network Information Center, 267

demo utilities, 396–423

Denmac Systems Inc., TrenData, 409–410

dependability, in system evaluation, 130

desk accessory, 452

DESKTOP.AFP directory, 295

Desktop Rebuild (Novell), 414

determination, 9

device code, 453

device drivers, 8, 452
for components after Windows 95 upgrade, 342–343
in new servers, 41, 58
NLMs as, 51

device numbering, 453

diagnostic tools, 49–50
fault-tolerance systems, 395
information resources about, 385–386
managing without, 277–278
protocol analyzers, 274–275, 393–394
utilities, 408–413
virus detection software, 387–389
for WANs, 273–278
workstation utilities, 390–391

diagrams of network, tools for, 413

dial-back systems, 225

dial-in access, 257
and network security, 225

dial-in/dial-out servers, 264–265

digital, 453

digital audio tape (DAT), 451

Digital Signal (DS), 455

digital telephone connections, 257
dial-up, 258

DIR command, DOS vs. NetWare file display, 350

direct memory access (DMA), 454

directory maps, 282

Directory Services trace utility (DSTRACE), 47

directory structure
application expectations of, 315
copying for applications on network, 314
default maximum tree depth for NetWare, 334
map of, 213

directory table, 453

disaster recovery, 230–248. *See also* prevention of disaster
after mechanical failure, 232–239
attitude, 231
data recovery, 235–236
from backups, 236–239
emergency kit for, 232–233
first efforts, 233–234
hardware failures other than server, 241
off-site storage of backups for, 204, 233, 246
physical recovery, 234
planning, 226–227
reconstruction, 242
software problems and user errors, 240–241
tools for, 396
viruses, 243

disk access time, with mirroring and duplexing, 52–53

disk coprocessor board (DCB), 22, 28

disk driver, 454

disk drives. *See also* partitions
accessibility after NetWare loading, 20
data recovery from, 230
external, 361
fault point chain, 59
INSTALL problems from previously formatted, 60
preparing for NetWare install, 39–40
protection from failure, 212

disk duplexing, 454

Disk-Full Early Warning, 218, 219

disk icon with question mark, on Macintosh, 97

Disk Manager (OnTrack), 349

disk mirroring, 454. *See also* mirroring

Disk Request Serviced From Cache, 216

disk space
in server, 216
for Windows 3.*x* on server, 316

Disk Watcher 3.1 (Backwoods Software), 398

Distributed Computing Environment (DCE), 482

Distributed Management Environment (DME), 482

Distributed Queue Dual Bus (DQDB), 455

DLLPATH statement, 292

DMA (direct memory access), 454

DME (Distributed Management Environment), 482

DNS (Domain Naming System), 455

DocNLM (Thompson Network Software), 423

documentation. *See also* information resources; record keeping
for adapters, 82
of cabling, **140–141**
creation during NetWare upgrade, **326–327**
of disaster plan, **247–248**
of network, **213–214**
for network cards, 8
for WAN printer configuration, 279
when installing, 105

Domain Naming System (DNS), 455

DOS, 39
age of, 107
booting by server, 20
boot record, 455
hard drive support limitations, 84
loading, 66
MODE command, 169
PRINT command, 179
printing to print server, 159
unloading, 223
variation in, **85–86**
version, 75–76
on workstation, 91

DOS partition, for NetWare 2, 28

DOS Requester, 89

downsizing, 278

DQDB (Distributed Queue Dual Bus), 455

DrivePro (Micro House), 84

drivers. *See* device drivers

DriveSpace, 353

DS (Digital Signal), 455

DSARC and DSREST backup (Palindrome Corporation), 405

Dspace (NetTech Australia), 402

DSR (Data Set Ready), 456

DSREPAIR, 48, 235, 362

Dsrepair.NLM (Novell), 414

DSTRACE (Directory Services trace utility), 47

DSU/CSU (data service unit/channel service unit), 456

DTE (Data Terminating Equipment), 456

DTR (Data Terminal Ready), 456

dual-bus PCI systems, 33

Dubios, Christophe, Wdspace, 399

Dupbind (Novell), 419

DUPBIND utility, 327

duplexed drives, 212

duplexing, 52–53, 454

duplicate network addresses, 41

Dupuis, Laurent, Net Tree, 414

dust, **209**

Dynamic Memory Pool Statistics Peak Usage, 216

DynaText, 369

Ē

Eastern Europe, 260

ECNE (Enterprise Certified NetWare Engineer), 382, 456

Edbin (Fachhochschule Hamburg), 406

EIDE (Enhanced IDE), 84

EISA (Extended Industry Standard Architecture), 32–33, 456
and interrupt problems, 38, 82–83

electromagnetic interference, 137, 138
and garbled token, 148

electronic mail, **317–318**

ElectroText (DynaText), 369

EliaShim Microcomputers, ViruSafe LAN, 388

embedded SCSI, 457

emergency, replacement of server parts, 109

emergency kit, for disaster recovery, **232–233**

EMM386.EXE, 351

EMMEXCLUDE command, 82, 90

EMSNET*x*.COM, 87

EMS Professional Shareware Libraries, NetWare CD-ROM, 386

encapsulation, 457

Enhanced Small Device Interface (ESDI), 457

Enterprise Certified NetWare Engineer (ECNE), 382, 456

ENTRY.NDS file, 50

EPROM, 22

equipment. *See* hardware

Error Correction Code (ECC) memory, 24

error messages. *See* messages

ESDI (Enhanced Small Device Interface), 457

Ethernet, **130–132**
AppleTalk on, 128
cabling for, 131
configuration, 457

Ethernet 802.2, 362

Ethernet card, 62

EtherTalk, 296, 458
on Macintosh, 102, 193
SCSI adapter on Mac for, 99

Ethervision (Triticom), 394

Event Monitoring NLM for NW3.*x* (Danasoft), 399

EVERYONE group, 278, 284, 357

existing systems, **8–9**
maintenance, **60–64**
fault point chain for, 63
scenario on failure of portion, **144–146**
server in, 21, **44–49**
hardware problems, **44–46**
software problems, **46–48**

expandability, in system evaluation, 130

expanded memory, on PC workstation, 87

Expert Sniffer Analyzer (Network General), 393

EXPORTS file, 299

Extended Industry Standard Architecture (EISA), 456

extended memory, on PC workstation, 87

extensions on Macintosh, **101–102**
   booting with settings off, 71

External Data Representation (XDR), 299

external drives, 361

F

Fachhochschule Hamburg, Edbin, 406

fake root, 315, 458

FAQ (Frequently Asked Questions), 377

fast Ethernet, 458

FAT (file allocation table), 235, 349, 458

fault point chain
   for AppleTalk, 154–155
   for cabling, 143–144
   for existing physical network, 146
   for Macintosh printing, 194
   for Macintosh workstation, **113–114**
   for network printing, *167*
   for new installation, 59–60
   for physical network maintenance, 152
   for PostScript printer, **183–184**
   for remote printing, 189–190
   for router as print server, 187
   for system maintenance, 63
   for Token Ring network, **148**
   for troubleshooting servers, *16, 26*
   for workstations, 73
   maintenance, **109, 111**
   new installation, 106–107

print problems, 192
   in Windows, **115–116**

fault points, 6
   in NetWare, 26–27
   for network printing, **167–169**
   for networked modems, 319–320
   for physical network, **120–122**
   for problem area identification, 15
   for servers, **25–27**
   for UNIX-to-NetWare printing, 179
   of wide area networks, **262–269**
   for workstations, **72–78**

fault tolerance, 245, 458. *See also* System Fault Tolerance
   of 10BaseT Ethernet, 132
   maintenance, **211–213**
   in system evaluation, 130
   tools for, 395

fax machines, 319

fax modems, networked
   applications to access, 307
   fault points for, **320**

FCC Class, 459

FCONSOLE, 21, 22, 44–45, 214, 268, 276
   to monitor NetWare 2*x* server, 216–217

FDDI (Fiber-optic Data Distribution Interface), 259, 459

FDISK, 84

FDM (frequency division multiplexing), 459

fiber channel, 459

fiber-optic cabling, 138–139
   with repeater, 263

Fiber-optic Data Distribution Interface (FDDI), 259, 459

Fiber Optic Inter Repeater Link (FOIRL), 460

file allocation table (FAT), 235, 458
   corrupted, 359

File and Print Services for NetWare (FPNW), 291

file attributes, 300

file cache buffers, in NetWare 3.*x*, 28

File Contents to Byte Stream, 310

file creation mask, for UNIX users, 300

file locks, **308–309**, 459

file migration, 30

file rights, **224–225**

file server. *See* servers

File Server Statistics Summary, 216

file services, for network applications, **307–309**

file sharing, 308

file structure, in NetWare upgrades, **325–326**

file systems, backups of other, **204**

File Transfer Protocol (FTP), 300, 460

file translator, 255

files
   compression and decompression, 30
   corruption of, 267
   on Macintosh, 470
   restoring individual, **240–241**

FILESERV, 363

FilesFor (Coates), 403

FILES statement, in CONFIG.SYS, 91

Finder, 459–460

firewall, 127

First Aid 95 (CyberMedia), 391

Fix Any PC…Fast, 372

floppy disks, loading NetWare from, 28

FOIRL (Fiber Optic Inter Repeater Link), 460

fonts
   on Macintosh, location for, 112–113
   printing, 182

F-PROT (Frisk Software International), 421

fractional T-1 services, 259, 460

fractional T-3 services, 259

frame, 460

Frame Relay, 259, 261, 460

FRED (Carter), 415

freeware, **396–423**

freeze, 106, 107
   of Macintosh during startup, 113
   of print server, 183

frequency division multiplexing (FDM), 459

Frisk Software International, F-PROT, 421

Frye Computer Systems, Network Management, 392–393

FSTATS NLM v1.10 file server, 400

FTAM (File Transfer Access and Management), 460

FTP (File Transfer Protocol), 300, 460

FTP sites, 379

full backup, 204

FxREPEAT (ANTaLION Software), 419–420

G

Gateway Services for NetWare (GSN), 291

gateways, 140, 255, 461
    for AppleTalk, 296–297
    LANs connected with, 287, *288*
    problems with, 264
    software to connect networks, 287

Gibson Research, Spin-Rite II, 391

Global Virtual Private Network (GVPN), 461

GMCopy (Novell), 407

Gobbler (Ingenieursbr voor Informatica), 410

GOSIP (Government Open Systems Interconnection Profile), 461

Grouplist (AccuSys Computer Services), 405

groups
    configuration report for, 326
    login script for, 43
    setting mapping for, 315
    setup in NetWare 4, 29

GROUPS file, 299

.GRP files, 317

GSN (Gateway Services for NetWare), 291

GUEST user, 278

Guethlein, Bill, List Trustees, 405

GVPN (Global Virtual Private Network), 461

H

H+ BEDV GmbH, AVScan, 421

handle, 461

handshaking, 462

hanging printer, 177

Hans-Joachim Roy, IPX Diagnostics for Windows, 410

hard drives
    checking for failures, 216–217
    data recovery from, 232, 233
    fixing software problems on, 45
    increasing size when restoring, 237
    Mac problems recognizing, 98
    preparation on new servers, 36–37
    suballocation of blocks, 30
    type determination for PC SETUP, 84
    Windows use of, 91

hardware
    memory errors, self-correcting, 24
    physical network standards, 130–135
    quality of, 207–208
    requirements for NetWare upgrade, 327–328
    requirements for NetWare upgrades 2.15 to 3.12, 332
    requirements for Windows 95, 342
    security, 38
    upgrading, 338–339
    for Windows NT, 354

hardware-based diagnostic tools, 273–276
    protocol analyzers, 274–275

hardware port, 486

Hardware-Specific Module (HSM), 481

HawkNet Inc.
    NetReport, 400
    NetTune Pro Demo 2.2, 400–401

Hayes compatibility, 265

HBA (host bus adapter), 463

HCSS (High Capacity Storage System), 463

HDLC (High-level Data-Link Control), 462

header, 126, 462

help, by network management tools, 271

Hendrickson, David, Strustee and Rtrustee, 406

hexadecimal, 462

HFS (Hierarchical File System), 462

hidden directories, after NetWare upgrade, 333–334

Hierarchical File System (HFS), 462

High Capacity Storage System (HCSS), 463

High Performance File System (HPFS), 292, 464

HIMEM.SYS, 351, 463

history, daily log for, 12

Holmstead Partners, Mass User Management, 417

home page, of Web site, 379

hop count, 463

host, 463

host bus adapter (HBA), 463

HOSTS file, 297, 299

Hot Fix, 463

Hot Fix redirection area, 39–40, 212

HPFS (High Performance File System), 292, 464

HSM (Hardware-Specific Module), 481

hubs, 122, 139, 256, 464
    for 10BaseT Ethernet, 132

I

ICONDATA.AFP, 395

ICONINDX.AFP, 395

IDE (Integrated Drive Electronics), 464

IDE drives, 84

IDs
    for RAID system, 36
    for SCSI devices, 34, 100

IEC (International Electrotechnical Commission), 464, 468

IEEE (Institute of Electrical and Electronic Engineers), 465

IFCONFIG, 103

IF MEMBER OF construction, 43

"Inaccessible hard drive" message, 354

"Incorrect version of COMMAND.COM--reboot PC" error message, 91
incremental backups, 201, 204
Industry Standard Architecture (ISA), 467
informational objects, 282
information resources, 8, 13, 368–382
  900 numbers and consultants, 381
  books and catalogs, 373
  CD-ROM products, 372
  Certified NetWare Engineer Professional Association (CNEPA), 381
  Computer Select, 372
  Internet, 376–380
  magazines, 370–372
  NetWare Application Notes, 336, 369–370
  NetWare manuals, 369
  NetWare Users International (NUI), 381
  newsletters, 372
  Novell Research Reports, 370
  Novell Technical Bulletins, 370
  online, 373–376
  technical support databases, 380
  about tools, 385–386
  training, 382
InfoWorld, 371
Ingenieursbr voor Informatica
  Beholder, 410
  Gobbler, 410
.INI files, 317
Init, 113, 465
  conflict checks, 354–355
  fault points in conflicts, 114
InnerSpace (Priam Systems), 349
InocuLAN (Cheyenne Software), 389, 420
insects, 209
INSTALL
  problems from formatted drives, 60
  to create NetWare partition, 39
installing
  cabling, 135–137

new workstation, scenario, **104–107**
installing NetWare
  debugging failed process, **39–43**
  drive preparation, **39–40**
installing new system
  scenario, **55–60**
  fault point chain, **59–60**
Institute of Electrical and Electronic Engineers (IEEE), 465
"Insufficient Memory" message, on Macintosh, 356
Integrated Drive Electronics (IDE), 464
Integrated Services Digital Network (ISDN), 467
Integrity Master (Stiller Research), 423
Intel
  KAOS4 Virus Protection, 421
  LANDesk Express, 415
  LANDesk Manager, 393
Intel Corporation, LAN Desk Virus Protect, 388
interference, and cabling location, 122
intermittent problems, 119
  from cabling, 138
  with servers, 22, 48–49
internal network numbers, 267
International Electrotechnical Commission (IEC), 464, 468
International Standards Organization (ISO), 128, 259, 468
The Internet, 267, 297, 376–380, 465
Internet addresses, 127
internetwork, 465. *See also* WANs (wide area networks)
Internetwork, 371
Internetwork Packet eXchange (IPX), 128, 466
  on Macintosh, 293, 296
Internetwork Packet eXchange Open Data-link Interface (IPXODI), 182, 466–467
InterNIC, 127, 297, 466
interrupt (IRQ), 467
  conflict with, 56
  conflicts on PCs, **82–83, 347–348**

and EISA configuration, in new servers, 38
  for ISA card, 82
  for LAN adapter, 37
  parallel interface and, 175
  recording, 7
  for SCSI adapter, 34
  for VGA adapter, 37
  when installing new workstation, 105
INTRAK, ServerTrak, 394
IntraLink Corporation, LanScan, 401
inventory of network
  software for, 272
  tools, **394**
Inventry (Adair), 401
IOBENCH.NLM (Symbios Logic), 413
I/O Error Count, 216
IPX (Internetwork Packet eXchange), 126, 466
  on Macintosh, 293, 296
IPX address conflict, 269
IPX.COM, 170
  potential faults for freeze from, 107
IPX Diagnostics for Windows (Hans-Joachim Roy), 410
IPX external network number, 466
IPX internal network number, 466
IPX internetwork address, 466
IPX packets
  encapsulating, 298
  structure, *126*
IPX/SPX, **126**
IPXODI (Internetwork Packet eXchange Open Data-link Interface), 182, 466–467
IRQ (interrupt), 467. *See also* interrupt (IRQ)
ISA (Industry Standard Architecture), 467
  interrupts for bus, 38
  settings on cards, 82
  VGA card, 33
ISA slots, 32

ISDN (Integrated Services Digital Network), 266, 467
adapters, 258
I-Soft, LANDoc 1.1 Demo Network, 413
ISO (International Standards Organization), 128, 259, 468
isolation of problem, 14

J

jabbering, 277
Jacobi, Jens, Whathave 2.0, 417
JCLUTL (Leon), 417
Jones, Justin, SAPTrack, 410
jumpers, 105

K

KAOS4 Virus Protection (Intel), 421
KDS Software, LAN Hijack, 415
Kellner, Kurt
BS.EXE, 406
SNET.EXE, 411
kernel, 85
keyboards, 209
failure in, 26

L

LAN (local area network), 468
basic definition, 253
documenting physical and logical structure, 214
piecemeal development, 4
reasons to connect multiple, 253–255
worldwide connections, 260–261
LAN adapters
ability to send and receive packets, 21
on new servers, 37
LAN Auditor (Blue Lance), 398
LAN Computing, 371
LAN connection
bridges as, 254
between buildings, 256

gateway for, **255**
long distances, **256–260**
router for, **255**
telephone company services for, **257**
to form WANs, **253**
LAN Desk Virus Protect (Intel Corporation), 388
LAN Hijack (KDS Software), 415
LAN Magazine, 371, 385
LAN Management & Control System (Software Solutions), 403
LAN Technologies, Data Access Reliability Test, 401
LAN Technology, 371
LAN Times, 371
LAN Utilities (Brightworks Development), 392
LAN WorkGroup, 298, **315–316**
LAN WorkPlace 5 for MS Windows, 298
LAN WorkPlace for Macintosh, 298
LANalyzer for Windows, 269, 270, **276–277**, **393**
Lanbench (DAC Micro Systems), 409
LANdecoder/e (Triticom), 393–394
LANDesk Express (Intel), 415
LANDesk Manager, (Intel), 393
LANDoc 1.1 Demo Network (I-Soft), 413
LanScan (IntraLink Corporation), 401
Lantraffic (Borland), 411
LAP (Link Access Protocol), 440
Large Internet Packet (LIP), 468
laser printer, status of, 193
LASTDRIVE statement, in CONFIG.SYS, 89
LatticeNet, 134
LatticeNet transceiver, 77
LBA (Logical Block Addressing), 354
LCAD Demo Network (Network Performance Institute), 413
.LCK file extension, 308
leaf objects, 280–281, 468
types, 282

leased lines, 257, 261
analog connections, 258
digital connections, 258–259
ISDN connection, 259
Lee, Ray, Workstation Automatic Inventory, 402–403
Leon, John C., JCLUTL, 417
linear bus topology, *123,* 123, **125**
Line Printer Daemon (LPD), 300
line quality, for dial-in/dial out communications, 266
Link Access Protocol (LAP), 440
LINK DRIVER IPXODI entry, in NET.CFG, 88
Link Support Layer (LSL), 87, 469, 480
LIP (Large Internet Packet), 468
list server, subscribing to, 377
List Trustees (Guethlein), 405
LOAD command, 42
load on server, monitoring, 44
LOAD TCP/IP command, in AUTOEXEC.NCF, 301
loading
DOS, 66
Windows, 70
local area network (LAN), 4, 468.
See also LAN (local area network)
LOCAL PRINTERS setting, 181
LocalTalk, 128, **133–134**, 296, 469
lock out of supervisor account, 224
LOCKD (Lock Daemon), 300
locked-exclusive file, 308
locked-shareable file, 308
log
administrator's work, 62, 248
daily, 12
of error messages, 21
of network events, **214–215**
system error, **45–46**, 49, 61–62
in tracking failure points, 6
of workstation configuration, 106
Logical Block Addressing (LBA), 354
logical map, of network, 140, 145, 214
logical number, 453
logical topology, 124

Logical Unit number (LUN), for RAID
    system, 36
login
    multiple on WAN, 279
    problems with, 47, 69
    security, **223–224**
    to service in NetWare, 361
LOGIN.EXE, 292
login scripts, **360**, 469
    after NetWare upgrade, 337
    on new servers, **43**
    order of execution, 282
    when upgrading to NetWare 4, 334
long distance LAN connection, **256–
    260**
long file names
    backup system support of, 204
    for shared files, 309
    in Windows 95, **93**, 342
low-level format, 39
LPD (Line Printer Daemon), 179, 300
LPT1, 469
LSL (Link Support Layer), 469, 480
    driver, 87

M

McAfee Associates
    Clean, 421
    Netscan, 421
    Netshield, 388, 422
    NetTools, 416
    Scan, 422
    Virusscan, 422
    Virus Shield, 422
Macintosh
    booting with extensions off, 71
    connecting to, **293–297**
    corrupted system on, 102
    desktop files and volume access,
        295–296
    hardware, **96–101**
    configuration, **100–101**
    name space support, 332
    networking, **102**
    printer setup, snapshot, **163–164**

printing on, **102–103**
    scenario on problems, **192–194**
    to queue, 182
    problems with power-on
        sequence, 97
    removing or adding cards, 211
    scenario on system configuration
        information, **111–114**
    SCSI devices for, **99–100**, 99
    software, **101–103**
    extensions, **101–102**
    troubleshooting tips, **354–357**
    upgrading System on, 340
    utilities, **414**
    as workstation, **70–71**
    fault point chain for, **113–114**
Macintosh clients, **96–103**
Macintosh file, 470
MacIPX, 296
MacWeek, 371
Madonna, William Jr., WmWhoHas,
    418
magazines, **370–372**
MagnaRAM 2 (Quarterdeck), 390
mail directories, 318
    problems after upgrade, 337
mail gateway, 255
mail server, 318
maintaining workstations, scenario on,
    107–109, 110–111
MakeUser (Schreiber), 407
MAKEUSER utility, 329
MAN (metropolitan-area network),
    253, 470
management tools
    software for network, 141
    utilities as NLMs, 52
    for WAN (wide-area network), **270–
        273**
MAP statement, 315
    batch file for multiple logins, 279
    using within Windows, 313
mapping of network, software for, 272
Mass User Management (Holmstead
    Partners), 417
master lost, 34

Masters, P.T., Sysdoc, 402
MAU (Multi-Station Access Unit), 132–
    133, 147, 470
mechanical failure, recovery after, **232–
    239**
Media Access Unit (MAU), 125
Media Support Module (MSM), 481
Meg (Tolliver), 401
memory
    ABEND from insufficient, 47
    Error Correction Code (ECC), 24
    insufficient on Macintosh, 356
    maximum for NetWare 2.2, 360
    on new servers, **31–32**
    on server, 216
    running NetWare for Macintosh,
        294
    for Windows workstation, 115
memory address, for ISA card, 82
memory conflicts, in Windows, 90
memory handler, in Windows 3.1, 351
memory segments
    IRQ mapping to, 348
    for LAN adapter, 37
    records of, **7–8**
    for VGA adapter, 37
merging, NDS trees, 282
Message Handling Service (MHS),
    317, 471
messages
    "ATPS can't login ####," 356
    in boot process, 80
    "Inaccessible hard drive," 354
    "Incorrect version of
        COMMAND.COM--reboot
        PC," 91
    "Insufficient Memory", on Mac-
        intosh, 356
    log of, 21
    "Out of Memory," 352
    "Printer unavailable," 181
    Router Configuration Error: *Server
        is claiming my same internet
        address*, 41, 57
    "Router Configuration Error," 269

MESSAGES statement, using within Windows, 313

metropolitan-area network (MAN), 253, 470

MFM (Modified Frequency Modulation), 470

MHS (Message Handling Service), 317, 471

Michna, Hans-Georg, Remote Software Update, 416

Micro 2000, Microscope 6.11, 392

Micro Channel, 471

Micro Channel (PS/2) clients, **96**

Micro House
DrivePro, 387
Technical Library, 387

Microscope 6.11 (Micro 2000), 392

Microsoft
Mail, 318
NDS-compatible service, 93
NetWare client, 92
Windows 95 Resource Kit, **386–387**

microwave relays, 260

Migrate (Novell), 419

Minimum File Cache Buffer Report Threshold, 219

mirroring, 36, 52–53, 454
of drives, 34, 212
of partitions, 36
of servers, 30

mission-critical applications, server mirroring for, 54

mission-critical equipment, stand-by replacement for, 208

MLID (Multiple Layer Interface Driver), 473, 480

MODE command (DOS), 169

modems, **318–320**
access by, 264
fault points for networked, 319–320
network applications to access services, 307
software for networked, 319

Modified Frequency Modulation (MFM), 470

Modify DOS Attributes From UNIX option, 357

MONITOR, 21, 22, 39, 44, 268, 276
Available Cache Buffers, 217
for baselining, 214
LAN Information selection, 45

monitor (screen display)
failure in, 26
fault points for, 74

monitoring, server loads, 44

monochrome video board, 33

Mosko, Mark, NDSScan, 414

motherboards, 32, 75, 107
damage to, 108
RAM on, 31

Motif, 482

Motorola 68000-based servers, 28

Mount Protocol, in UNIX, 300

mounting disk, on Macintosh, 98

moving, adapter cards, 210

MPC (Multimedia PC) 1, 471

MPC (Multimedia PC) 2, 472

MPC (Multimedia PC) 3, 472–473

MSM (Media Support Module), 481

multiple-byte character, 473

Multiple Layer Interface Driver (MLID), 473, 480

multiple logins, on WAN, 279

multiplexer (MUX), 474

multiplexing, 473

Multi-Protocol Router, 264

Multi-Station Access Unit (MAU), 132–133, 147, 470

MUX (multiplexer), 474

N

NAECs (Novell Authorized Education Centers), 382

Name Binding Protocol (NBP), 440

name space, 473–474

name space modules, as NLMs, 52

name space support. *See also* long file names
backup software handling of, 237
for Macintosh, 355

memory for, 294
for OS/2, 292
for UNIX files, 299

naming conventions, after NetWare upgrade, 333

National Bureau of Standards, 478

National Institute of Standards and Technology (NIST), 478

NBDAEMON.EXE, 95

NBP (Name Binding Protocol), 440

NCard (Collins), 409

NCB (Network Control Block), 474

NCOPY, 314

NCP (NetWare Core Protocol), 475

NDS, 29. *See also* NetWare Directory Services

NDS database
back up and restoring, 237
DSREPAIR to repair, 235
repairing, 48

NDS objects, **281–283**

NDSScan (Mosko), 414

NDS tools, **414**

NDS trees, **280–281**, *281*, 474
merging, 282

Net Tree (Dupuis), 414

NET$BIND.SYS, 50

NET$BVAL.SYS, 50

NET$OBJ.SYS, 50

NET$OS.EXE, 39
backup of, 22, 213
corrupted, 46
for version 2.*x*, 28

NET$PROP.SYS, 50

NET$VAL.SYS, 50

NetBEUI (NetBIOS Extended User Interface), **127**, 474

NetBIOS.EXE, **127–128**, 475

NETBIOS.SYS, 95

NET.CFG, 75, 87, 475
CONNECTIONS=##, 362
LINK DRIVER IPXODI entry, 88
SHOW DOTS = ON statement, 313

NetCure (Artefact), 408

NetGuard Systems, SERVivor 3.5, 395
NetMagic (Netmagic Systems Inc.), 418
Net-Prot 2.1 (Command Software Systems), 388
NetReport (HawkNet Inc.), 400
Netscan (McAfee Associates), 421
Netshield (McAfee Associates), 388, 422
NETSTART.BAT, 85
NETSTAT, 103
NetTech Australia, Dspace, 402
NetTools (McAfee Associates), 416
NetTune Pro Demo 2.2 (HawkNet Inc.), 400–401
NetView, 475
NetWare, 27–30
    accessing services with network applications, 306–313
    cache buffers for, 216
    configuration files, 40
    debugging failed install, 39–43
    diagnostic tools for, 276
    failure points, 26–27
    growth, 24
    LANs connected with, 287, *288*, 289
    loading, 360–361
    memory recognition by, 58
    print utilities, 279, 309
    problems loading, 20, 22
    security within, 38
    tips for troubleshooting, 358–362
    upgrading, **51**
    utilities, 392–393
    version 2.*x*, 27–28
    error starting, 39
    monitoring server, 216–217
    troubleshooting tips, **360**
    version 3.*x*, 28–29
    monitoring server, 217–218
    troubleshooting tips, 360–361
    version 4.*x*, 29–30
    monitoring server, 218–219
    new structure for, 280–283
    print process, 170

troubleshooting tips, **361–362**
version structure differences, *29*
Windows 95 interface with, 341
NetWare Access, Network File System for, 298–300
NetWare Access Server, 319
NetWare Application Notes, 336, 369–370
NetWare Buyer's Guide, 380
NetWare Clear Connection (Smith), 418
NetWare clients, for Windows 95, 92–93
NetWare Connection, 381
NetWare Core Protocol (NCP), 475
NetWare Directory, managing, **50**
NetWare Directory database, 29
NetWare Directory Services, 278
    backup of database, **203**
    tracing errors, 47
    troubleshooting, **283–284**
    and WANs, **280–284**
NetWare Disk Usage 2.46 (Danen Software Services), 400
NetWare DOS/Windows Client Kit, 350
NetWare drivers, on PC workstation, 85, 87
NETWARE.DRV, 90
NetWare executable file. *See* NET$OS.EXE; SERVER.EXE
NetWare Express, 475
NETWARE.INI, 85
NetWare Loadable Module (NLM), 26, 46, 51–52, 478–479
NetWare for Macintosh
    printing from, **178**
    on servers, 293–296
NetWare Management Agents, 476
NetWare protocols, 476
NetWare Requester for OS/2, 476
NetWare Runtime, 477
NetWare System Monitor (C&P Software Systems), 399
NetWare Tools for Windows, 313

NetWare for UNIX, 302
NetWare UNIX client, NeXTStep and, 292
NetWare Users International (NUI), 381
NetWare VLM client, 92–93
NetWare Workstation Kit for DOS/ Windows (CompuServe), 351
NetWatch (Virtual Networks), 413
NetWire, 373–374, 477
network addresses, 268
    assignments in new servers, **41**
    conflicts, **269**
    for LAN, 126
network administrators, shortage of, 4
network analyzer, 147
network applications, 306–320
    accessing NetWare services with, 306–313
    electronic mail, 317–318
    file services, 307–309
    modems, 318–320
    print services, 309–312
    running from server, 313–317
Network Communications, LAN Network Probe 4.4, 394
Network Computing, 371
Network Control Block (NCB), 474
Network Custodian Pro, 396
network diagramming, tools for, **413**
network drivers
    age of, 107
    on workstation, 69
Network File System (NFS), 298, 478
    configuring for UNIX, 298–299
Network General, Expert Sniffer Analyzer, 393
Network Instruments
    Analyst/Probe, 411
    Observer, 402
network interface cards (NIC), 57, 477
    accessibility after NetWare loading, 20
    configuring, 8
    as physical network fault point, 122

network inventory program, 49
Network layer, in OSI, 129
Network Management (Frye Computer Systems), 392–393
network monitor, 146
Network News, 371
network node, 477
network operating system (NOS), 479
network performance, decline in speed, 45
Network Performance Institute, LCAD Demo Network, 413
network printing
    configuration files or attributes, 174
    fault points for, 167–169
    multiple printers, 310
    printer accessibility, 168
    snapshots for, 158–164
network security. *See* security
Network Support Encyclopedia (NSE), 380, 477–478
Network World, 371
networked modems, fault points for, 319–320
networking hardware, security for, 139
Networking Management, 372
networking software
    on PC-compatible workstation, 86–89
    upgrading, 340–341
networks
    configuration worksheet, *433*
    documenting, **213–214**
    essential links in, 15
    growth of PC-based, 24
    growth in use, 4
    logical map of, 140, 145
    Macintosh printer connection to, 163
    running Windows form, 90
NETWORKS file, 299
NETX.COM, 87, 182, 478
NET*x*.COM, 87, 170
new installation, evaluating physical aspects, 130

new network, cabling on, 118
new servers, 30–43
    bus type, **32–33**
    configuration files in, **40–41**
    device drivers in, **41**
    hard drive preparation on, **36–37**
    hardware problems in, **31–38**
    interrupts and EISA configuration, **38**
    LAN adapters on, 37
    login scripts on, 43
    memory on, **31–32**
    multiple protocols on, **41–42**
    NetWare permissions on, 42
    network address assignments in, 41
    RAID (Redundant Array of Inexpensive Disks) systems on, 35–36
    SCSI adapters on, **33–34**
    SCSI devices on, **34–35**
    software problems in, **39–43**
    VGA adapter on, 37
new systems, 7–8
    installing workstations, **78**
    server in, 20
    tracking configuration details, 7–8
newsgroups on Internet, 377–378
newsletters, **372**
NeXTStep, 85, 289
    and NetWare UNIX client, **292**
NFS (Network File System), 298, 478
    configuring for UNIX, **298–299**
NFSADMIN utility, 357
NIC (network interface card), 477
    driver for, 32
    on Macintosh, 98
    on server, 25–26
Nicinfo (Auto Exec), 409
NIST (National Institute of Standards and Technology), 478
NLM (NetWare Loadable Module), 26, 46, **51–52**, 478–479
NMI (non-maskable interrupt), 479
NMPIPE.SYS, 95
NOBODY user, 357

node number, 479
non-maskable interrupt (NMI), 479
Norton Utilities (Symantec), 390
NOS (network operating system), 27, 479
NOTIFY.XXX file, 174
Novell
    B2DS, 407
    Comchek Utility, 411
    Desktop Rebuild, 414
    Dsrepair.NLM, 414
    Dupbind, 419
    GMCopy, 407
    Migrate, 419
    Network Support Encyclopedia Pro, 386
    Printgrp, 419
    Printuser, 419
    tech support, 368
    Uimport.Exe for NetWare, 419
Novell Authorized Education Centers (NAECs), 382
Novell Check (Carra Bussa), 398
Novell DCB, 20
Novell Multi-Protocol Router, 140
Novell NetWare Client for Windows 95, 93
Novell Research Reports, 370
Novell Technical Bulletins, 370
Novell technical support, 13
NPRINTER.EXE, 168
NPRINTER.NLM, 173
NPSERVER.SYS, 95
NSE (Network Support Encyclopedia), 380, 477–478
NT servers, Windows clients and, **290–291**
NuBus, 480
NUI (NetWare Users International), 381, 480
Nutilize (Auto Exec), 409
NWADMIN, 45, 188, **283**
NWSETUP, 351
NWTOOLS program, 312, 313
Nwuserlist (Ridderhof), 418

O

objects, in NDS, 29
Observer (Network Instruments), 402
ODI (Open Data-link Interface), 480–481
ODI drivers, 289
    on PC workstations, 87–88
ODINSUP (Open Data-link Interface/Network driver interface specification SUPport), 481
offline UPS, 503
off-site storage, of backups, 204, 233, 246
On Technologies, Editor's Choice Catalog, 386
online help, by network management tools, **271**
online information resources, **373–376**
online UPS, 503
Ontrack Disk Manager, 84
Open Data-link Interface (OPI), 480–481
Open Data-link Interface/Network driver interface specification SUPport (ODINSUP), 481
Open Software Foundation (OSF), 482
Open System Interconnection (OSI) Model, **128–129**, 483
operating systems
    as failure point, **75–76**
    restoring after disaster, **238–239**
    shutting down, 210
    upgrading, **340–341**
optical disk, 481
organization, 482
Organization container object, 282
organizational role leaf object, 282
organizational unit, 482
Organizational Unit container object, 282
OS/2, 85, 289
    file names in, 309
    and NetWare access, **292**
    Warp, 95

OS/2 clients, **95–96**
OS/2 Requester, 95, 292
OSF (Open Software Foundation), 482
OSI (Open System Interconnection) Model, **128–129**, 483
"Out of Memory" errors, 352
Outrider (BlueSky Shareware), 398

P

Packet Burst Protocol, 483–484
packet monitoring, by network management tools, **271**
Packet Receive Buffers statistics, 218
packet switching, 484
packets, 126, 483
Palindrome Corporation
    DSARC and DSREST backup, 405
    Storage Manager 4.0, 395
PAP (Printer Access Protocol), 440
parallel port, 484
    or AppleTalk for printer, 181
    for printer, 174–175
parity, 484
parity drive, 36, 54
PARTITIO.NDS file, 50
partitions, 36–37, 454
    backup and restore, 362
    corrupted, 349
    for NetWare, 39
    when upgrading NetWare, 331
passive hubs, 464
    for ARCnet, 134–135
passive star, 485
passwords, **223–224**
    problems changing, 47
patch panel, **139**
path, 485
    for network file services, 307
PATH command, 347
PAUSE command, 347
PC adapter cards, 75, **81–82**
    default IRQ, 348
PC Agent/SNMP (Standard Microsystems), 412

PC-compatible systems
    DOS PRINT command, 179
    network growth, 24
    tips for troubleshooting, **346–348**
    variety, 72
    workstation on, 67
PC-compatible workstations, **79–85**
    AppleTalk support on, **296**
    basic structure, 79
    boot sequence, **80**
    configuring with SETUP, **83–84**
    networking software on, **86–89**
    OS/2 clients, **95–96**
    Plug and Play, **84–85**
    vs. NetWare server, 31
    software, **85–89**
    updating operating system, 340
    Windows and NetWare, **89–94**
PCI (Peripheral Component Interconnect), 8, 485
PCI bus, 33
    on Macintosh, 96
PCI cards, 34
    and interrupts, 38, 83
    vs. LAN adapter, 37
PCI slots, 32
PCONSOLE, 158, 186, 279
    printer configuration, 363
    printing DOS text file from, 160
    print jobs sent to queue by, 161
    Print Queue Information window, 172
PC operating systems
    connecting to systems with, **289–293**
    standardizing, 86
Pcscan (Trend Micro Devices Inc.), 423
PC Week, 371
peer-to-peer security, in Windows 95, 343
Pentium PC, as server, 332
Percentage of Utilization statistic, 217
Peripheral Component Interconnect (PCI), 485

permissions, 240, 291
in e-mail directory, 318
on new servers, **42**
structure change in NetWare versions, 51
in UNIX, and NetWare, **300–301**
on UNIX workstations, 357
phone lines, protection of, 207
PhoneNET, 485
physical address, 453
Physical layer, in OSI, 129
physical layer protocol, 126
physical network. *See also* cabling
data communication protocols, **125–129**
documenting, 214
fault point chain for, 146, 152
fault points for, **120–122**
hardware standards, **130–135**
scenario on growth, **148–152**
scenarios, **141–155**
snapshot for, **118–119**
topologies, **122–125**
physical security, 38, **223**
Physical Unit (PU), 487
Pinch (Adair), 422–423
PING, 103, 485
PKWare, PKZIP, 390
planning
for disaster recovery, 198–199, **226–227**
NetWare 4.*x* network, 282
upgrading NetWare, 324–325
Plug and Play, 8, 33, **84–85**, 486
polarity error, 143
port, 486
for printer on workstation, 169
Portable NetWare, 302
portable tape drive, 205
POST (power-on self test), 66, 68, 76, 486
for Macintosh workstation, 70
messages, 346–347
Post-Probe (Micro 2000), 392

PostScript printing, 176, **177**, 310, 486
fault point chain for, **183–184**
scenario for setup, **180–184**
pound sign (#), to comment out configuration file line, 40
power, evaluating system requirements, 207
power failure, 206
UNIX workstations after, **359**
power protection management, **206–207**
power supply link, 25
power surge, 108, 244
intermittent problems from, 48
PowerBooks, external SCSI devices on, 100
power-on sequence, Macintosh problems with, 97
Preferred Systems, AuditWare, 394
Presentation layer, 129
prevention of disaster, **198–227**
backup system in, **199–205**
baselining, **215–220**
equipment quality and, **207–208**
fault tolerance maintenance, **211–213**
network plans and logs in, **213–215**
network security in, **222–226**
power protection management in, **206–207**
preparedness in, **246–248**
tools and techniques, **244–245**
user training, **220–221**
virus protection, **221–222**
preventive maintenance, 208–211, 244
anti-static precautions, **209–210**
of connections, **209**
dust and other contaminants, 209
justifying a cost of, 270
manufacturer's directions, **210**
Primary Rate Interface (PRI), 467
PRI (Primary Rate Interface), 467
PRINT HEADER setting, 171, 177
Print Queue Information window, in PCONSOLE, 172

print queues, 168, **172–173**
configuration worksheet, *436*
direct access, **310–311**
for Macintosh printer, 295, 356
in NetWare 2.*x* and 3.*x*, 363
placing jobs directly into, 158
print server, 170, **173–174**
configuration worksheet, *436*
existing setup, 161
in fault point chain, 184
printing from DOS on, 162
router as, **184–187**
Print Server directory, 174
print server software, 168. *See also* PSERVER
PRINT TAIL setting, 171, 177
PRINT.XXX file, 174
PRINTCON, 172, 279, **359**
Printer Access Protocol (PAP), 440
printer driver, fax modem software support of, 319
printer names, 294–295
printer-related objects, 282
printer type, and garbled text, 310–311
"Printer unavailable" message, 181
printers, **175–176**
accessibility to network, 168
cable for, 168
configuration worksheet, *435*
problems from, 153, 154
serial or parallel interface for, **174–175**
snapshot for existing setup, **160–163**
snapshot for Macintosh setup, **163–164**
snapshot for new setup, **158–160**
Printers Control Panel, in Windows, 313
PRINTGROUP utility, 326
Printgrp (Novell), 419
printing, **169–176**
by network applications, **309–312**
fonts in network applications, **311**
from NetWare for Macintosh, 178

from Windows applications, 311–312

on Macintosh, **102–103**

problems printing last page, 171

scenario for remote, 187–190

troubleshooting tips, 362–363

in UNIX, **178–179**

on WANs, 278–279

workstation problems when, 190–192

Printuser (Novell), 419

PRINTUSR utility, 326

processor, for Windows workstation, 115

Processor Utilitization statistic, 219

profile login script, 43, 282

PROM (programmable read-only memory), 28, 486

protected mode, 30, 487

protocol analyzers, 274–275, 393–394, 487

protocols

  for AppleTalk, 440

  for data communication, **125–129**, 265

  multiple on new servers, **41–42**

  for Windows clients of NT servers, 290–291

PS/2 (microchannel) clients, **96**

PSERVER.EXE, 168, 170, **173**, 173, 363

  print server lockup by, 161

  queue connection, 158, 162

PSERVER.NLM, 173

PSERVER.VAP, 170, 186

PU (Physical Unit), 487

public domain Init program, 112

punch-down block, 139

Q

QEMM (Quarterdeck Expanded Memory Manager), 82, 390

quality of equipment, 244

  and disaster prevention, 207–208

Quarterdeck, 390

  CleanSweep, 391

  WINProbe, 390

QUEUE.XXX file, 174

Quota (Coates), 403

R

RAID (Redundant Arrays of Independent Disks), 487–488

  for fault tolerance, 53–54

  levels of, 36

  on new servers, 35–36

RBOC (Regional Bell Operating company), 488

read-after-write verification, 212

read-only file, 224–225

read-only memory (ROM), on workstation, 76

read request, 217

README files, 8, **369**

  for adapter cards, 33

real-life scenarios, **16–18**. See also scenarios

RealTech Systems Corporation, SAP-Track, 411

rebooting servers, 21

  to bypass security, 223

record keeping, **10–12**, 56, **213–215**. See also documentation

  daily log, 12

  forms for, **426–436**

  of interrupts and memory segments, 7–8

recovery services, **239**

  relationship with, **227**

redirection, 488

  shell-printer, **170–171**

redirection blocks, 39–40

Redundant Arrays of Independent Disks (RAID), 487–488

REGEDIT.EXE (Registry Editor), 211

Regional Bell Operating company (RBOC), 488

REGISTER MEMORY command, 32, 58

registry, 488

  text file as backup, 211, 352

Registry Editor (REGEDIT.EXE), 211, 352

rekeying data, 242

reliability, of backup system, 203

remote connection, 488

remote management, of workstations, **415**

remote printing, scenario, 187–190

Remote Procedure Call (RPC), 489

Remote Software Update (Michna), 416

RENMDIR utility, 337

Repeat Program Group (ANTaLION Software), 420

repeaters, 122, 139, 145, **256**, 489

  problems with, **263**

  Thin Ethernet using, *145*

replication, in version 4, 30

Report-Generator (TGB), 404

Request to Send (RTS), 490

Rescue, 408

ResEdit (Resource Editor), 489

resource fork, 470

resources for troubleshooting, 13. See also information resources

restoring

  individual files, **240–241**

  workstation data, **237–238**

restoring from backups, 236–239

return path, when upgrading, 211

RG-58 cable, 135

RG-62 93 ohm coaxial cable, 135

Ridderhof, Ric, Nwuserlist, 418

rights, when upgrading NetWare, 331

rightsizing, 278

ring topology, *123*, 123, **124**

RIP (Router Information Protocol), 490

RLL (Run-Length Limited), 489

ROM (read-only memory), on workstation, 76

root object, 281

router, 140, 489

  defective, 241

  as print server, **184–187**

"Router Configuration Error" message, 269

"Router Configuration Error: *Server* is claiming my same internet address" error message, 41, 57

Router Information Protocol (RIP), 490

routers, 255

    problems with, 264

    upgrading, 267

Routing Table Maintenance Protocol (RTMP), 440

RPC (Remote Procedure Call), 489

RPRINTER.EXE, 87–88, 168, 170, 363

    print server lockup by, 161

RS-232-C, 490

RS-232 interface, 174

RTMP (Routing Table Maintenance Protocol), 440

Rtrustee (Hendrickson), 406

RTS (Request to Send), 490

Run-Length Limited (RLL), 489

Ryu Consulting, Snoop, 412

S

SAA (System Application Architecture), 490–491

SafetyNet Inc., VirusNet LAN, 423

SALVAGE utility, 199, 241

SAP (Service Advertising Protocol), 492

SAPTrack (Jones), 410

SAPTrack (RealTech Systems Corporation), 411

satellite services, 259–260, 261

Save As command, for locked file, 308

Save/Restore Trustee Info (Computer Tyme), 406

SaveUser (Schreiber), 407

SBACKUP, 362

SCANDISK, 238

Scan (McAfee Associates), 422

scanners, 34

    SCSI on Mac for, 99

SCAN software (McAfee Associates), 388

scenarios, 16–18

    AppleTalk, 152–155

    big company, 17–18

    cabling, 141–144

    existing system maintenance, 60–64

    fault point chain, 63

    failure of portion of existing network, 144–146

    Macintosh printing problems, 192–194

    Macintosh system configuration, 111–114

    new workstation installation, 104–107

    physical network, 141–155

    PostScript printer, 180–184

    remote printing, 187–190

    router as print server, 184–187

    small company, 17

    system installation, 55–60

    Token Ring network, 146–148

    Windows workstation, 114–116

    on workstation maintenance, 107–109, 110–111

    workstation printing problems, 190–192

Schreiber, Wolfgang

    SaveUser and MakerUser, 407

    Vspace, 408

screen savers, 354

SCSI (Small Computer System Interface), 491

    embedded, 457

SCSI adapters

    compatibility of, 81–82

    device driver for, 32

    on new servers, 33–34, 57, 58

SCSI devices

    bootable drives, 20

    changing connections, 35

    connecting or disconnecting, 100

    hard drive, 84

    for Macintoshes, 99–100, 99

    on new servers, 34–35

    termination of, 34, 56, 100

SDLC (Synchronous Data-Link Control), 491

SECURE CONSOLE command, 223

security, 222–226, 245. *See also* permissions

    dial-in access, 225

    file rights, 224–225

    for network hardware, 139

    passwords, 223–224

    physical, 38, 223

    trustee rights, 224–225

    of Windows 95, 291

Security Integration, VirusNet, 387

SEND statement, using within Windows, 313

Sequenced Packet Exchange (SPX), 496–497

serial communication, 492

serial interface, for printer, 174–175

serial port, 265, 492

serialization, 492

server applications, as NLMs, 52

SERVER.CFG, in version 2.*x*, 28, 40, 51

SERVER.EXE, 28, 39, 57

    backups of, 213

    corrupted file, 46

    messages from, 22

Server Message Block (SMB), 493

server-related objects, 282

servers. *See also* new servers

    assigning network numbers to, 49

    backups of, 200

    configuration worksheet, *11–12, 427–430*

    to connect existing networks, 253

    data recovery after mechanical failure, 235

    dial-in/dial-out, 264–265

    documenting software configuration, 213

    duplicating, 212

    emergency part replacement, 109

    in existing system, 21

fault point chain, *16*, **25–27**, *26*, *59–60*
first check of, 14
improper shutdown, 359
information to recreate, 326
intermittent problems on, 22, **48–49**
with LAN cards as router, 140
management tools for, 272–273
memory for running NetWare for Macintosh, 294
mirroring, **54**
monitoring, 44, **216–219**
NetWare for Macintosh on, 293–296
for NetWare upgrade to version 4, 334
in new systems, 20
NIC (network interface card) on, 25–26
overloading, 46
vs. PC workstation, 31
printer attachment to, 168
protecting from viruses, 243
rebooting to bypass security, 223
recovery, **234**
with backup restore, **236–237**
requirements for, 332
running network applications from, **313–317**
running Windows 3.*x* from, 316–317
scenarios, **55–64**
user data storage on, 205
workstation login, 67
zone name when configuring, 356
Server Sentry v.6.0 (Circuit Masters), 399
ServerTrak (INTRAK), 394
Service Advertising Protocol (SAP), 492
Service Process statistic, 217–218
SERVivor 3.5 (NetGuard Systems), 395
SERVMAN, 44, 219
Session layer, in OSI, 129
SESSION statement, 313
SETPASS statement, 313

SETUP, 492
to configure PC workstation, 83
to configure print server, 183
Setuser (Barnes), 417
SETVER.EXE command, 340
SFT (System Fault Tolerance), **52–54**, **211–213**, 499
level III, 54, *55*
shadow BIOS, 37
shareware, **396–423**
payment for, 220
SHELL.CFG, 87, 91
backups of, 213
SHOW DOTS = ON statement, 313, 350
shell-printer redirection, **170–171**
SHELLGEN, 87
shielded twisted-pair cabling, 133
shipping workstations, 82
SHOW DOTS = ON statement, 313, 350
Showevent (Cyco Automation), 399
shut down of system, procedure for, 210
SIMM (Single-In-line Memory Module), 493
Simple Mail Transfer Protocol (SMTP), 493, 318
Simple Network Management Protocol (SNMP), 139, 241, 272, 495
simulated sine wave power supplies, 206
sine wave power supplies, 206
Single-In-line Memory Module (SIMM), 493
Single In-line Package (SIP), 493
single-route broadcasting, 496
SIP (Single In-line Package), 493
slave slot, 34
Small Computer System Interface (SCSI), 33, 491
SmartCOPY (Clerc), 416
SMARTDRV.SYS, 349
SMB (Server Message Block), 493

SMDS (Switched Multimegabit Data Services), 493
Smith, Stephen, NetWare Clear Connection, 418
SMT (Station ManagemenT), 493
SMTP (Simple Mail Transfer Protocol), 493, 318
Smulders, Maurice, Complete 4.*x* Tree Update, 416
SNA (Systems Network Architecture), 494–495
SNA Distribution Services (SNADS), 495
snapshots, **14**
for existing printer setup, **160–163**
for network printing, **158–164**
for physical network, **118–119**
for server, **20–22**
for workstations, **66–71**
SNET.EXE (Kellner), 411
SNMP (Simple Network Management Protocol), 139, 241, 495
Snoop (Ryu Consulting), 412
socket, 495
software
access to NetWare print services, 169
for backups, **202**
documenting on server, 213
documenting workstation configuration, 213
as failure point, **75–76**
on Macintosh, **101–103**
maintaining archive of, 11
management tools, **415–416**
for networked modems, 319
for network management, 141
on PC-compatible workstations, **85–89**
for printers, 176
problems on existing servers, **46–48**
problems in new servers, **39–43**
recovery after problems from, **240–241**
restoring after disaster, **238–239**

server crash from, 27
standardizing, 17
system crash from, 47
upgrading, **339–343**
for WANs, **267–269**
when upgrading NetWare, 332
software-only diagnostic tools, for
WANs, **276–277**
software port, 486
Software Solutions, LAN Management
& Control System, 403
Software Systems, Card-Network
Scanner, 412
Solaris for Intel, 85
solutions, searching for, **6**
SONET (Synchronous Optical
NETwork), 495
source routing, **495–496**
sparse file, 496
speed, of backup system, **201–202**
SpeedStor, 349
Spin-Rite II (Gibson Research), 391
SPS (Standby Power System), 496
SPX (Sequenced Packet Exchange),
126, **496–497**
SPX CONNECTIONS setting, 171
SS.EXE (Adair), 402
SSCP (System Services Control Point)
software, 494
ST412, 497
ST506, 497
ST506 RLL, 497
Stacker, 353
Standard Microsystems, PC Agent/
SNMP, 412
standardizing
applications, 17
PC operating system, 86
workstations, 9
Standby Power System (SPS), 496
StandbyServer32 (Vinca), 395
star network topology, *123*, **125**, 497
startup, Macintosh freeze during, 113
STARTUP.CMD, 497
Startup document, on Macintosh, 102

STARTUP.NCF, 360
increasing buffers with, 218
in version 3, 28, 40, 51
static safety precautions, 81
Station ManagemenT (SMT), 493
statistical multiplexer, 498
status lights, 81
Stiller Research, Integrity Master, 423
stop bit, 498
storage, of backups, 204, 233, 246
Storage Manager 4.0 (Palindrome Corporation), 395
STP (shielded twisted pair), 498
Strustee (Hendrickson), 406
Sun Microsystems, 298
superservers, 24
SUPERVISOR
limits on testing applications as, 315
to set up WAN printing, 279
supervisor password, 224
support, for backup system, 203
Support On Site, 380, 387
surge protector, 206, 244, 498
SVGA monitor, 210
swap file, in Windows, 352
Switched Multimegabit Data Services
(SMDS), 493
switching hubs, 139–140
Symantec
Anti-virus for Macintosh, 389
Norton Utilities, 390
Untouchable Network, 389
Utilities for Macintosh, 389
Symbios Logic, IOBENCH.NLM, 413
Synchronous Data-Link Control
(SDLC), 491
Synchronous Optical NETwork
(SONET), 495
synchronous protocol, 498
synchronous transmission, 498
SYS:_NETWARE directory, 50
SYS volume, 323, 326
SYSCON, 45, 318, 358
Sysdoc (Masters), 402
SYSLOAD for NetWare, 403

System 7, reinstalling, 102
System Application Architecture (SAA),
490–491
System Commander (V Communications), 391
system configuration, information
about, **111–114**
system directories, after NetWare
upgrade, 333–334
system error log, 45–46, 49, 61–62
System Fault Tolerance (SFT), 52–54,
211–213, 499
level III, 54, *55*
system folder, 499
extensions in, 101
system freeze, 106
SYSTEM.INI file, 82, 85
[386Enh] section, EMMEX-
CLUDE, 90
backups of, 213
system login script, 43
system maintenance, fault point chain
for, 63
System Messages manual, 47
System Services Control Point (SSCP)
software, 494
system software, on Macintosh, 98
Systems Network Architecture (SNA),
494–495

T

T-1, 258, 499
T-3, 258, 499
Tab characters, NetWare print utility
conversion, 310
tape drives, 34
for backup, 201
cost of, **202–203**
portable, 205
tapes, cost for backup, 202
Taylor, Scott, TestNet, 412
T-carrier, 499
T-connector, 123, 146
TCPCON, 268, 276, 301

TCP/IP (Transmission Control Protocol/Internet Protocol), 103, **127**, 500
    internal network numbers in, 267
    and Unix connectivity, **297–302**
    in WAN environment, 42
TCP/IP address conflict, 269
TCP/IP connections, UNIX with NetWare server, **301–302**
TDM (time division multiplexing), 500
TDR function, 275
technical support databases, **380**
telecommunications service providers, **266–267**
telecommunications standards, for dial-in/dial-out connections, 265
telecommuting, and security, 225
telephone company services, for LAN connection, **257**
Telnet, 300
terminate and stay resident (TSR), 502
termination, 500
    of cabling, 149
    of SCSI devices, 34, *56*, 100
testing
    backups, 247, 329
    for component failure, 108, 109
    equipment for, 143
TestNet (Taylor), 412
TGB, Report-Generator, 404
Thick Ethernet, 123, **131**
    cabling requirements, 131
    with repeater, 263
thin Ethernet, 122, **132**, 149
    cabling requirements, 131
    with repeater, *145*, 263
Thompson Network Software, DocNLM, 423
Thompson Software Inc., Volumes 1.1, 404
throughput, in system evaluation, 130
time division multiplexing (TDM), 500
token passing, 500

Token Ring network, 124, **132–133**, 501
    AppleTalk on, 128
    cabling requirements, 134
    fault point chain for, **148**
    scenario, **146–148**
Token Talk, 501
Tolliver, Jim, Meg, 401
Topology-Specific Module (TSM), 481
topologies, 501
    of physical network, **122–125**
Track-it for Windows (Blue Ocean Software, Inc.), 398
trade publications, 13
traffic, reducing with bridge, 254
trailer for packet, 126
training, **382**
    for users, **220–221**, 245
Tran Nga, Tammy, Base12, 404
transceivers, 122
transfer method, to upgrade NetWare version 2 to version 3, **328–329**
Transmission Control Protocol/Internet Protocol (TCP/IP), 500
Transport layer, in OSI, 129
trend analysis, by network management tools, 271
Trend Micro Devices Inc., Pcscan, 423
TrenData (Denmac Systems Inc.), 409–410
Triticom
    ARGUS/n 1.5, **404**
    Ethervision, 394
    LANdecoder/e, 393
Trojan horse, 501
troubleshooting
    aids for, **14–18**
    approach to, **5–6**
    attitude when, **9–10**
    resources for, **13**
    trying different solutions, **6**
trustee entry, for UNIX directory, 358
trustee rights, **224–225**, 300
    problems changing, 47
TSM (Topology-Specific Module), 481

TSR (terminate and stay resident), 86, 502
tunneling, 127, 298
twisted-pair cabling, 122, 138, 502
twisted-pair Ethernet, 123, **132**
    cabling requirements, 131
twisted-pair Token Ring network, hub in, 122
TxRepeat (ANTaLION Software), 420

U

UDP (User Datagram Protocol), 502
Uimport.Exe for NetWare (Novell), 419
unattended backups, 201
UNDELETE, 238
uninterruptible power supply (UPS), 56, 198, 206, 244, 503
UNIX
    Macintosh freeze on attempted volume access, 355
    printing in, **178–179**
    TCP/IP and connectivity, **297–302**
UnixWare, 289
    and NetWare support, 293
UNIX workstations, **103**
    access to NetWare volumes, 298
    troubleshooting tips, **357–358**
unknown objects, 283
unloading DOS, 223
unshielded twisted-pair cable, 133
Untouchable Network (Symantec), 389
upgradability, in system evaluation, 130
upgrading, **322–343**
    hardware, **338–339**
    return path when, **211**
    software, **339–343**
    to Windows 95, **341–343**
    utilities for, **418–419**
upgrading NetWare, 51, **323–337**
    backups before, 51, **327**
    creating documentation during, **326–327**
    hardware requirements for, 327–328

planning, 324–325

preparation, 325–328

troubleshooting after, 333–334

version 2.*x* to 3.*x*, 328–329

example, 331–334

version 3.*x* to 4.*x*, 329–331

example, 334–337

troubleshooting after, **337**

without work flow disruption, 323–324

upper memory, automatic loading of BIOS in, 37

UPS (uninterruptible power supply), 56, 198, 206, 244, 503

UPS monitoring, 503

user accounts

problems modifying, 47

setup in NetWare 4, 29

User Datagram Protocol (UDP), 502

User Definition File (UDF) directory, 316–317

user errors, **76**

recovery after, **240–241**

user information, in binderies, 50

user login script, 43

user-related objects, 282

UserDump (Coates), 407

USERLIST statement, using within Windows, 313

users

configuration report for, 326

data storage on file server, 205

information accuracy, 111

information configuration worksheet, *434*

information from when troubleshooting, 9

information on upgrade, 333

management tools, **416–418**

minimizing network downtime for, 323–324

path name information for, 307

problems from, 146

system changes by, 191

training, 220–221, 245

understanding of locked files, 308

USERS file, 299

UTP Ethernet cabling, 138

V

V.22, 503

V.22bis, 504

V.32, 504

V.32bis, 504

V.35, 504

V.42, 504

V.42bis, 505

V Communications, System Commander, 391

value-added process (VAP), 27, 293–294, 505

VALUE.NDS file, 50

VCPI (Virtual Control Program Interface), 505

ventilation, 209

very small aperture satellite terminal (VSAT), 505

VFeatures Deluxe (Golden Bow), 349

VGA adapter, on new servers, 37

video boards, 33

Vinca, StandbyServer32, 395

Virtual Control Program Interface (VCPI), 505

Virtual Loadable Module (VLM), 505

Virtual Networks, NetWatch, 413

Virtual Telecommunications Access Method (VTAM), 494, 505–506

virus detection software, 86, 152, **221–222**, 387–389, 419–423

Virus Shield (McAfee Associates), 422

ViruSafe LAN (EliaShim Microcomputers), 388

viruses, **243**

VirusNet LAN (SafetyNet Inc.), 423

VirusNet (Security Integration), 387

Virusscan (McAfee Associates), 422

VIRx (Datawatch Corporation), 420

VLMs (Virtual Loadable Module), 505

loading, 88–89

VOLINFO statement, using within Windows, 313

voltage checkers, 276

Volume Low Warning Reset Threshold, 218

Volume Low Warning Threshold, 218

Volumes 1.1 (Thompson Software Inc.), 404

volumes

names on Macintosh, 355

size of, 40

VPICD.386 driver, 351

VPICDA.386, 91

VREPAIR, **45**, 62, 233, 235, 359

screen blanks after, 360

VSAT (very small aperture satellite terminal), 505

Vspace (Schreiber), 408

VTAM (Virtual Telecommunications Access Method), 494, 505–506

W

wait state, 506

WAN analyzers, 49

WAN (wide-area network), 42, 252–284, 506

diagnostic tools, 273–278

hardware troubleshooting, 262–266

LAN connection to form, 253

management tools, 270–273

multiple logins, 279

NetWare directory services and, 280–284

piecemeal development, 4

printing on, 278–279

software for, 267–269

Warp (OS/2 3.0), 95. *See also* OS/2

Warp Connect, 95, 292

watchdog, 506

watt, 506–507

Wdspace (Dubios), 399

Web page, for Novell, 13

Western Europe, 260

Whathave 2.0 (Jacobi), 417

Wide area networks. *See* WAN (wide area network)

WIN.COM, 317

WIN.INI, 85
  backups of, 213
WINA20.SYS, 351
Windows (Microsoft), 76, 85
  applications bypassing DOS LPT
    port, 309
  checking for NetWare configu-
    ration, 351
  loading, 70
  memory conflict with video
    adapter, 82
  and NetWare, 89–94
  setup consistency for, 115
  troubleshooting before 3.1, 349–
    350
Windows 3.1
  accessing NetWare services from,
    312–313
  Enhanced mode, 351
  tips for troubleshooting, 350–352
Windows 3.*x,* running from server,
    316–317
Windows 95, 80, 85, **91–94,** 289, 290,
    316
  accessing NetWare services from,
    312
  applications and, **94**
  backup of registry as text file, 211
  long file names support, 93, 309
  NetWare clients for, **92–93**
  network printing from, 188
  other network protocols under, 94
  security of, 291
  shut down, 353
  troubleshooting tips, 352–353
  upgrading to, 341–343
Windows 95 Resource Kit, 386–387
Windows applications, printing from,
    311–312
Windows clients, and NT servers, 290–
    291
Windows NT, 89, **94,** 289, 290, 353–
    354
Windows for Workgroups (WFW), 89,
    90, 290, 350

accessing NetWare services from,
    312
  security of, 291
Windows workstation
  fault point chain for, **115–116**
  scenario, **114–116**
WINProbe (Quarterdeck), 390
WINSTART.BAT, 351
wiring. *See* cabling
WmWhoHas (Madonna), 418
work log, 62
worksheet
  network configuration, *433*
  printer configuration, *435*
  print server and queue configu-
    ration, *436*
  server configuration data, *11–12,*
    427–430
  user information configuration, *434*
  workstation configuration, *431–432*
Workstation Automatic Inventory
    (Lee), 402–403
workstations
  backup systems for, **205**
  booting, 66
  checking for changes, 78
  configuration worksheet, *431–432*
  connection with physical network,
    118
  connection to network as failure
    point, 74–75
  connections in, 77–78, **81–82**
  data recovery from, **235-236**
  determining problems on multiple,
    14
  documenting software configu-
    ration, 213
  fault points, 72–78
  BIOS failure, 75
  motherboard, 75
  operating system and software, 75–
    76
  PC card, 75
  interrupt conflicts on, **82–83**
  log of configuration, 106

log in to server, 67, 69
  Macintosh as, 70–71
  migrating as upgrade method, **330**
  NetWare upgrade and, 328
  network drivers on, 69
  new installations, 78
  PC-compatible, 79–85
  for print server, 181
  printing from, 159, 162
  printing from DOS on, 160
  printing problems from, 190–192
  recovery, **234**
  remote management utilities, **415**
  restoring data, 237–238
  scenario,
  installing new, 104–107
  Macintosh, 111–114
  on maintenance, 107–109, 110–111
  shipping, 82
  snapshot, **66–71**
  standardizing, 9
  troubleshooting basics, 76–78
  for UNIX, **103**
  upgrading networking or system
    software on, 340
  utilities, 390–391
  with virus, 86
World Wide Web, 379–380
World Wire, 376
WSCDiag (ASC), 408

X̄

X.25, 507
X.25 CCITT standard, 260–261
X.32, 507
X.400, 507
X.500, 507
XDR (External Data Representation),
    299
Xmodem, 507–508
XMSNET*x*.COM, 87
XON/XOFF, 508

Y

yahoo Web site, 379
Ymodem, 508

Z

Ziff Desktop Information, 380, 387
ZIP (Zone Information Protocol), 440

Zmodem, 508
Zone Information Protocol (ZIP), 440
zone name, 294
   when configuring server, 356
zone number conflicts, and Macintosh
   printing, 178
ZTEST, 39

What's on the CD-ROMs

The two CD-ROMs that accompany this book contain demos of some excellent programs that will come in handy as you troubleshoot NetWare systems.

CD 1 contains:

The Micro House Technical Library Encyclopedia of I/O Cards (©1993-1995 Micro House International, Inc.) and demo versions of the following products:

- Micro House Technical Library (©1993-1995 Micro House International, Inc.). As mentioned in Appendix B, the Micro House Technical Library is an extremely useful reference for finding jumper settings on boards and hard drives for which you no longer have documentation.

- Support On Site for Hardware (©1995 Micro House International, Inc. and Ziff-Davis Interactive). This product contains manuals for many different manufacturer's boards, hard drives, and other items.

For information on installing and running these Micro House products, consult the *readme.txt* file located in the root directory.

The catalog of the Charles River Media CD-ROM (©1995 Charles River Media, Inc.). It is a useful tool in itself because it may show you tools that you may not know existed. For information on installing the Charles River catalog, and for CD warranty information, consult the *readme.txt* file located in the root directory.

CD 2 contains a five-use trial edition of Computer Select (©1996 Information Access Company), a digest of computer magazine articles. To install the program, run SETUPW.EXE from Windows and follow the on-screen instructions. Because this is a limited-use trial edition, plan your research carefully, so as to make the most of each use.